Using MacWrite®

Mark K. Bilbo

que®
CORPORATION
LEADING COMPUTER KNOWLEDGE

Using MacWrite®

Copyright © 1990 by Que® Corporation

Library of Congress Catalog No.: 90-60504

ISBN 0-88022-547-5

93 92 91 90   8 7 6 5 4 3 2 1

Interpretation of the printing code: the rightmost double-digit number is the year of the book's printing; the rightmost single-digit number, the number of the book's printing. For example, a printing code of 90-1 shows that the first printing of the book occurred in 1990.

Using MacWrite is based on MacWrite II Version 1.1.

DEDICATION ▼

To Grandma and Grandpa, with love

Publishing Director

Lloyd J. Short

Acquisitions Editor

Karen A. Bluestein

Product Director

Shelley O'Hara

Production Editor

Jeannine Freudenberger

Editors

Sara Allaei
Sharon Boller
Kelly Currie
Daniel Schnake

Technical Editor

Daniel Zoller

Indexer

Hilary Adams

Book Design and Production

Dan Armstrong
Bill Basham
Claudia Bell
Brad Chinn
Don Clemons
Sally Copenhaver
Tom Emrick
Dennis Hager
Tami Hughes
Bill Hurley
Charles Hutchinson
Jodi Jensen
Larry Lynch
Lori A. Lyons
Jennifer Matthews
Cindy L. Phipps
Joe Ramon
Dennis Sheehan
Louise Shinault
Bruce D. Steed
Mary Beth Wakefield
Nora Westlake

Composed in Garamond and Excellent No. 47
by Que Corporation

ABOUT THE AUTHOR ▼

Mark K. Bilbo

Mark K. Bilbo is free-lance technical writer and computer consultant. He also has been on the writing staff for the CBS show *Tour of Duty*. He has worked in technical support and product development at Monogram Software. He is the author of *Using Dollars and Sense*, Macintosh Version, published by Que Corporation.

CONTENTS AT A GLANCE

TABLE OF CONTENTS

II Document Design

ACKNOWLEDGMENTS

I want to acknowledge D. Lynn Smith and Joseph A. Will for their help with the graphics in this book. I also want to thank Lee, Bryan, Kerma, Shana, Cindy, and Luke of the AISC at Cal State Long Beach—new friends—for being there.

And to Lloyd, Karen, Shelley, and Jeannine of Que who hounded this book out of me. Thanks.

TRADEMARK
AKNOWLEDGMENTS

Que Corporation has made every effort to supply trademark information about company names, products, and services mentioned in this book. Trademarks indicated below were derived from various sources. Que Corporation cannot attest to the accuracy of this information.

Apple, ImageWriter, LaserWriter, and Macintosh are registered trademarks and Finder and MultiFinder are trademarks of Apple Computer, Inc.

AppleWorks is a registered trademark of Apple Computer, Inc., licensed to Claris Corporation.

Claris is a trademark and FileMaker II, MacDraw, MacPaint, and MacWrite are registered trademarks of Claris Corporation.

Helvetica is a registred trademark of Linotype Co.

IBM is a registered trademark of International Business Machines Corporation.

Microsoft is a registered trademark of Microsoft Corporation.

Word Finder is a trademark of Microlytics, Inc.

WordPerfect is a registered trademark of WordPerfect Corporation.

WriteNow is a trademark licensed to T/Maker Company.

Introduction

In the early days of the Macintosh, choosing a word processor package was simple. Only one existed—MacWrite—and it came with the Macintosh.

The MacWrite of those days was not what you would call a "powerhouse" program by today's standards. It didn't have a great many features and was certainly not a desktop publishing program. But MacWrite was easy to use, and Mac users could write and edit letters, reports, scripts, and even books with an ease no one had expected from a computer.

As the Macintosh gained acceptance, other word processing packages began to appear on the market. Software publishers, in the rush to compete, added features that enabled users to check document spelling; add headers, footers, and footnotes; and do complex searches and replacements. Subsequent generations of Macintosh computers made possible the addition of still more features and power to the programs.

MacWrite seemed likely to be left in the backwater of word processing, used only by a few diehards who neither wanted nor needed to be swept into the desktop publishing tide. Even Apple dumped the program, sending it off with the newly formed Claris Corporation.

Claris, however, had no intention of allowing MacWrite to languish. Almost immediately, Version 5.0 of the program was released in order to address some of the more pressing issues of users. But that version was not the end of the matter.

One problem with the desktop publishing revolution is that word processing programs have become so sophisticated and powerful that the average user has been rapidly left behind. If you want to produce advertisements, mass mailings, books, pamphlets, and the like, a wide variety of word processors are available to you. If your needs are simpler—you want to write a letter now and then, write a term paper, or prepare a resume—you may find yourself in the proverbial position of swatting a fly with a bazooka and paying high-powered artillery prices.

In 1989, Claris came to the rescue of the average user by introducing Mac-Write II. The program is powerful enough to satisfy users who need spelling checking, hyphenation, complex paragraph formatting, search-and-replace functions, and other features—including graphics—yet MacWrite II remains true to the original MacWrite ideal of simplicity and ease of use.

You could say, to paraphrase Apple Corporation's earlier advertisements, that MacWrite II is the word processor for the rest of us.

The Power of MacWrite II

To support the assertion that MacWrite II is indeed an attractive word processor for the average user, here's a partial list of the program's features:

- Full compliance with the Macintosh User Interface guidelines, which provide for easy-to-use graphic and menu-driven controls and commands

- Custom, user-defined styles with color support

- Multiple "snaking" columns, up to 10 in a document

- Spelling checking, including the option to check the spelling of words as they are typed

- Variable font sizing, from 2 to 500 points in 0.25-point increments

- Search-and-replace capabilities, using font and other style attributes

- Hyphenation, including automatic hyphenation with user-definable exceptions

- Data merging to create form letters

- Paragraph formatting with first-line and hanging indents, four different types of tabs, variable line spacing, and the standard four types of justification

These features are, of course, in addition to the editing capabilities now common to Macintosh software—selecting, cutting, pasting, and so on.

With these features and others that are explored in this book, you can create a variety of useful documents ranging from the simple to the complex. Some examples of the kinds of documents you can create include

- *Letters*. From informal letters to friends and relatives to formal business letters with company logos

- *Reports*. From term papers to business reports, including charts, graphs, and title pages

- *Booklets and Pamphlets*. From small advertising fliers for community events to instructional or procedural manuals with illustrations and logos for your company

- *Newsletters*. For your homeowner's association, club, or even your family

- *Form Letters*. Letters customized for each person on mailing lists for associations, clubs, charities, and small businesses

The program has many other uses, which become apparent as you grow more familiar with MacWrite II. During your exploration of the program, you should work through the quick starts in this book. They will serve as your introduction, giving you the knowledge necessary to apply MacWrite II to your specific needs.

The Purpose of This Book

MacWrite II has remained faithful to the company's original intent of providing an easily learned and operated program. Users already familiar with the Macintosh may find that they can begin using MacWrite II without even opening the manual—high praise for a Macintosh software package.

The manual provided by Claris is clearly written and well designed and does a good job of covering the program's features. It is an excellent reference tool, which you should keep handy at all times. The Help facility provided in MacWrite II is also well done and easy to use.

The purpose of this book, *Using MacWrite*, is to bridge the gap between these basic reference materials and actual applications. In this book, features are explained within the context of using them to create all types of sample documents. The aim is to give you an understanding of the program's features as tools ready to help you create useful documents.

Who Should Use This Book

All MacWrite II owners can benefit from *Using MacWrite*.

If you're a beginning Macintosh user, you can use this book as an introduction to the MacWrite II program. You learn the basic concepts and skills needed to create and edit documents, as well as other features tailored to your specific needs.

Keep in mind, however, that this book does not attempt to teach the basics of using a Macintosh, although some items are covered as needed within the context of the features discussed. Your best sources for learning the Macintosh computer itself are provided by Apple. A "tour" disk introduces the basic Macintosh computer system concepts, including dragging, clicking, and double-clicking. The manual included with the machine is also a well-written, easy-to-follow introduction to the functions and concepts you need in order to gain full use of the Macintosh. If you are just starting out with the Macintosh, use both the "tour" disk and the manual as your starting points. This book uses terms explained and illustrated by these two sources.

If you're an intermediate user, you're probably already familiar with the necessary terms and functions used in the book but not with their specific applications in the MacWrite II program. You may have used MacWrite II in some limited fashion, but with this book you can learn to apply the program's features more skillfully.

If you're a more advanced user, you also can gain useful information from this book. Although you may already be accustomed to using the Macintosh and various software programs and may have used the MacWrite II program (or earlier versions), you still may be unfamiliar with some of its functions. Or you may find uses and applications in this book that you have not yet explored.

The Organization of This Book

This book is divided into 3 parts consisting of a total of 15 chapters, 4 appendixes, a glossary of terms, and a tear-out keyboard command guide. The following paragraphs provide a sort of road map to give you an idea of the topics and examples covered in each area of the book.

Part I, "Document Basics," consists of six chapters that cover the basic concepts of documents and the MacWrite II implementation of these concepts. Beginning with a simple tutorial, this part of the book explores the MacWrite II working environment and its use in creating, working with, and editing documents.

Chapter 1, "Quick Start: Writing a Letter," is a hands-on tutorial. In this chapter, you create, edit, save, and print a basic informal letter. If you're a beginning user, you should use this chapter to familiarize yourself with MacWrite II before proceeding to subsequent chapters.

Chapter 2, "Creating a MacWrite II Document," covers the basics of the program in order to enable you to begin creating your own documents. You learn about the MacWrite II working environment: the document window, the tab icons, the line spacing icons, and the text alignment icons. The chapter also covers the basic building blocks of documents. Setting page margins, page breaks, paragraph indentions, tabs, and spacing are explored, as are saving and printing documents.

Chapter 3, "Editing a Document," begins your exploration of the editing features of the program, starting with the basics of selecting text and working with selected text. The chapter discusses deleting, copying, and moving blocks of text and describes how to edit paragraph formats by using the ruler, the Paragraph dialog box, and the "invisible" formatting characters.

Chapter 4, "Correcting Spelling, " explains how to use MacWrite II's spelling-checking feature. You learn how to install dictionaries, check the spelling of your documents, and create your own dictionaries.

Chapter 5, "Advanced Document Editing," explores the more complicated aspects of editing documents. Included in this chapter are the use of the search-and-replace and thesaurus functions, hyphenation, and special characters.

Chapter 6, "Working with Documents," covers several document-specific functions of the program, including working with more than one document, translating to and from other program file formats, inserting text from other files, creating and using stationery, and using the View menu.

Part II, "Document Design," consists of four chapters that cover laying out, designing, and enhancing documents.

Chapter 7, "Quick Start: Creating a Booklet, " is a hands-on tutorial that leads you through the creation of a small booklet. In this chapter, you gain experience in using title pages, headers and footers, fonts, and footnotes.

Chapter 8, "Designing the Page Layout," explores how to set page size, use left and right pages, set page margins, and set tabs.

Chapter 9, "Adding Other Document Elements, " is a continuation of the discussion of the building blocks of documents. The chapter explains how to create title pages, headers and footers, and footnotes, and how to insert current dates and times and page numbers.

Chapter 10, "Enhancing Documents," covers the use of fonts and styles to improve the appearance of your documents. The chapter also explores the MacWrite II feature of custom styles and the program's capability to search for and replace fonts and styles.

Part III, "Specialized Documents," consists of five chapters that deal with multicolumn documents, graphics, and form letters (also called *mail merge*).

Chapter 11, "Quick Start: Creating a Newsletter," serves as a step-by-step introduction to working with multicolumn documents and graphics. In this chapter, you create a newsletter to gain experience in working with these features in MacWrite II.

Chapter 12, "Working with Columns and Graphics," takes an in-depth look at documents having more than one column. Also covered are the graphic-handling features of the program.

Chapter 13, "Creating Tables," covers creating, entering, and editing tables in MacWrite II.

Chapter 14, "Quick Start: Creating a Company Mailing," is a hands-on introduction to the mail-merge (form letter) capability of the program. You are introduced to data files and form letters by learning step-by-step how to create a mailing for a fictional company.

Chapter 15, "Creating Form Letters," describes how to create data files, explores the different methods of editing form letters, explains the available commands, and shows you how to put form letters to use.

Appendix A is a guide to installing MacWrite II on your Macintosh system—something you may want to look at before reading further. Appendix B is a Quick Reference procedural guide to the commands in the MacWrite II program. Use this guide to locate a quick step-by-step guide for the major procedures. Appendixes C and D are guides to the menus and windows of the program, respectively. Each menu and window in the program is shown with an explanation (and chapter references) of the function of each part. Finally, the glossary defines the terms used in this book. This book also includes a tear-out card that shows the keyboard equivalents for each command.

This book has been written for use on two levels: as a hands-on tutorial and as a reference source. Several quick-start tutorial chapters allow you to get your feet wet by using the commands to create real documents. If you're a more advanced user, you may want to skip the quick starts and go straight to the "meat." But if some concept or function proves difficult to understand, the quick starts can serve as examples to help orient you.

Although skipping around in the book as you see fit is perfectly acceptable, if you're a beginning user you should start with Chapters 1 and 2 and follow them all the way through. These chapters cover the basic concepts you need in your exploration of MacWrite II.

Part I

Document Basics

Includes

Quick Start: Writing a Letter

Creating a MacWrite II Document

Editing a Document

Correcting Spelling

Advanced Document Editing

Working with Documents

Quick Start:
Writing a Letter

Although MacWrite II is certainly powerful enough to handle more difficult word processing projects, such as newsletters, reports, booklets, and the like, the program's ease of use also lends itself to simpler, less complicated tasks like writing a letter to a friend.

This quick start concerns just such an example—an informal letter. With this example, you see the process of starting the program, the one-time customization screen, the basics of the document window, and various menus. As you create the document, you also learn the basics of using MacWrite II's Insert Date command, indenting paragraphs, editing text, checking spelling, and saving and printing the document.

Starting MacWrite II

After installing MacWrite II (see Appendix A for more information), you should see something similar to figure 1.1 on your Macintosh screen. The figure shows a work disk created for floppy disk drive users. If you have a hard drive, the window will be slightly different. The important thing at this point is to note the MacWrite II icon, shown in figure 1.1 in the upper left of the window. The icon, or picture, of the MacWrite II program is that of a written document and a pencil. The box that surrounds the icon is part of the Claris Corporation logo.

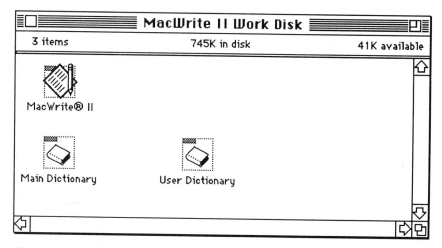

Fig. 1.1. *The MacWrite II Work Disk screen.*

To start the MacWrite II program, follow these steps:

1. Double-click the MacWrite II icon. The program presents a screen that asks you to personalize your copy of the program (see fig. 1.2). You see this screen only once—the first time you run the program.

Fig. 1.2. *The MacWrite II customization screen, where you personalize your copy of the program.*

2. Type your name. (The cursor is automatically in the proper typing area.) Notice that until you type your name, the OK button in the lower right of the screen remains "grayed out," which means that the option is unavailable.

3. If you want to include a company name, press Tab to reach the Company field, and type your company name.

4. To start the program, click the OK button. A screen displaying the Claris Corporation logo and your name and company appears briefly as the program starts.

Exploring the MacWrite II Environment

After the program starts, the MacWrite II document window appears (see fig. 1.3). In subsequent sessions, you don't see the customization screen when you start MacWrite II. Instead, the program starts with the Claris logo and this document window.

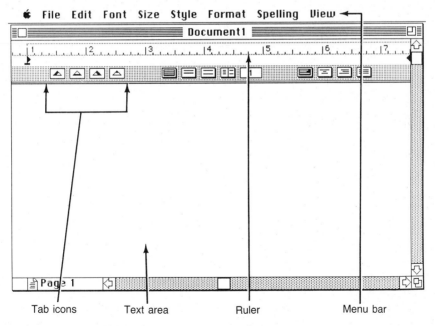

Fig. 1.3. The MacWrite II document window.

Figure 1.3 points out a few parts of the screen, which you use when creating the sample document in this chapter. In the following sections, each part is discussed briefly.

The Menu Bar

The *menu bar* is not part of the document window but is an important part of the program. You use the menu bar, your command center, to control the program's operation. The menu bar is one constant you see time and time again in your use of the Macintosh. Understanding how to use the menu bar is crucial.

You operate the MacWrite II menu the same way you operate menus in other Macintosh programs and the desktop, the Macintosh operating system. To make a selection from the menu bar, you place the mouse pointer (the small arrow you move by sliding the mouse) on the menu name, press and hold the mouse button, move the mouse pointer down to the command to be executed, and release the mouse button.

For a quick example, move the mouse pointer to the small apple in the upper left corner of your screen; the apple represents the Apple menu. Then press and hold the mouse button to "pull down" the menu (see fig. 1.4). As long as you hold down the mouse button, the menu stays down.

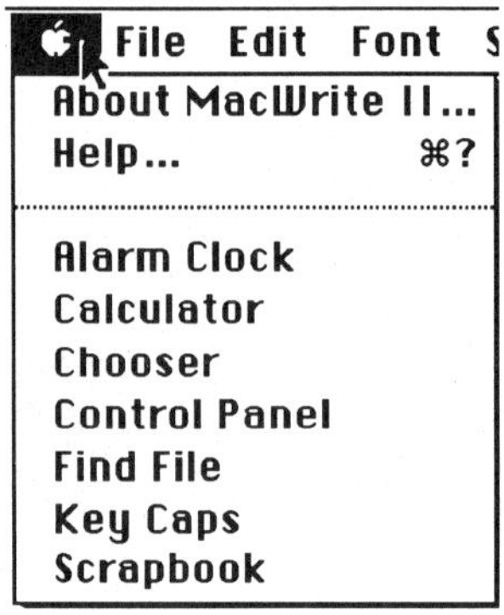

```
 ⌘   File   Edit   Font   S
About MacWrite II...
Help...                 ⌘?
..............................
Alarm Clock
Calculator
Chooser
Control Panel
Find File
Key Caps
Scrapbook
```

Fig. 1.4. The Apple menu.

While holding down the mouse button, move the mouse pointer to the About MacWrite II command. A dark band of highlighting appears around the command. When you release the mouse button, the Claris logo and information about the MacWrite II copyrights appears. Click anywhere in this window to make it disappear and to return to the document window.

At this point, you may want to explore the menus by moving the mouse pointer to each menu name and pressing and holding the mouse button. This way, you can see the commands available in each menu. Understanding all of them is not important yet, but you can get at least an idea of the commands and their locations.

The Ruler

Just below the name of the current document (in this case,
Document1—the default name) is the *ruler*, which shows measurement
units in inches. (You can change the units of measure; see Chapter 2,
"Creating a MacWrite II Document.") The ruler operates just as if you laid
a ruler across the top of a sheet of paper with the left edge of the ruler
against the left edge of the paper. You use the ruler to change margins, set
tabs, and set indents.

A regular-size piece of paper in the United States is 8.5 inches across and
11 inches long. As you can see in figure 1.3, the ruler in this case shows
the part of the "paper" from the 1-inch marker to the 7.5-inch mark. You
thus have a 1-inch margin on each side of the page. Each margin is marked
by a black triangle on the ruler.

The Tab Icons

In the gray area below the ruler are several *tab icons*. From left to right,
the first four icons represent four different types of tab settings you can
select: left-aligned, centered, right-aligned, and decimal-aligned. (The next
five icons enable you to set the spacing—single-spacing, double-spacing,
and so on—of the lines in the document. The last four icons control the
text justification. All these icons are discussed in detail in Chapter 2.)

To use one of these tab icons, you just move the mouse pointer to the
appropriate icon, and drag the icon to the location on the ruler where you
want a tab set.

The Text Area

The largest part of the document window is the *text area*. This "white"
space is the area in which you type text, paste graphics, and edit.
Obviously, most of your time with MacWrite II is spent working in this
part of the window.

The text area is the electronic equivalent of a blank sheet of paper waiting
to be written on. At present, the only item in the text area is the
cursor—the blinking bar that indicates where text will be inserted when
you type.

Creating a Letter

With the document window on-screen, you are ready to begin creating your letter. The first step is to address the letter. This example uses a standard letter form similar to what is taught in many typing classes. You therefore need to set a tab to align the date and return address.

Setting a Tab

The program provides some tabs already set in each new document. These tabs are called the *default tabs*, and they are located at each half-inch mark on the ruler. Unless you set other tabs, these settings remain in effect.

Because you want the date and return address to align at the 4.5-inch mark, setting a tab at that location is easier than pressing the Tab key the seven times necessary to reach the 4.5-inch mark on each line.

To set the tab, follow these steps:

1. Move the mouse pointer to the first tab icon, the triangle that has the thick left side.

2. Press and hold the mouse button.

3. Drag the tab icon to the ruler and move the pointer along the ruler, still holding down the mouse button, until the pointer reaches the midway point between 4 inches and 5 inches. As you move the mouse pointer, a copy of the tab icon moves with the pointer.

4. Release the mouse button. The icon is now "stuck" to the ruler at the 4.5-inch mark.

Press Tab once, and the cursor jumps immediately to the 4.5-inch mark. You are going to place the date here. Although you can just type it, MacWrite II provides another method of entering the current date.

Entering the Current Date

To enter the date, you first need to select a date format. Then you can use a MacWrite command to enter the current date. Follow these steps to select a date format:

1. Open the Edit menu, which is shown in figure 1.5. (Remember, move the mouse pointer to Edit in the menu bar, and press and hold the mouse button.)

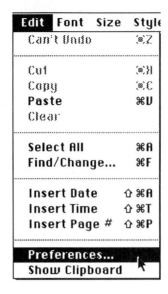

Fig. 1.5. The Edit menu.

2. Choose the Preferences command (drag the mouse pointer to that command) to open the Preferences dialog box, shown in figure 1.6.

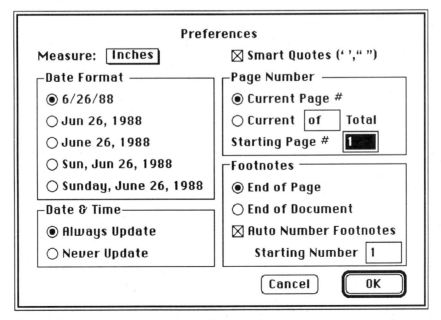

Fig. 1.6. The Preferences dialog box.

You can set several different options in this dialog box. At this point, however, you are concerned only with the Date Format options. Five are available, and each shows a sample of the date format. The numbers here are not important; they are used only to illustrate the format.

3. For this example, choose the June 26, 1988, format. This option provides a date format with the month name spelled out and followed by the day and then the year. Choose this format by clicking the small circle to the left of the format. The small black dot moves to the circle you have clicked, indicating that MacWrite II will use this date format.

4. To close the Preferences dialog box, click the OK button in the lower right of the box (as an alternative, press the Return key). The box closes, and you are returned to the document window.

To insert the date, open the Edit menu and choose the Insert Date command. The current date appears at the cursor position.

Typing the Addresses and Greeting

You are now ready to type the addresses and greeting of the letter. To do so, follow these steps:

1. Press Return twice to leave a blank line between the date and the return address. (Note that on some Macintosh keyboards, the Return key is labeled Enter.)

2. Press Tab, and type the following return address. Remember to press Return at the end of the street address and then press Tab before typing the city, state, and ZIP code.

   100 Pine Tree Street
   Long Beach, CA 90800-1234

3. Press Return twice to leave a blank line between the return address and the inside address.

4. Type the following inside address. Do not press Tab before these lines; you want them positioned against the left side of the page. Do remember to press Return after each line.

   Linda South
   3000 Rock Lane
   Rio Tornado, CA 91000

5. After you press Return at the end of the third line, press Return again to add a blank line after the address.

6. Type the greeting

   Dear Linda,

   Figure 1.7 shows your progress so far.

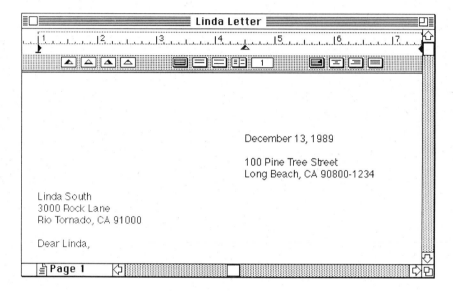

Fig. 1.7. *Your partially completed letter.*

You are now almost ready to type the body of the letter itself. But first press Return twice to place a blank line between the greeting and the letter body. Users of computer models with standard built-in screens, such as the Macintosh Plus and the SE, will see the document move up to provide more working space. Users of other monitors will see this movement at a different point, depending on how big the monitor is and how much of the document fits on the screen.

This movement is called *scrolling*. Regardless of the size monitor you use, the program automatically moves the document each time you need more room to work. You also can scroll the document yourself. Scrolling is mentioned in this chapter's section on "Editing the Letter" and is covered in detail in Chapter 2, "Creating a MacWrite II Document."

Setting the First-Line Indent

You need to make a change before you type the body of the letter. In an informal letter (and in many formal ones), the first line of each paragraph is indented. You can make this indention by pressing Tab before typing the first line just as when you are using a typewriter. But MacWrite II offers another way of indenting the first line of a paragraph, that saves you this step while at the same time ensuring the same automatic indent for each paragraph.

Note on your screen that the ruler contains two black triangles, one at each side. The left triangle beneath it has a small bar that the right triangle does not have. This bar is actually an upside-down T that is partially hidden by the left-margin triangle. This T symbol is the *first-line indent marker*. To change the indent, follow these steps:

1. Move the mouse pointer to the small bar below the left triangle.

2. Press and hold the mouse button.

3. Drag the indent marker to the 1.5-inch mark, and release the mouse button.

All that is necessary to "grab" the first-line indent marker is to have the tip of the arrow-shaped mouse pointer touching the small bar of the marker when you press the mouse button. But grabbing only the indent marker can be tricky. If you notice the black triangle moving with the marker, move the mouse pointer back to the triangle's original location (the 1-inch mark), release the mouse button, and start over.

After you move the marker, notice that the cursor has moved half an inch.

Typing the Letter Body

Type the following two paragraphs. Remember, you do not have to press Tab at any time. Press Return only at the end of each paragraph, not at the end of each line. Resist the temptation to correct any spelling or other goofs in the letter. These errors are intentional and will serve as examples for the spelling-checking and editing tutorials later in the chapter.

Hope this letter finds all well with you and the kids. It's been much too long since we've seen you dispite the fact we moved only last. Having to leave you and Jeff behind is probably the our only regret with the move. Guess I'm going to have to sharpen my letter-writing skills now that you're a toll call away!

I'll be killing two birds with one stone by writing. We just bought MacWrite II for our Macintosh, and I've decided to learn how to use it. It's easier than I thought! Already I'm setting "tabs" and "first-line indent markers." Sound like a real "computer whiz" right? Just promise me one thing. If I start sounding like one of those commercials, shoot me!

Notice that as you type, the program automatically moves to the next line words that would have passed the right margin. This feature is called *word wrap* because the words are wrapped around to fit within the margins.

Notice also that because of the location of your first-line indent marker, when you press Return to end a paragraph, the cursor automatically moves in half an inch to indent the first line of the next paragraph. (Other uses of the first-line indent marker are covered in Chapter 2.)

Entering the Closing

You are now ready to type the closing of your letter. Follow these steps:

1. Press Return to leave a blank line between the last paragraph and the closing.

2. As you can see in the ruler, the original tab setting at 4.5 inches is still in effect. Press Tab and type *Best Wishes,* as your closing.

The letter is now complete. Figure 1.8 shows the body and closing. In the figure, the program has scrolled the first lines of the letter out of the document window. If you have a larger monitor, you may be able to view more of your document at one time, and your screen will appear slightly different. The part of the document that has scrolled out of the document window has not disappeared but is only temporarily out of view.

Editing the Letter

Unless you are an absolutely perfect typist and never make mistakes, your typing will undoubtedly need some corrections. Here is perhaps the greatest strength of using a word processor as opposed to a typewriter: nothing has yet been committed to paper. You can make corrections and

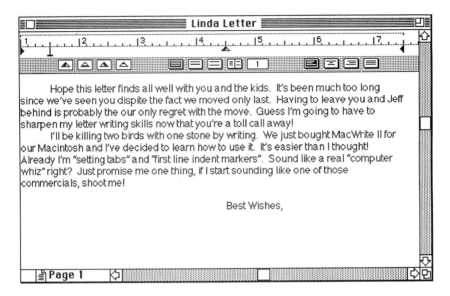

Hope this letter finds all well with you and the kids. It's been much too long since we've seen you dispite the fact we moved only last. Having to leave you and Jeff behind is probably the our only regret with the move. Guess I'm going to have to sharpen my letter writing skills now that you're a toll call away!

I'll be killing two birds with one stone by writing. We just bought MacWrite II for our Macintosh and I've decided to learn how to use it. It's easier than I thought! Already I'm "setting tabs" and "first line indent markers". Sound like a real "computer whiz" right? Just promise me one thing, if I start sounding like one of those commercials, shoot me!

Best Wishes,

Fig. 1.8. *The letter's body and closing visible on-screen.*

changes quickly and easily without retyping the entire document or using correction fluid.

Depending on the size of your monitor, you may need to scroll the letter's text so that the entire letter body is visible on-screen. Scrolling is the method by which you move the document up and down in the document window.

On the right side of the document window, you see two small arrows (again see fig. 1.8). An arrow pointing up is near the upper right corner of the window, and an arrow pointing down is near the lower right corner. These *scroll arrows* permit you to move the document in the document window. Think of the document as a piece of paper being moved up and down behind a window frame. When you place the mouse on the up scroll arrow and click, you move the document up by about a line and a half. This movement permits you to see more of the document that is below the bottom of the window. Clicking the down scroll arrow moves you down through the document.

Inserting Text

To insert text into your letter, follow these steps:

1. Click the up scroll arrow a few times until you can read the entire letter body, the part that begins with "Hope this letter...."

Notice that the second sentence appears to have a word missing after the word *last*.

2. To insert the word *month* into the sentence, move the mouse pointer to the end of the word *last*. As you move the pointer in the text area of the document window, notice that the black arrow has become an *I-beam*. You use this I-beam pointer to place the cursor at the location at which you want to insert text.

3. When the I-beam is between the letter *t* and the period, click the mouse button. The vertical blinking cursor appears, indicating that text you type will be inserted at this location.

4. Press the space bar, and type the word *month*.

You can use this method of inserting text to insert a space between words, a skipped letter within a word, an entire sentence, or even an entire paragraph.

Simple enough. But as you read the next sentence, you encounter the reverse situation: text that needs to be removed.

Deleting Text

The third sentence in the letter reads:

Having to leave you and Jeff behind is probably the our only regret with the move.

Obviously, "the our" is not what was intended. The word *the* needs to go. To delete the word, follow these steps:

1. Move the I-beam pointer to the end of the word *the*.

2. Click the mouse button to place the cursor at the end of the word.

3. Press the Backspace key (on some keyboards this key is labeled Delete or Del) until the word is gone. Remember to remove the space that precedes the word; otherwise, two spaces appear between *probably* and *our*.

Again, you can use this method to delete any amount of text, from a single character to the entire document. The technique is best used, however, for single characters or a small word. A quicker method for deleting an entire word is discussed in the next section and in Chapter 3.

Replacing Text

The sentence you have been working on ends with the phrase ". . . our only regret with the move." After looking at it, suppose that you decide you should have said *about* rather than *with*.

To select and replace the entire word, follow these steps:

1. Move the I-beam pointer until it is approximately in the middle of the word *with*. (You do not have to be exactly accurate.)

2. Double-click the mouse button. A dark band appears around the word. This action is referred to as highlighting, or *selecting*, the word.

   Now that the word is selected, you can do a couple of things. You can delete the word by pressing the Backspace (or Delete) key. Or you can just replace the word by typing a new one.

3. With the word *with* selected, type the word *about*. MacWrite II automatically replaces the old word with the new one.

When you make a selection and type, whatever you type replaces the selected text. This point is an important one to remember when you edit. You want to make sure that the correct text is selected before you start typing.

Double-clicking to select a word is only one of several selection methods available in MacWrite II. In Chapter 3, "Editing a Document," making selections and using them to edit documents is explored in greater depth.

Checking Your Spelling

To check the spelling of the letter, open the Spelling menu and then choose the Check All command (see fig. 1.9). The program begins checking the document's spelling immediately.

Note: If the Check All command is grayed out, the program is unable to locate the main dictionary. You therefore need to copy the main dictionary to your working disk or your hard drive. Refer to Appendix A. (The main dictionary is supplied on the MacWrite II Program Disk. If you use the installation instructions in Appendix A, the dictionary should be on the same disk—and in the same folder, if any—as the MacWrite II program.)

When you choose Check All from the Spelling menu, a dialog box appears, as shown in figure 1.10. This Spelling dialog box is the area where misspelled or otherwise questionable words appear and where you can correct them.

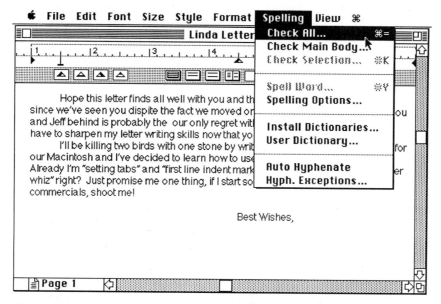

Fig. 1.9. *Selecting Check All to tell MacWrite II to begin checking spelling.*

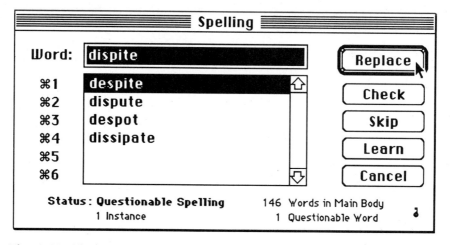

Fig. 1.10. *The Spelling dialog box.*

In figure 1.10, the program has detected a questionable spelling, which is shown near the top of the dialog box in the Word field. You probably noticed while typing the letter that the word *dispite* is incorrect.

MacWrite II has suggested some alternative spellings in the list box below the questioned word. The first suggested spelling, *despite*, is correct and is already selected by the program. Click the Replace button to replace *dispite* with *despite*. The program then moves on.

This word is the only questionable one in the example. When MacWrite II reaches the end of the document and finds no other unrecognizable words, the Replace button changes to Done (see fig. 1.11). Click the Done button to close the Spelling dialog box and to return to the document.

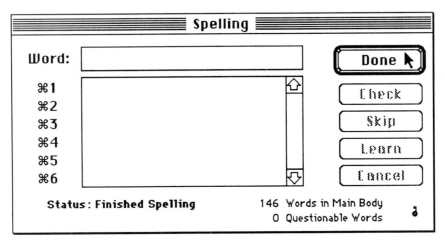

Fig. 1.11. Click the Done button to complete the spelling-checking process.

Saving the Letter

Saving the letter is a simple process. Open the File menu, and select the Save command (see fig. 1.12). The program responds by displaying the dialog box shown in figure 1.13.

This dialog box is the standard one supplied by the Macintosh System software. If you are unfamiliar with the Save dialog box, you should read the manual supplied with your computer. This chapter explains the dialog box only briefly.

At the top of the box is the name of the disk or folder currently being used. In the example, this disk is the MacWrite II Work Disk. (The name of the current disk also appears above the Eject button on the right side of the box.)

The list box below the name of the current disk or folder contains a list of files located on the disk or in the folder. In figure 1.13, you can see the MacWrite II, Main Dictionary, and User Dictionary files.

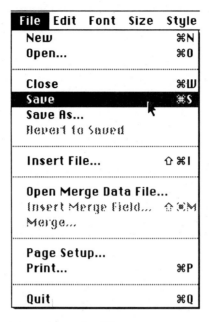

Fig. 1.12. Selecting Save from the File menu.

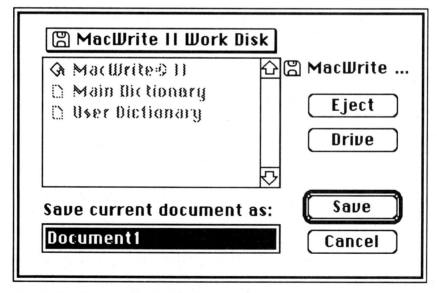

Fig. 1.13. The Save dialog box.

Four buttons are located along the right side of the dialog box. The Eject button ejects the current disk from the machine. This button is grayed out and unavailable if you are working on a hard drive. The Drive button enables you to switch to a different disk. Each click of this button switches you to another disk drive so that you can choose the disk on which you want to save the file. Clicking the Save button causes the program to save your file with the name you have given it. The Cancel button cancels the save process and returns you to the document.

The last part of the dialog box is the Save Current Document As field. In this field, you type the name under which you want to save the document. Notice in figure 1.13 that the program has supplied the name Document1. Because this document is a letter to your mythical friend Linda, name the document after her, and type *Linda Letter* in the field. As you type, note that the name Document1 vanishes and is replaced by what you type.

Now, to save the document, click the Save button. The new name, Linda Letter, is displayed immediately in the document title bar at the top of the document window and will appear there any time the document is opened.

Printing the Letter

Finally, the letter is ready to be printed and mailed. To print the document, choose the Print command from the File menu. You see a Print dialog box similar to that shown in figure 1.14. The exact appearance depends on your particular Macintosh system.

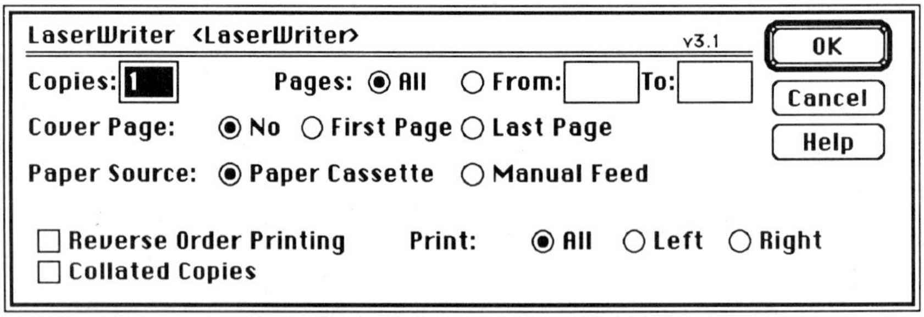

```
┌─────────────────────────────────────────────────────────────┐
│  LaserWriter <LaserWriter>                    v3.1  ┌──────┐  │
│                                                     │  OK  │  │
│  Copies:[1▌]      Pages: ◉ All  ○ From:[    ]To:[    ]└──────┘  │
│                                                     ┌──────┐  │
│  Cover Page:    ◉ No  ○ First Page ○ Last Page      │Cancel│  │
│                                                     └──────┘  │
│  Paper Source: ◉ Paper Cassette  ○ Manual Feed      │ Help │  │
│                                                     └──────┘  │
│  □ Reverse Order Printing     Print:  ◉ All ○ Left ○ Right    │
│  □ Collated Copies                                           │
└─────────────────────────────────────────────────────────────┘
```

Fig. 1.14. The Print dialog box for a LaserWriter printer.

No matter which Print dialog box appears on your screen, for now just click the OK button. The program notifies you that the document is printing, and you soon have your first MacWrite II document in hand.

If you have trouble printing, check your printer's manual. Covering the various printers and their configurations is beyond the scope of this book. Here, however, are a few tips:

- Make sure that your cables are tightly connected. Don't just assume that they are.

- Check the setting in the Chooser desk accessory. This desk accessory, covered in the Macintosh manuals and the printer manual, determines where the program attempts to print. If the Chooser is set incorrectly, you may be attempting to print to a nonexistent printer.

- Make sure that you have installed your printer drivers correctly. Drivers, which are software items supplied by the printer manufacturers, must be present in your System Folder to allow any program to print.

Quitting MacWrite II

With the letter saved to disk and printed, you are ready to leave MacWrite II. Open the File menu, and select Quit (see fig. 1.15). The program quits, and you are returned to the Macintosh System desktop.

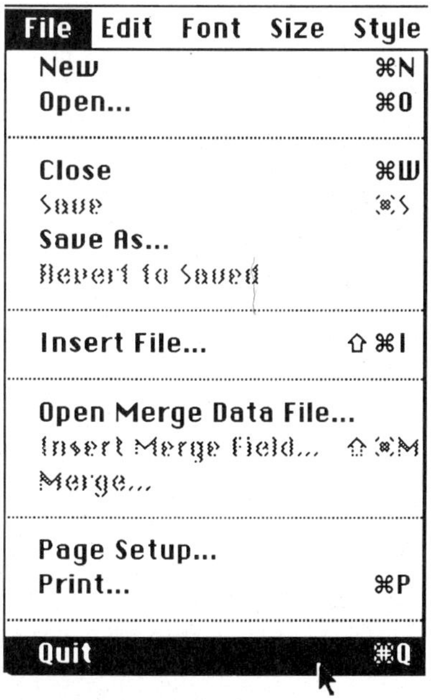

File	Edit	Font	Size	Style
New				⌘N
Open...				⌘O
Close				⌘W
Save				⌘S
Save As...				
Revert to Saved				
Insert File...				⇧⌘I
Open Merge Data File...				
Insert Merge Field...				⇧⌘M
Merge...				
Page Setup...				
Print...				⌘P
Quit				⌘Q

Fig. 1.15. *Selecting Quit from the File menu.*

You are now ready to turn to a more detailed discussion of the MacWrite II environment and the use of MacWrite II in creating and editing documents.

Creating a MacWrite II Document

This chapter covers the basics of MacWrite II so that you can begin creating basic documents like the letter in Chapter 1.

The MacWrite II environment is discussed first. In this section, you gain an understanding of the program and its tools. Next, you see how to use the document elements—pages and paragraphs—to create a document. You learn what changes you can make to the page and to the paragraphs. After completing these two sections, you should have an understanding of how to use MacWrite II to create documents. The final two sections deal with saving and printing documents.

If you skipped Chapter 1 and find some of the concepts presented in this chapter difficult to follow, you may want to use Chapter 1 as a hands-on tutorial. If you need information on installing or starting the program, see Appendix A.

Understanding the MacWrite II Environment

When you start MacWrite, you see a blank document screen. The environment of MacWrite II consists of the document window, the ruler, the tab icons, the text alignment icons, and the menus. You encountered these elements in the preceding chapter as you created the example letter. The following sections cover each element in greater detail.

31

The Document Window

The window is one of the fundamental parts of the Macintosh user interface. Users familiar with the Macintosh may find the following section something of a rerun, because MacWrite II adheres to Apple standards.

Figure 2.1 shows the parts of the window. The basic activities for the window are discussed in the following sections.

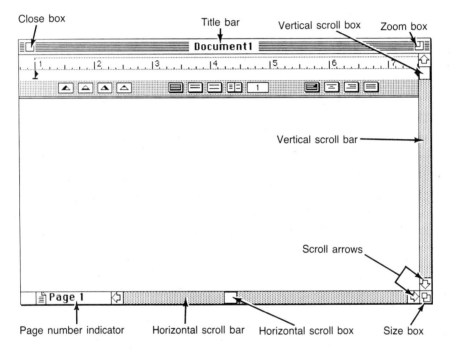

Fig. 2.1. *The document window.*

Moving the Document Window

At the top of the document window, you find the name of the document in the title bar. Documents that have not yet been named bear the name *Document* and a number. Documents are named when you select the Save option from the File menu (see "Saving Documents," later in this chapter).

The title bar is also the part of the document window you grab in order to move the window. When you have more than one window open or when you want to see a window that is temporarily behind a dialog box or menu, you may want to move the window.

To move a window, follow these steps:

1. Place the pointer in the title bar.

2. Press and hold the mouse button.

3. Drag the outline of the window to the desired location.

4. Release the mouse button.

Resizing the Document Window

Just as you may want to move a document window, you also may want to change the size of the window in order to work more efficiently. On the far right end of the title bar is a box-within-a-box icon called the zoom box, which works with the size box in the lower right corner of the document window. The size box enables you to change the size of the document window with the following steps:

1. Place the mouse pointer in the size box.

2. Press and hold the mouse button.

3. Move the mouse, dragging the outline of the window to the desired size.

4. Release the mouse button.

After you have shrunk a document window by using the size box, you can restore the window to its full size by clicking the zoom box. Click the zoom box again to shrink the window. Each click on the zoom box toggles between the normal document size and the last size you set using the size box.

Scrolling the Document

The vertical and horizontal scroll bars enable you to move your document within the document window. Clicking one of the small scroll arrows moves the document up, down, left, or right by about .25 inch.

Clicking the gray area above or below the scroll box in the vertical scroll bars moves your document up or down by one screenful of text. Clicking to the left or right of the scroll box in the horizontal scroll bar moves to the left or right edge of the page (or to other pages if you use the Side By Side option in the View menu—see Chapter 5).

The fastest method for moving through your document is to drag the scroll box through the vertical or horizontal scroll bar. When you drag the vertical scroll box, the page number indicator in the lower left corner of the document window indicates what page you have reached. You can move quickly to a particular page by following these steps:

1. Place the pointer in the vertical scroll box.

2. Drag the vertical scroll box (up or down) until the desired page number appears in the page number indicator.

3. Release the mouse button.

The specified page appears in the window.

Closing the Document Window

The close box is in the upper left corner of the window. Clicking the box puts away the document contained in the window but does not quit MacWrite II. For more information on closing and saving your document, see the section "Saving Documents," later in this chapter.

The Ruler

In addition to the document window parts, the screen also displays a ruler. Referring to figure 2.2, you can see that the ruler consists of three parts: the page margin indicator, the ruler measurements, and the icon bar. At the top of the ruler is a dotted line that indicates the maximum width of the document. The width is limited by the left and right margins of the document.

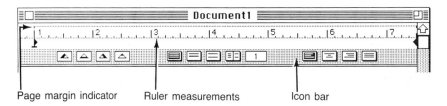

Page margin indicator   Ruler measurements   Icon bar

Fig. 2.2. The ruler.

The document margins are set automatically to the standard 1 inch of space to the left and right of the text. Because the document page is 8.5 inches wide (the size of a standard piece of paper), the dotted line indicates that the maximum width of text in this document begins at the 1-inch mark and ends at the 7.5-inch mark. You can change these margins (see "Setting Page Margins," later in this chapter).

The main part of the ruler consists of the measurements themselves. These marks indicate the width of the document and aid in the placement of page margins, paragraph indents, and tabs. The unit of measure is automatically set to inches. The ruler, therefore, extends from 0 inches to 8.5 inches with one-eighth inch divisions.

Throughout this book, the inches are used as the unit of measure. You can, however, change this unit. First, you select the Preferences option in the Edit menu. The program responds with the Preferences dialog box (see fig. 2.3).

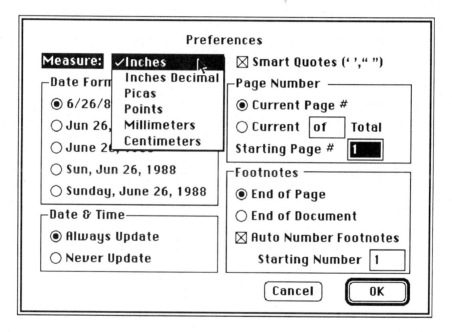

Fig. 2.3. *The Preferences dialog box.*

In the upper left part of this box is a pop-up menu next to the word *Measure*. The current unit of measure—inches—is in the shadowed box of the pop-up menu. To access this menu, move the pointer into the shadowed box and then press and hold the mouse button. This action brings up a menu with the six different units of measure available.

After highlighting the unit of measure you want, release the mouse button. That unit of measure is displayed in the shadowed box. After you click the OK button, the ruler changes to the chosen unit of measure.

The available units of measure are the following:

- *Inches.* The default unit of measure. The page is measured in inches with one-eighth-inch subdivisions.

- *Inches Decimal.* The page is measured in inches, but each inch is divided into tenths rather than eighths.

- *Picas.* Typists may be familiar with this measure. Basically, 1 pica is one-sixth inch. The ruler is divided into 12 subdivisions (half-picas) per inch.

- *Points.* An inch contains 72 points. The ruler is divided into 12 subdivisions per inch.

- *Millimeters.* The ruler is labeled every 10 millimeters with 5 subdivisions indicating 2 millimeters each.

- *Centimeters.* The ruler is labeled in centimeters with 5 subdivisions per centimeter indicating 2 millimeters each.

Changing the unit of measure has no effect on the document or placement of any document element. The unit of measure exists solely as a guide to help you place the various document elements.

Below the ruler, you see three sets of formatting icons: the tab icons, the line spacing icons, and the text alignment icons. MacWrite uses four tab icons: Left, Center, Right, and Align On tab. You use these icons to place tabs on the ruler. See the section "Setting Tabs" for more information.

The next set of icons controls the line spacing. From left to right, the first three icons represent single-spacing, one-and-one-half-line spacing, and double-spacing. The section "Specifying Paragraph Spacing" discusses changes you can make to line spacing.

The four text-alignment icons control the overall alignment and appearance of text. Each icon corresponds to one of the four types of alignment available in MacWrite II. The alignments are discussed in the section "Setting Paragraph Indents."

The Menus

The menu bar across the top of the screen is your control center for MacWrite II. All functions and commands are accessed through the menus in the menu bar.

Some menu selections bring up submenus or windows or dialog boxes in which you can set various options. The menu selections that bring up submenus are followed by ellipses (three periods). In the File menu, the Open, Save As, and Print commands are three such menu selections. Appendix D of this book contains explanations of dialog boxes and windows in MacWrite II. If you encounter one that you are not familiar with, refer to this appendix.

Making Menu Selections

The menus are pull-down; when you place the pointer on a menu name and press the mouse button, the menu drops down from the menu bar (see fig. 2.4).

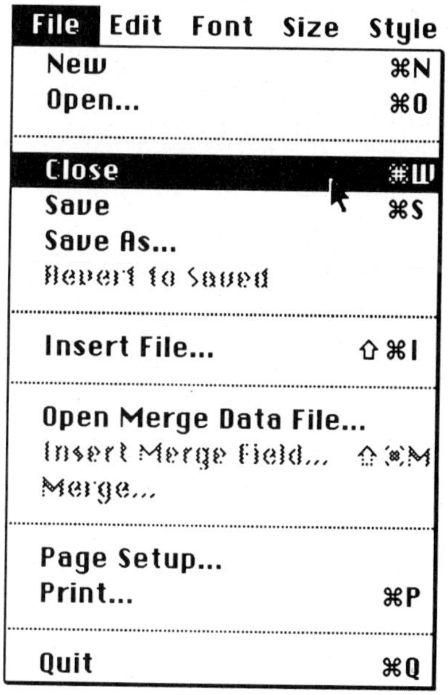

File	Edit	Font	Size	Style
New				⌘N
Open...				⌘O
Close				**⌘W**
Save				⌘S
Save As...				
Revert to Saved				
Insert File...				⇧⌘I
Open Merge Data File...				
Insert Merge Field...				⇧⌘M
Merge...				
Page Setup...				
Print...				⌘P
Quit				⌘Q

Fig. 2.4. The File menu.

In figure 2.4, the Close command is being selected on the File menu. To select an option, pull down the menu by pressing and holding down the mouse button and then slide the mouse pointer to the command. To select the command, release the button when the dark band highlights the command name. Appendix C lists each menu and its commands.

Making Keyboard Menu Selections

A keyboard equivalent enables you to choose certain menu commands from the keyboard. To the right of the New command on the File menu, for instance, you see a small four-leaf clover symbol followed by the letter *N*. The four-leaf clover refers to the Command key. The Command key on the keyboard has the same symbol imprinted on the key top. On some keyboards, an apple symbol may appear on the Command key.

To select the New command from the keyboard, hold down the Command key and press the letter N (lowercase). This key combination accomplishes the same thing as choosing New from the File menu (that is, a new, blank document is created). Other keyboard equivalents operate in the same manner.

An up arrow preceding the Command key symbol on the menu indicates that you also must hold down the Shift key to operate the command from the keyboard. An example of a Shift-Command key equivalent is the Insert File command. To choose Insert File from the keyboard, you hold down the Command key and the Shift key and then press the letter I (Shift-Command-I).

Creating a Document

The main part of the MacWrite screen is the *text area*. In this large, initially blank space, you type text, paste graphics, and edit. To create a document, you just begin typing your text in the text area. As you type, note that you do not have to press Return at the end of each line. The program automatically moves words that would pass the right margin to the next line, a capability called *word wrap*.

To insert text, place the I-beam pointer where you want the new text, click the mouse button, and type the new text. To delete text, use the I-beam pointer to place the cursor after the text you want to delete, and backspace over the text. Other editing changes are covered in Chapter 3.

If you simply want to commit words to the page, you can save and print your document after you type it. But MacWrite offers other features you can use to control how your text appears on-screen and in printed form. A document is built of certain elements. The two elements covered in this chapter are pages and paragraphs, two basic elements of any document.

Remember that each document element can have its own formatting. These elements work together and affect each other. For example, the page margins limit the margins you can set for paragraphs. The next two sections discuss changes you can make to pages and paragraphs.

Formatting Pages

The largest document element is the page. A document is first broken down into pages. Whether a document is a single-page resume or a dictionary-sized book, the first question considered is the number of pages in the document.

You can format your document pages. For instance, you can set page margins and adjust the amount of text on a page by inserting and removing page breaks. These topics are covered in this section.

Setting Page Margins

Page margins determine the maximum width and height of text and graphics on the page. You set this limit by specifying the amount of space from the edge of the page to the beginning of the text on the page. You set the margins for an entire document through the Page dialog box.

You should determine the page margins before you begin to work on a document. You can change your mind and use the dialog box to alter the page margins, but changes in these margins can affect the formatting of text you have already typed, and you may have to do extensive editing. To prevent this problem, you may want to sketch out your planned pages.

Accessing the Page Dialog Box

To access the Page dialog box, select Page from the Format menu. The program responds with the Page dialog box (see fig. 2.5). The options available in this dialog box include

- *Left/Right Pages*. An X in this box—called a check box—determines whether the document has left and right pages (see Chapter 8 for more information).

- *Title Page*. This option determines whether the first page of the document is a title page. An X in this box, placed by clicking it, means that the first page is a title page (title pages are covered in Chapter 8).

- *Margins*. These four measurements determine the amount of space that surrounds your document. Typing a number in any of these four fields places that amount of space between that edge of the paper and the text in your document.

- *Columns*. These two options are covered in Chapter 12. Basically, they enable you to create newspaperlike columns in your document and determine the amount of space between them.

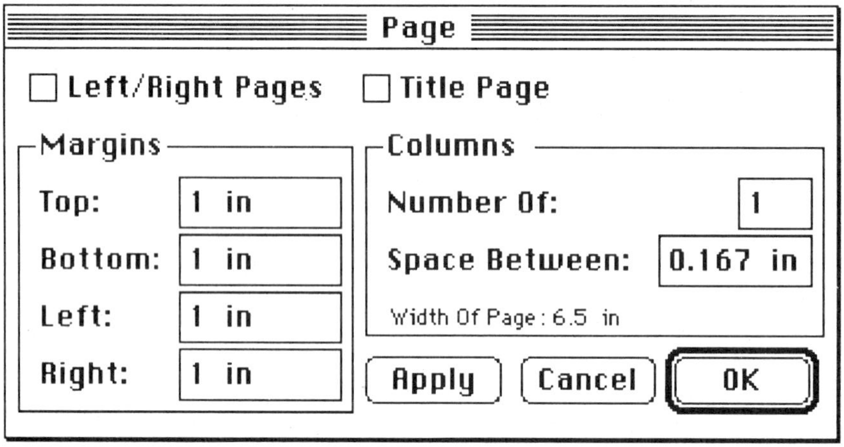

```
┌─────────────────────────────────────────────────────┐
│ ≡≡≡≡≡≡≡≡≡≡≡≡≡≡≡≡≡≡≡≡≡≡  Page  ≡≡≡≡≡≡≡≡≡≡≡≡≡≡≡≡≡≡≡≡≡ │
│ ☐ Left/Right Pages    ☐ Title Page                   │
│ ┌─Margins────────────┐ ┌─Columns──────────────────┐ │
│ │ Top:      [1  in]  │ │ Number Of:        [  1 ] │ │
│ │ Bottom:   [1  in]  │ │ Space Between: [0.167 in]│ │
│ │ Left:     [1  in]  │ │ Width Of Page : 6.5  in  │ │
│ │ Right:    [1  in]  │ │ ( Apply ) ( Cancel ) ( OK )│ │
│ └────────────────────┘ └──────────────────────────┘ │
└─────────────────────────────────────────────────────┘
```

Fig. 2.5. *The Page dialog box.*

The Width Of Page line in the Columns section of the Page dialog box does not apply solely to columns. If your document contains only one column, this line reports the total width of the page in which you can enter text and graphics.

In figure 2.5, the line reads Width Of Page: 6.5 in. Remember that a sheet of paper is 8.5 inches wide. The left and right page margins are set to 1 inch each. Because these page margin settings put 1 inch of space on each side of the text, this setting leaves 6.5 inches in which you can enter text and graphics.

Finally, the buttons of the Page dialog box are the following:

- *Apply*. This button applies the settings in the Page dialog box to your document so that you can see the results. You can experiment with the settings by trying different combinations and clicking Apply to see the results. The Page dialog box stays on the screen. You can move the Page dialog box around to see the changes by dragging in its title bar.

- *Cancel*. Clicking this button loses any changes you have made since bringing up the dialog box. The document reverts to the last settings of the Page dialog box. You are returned to your document.

- *OK*. Accepts the settings in the Page dialog box. The new settings are applied to your document, and you are returned to it. You can select Page from the Format menu and make any other changes you want—they are not written in stone after you click OK.

Entering Page Margins

After you select Page from the Format menu, setting page margins is simple. When the Page dialog box appears on-screen, the dark highlighting band is already in the Top Margins field. Type the measure of the amount of space you want above the text on each page of your document. If you want a two-inch top margin on each page, type *2*, and press the Tab key to move to the next setting box.

You enter the remaining three settings—the Bottom, Left, and Right Margins settings—in the same manner. The dark highlighting band moves to each field in turn as you press Tab. Type the number representing the amount of space you want on the bottom, left, or right side of each page of your document. Press Tab to accept the value and move to the next field.

You do not have to type the *in* you see in the fields. This abbreviation represents inches—the current unit of measure. (For information on changing this unit, see "The Ruler," in this chapter.) When you type a number in any of the four margin fields, the program assumes that you are entering a number in the current unit of measure.

You can override this default by typing a number followed by an abbreviation representing one of the other units of measure available in the program. Table 2.1 shows the acceptable abbreviations and their meanings.

Table 2.1
Units of Measure

Abbreviation	Unit of Measure
in	inches
i	inches
"	inches
p	picas
pt	points
mm	millimeters
m	millimeters
cm	centimeters
c	centimeters

For example, if the unit of measure is set to inches, you can set a two-centimeter top margin by typing *2 cm* in the Top Margins field. To accept the margin settings, click the OK button or press the Return key.

If you make an error setting one of the margins, a dialog box appears after you click the OK button or press Return (see fig. 2.6). The error message gives you the acceptable values for the field. Click OK to return to the Page dialog box. The incorrect setting is highlighted to indicate where the correction should be made.

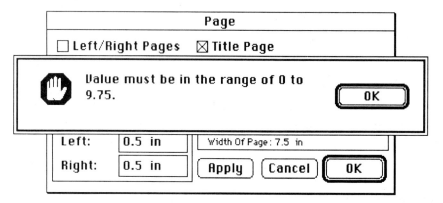

Fig. 2.6. *An incorrect value has been entered.*

Inserting Page Breaks

A *page break* is the location where a page ends and another begins. Normally, the program handles page breaks for you. After the page is filled with text, the program moves to another page and places text on that page.

You can adjust these page divisions yourself. For instance, you may find that the program breaks paragraphs and places the parts on two different pages, sometimes leaving a single line alone on one of the two pages. In many word processing programs this problem is addressed with what is called widow and orphan control. Although MacWrite II does not have these options, you can control widows and orphans by using the Insert Page Break command.

Consider the text in figure 2.7. At the bottom of the window, you can see that the bottom page (page 3) begins with a single line that belongs to the paragraph at the bottom of the first page (page 2). This single separated line is called as a *widow*. The reverse situation—the first line of a paragraph left at the bottom of a page—is called an *orphan*.

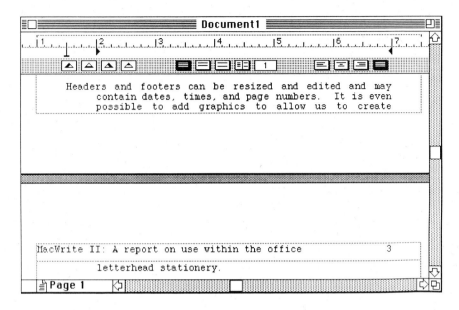

Fig. 2.7. *A widow on page 3.*

Because page 2 is full, the best solution is to force the entire last paragraph to page 3. To do so, insert a page break before the paragraph that begins *Headers and footers* by following these steps:

1. Place the mouse pointer just before the first word of the paragraph (the word *Headers*).

2. Press the mouse button. This process puts the cursor just before the paragraph's first word.

3. Select the Format menu and choose the Insert Page Break command.

The paragraph is moved to the next page. You have inserted an invisible page break character before the paragraph's first word. The page break character indicates to the program where the next page is to begin.

Deleting a page break character is simple. Click the mouse at the point after the page break. For the preceding example, click the mouse at the beginning of the word *Headers*. Press the Backspace key (Delete on some keyboards) to delete the page break.

Although deleting page breaks is a simple task, finding them after you have inserted them may not be so simple. Page breaks are part of a class of MacWrite II characters called *invisibles*. These invisible formatting characters are covered in Chapter 3. For now, simply select Show Invisibles from the View menu to make the page break character visible so that it can be edited.

Figure 2.8 shows how the page break character appears after Show Invisibles is selected. The page break character is the double arrow pointing downward, the last character on page 2. Now that the character is visible, you can delete it as you delete any other character. You can backspace over it, or you can double-click it and press the Backspace key.

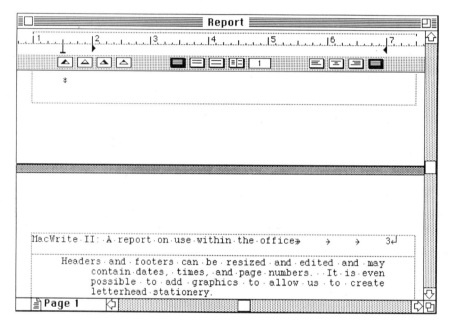

Fig. 2.8. *Displaying the invisible page break character.*

To restore the previous view—to make the invisibles invisible again—select Hide Invisibles from the View menu.

Formatting Paragraphs

Paragraphs are probably the most important document elements. In MacWrite II, all text in a document is part of some paragraph. Most formatting is paragraph oriented, and each paragraph can have its own formatting.

MacWrite II considers any group of characters ending with a carriage return to be a paragraph. Therefore, each time you press the Return key (Enter on some keyboards), you create a new paragraph. Even if you type a single letter and press Return, MacWrite II considers that letter a paragraph.

The Paragraph dialog box brings all the paragraph-specific formatting together into one location. To display this box, choose Paragraph from the Format menu. The Paragraph dialog box is divided into three parts: the indent settings, the spacing settings, and the control buttons (see fig. 2.9).

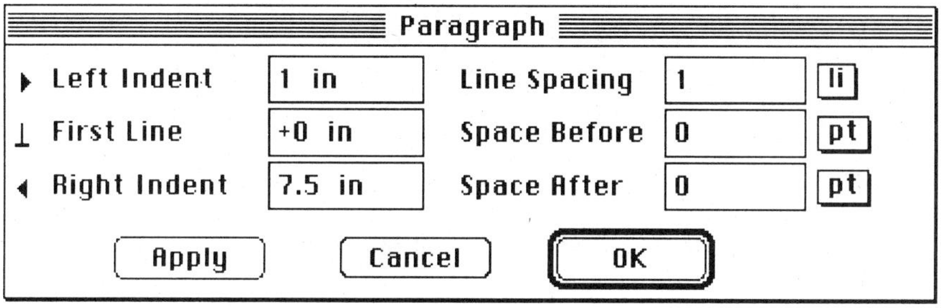

Fig. 2.9. The Paragraph dialog box.

In brief, the indent settings are as follows:

- *Left Indent*. Controls the left margin of the text of the paragraph. Corresponds to the left black triangle in the ruler.

- *First Line*. Sets the first-line indent of the paragraph. Corresponds to the upside down T in the ruler.

- *Right Indent*. Sets the right margin of the paragraph's text. Corresponds to the right black triangle in the ruler.

The spacing settings are the following:

- *Line Spacing*. Controls the amount of space each line receives. You also can set this spacing from the ruler with the line spacing icons. In the dialog box, you enter a number to set Line Spacing.

- *Space Before*. Enables you to specify an amount of space to precede the paragraph

- *Space After*. Enables you to specify an amount of space to follow a paragraph

To the right of each spacing setting is a pop-up menu that enables you to choose the unit of measure for each. These settings are covered in another section in this chapter.

The buttons should be familiar:

- *Apply.* Enables you to apply the settings to a paragraph to see the results. The dialog box remains on the screen. You may have to move the dialog box by dragging the title bar so that you can see the paragraph in question.

- *Cancel.* Loses any changes you have made in the Paragraph dialog box and closes the box. Note that holding down the Command key and pressing the period key is the same as clicking the Cancel button.

- *OK.* Confirms the settings you have made, applies them to the paragraph, and closes the Paragraph dialog box. Pressing the Return key produces the same results.

An interesting aspect of the Paragraph dialog box is that it can be called up by double-clicking any indent marker in the ruler: the left indent triangle, the first-line indent upside-down T, or the right indent triangle. Double-clicking one of these markers is the same as selecting Paragraph from the Format menu.

Setting Paragraph Indents

The Left and Right Indent settings determine the left and right limits to the text of the paragraph. Setting the Left Indent to two inches means that the paragraph text will not cross to the left of the two-inch mark on the ruler.

The First Line indent setting controls the starting point for the first line of the paragraph. With this setting, you can create two types of indents—the regular indent, where the first line begins to the right of the left edge of the text, and hanging indents, where the first line begins to the left of the left edge of the text.

You can use one of three different approaches to set paragraph indents. You can use the indent markers in the ruler, the Paragraph dialog box, or a combination of the first two methods.

Using the Ruler

Contained in the ruler are three markers that correspond to the three types of paragraph indents (see fig. 2.10). To set any marker, drag it to the desired location.

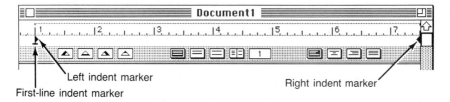

Fig. 2.10. *The ruler paragraph indent markers.*

For example, to make the left edge of your paragraphs begin at the two-inch mark, do the following:

1. Place the mouse pointer on the left indent marker.

2. Drag the indent marker to the desired location (the 2 mark).

As you drag the left indent marker, you may notice that the first-line indent marker moves with the left indent marker. Setting the first-line indent marker separately is covered later.

Unlike pages where the margin settings apply to the entire document, paragraph indents apply until changed. That is, you can set the paragraph indents, type a paragraph, and then change the indents for the next paragraph. Each paragraph in your document can have unique indent settings.

The majority of your paragraphs will have the same indent settings. You do not have to set the indent markers before typing each paragraph. The program assumes that the current settings apply to each paragraph until you make a change.

Using the Paragraph Dialog Box

The other two methods of setting the paragraph indents use the Paragraph dialog box. These two methods give you greater precision in setting the indents (up to three decimal places).

After you choose Paragraph from the Format menu, the Paragraph dialog box appears. You then can enter the position of the left and right indent markers as measurements. In the preceding section, you moved the left indent marker to the 2 position on the ruler by dragging. You can make the same change with the Paragraph dialog by typing *2* in the Left Indent field and clicking the OK button. You can set the right indent of the paragraph in the same manner. To reach the field, press the Tab key until the number in the Right Indent field is highlighted. Type the new position of the right indent. Click OK to confirm the setting.

You can set both indents at the same time. Before clicking the OK button, type both settings. Use the Tab key to move from field to field. If you want, you can click the Apply button to see the effect of the settings. The two indent markers in the ruler move to the positions you enter.

Using Both the Paragraph Dialog Box and the Ruler

You also can drag the indent markers in the ruler while the Paragraph dialog box is open. As you drag either indent marker, the field to which that marker corresponds shows the position of the marker. You may want to use this method when you have an idea of where the marker needs to be but are not certain of the exact location. After you have placed the indent markers, you can make adjustments by changing the measures in the Left and Right Indent fields in the Paragraph dialog box.

Keep in mind that the Paragraph dialog box allows three decimal places for positioning indents. For example, the left indent marker at the 2 1/8 position is entered as *2.125* in the Left Indent field.

Setting First-Line Indents

The first-line indent applies only to the first line of a paragraph. If you read Chapter 1 and followed along with the quick start, you saw how you can use the first-line indent marker instead of a tab to indent the first line of each paragraph.

Using the first-line indent setting can save you time and effort. Instead of pressing the Tab key at the beginning of each paragraph to indent the first line, you can indicate to the program where the first line should begin. The remaining lines of the paragraph follow the left indent setting for their starting position.

Setting the first-line indent is similar to the process used for the left and right indents. Consider the paragraph in figure 2.11.

As you can see, the paragraph's first line begins at the 1.5-inch position, but the rest of the paragraph's lines begin at 1 inch. Using the ruler, you accomplish this indention by following these steps:

1. Place the mouse on the small bar below the left indent marker (the bottom of the upside-down T).

2. Drag the first-line indent marker (the upside-down T) to the position where you want the first line to begin (1.5 inches).

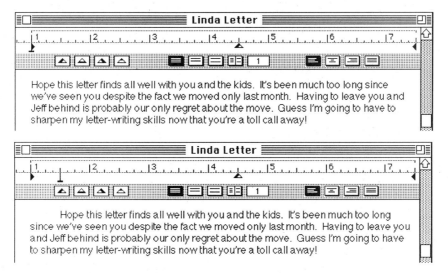

Fig. 2.11. *An indented paragraph.*

3. Release the mouse button.

The first line of each paragraph then automatically begins at 1.5 inches—you do not have to press the Tab key.

You also can use the Paragraph dialog box to set the first-line indent. Consider figure 2.12, which shows the settings for the same paragraph.

Note that the first-line indent is set relative to the left indent position. In the figure, the left indent is set at 1 inch (and you see the marker at that point on the ruler). The First Line field reads +0.5 in. This setting means that the first-line indent is positioned .5 inch to the right of the left indent position, or 1.5 inches from the margin.

You always enter the First Line field relative to the Left Indent field. If after setting the left indent position, you decide that you want the first line of each paragraph to indent one-quarter of an inch, you enter +0.25 in the First Line field.

You also can drag the first-indent marker in the ruler with the Paragraph dialog box on the screen. The First Line field shows the numeric measure of the marker's position. You can use as many as three decimal places

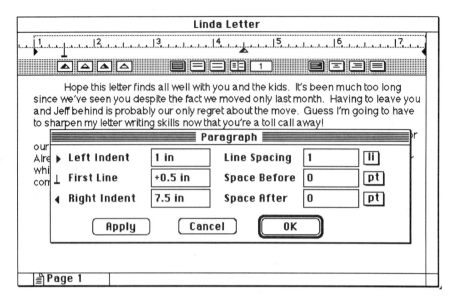

Fig. 2.12. *The sample paragraph's indent setting.*

when adjusting a first-line indent after dragging the marker. For example, you enter a first-line indent of three-eighths as +*0.375.*

You can enter a negative number for the first-line indent position to create a *hanging indent.* A *hanging indent* has the first line of the paragraph extending to the left of the body of the paragraph. The first line hangs out over the rest. Figure 2.13 shows an example of a hanging indent and the Paragraph dialog box settings used to accomplish it. Note that the First Line indent setting is a negative number—the first-line indent marker is .5 inch to left of the left indent marker.

If the left indent marker is at the edge of the page margin, you cannot set the first-line indent to the left of the left indent marker. To achieve a hanging indent, as in figure 2.13, you must first position the left indent marker. Then you can place the first-line indent.

When you move the left indent marker, the first-line indent marker moves with the left indent marker, maintaining its relative position. In the figure, you cannot position the left indent marker at 1 inch (the left margin) by entering 1 in the Left Indent field, because the first-line indent marker does not have room to move .5 inch to the left of the left indent marker.

This problem occurs only when you are using the Paragraph dialog box to position the indent markers. If you drag the left indent marker in the ruler,

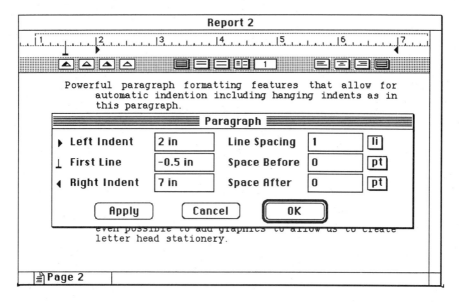

Fig. 2.13. *A hanging indent.*

the marker scoops up the first-line indent as the marker passes over the first-line indent. The two markers then move together.

If you want to reposition the left indent marker by dragging in the ruler but do not want the first-line indent marker to move with the left indent marker, do the following:

1. Place the mouse pointer on the left indent marker.

2. Press and hold the Option key on the keyboard; then press and hold the mouse button.

3. Drag the left indent marker to a new position.

4. Release the mouse button.

This process (sometimes called Option-clicking or Option-dragging) moves only the left indent marker. The first-line indent marker maintains its position.

Setting Paragraph Spacing

Each paragraph can have its own spacing. In addition, you can specify an amount of space to precede or follow a paragraph. The following sections discuss these paragraph spacing changes.

Setting the Unit of Measure

Each of the three spacing settings has five units of measure. The units of measure are accessed through pop-up menus. The three shadowed boxes containing the unit of measure for each spacing setting are menus. Moving the mouse pointer to one and then pressing the mouse button brings up a menu revealing the units available (see fig. 2.14).

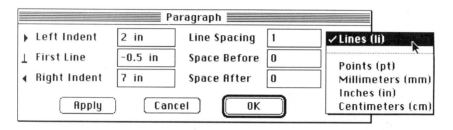

Fig. 2.14. *The pop-up Unit of Measure menu.*

Each spacing setting has five available units of measure:

- *Lines (li)*. The spacing is set in number of lines. The actual height of a line is determined by the font used.

- *Points (pt)*. The spacing is set as a number of points. A point is equal to 1/72nd of an inch. This measure is absolute; no adjustment is made for font sizes.

- *Millimeters (mm)*. The spacing is set in millimeters. One millimeter is equal to about 0.039 inches, or 2.835 points. This measure is absolute.

- *Inches (in)*. The spacing is set in inches. Inches are an absolute measure.

- *Centimeters (cm)*. The spacing is set in centimeters. One centimeter is 10 millimeters, about 0.39 inches, or 28.35 points. Centimeters are an absolute measure.

All the units of measure except lines are absolute. Remember that a line is adjusted for the fonts you use, and all fonts are not the same height. When you use the lines unit of measure, one line is defined as the height of the font plus some extra space to leave room between lines.

If you use an absolute measure for the line spacing setting, you may have to adjust fonts to keep from cutting off the tops of characters that do not fit within the height for the line.

Because the Space Before and Space After settings determine the amount of space before and after paragraphs, clipping characters is not a problem between paragraphs.

To select a unit of measure, follow these steps:

1. Place the mouse pointer on the unit of measure in the shadowed box.

2. Press and hold the mouse button to cause the menu to pop up.

3. Continuing to hold down the mouse button, move the mouse to slide the dark highlighting band to the chosen unit of measure.

4. Release the mouse button.

The chosen unit of measure appears in the shadowed box.

When you change the unit of measure, the program converts the entries in the Line Spacing, the Space Before, and the Space After fields to the approximate equivalent of the entry in the new unit of measure. Do not assume, however, that the conversion is exactly accurate.

When you change to or from lines as the unit of measure, the new entry in the field is approximate. Remember that lines are a relative measure. The amount of space represented by a line is adjusted to fit the document's font. The other units—points, millimeters, inches, and centimeters—are absolute. For example, if you have 1 in the Line Spacing field and the unit of measure is changed from lines to points, the number changes to 16, because 16 points is approximately equal to single-spacing.

Unless you need to use one of the other units of measure, you should stick with lines. Lines are the easiest unit of measurement to use, eliminating the worry of font heights and similar concerns.

Setting the Line Spacing with the Ruler

On the ruler, you find three line spacing icons (see fig. 2.15). Clicking one of the line spacing icons sets the line spacing to the familiar numbers (for typewriter users). These spacings operate as follows:

- *Single-spacing.* Leaves no blank lines between lines of text. Essentially, each line of text receives one line of room.

- *One-and-one-half spacing.* Leaves a blank half line between lines of text. That is, each line of text receives one and one-half lines of room.

- *Double-spacing.* Leaves a blank line between lines of text. Each line of text receives two lines of room.

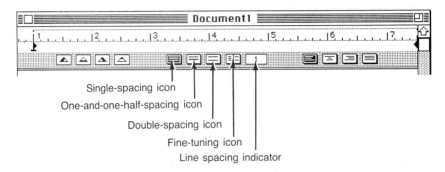

Fig. 2.15. *The line spacing icons.*

The current line spacing is indicated by a darkened icon and a number in the line spacing indicator. A 1 in the indicator shows that single-spacing is in force, a 1.5 shows that one-and-one-half-line spacing is being used, and a 2 shows double-spacing.

Fine-Tuning Line Spacing

The fine-tuning icon is a two-part icon. The left side has lines closer together than the right side. You can increase or decrease line spacing by clicking the appropriate side.

To decrease the line spacing, click the left side of the fine-tuning icon. Each click decreases the line spacing one-half line. To change the line spacing from double-spacing to single-spacing, for example, click the left side twice.

To increase line spacing, click the right side of the fine-tuning icon. Each click increases the line spacing by one-half line.

Using the fine-tuning icon, you can increase the line spacing up to 10 lines of space for each line of text.

Setting Line Spacing with the Dialog Box

To enter a Line Spacing setting using the Paragraph dialog box, type a number in the Line Spacing field. You then can tab to another field or click OK to confirm the setting. A number entered without an abbreviation is set in the unit of measure displayed in the shadowed box next to the Line Spacing field.

Lines (abbreviated li) is probably the best and easiest unit of measure to use. Single-spacing and double-spacing are the units of measure you probably are accustomed to. With the unit of measure set to lines, a 1 in this field indicates single-spacing, a 2 indicates double-spacing, a 3 triple-spacing, and so on.

You can enter fractional amounts. For example, you can enter *1.5* for one-and-one-half spacing. Up to three decimal places are available.

Unlike the page margin settings and the indent settings, spacing cannot be entered with an abbreviation. You must use the menus to set the unit of measure. In other words, if you want to use centimeters as your unit of measure for line spacing, you must select Centimeters from the pop-up menu and then enter the amount in the Line Spacing field. You cannot type *2 cm* while the unit of measure is set to Lines.

Setting Space before and after a Paragraph

Although you can press Return twice at the end of each paragraph to leave a blank line between paragraphs, the Space Before or Space After setting can save you the extra keypresses by making the program leave a blank line for you. Open the Paragraph dialog box and enter a number in the Space After field.

What number should you enter in the Space After field? To find the answer to that question when the unit of measure is points (the default unit of measure), recall that a point is 1/72nd of an inch. A standard 11-inch sheet of paper has 66 single-space lines. A single-space line is, therefore, 1/6th of an inch. To get a single blank line to follow each paragraph, enter 12 in the Space After field (12/72 = 1/6).

Although fonts are measured in points, this method may not always result in the best-looking spacing for your paragraphs. For example, 2 fonts with a measure of 12 points may not be the same height. A 12-point space after (or before) your paragraphs may not look like a single blank line, appearing too small or too large. Several attempts may be necessary to find the correct measurement. Use the Apply button to experiment. Fonts and font sizes are covered in Chapter 9.

An easier way exists. Use the Lines unit of measure. MacWrite II automatically adjusts lines to fit the font and font size. If you use the Lines unit of measure for adding space before or after a paragraph, you can use *1* for one blank line, *2* for two blank lines, and so on. You can use up to three decimal places. For example, entering *1.125* yields one-and-one-eighth blank line.

Setting Paragraph Tabs

MacWrite II automatically places left tabs every half inch along the ruler. You can use these tabs without making any settings; simply press the Tab key.

After you make a tab setting (using the icons), the default tabs to the left of the tab icon are turned off. This change occurs each time a tab is set using one of the tab icons.

You set tabs on the ruler. You should determine the tabs necessary for a paragraph and set them (by dragging the icon to the ruler) before typing the paragraph. Remember that MacWrite II sets left tabs every half inch. Keep in mind, however, that these default tabs are not adjusted to fit the indents you set for the paragraph. If you indent the left edge of a paragraph to 2.25 inches, for example, the next default tab remains at 2.5 inches. If you want to tab one-half inch right from your indent marker, you must set a tab at 2.75 inches.

As with other paragraph formatting, when you start a new paragraph by pressing Return (Enter on some keyboards), the tabs are carried over to the new paragraph. When you encounter a paragraph that needs different tab settings, you must change the settings before typing that paragraph.

Each tab icon represents a different type of tab (see fig. 2.16). From left to right, the four tab types are the following:

- *Left.* The left edge of the text aligns at the tab position.

- *Center.* The text centers at the tab position.

- *Right.* The right edge of the text aligns at the tab position.

- *Align On tab.* The text aligns on a particular character. MacWrite II automatically sets this character to a decimal point. You can change this character (see Chapter 7).

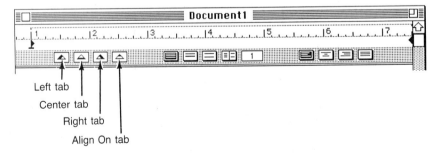

Fig. 2.16. The tab icons.

Figure 2.17 shows examples of each type of tab. The first three lines have
been created using the first tab type, the Left tab (represented by the
triangle icon with the darkened left side). The Left tab corresponds to the
tab settings used by typewriters.

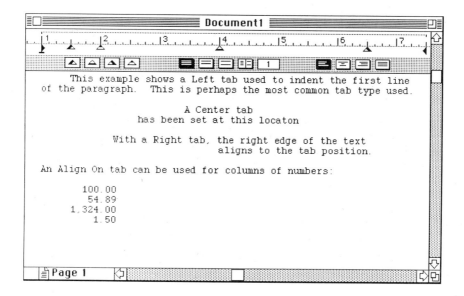

Fig. 2.17. Examples of the four tab types.

The second set of lines were created by using the Center tab type
(represented by the triangle with a darkened bottom). After you set a
Center tab, pressing Tab places the cursor at that position. Text centers
around the tab position. Center tabs are useful for centering titles and
headings. Rather than counting letters and figuring the space needed to
center the text, you simply place a Center tab at the location where you
want text to center, tab to the Center tab, and type.

The third set of lines in figure 2.17 use a Right tab (represented by a
triangle with the right side darkened). After setting the Right tab, when
you press Tab, the cursor jumps to that position. Any text typed moves
from the tab position to the left, leaving the right edge of the text at the
tab position. You can use this type of tab to create those right-side
quotations you may have seen in books and pamphlets.

The column of numbers demonstrates the Align On tab (represented by
the triangle with the darkened point). After placing this tab, you can align
a series of numbers by pressing the Tab key and typing the numbers. The
program automatically shifts the numbers so that the decimal points align.

Align On tabs are of great use in reports and invoices or any other type of document where you need to align columns of numbers. You can set several Align On tabs, and create columns of numbers for comparison of budgeted versus actual expenditures on a project, for example.

Setting Tabs

You set all four tab types with the same procedure. After deciding the type of tab you need, set a tab by following these steps:

1. Move the mouse pointer to the tab icon.

2. Drag the tab icon (actually a copy of the icon) on to the ruler.

3. Move to the desired location of the tab on the ruler.

4. Release the mouse button.

As you drag a tab icon on to the ruler, notice that the icon jumps toward the ruler measurements. At this point, you can make fine adjustments to the tab's position by moving the mouse left or right while holding down the mouse button.

Changing and Removing Tabs

After you place a tab icon on the ruler, you can move the icon to adjust the tab setting or remove the icon from the ruler. To move a tab, follow these steps:

1. Place the mouse pointer on the tab icon you want to move.

2. Press and hold down the mouse button.

3. Move the mouse left or right (holding down the mouse button) to move the tab icon.

Removing a tab is a similar procedure: Place the cursor on the tab icon and press and hold down the mouse button. Then move the tab icon down off the ruler until the icon disappears. You do not have to return the icon to any position.

Setting Paragraph Text Alignment

Four different types of text alignment are available in MacWrite II (see fig. 2.18). You can use any of the four, although a single paragraph can have only one alignment. The text alignment icons from left to right are

- *Flush left*. Text is aligned against the left side of the paper, leaving the right side ragged.

- *Center*. Text is centered in the middle of the page (centered from left to right, but not top to bottom).

- *Flush right*. Text is aligned against the right side of the paper, leaving the left side ragged.

- *Justified*. The left and right sides of the text are aligned, producing a smooth, newspaper-column look.

Figure 2.19 shows samples of each alignment. Each line of a left-justified paragraph begins at the left indent setting, creating a straight edge vertically. The right edge of the paragraph is jagged—the last word of each line is not aligned to the right indent marker.

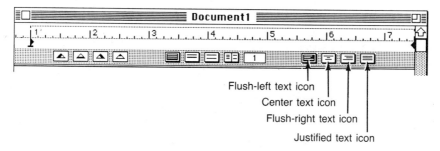

Fig. 2.18. The text alignment icons.

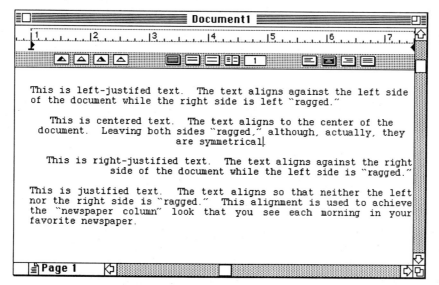

Fig. 2.19. Samples of text alignments.

This alignment is good for letters, memos, and other basic documents. Professional writers frequently use this alignment for stories and books because left-justified text is easier to deal with when typesetting.

The center text alignment centers the paragraph's text between the left and right indent settings. Centered text is best used for elements such as titles, column headings, header text, and the like. You probably will not use centered text in the body of a document unless you want a special effect like a Christmas greeting or poem.

You also see centered text used in headers and footers. The header and footer text can be centered over each page of your document. The use of headers and footers is covered in Chapter 8.

Right-justified text (flush-right text) is not used often. This setting causes the right edge of text to align to the right indent setting. You see right-justified text in footers where the page number and associated text are forced to the right side of the page.

Justified text is an excellent choice for memos, letters, reports, and multiple-column documents (covered in Chapter 11). Businesses use justified text for formal correspondence. Justified text produces a blocky look for each paragraph because the edges are aligned to the left and right indent settings.

To select a text alignment, click the icon of the text alignment you want to use. For example, to change to center text alignment, click the center text icon. The icon darkens to indicate which text alignment has been chosen.

You can change text alignment at any time as you create the document; the change applies from the current paragraph until another text alignment is chosen. Changing the text alignment of a previously typed paragraph is covered in Chapter 3.

As with other paragraph formatting, when you press Return, the alignment is carried over to the next paragraph, so you do not have to reselect the alignment at the beginning of each new paragraph. Selecting an alignment is necessary only for paragraphs with a different alignment.

Saving Documents

Saving a document is storing its contents on a floppy or hard disk drive. MacWrite II, like other computer programs, works with information while it is stored in memory circuits. These circuits are much faster than disk drives when storing and retrieving information. Unfortunately, when you shut off the power, the circuits lose whatever is stored in them. Hence, the need for disks.

When you are working on a document, you should remember to save it frequently. You never know when the power may go out (or even fluctuate), and your document may simply vanish. The rule of thumb is to save at the point at which you are unwilling to redo the work. For many people, this rule means saving every 15 minutes or so. Few things are more frustrating than having several hours of work wiped out by a momentary power failure.

Saving a New Document

When you begin a new document, MacWrite II names it Document followed by some number. As you type, edit, insert graphics, or perform any other command, the program stores the information in memory. Until the first time you save the document, no file exists on disk.

You can use one of two methods to save your document. You can save and name the document when you close it. To close a document, click the close box—the small box in the upper left of the document window—or select Close from the File menu.

If you make changes to the document and click the close box, the program responds with the dialog box shown in figure 2.20. MacWrite II wants to make sure that you save your changes before you close the document.

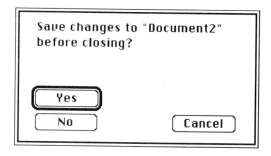

Fig. 2.20. *The Save Changes dialog box.*

Clicking the No button in this dialog box closes the window without saving the changes you have made to the document. Clicking the Cancel button returns you to the document.

To save the changes made to your document, click the Yes button or press the Return key on the keyboard. If you have saved the document before, the program saves the new version of the document over the old one, replacing it on disk.

This approach is best used for short documents—a short letter or memo. Longer documents—because of the amount of work involved in them—should be saved to disk long before you close them.

The second approach is to select Save from the File menu and save the file to disk immediately (see fig. 2.21). Note that you can select this command from the keyboard by holding down the Command key (the four-leaf clover symbol) and pressing the letter S.

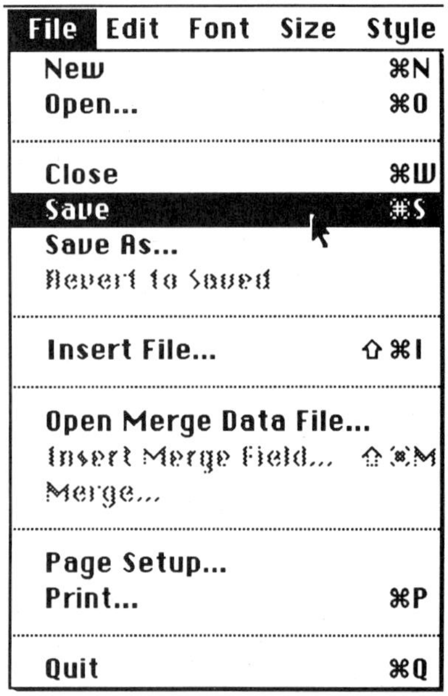

File	Edit	Font	Size	**Style**
New				⌘N
Open...				⌘O
Close				⌘W
Save				⌘S
Save As...				
Revert to Saved				
Insert File...				⇧⌘I
Open Merge Data File...				
Insert Merge Field...				⇧⌘M
Merge...				
Page Setup...				
Print...				⌘P
Quit				⌘Q

Fig. 2.21. Selecting Save.

Regardless of the approach you use to save a new document, you see the dialog box shown in figure 2.22. In this dialog box, the program prompts you to name and specify the location of the new document. At the top of the dialog box is the name of the current disk or folder. Below the document name in the small window is a list of the files on that disk or in that folder. The names are gray because the function of this dialog box is to save a file to disk, not to open or insert a file that is already on disk.

You can use this window to verify that you are not attempting to use a file name that has already been taken.

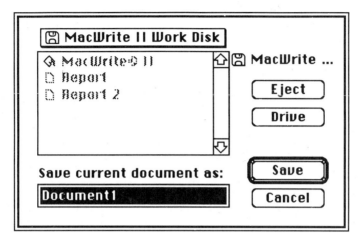

MacWrite II Work Disk

◇ MacWrite II
☐ Report
☐ Report 2

MacWrite ...
Eject
Drive

Save current document as:
Document1

Save
Cancel

Fig. 2.22. *The Save File dialog box.*

In the field below the line Save current document as is the name with which the document will be saved. The first time you save a document, the program automatically inserts the name that the program assigned when the document window was opened.

Because the name you give the document is the one that will appear with the document on disk, you should use a descriptive name (up to 31 characters long) that will help you remember the document's contents. The name can contain spaces and any character except the colon (:). You type a name and then click the Save button to save the document to disk. Pressing the Return key has the same effect as clicking the Save button.

When you click Cancel, the program does not save the file to disk. Instead, the program returns you to the document. Holding down the Command key and pressing period is the same as clicking the Cancel button.

The Eject button ejects the current disk from the computer. (The name of the current disk is shown above the Eject button.) Clicking the Drive button switches disk drives so that you can choose the disk on which you want to save the file.

Saving a Copy of a Document

Sometimes you may want to save a copy of a document that has already been stored to disk. You may make changes and want to keep the original or perhaps want a backup copy. To do so, simply select the Save As option from the File menu. The program responds with the dialog box shown in figure 2.23.

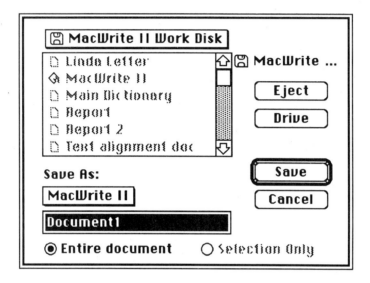

Fig. 2.23. *The Save As dialog box.*

Note that the dialog box has MacWrite II, the default file format, beneath the Save As line. You can select different file formats for storing the document (see Chapter 5). Below this line is the current document name, which you change to reflect the fact that you are saving a second copy of this document.

Below the name field, you see two buttons. If you select Entire Document, the entire document will be saved to disk. You can save sections of a document by selecting the section and clicking the Selection Only button. This button becomes available after a selection is made. Making and working with selections is covered in the next chapter of this book.

After you have given the document copy a new name, click the Save button (or press the Return key) to store the copy to disk.

Reverting to Saved

Now and then you may find that you have made changes that you do not want. You can return to the last-saved version of the document two ways. The first method is the following:

1. Close the document by clicking the close box or selecting Close from the File menu.

2. Click the No button when the program asks whether you want to save the changes you made.

3. Open the document again.

You can use a much simpler version of this procedure. Choose Revert to Saved from the File menu. The program responds with a dialog box asking for confirmation. To return to the last version of the document that was saved to disk, click the OK button (or press the Return key). Keep in mind that any changes made since the last time you saved the document to disk will be lost.

Clicking Cancel aborts the Revert command and returns you to your document with your changes intact.

Printing a Document

A word processor, no matter how easy to use or how powerful, would be of little use without the capability to print your document on paper. Here again, MacWrite II shows its ease of use.

The easiest way to print a document is to perform the following steps:

1. Select Print from the File menu.

2. Click the OK button in the dialog box that appears.

The program prints one copy of your document. Printing more than one copy or printing only part of your document requires that you set a few print options.

Only a few options are associated with printing in MacWrite II; the options appear in two locations. The first location is the Page Setup dialog box. If you choose to alter the options in the Page Setup dialog box, you should do so before attempting to print your document. The second location is the Print dialog box that appears after you select Print from the File menu.

Using the Page Setup Options

To access the Page Setup dialog box, select Page Setup from the File menu. The Page Setup dialog box for the LaserWriter is shown in figure 2.24.

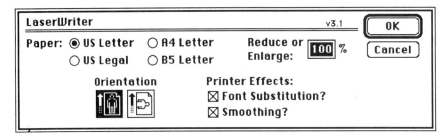

Fig. 2.24. *The Page Setup dialog box for a LaserWriter printer.*

The specific dialog box you see depends on the printer you have. Because of the number of printers now available for the Macintosh, covering print options for every printer is impossible. You must check your printer manual for explanation of options specific to your printer.

Some of the options, however, are seen in some form in just about every printer's Page Setup dialog box. Common options are covered in the following sections.

Setting Paper Size

The Paper option enables you to choose the paper type you are using in the printer. US Letter and US Legal, shown in figure 2.24, are the most common paper types. A4 Letter and B5 Letter are European standard paper sizes and are rarely used in the United States.

Choose a paper size by clicking the small circle next to the name of the paper you are using. Most LaserWriter users do not need to change the default option, US Letter (the standard 8.5-by-11-inch paper).

Note that other printers can have different paper size options available. In figure 2.25, the Page Setup dialog box is shown for the ImageWriter LQ.

Some of the paper sizes are the same as for the LaserWriter: US Letter, US Legal, and A4 Letter. Now, however, you see Computer Paper, International Fanfold, and even an Envelope (#10) option. Most ImageWriter users probably will choose the Computer Paper option. This type of paper

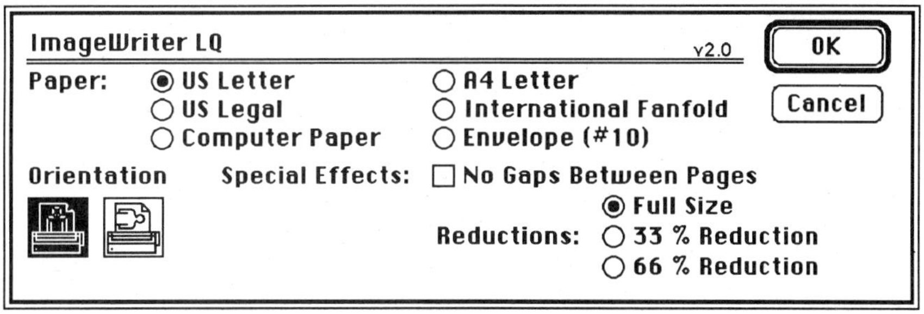

```
┌─────────────────────────────────────────────────────────────────┐
│ ImageWriter LQ                                 v2.0    ┌─────────┐│
│                                                        │   OK    ││
│ Paper:    ⊙ US Letter          ○ A4 Letter            └─────────┘│
│           ○ US Legal           ○ International Fanfold  ┌────────┐│
│           ○ Computer Paper     ○ Envelope (#10)        │ Cancel ││
│                                                         └────────┘│
│ Orientation    Special Effects:  ☐ No Gaps Between Pages          │
│                                              ⊙ Full Size          │
│  [🖶] [🖶]                      Reductions:  ○ 33 % Reduction      │
│                                              ○ 66 % Reduction     │
└─────────────────────────────────────────────────────────────────┘
```

Fig. 2.25. *The ImageWriter LQ Page Setup dialog box.*

comes in a continuous stream and is pulled through the printer by use of the holes along the side. Click the circle next to the paper option you want.

After you have chosen the paper, this information is saved with the document, so you do not have to set paper size again for that document.

Changing the paper size for a completed document can change the formatting. After all, if you create the document with the Paper option set to US Letter, the program places page breaks based on a paper size of 8.5 by 11 inches (minus the page margin settings). If you choose the US Legal option before printing, you are indicating to the program that the paper is 3 inches longer than before. MacWrite II adjusts the text to fit on the longer page, moving page breaks as needed.

Enlarging and Reducing Documents

Most Page Setup dialog boxes enable you to adjust the size of the printed document on the page. The LaserWriter Page Setup has a field in which you enter a number representing the percentage size of the printed document. That is, to print the document at one half its normal size, you enter *50*. To double the document's size, enter *200*. Enlarging and reducing a document increases the time required to print it.

Some printers, including ImageWriters and other dot-matrix printers, provide only limited adjustment of the printed size of your document. If you refer to figure 2.25, you see that the ImageWriter LQ has only three choices: Full Size, 33% Reduction, and 66% Reduction. Enlargements on the ImageWriters are not possible.

Because changing the size of the document affects the ruler and margin settings, the new size can appear confusing at first. After changing the size and returning to the document, the ruler and page margins are changed to fit the new document size.

To see the effect of enlarging or reducing a document, consider a couple of examples. First, assume that you have decided to enlarge the document by 50 percent (this example assumes that you are using a LaserWriter). Figure 2.26 shows the document before it is enlarged.

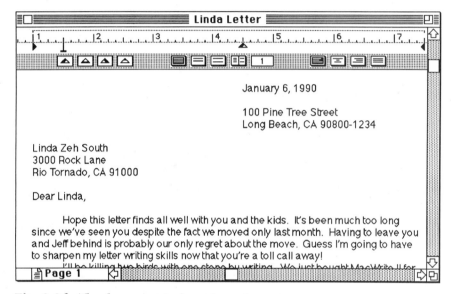

Fig. 2.26. The document to be enlarged.

Note that the page margins are set to 1 inch. This setting leaves the area of the page from the 1-inch position to the 7.5-inch position to be used for text. The 50 percent enlargement is accomplished by following these steps:

1. Select Page Setup from the File menu.

2. Type *150* in the Reduce or Enlarge field.

3. Click the OK button.

Figure 2.27 shows the results of the enlargement.

Because the text of the document is being increased in size by 50 percent, the ruler has been decreased in length. The purpose of the adjustment is to make the image of the document on the screen conform to what will be printed. Everything in the document—including the page margins you set—is going to be increased by 50 percent. The ruler is now 5.67 inches wide. As the document is printed, the printer increases the text by 50 percent. A 50 percent increase in size of a ruler 5.67 inches wide results in a page width of 8.5 inches (5.67 × 1.5 = 8.5).

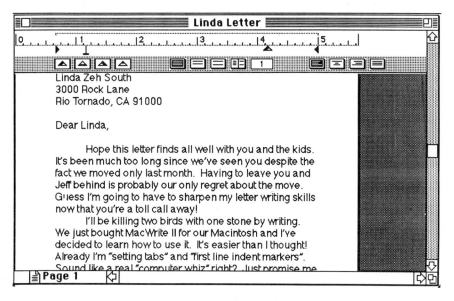

Fig. 2.27. *The enlarged document.*

A similar change occurs for a reduction in the document size. Entering *50* in the Reduce or Enlarge field results in an apparent doubling of the ruler length (from 8.5 inches to 17 inches) and page margins. This enlargement is simply to show that twice as much text now fits on the paper because the size of the text has been cut in half.

Perhaps the best course is to familiarize yourself with the effect of reducing or enlarging your page by trying a few different settings and printing a test document.

Orienting Your Document

The two Orientation settings in the Page Setup dialog box are portrait and landscape. Portrait is the standard orientation. The short sides of the page are at the top and bottom; the long sides are the left and right sides of the page. The landscape orientation is a 90-degree rotation. The page is printed with the long sides of the paper as the top and bottom edges and the short sides to the left and right—in other words, the page is sideways.

You choose an orientation by clicking one of the two icons. Keep in mind that landscape orientation requires more time to print than portrait (see Chapter 7). After you have set the Page Setup options, click the OK button (or press Return) to confirm your choices.

Using the Print Dialog Box Options

After you select Print from the file menu, a dialog box similar to the one in figure 2.28 appears. The dialog box shown is for Apple LaserWriters. If you have a different printer, the Print dialog box will be slightly different. Consult your printer manual for a description of options unique to that printer.

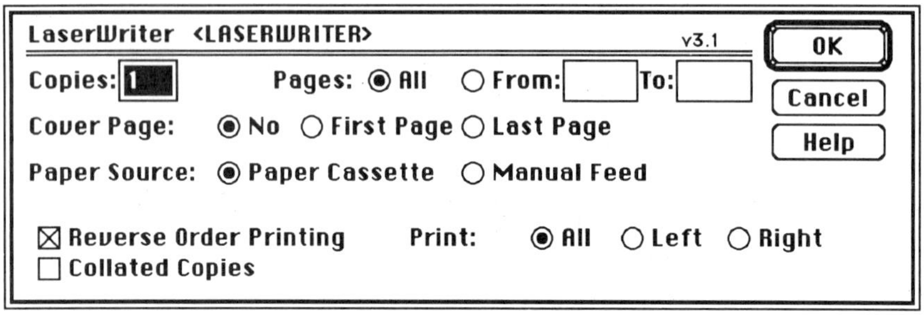

```
┌────────────────────────────────────────────────────────────────┐
│ LaserWriter <LASERWRITER>                    v3.1    ╭───────────╮│
│                                                      │    OK     ││
│ Copies:▐1▌        Pages: ◉ All   ○ From:    To:      ╰───────────╯│
│                                                      ╭───────────╮│
│ Cover Page:    ◉ No  ○ First Page ○ Last Page        │  Cancel   ││
│                                                      ╰───────────╯│
│ Paper Source: ◉ Paper Cassette  ○ Manual Feed        ╭───────────╮│
│                                                      │   Help    ││
│                                                      ╰───────────╯│
│ ☒ Reverse Order Printing      Print:   ◉ All  ○ Left  ○ Right    │
│ ☐ Collated Copies                                                │
└────────────────────────────────────────────────────────────────┘
```

Fig. 2.28. *The Print dialog box for an Apple LaserWriter printer.*

Several options appear regardless of the printer you have. In the figure, these are labeled

- *Copies.* Enables you to specify the number of copies of your document you want to be printed

- *Pages.* Enables you to specify a range of pages to be printed

- *Reverse Order Printing.* Determines the order in which the pages are printed

- *Collated Copies.* Collates copies; available only on laser printers

- *Print.* Buttons enable you to print left pages, right pages, or all pages in the document. Left and right pages are discussed in Chapter 7. Click the button next to your choice.

After you have set the options, click the OK button (or press Return), and the program prints your document.

Printing Multiple Copies and Collating

To print more than one copy of your document, type the number you want in the Copies field. For a couple of copies of a document, this procedure is fine. If you have a long document, however, you may want to print one copy and use a copy machine to produce the rest.

The Collated Copies option is available to users of the LaserWriter (or similar laser printers). Normally, when the program prints more than one copy of a multipage document on a LaserWriter, the first page is printed the number of times specified. Then the second page is printed the number of times specified. The program proceeds to the end of the document, printing each page according to the setting in the Copies field.

This method leaves the collating—putting the copies together—to do by hand. Clicking the Collated Copies box gives the job to the program. This option causes the program to print pages 1, 2, 3, and so on, to the end of the document before proceeding to print the next copy.

Using this option increases the amount of time required to print the copies of the document. If you have graphics in your document, using the Collated Copies option may slow your printing intolerably.

Using the Reverse Order Option

The Reverse Order option does exactly as its name implies. The pages of the document are printed in reverse order. The program begins at the end of the document and works back to the beginning. The purpose of this option is to accommodate the stacking order of printers. You can print the last page first, and your document will stack in proper order.

The stacking order is different among different printers (even among Apple's original LaserWriters and the LaserWriter II series). You must experiment to see whether this option should be on or off to print your documents in the proper order.

Using Print Ranges

The print range (Pages) option is one of the easiest to use. This option enables you to choose the range of pages you want to print. For example, if you want to print pages 3 through 8 of a 15-page document, do the following:

1. Click the small circle next to the From field.

2. Type the number of the first page (3) you want printed and then press Tab.

3. Type the number of the last page (15) you want printed.

4. Click the OK button (after setting any other options you choose).

Canceling Printing

Unless you are using MultiFinder, after the program has begun printing a document, you see a dialog box stating that you can cancel printing by holding down the Command key and pressing the period (.) key. The printer may take a few moments to stop after you cancel.

If you are using MultiFinder, you must cancel printing through the Print Manager—a part of the System software. Covering the functioning of this item is beyond this book. However, the Apple manuals do an excellent job covering the System software.

Summing Up

In this chapter, you have begun your exploration of the power of MacWrite II. You began with the MacWrite II working environment. You should now have a basic knowledge of the document window, the ruler, the tab icons, the line spacing icons, and the menu bar.

You also covered the basic elements of documents—pages and paragraphs. You now should understand page margins, page breaks, line spacing, and text alignment. Finally, saving and printing documents are covered.

Armed with an understanding of these basics, you should be ready to create and print your own MacWrite II documents. And you should be ready to turn your attention to the editing features of the program.

3

Editing a Document

The capability to change your document before it hits paper is probably the single biggest reason that word processors have attained their current popularity. Anyone who has had to retype a page or an entire document because of mistakes or has dealt with correction fluids, tapes, and other correction materials quickly realizes the advantages word processors have over the typewriter.

But even after the advent of word processors, the search for quick, painless editing went on. Apple Computer's introduction of the pointing device and the graphic (pictorial) interface was a landmark event for the personal computer. Making changes—editing—became a matter of pointing and clicking rather than using arcane strings of command words and numbers.

Continuing in the tradition of Apple, Claris has taken full advantage of the text-editing capabilities of the Macintosh computer with MacWrite II. The result is a word processor that makes editing documents about as painless as possible with current technology.

If you are just now making the transition from typewriter to word processor or from one of the older, more difficult software programs, some of the concepts may be new and a little confusing. Rest assured, however, that you soon will wonder how you ever managed without them.

Editing Text Selections

In the quick start in Chapter 1, you encountered some of the simpler text editing concepts offered by MacWrite II. These concepts are covered again in this chapter in the broader context of editing text selections.

A *text selection* is text you choose from a document. A text selection can consist of as little as a single character or as much as the entire document. You can select words, sentences, paragraphs, and more with the keyboard or the mouse. Selected text is highlighted on-screen.

Selecting Text

You select text primarily by using the mouse; however, you also can use keyboard methods to select text. If you are just learning the Macintosh computer, you should probably start by using the mouse to make text selections. The mouse is the most intuitive method. As you progress, you can experiment with the keyboard method to determine whether using the mouse, the keyboard, or a combination of both is best for you. (The keyboard selection commands rely on keys that date from the Macintosh Plus keyboard to the present. If you have one of the older keyboards, these commands are not available.)

Selecting Text by Using the Mouse

You can select any amount of text by dragging the pointer across the text with the mouse button held down. For example, in figure 3.1, you see the first page of text of a sample report. The first part of the third line of the first paragraph has been selected. You know that this text is selected because the selected words are highlighted.

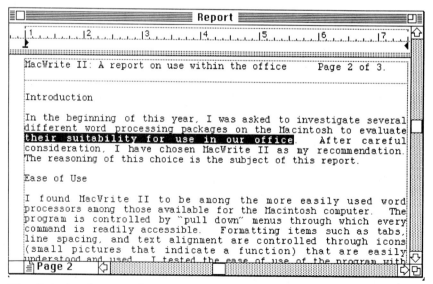

Fig. 3.1. *A selection of text.*

To make this selection, follow these steps:

1. Move the mouse pointer to the point immediately before the word you want to select—for example, the letter *t* of the word *their*.

2. Press and hold the mouse button.

3. Continue to hold down the mouse button while you move the mouse pointer across the line of text until you reach the end of the text you want to select—for the example, the word *office*.

4. Release the mouse button.

You use these same steps to select any amount of text. You can start and stop at any point in your document, except the selection cannot cross certain document elements. Although a selection can cross from paragraph to paragraph or from page to page, a selection cannot also include headers, footers, or footnotes (see Chapter 8). You can make selections within any of these elements, but you cannot make a selection that crosses from one to another.

You must select and work with headers and footers separately from the pages on which they appear. In figure 3.2, you can select any of the text in the footer. If you move out of the footer's box, however, you scroll the document. No text is selected outside the box.

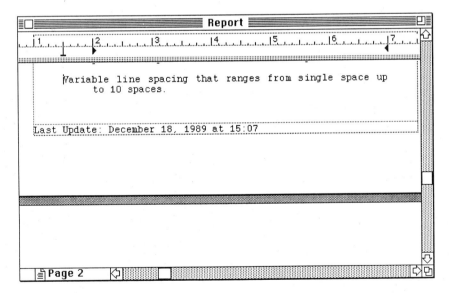

Fig. 3.2. *Footer text cannot be selected with body text.*

Within these limitations, you can use mouse shortcuts to select certain groups of text. You can select a word, line, or paragraph by placing the mouse pointer anywhere within one of these groups of text and clicking the mouse a number of times. The shortcuts are

- *Word*. Place the mouse pointer on the word and quickly press and release the mouse button twice (double-click).

- *Line*. Place the mouse pointer on the line and quickly press and release the mouse button three times (triple-click).

- *Paragraph*. With the mouse pointer anywhere in the paragraph, quickly press and release the mouse button four times (quadruple-click).

Note that *line* in this case does not refer to a sentence. A line is the text that stretches from one side of the page to the other, whether that length means a sentence, a part of a sentence, parts of two sentences, or whatever. MacWrite II has no shortcut for selecting a sentence.

Selecting Text by Using the Keyboard

Making text selections with the keyboard depends on the positioning of the cursor. The following section explains how to move the cursor; the next section describes how to select text with the keyboard.

Keyboard Cursor Movement

Beginning with the Macintosh Plus computer, Macintosh keyboards (including those supplied by companies other than Apple) have included four arrow keys. These keys, as the name implies, have arrows imprinted on the top, pointing in the four directions: up, down, left, and right.

These keys move the cursor in the direction indicated by the arrow. Press a key; the cursor moves one space in that direction. For the up- and down-arrow keys, the cursor moves one line. For the left and right keys, the cursor moves one character (or space). Holding the key down repeats the movement as long as the key is pressed. (If the keys on your computer do not repeat, check your Macintosh manual for the keyboard settings in the Control Panel.)

You can duplicate the left-arrow key's movement by holding down the Control key and pressing the backslash (\) key. Holding down the Control key and pressing the right bracket (]) key duplicates the function of the right-arrow key.

Other cursor movements possible from the keyboard are listed in table 3.1. You also will find these keys included on the tear-out reference card in the back of this book.

Table 3.1
Cursor-Control Keys

To Move	Press
Left one character	Left arrow or Control-\
Right one character	Right arrow or Control-]
Up one line	Up arrow
Down one line	Down arrow
Left one word	Option-left arrow
Right one word	Option-right arrow
To beginning of a line	Command-left arrow
To end of a line	Command-right arrow
Up one paragraph	Option-up arrow
Down one paragraph	Option-down arrow
To beginning of document	Command-up arrow
To end of document	Command-down arrow
To main text of document	Command-Return

With the number of different keyboards now available for the Macintosh, you may need to check your manual for the exact location of some of these keys if you are not familiar with them. The Command key usually has a four-leaf clover symbol printed on top, sometimes with an apple symbol alongside the clover symbol. On some keyboards from suppliers other than Apple, the key may simply be stamped with the word *Command*. The Option key may be indicated by *Opt* or *Option*, and the Control key usually has *Ctrl*, *Ctl*, or *Control* printed on the top.

The Command, Option, Control, and Shift keys are referred to as *modifier keys*. That is, they modify or change the meaning of the second key. In this book, a hyphen (-) between two keys indicates that you press the keys together. Usually, you press and hold any modifier keys before pressing the last key.

Command-Return is useful when you have just created or edited a document element such as a header, footer, or footnote. Using Command-Return moves you from the document element to the main text, returning you to your last cursor position within the text.

Keyboard Text Selection

After the cursor is positioned at the beginning of the text you want to select, you make the selection by using commands similar to the cursor-movement key combinations, except that the Shift key is usually added. The text-selection key combinations are listed in table 3.2.

Table 3.2
Keyboard Text-Selection Commands

To Select	Press
One character left	Shift-left arrow or Shift-Control-\
One character right	Shift-right arrow or Shift-Control-]
One line up	Shift-up arrow
One line down	Shift-down arrow
One word left	Shift-Option-left arrow
One word right	Shift-Option-right arrow
To beginning of a line	Shift-Command-left arrow
To end of a line	Shift-Command-right arrow
One paragraph up	Shift-Option-up arrow
One paragraph down	Shift-Option-down arrow
To beginning of document	Shift-Command-up arrow
To end of document	Shift-Command-down arrow

Holding the keys down causes the selection action to repeat at the repeat rate set in the Control Panel.

In figure 3.3, you see part of a sample report. To select the phrase as shown in figure 3.3, follow these steps:

1. Starting from the beginning of the word *Introduction*, press the down arrow five times to move to the beginning of the word *consideration*.

2. Press Option-right arrow to move to the word *I*.

3. Press Shift-Option-right arrow eight times to select each word in the phrase.

or

Press Shift-Command-right arrow to select from the current cursor position to the end of the line.

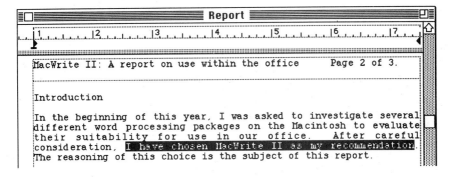

Fig. 3.3. *A selection made with the keyboard.*

Working with Selected Text

After you have made a text selection, you can work with that selection. You can include more text or reduce the amount included in the selection. You can delete, replace, move, or copy the selection to other parts of your document.

Much of this section deals with the upper part of the Edit menu. From the Edit menu, you choose most of the commands that operate on selected text. Keyboard equivalents for these operations are pointed out as each function is discussed. Refer to the command card for a complete list.

Extending Text Selections

After selecting text with the mouse or the keyboard, you may find that you want to include more text in the selection. You can use the mouse or the keyboard to extend your selection, regardless of which one you used to make the initial selection.

Extending Selections with the Mouse

Using the mouse to extend a selection is similar to the procedure for using the mouse to create a selection to begin with. Figure 3.4 shows a sample selection.

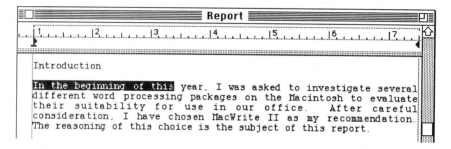

Fig. 3.4. A sample selection to be extended.

After making the selection shown in the figure, suppose that you decide that you want to include the word *year*. To extend the selection, follow these steps:

1. Position the mouse pointer at the end of the word *year*.

2. Press and hold the Shift key.

3. Click the mouse button.

Immediately, the black highlighting band encompasses the word *year*. This operation is referred to as *Shift-clicking* and can be used to extend a selection. Remember that you are extending a selection from the starting point you chose when you first made the selection, and the selection must be continuous (except for skipping headers, footers, and footnotes). The starting point of a selection acts as an anchor for the selection. Any extension stretches from that anchor to the new location you choose.

Extending Selections with the Keyboard

To extend a selection using the keyboard, you use the keystrokes you use to make a selection. Refer to table 3.2 or the command reference card if you need to review the commands.

To make the selection in figure 3.4, you use the Shift-Option-right arrow command to include each word of the text. Extending the selection is merely a matter of using the keyboard selection commands. Because the word *year* is to be included in the selection, you use the command to select one word to the right. This command is Shift-Option-right arrow, the command used to make the first selection.

In general, to add to a text selection, use the keyboard command that corresponds to the amount of text you want to add. To add a single character, use Shift-right arrow (or Shift-Control-]); to add the remainder of the line, use Shift-Command-right arrow, and so on.

Shortening Text Selections

Shortening a selection uses essentially the same commands as extending a selection. Again, you can use the mouse or the keyboard. The mouse command for shortening a selection is the same as for extending a selection—Shift-click.

Suppose that you want to remove the words *as my recommendation* from the selection shown in figure 3.3. To shorten the selection, follow these steps:

1. Position the mouse pointer on the end of the name *MacWrite II*.

2. Press and hold the Shift key.

3. Click the mouse button.

The words are removed from the selection. The selection in figure 3.3 was begun at the word *I*. By Shift-clicking, you indicate where the new end of the selection should be.

To shorten the text selection by using the keyboard, use the Shift-Option-left arrow command to select one word to the left. Hold down the Shift and Option keys; then press the left-arrow key three times.

Deleting and Replacing Text Selections

Two of the simplest operations you can perform on a selection of text are delete and replace. After a text selection has been deleted or replaced, you can reverse the action with the Undo command, which is covered later in this chapter.

To delete a section of text, do the following:

1. Select the text with the mouse or keyboard.

2. Press the Backspace key (labeled Delete on some keyboards).

   or

   Select Clear from the Edit menu (see fig. 3.5).

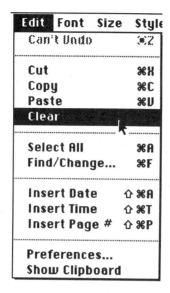

Fig. 3.5. *Selecting the Clear command from the Edit menu.*

The text selection is erased.

Replacing text is a similar operation. Consider the text selection in figure 3.6.

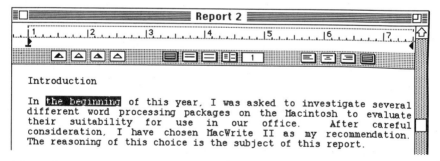

Fig. 3.6. *A selection to be replaced.*

In this example, suppose that you want to replace the words *the beginning* with the word *January*. The procedure is simple:

1. Make the text selection (already done in the figure).

2. Type the new text.

After making the selection, anything you type replaces the selected text. "Anything you type" includes results of such actions as inserting tabs and pressing Return, as well as numbers and letters. You can restore replaced or deleted text by using the Undo command (discussed later this chapter).

After you make a selection, pressing any key on the keyboard (with the exception of Shift, Command, Control, and Option) erases the selection and replaces it. The Backspace key simply erases the selection.

Moving Text Selections

In addition to replacing and deleting text, you may want to move text. For example, while editing a term paper, you may decide that a paragraph in the middle will serve better as the paper's introduction. Instead of retyping the paragraph, you can move it from the middle to the beginning of the paper. To move a paragraph, you "cut and paste" your text. In essence, text is cut from the document and then pasted into a new location.

To move text, follow these steps:

1. Select the text with the mouse or keyboard.

2. Select the Cut command from the Edit menu.

3. Move the cursor to the desired new location of the text.

4. Select the Paste command from the Edit menu.

When you select Cut from the Edit menu, the text is removed from the document and placed in a temporary area called the Clipboard. Text stays in the Clipboard until the next cut operation replaces the old text with new text or until you turn off the Macintosh.

After text is placed in the Clipboard, selecting Paste from the Edit menu puts the text into the document at the current cursor position. Because the text remains in the Clipboard until the next cut operation, you can paste the text any number of times in the document or other documents (see Chapter 5).

Deleted text (see "Deleting and Replacing Text Selections") is not placed in the Clipboard and cannot be pasted.

Copying Text Selections

You can place selections of text in the Clipboard and paste them into other locations in your document without removing them with the Cut command. This feature is useful for documents in which you need to preserve exact wording. To copy a selection of text to another area of your document, use the following steps:

1. Select the text you want to copy, with the keyboard or mouse.

2. Choose the Copy command from the Edit menu.

3. Position the cursor at the correct location.

4. Select Paste from the Edit menu.

The Copy command copies the text to the Clipboard without removing the text from the document. The Paste command, as before, places the Clipboard text into your document at the current cursor position. Again, you can use Paste as many times as you want. The text in the Clipboard remains the same until the next Cut or Copy command or until you turn off your machine.

Viewing the Clipboard Text

Sometimes you may want to check the text that is in the Clipboard. Because the text is not replaced until the next cut or copy operation, you may forget what the selection is.

You can view the text in the Clipboard by choosing the Show Clipboard command from the Edit menu. The Clipboard appears, showing the last selection of text cut or copied (see fig. 3.7).

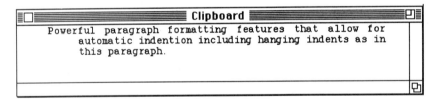

Fig. 3.7. *Viewing the contents of the Clipboard.*

You cannot edit text in the Clipboard window. The Show Clipboard command only shows the contents of the Clipboard.

To put away the Clipboard, click the close box in the upper left corner of the Clipboard window or select the Hide Clipboard command. (The Hide Clipboard command replaces the Show Clipboard command in the Edit menu when the Clipboard is visible.)

Using the Undo Command

With the Undo command, you can reverse operations, such as accidental deletions, replacements, and cuts. The command's actual power goes beyond these simple examples. Almost any command—whether deleting, replacing, cutting, formatting, or even typing—can be reversed to restore the text to its previous condition.

For example, consider the text of figure 3.8. Suppose that you have selected the text to move it to another location in your document. Accidentally, you press the Z key as you reach for your cup of coffee, replacing the selection with a *z* (see fig. 3.9).

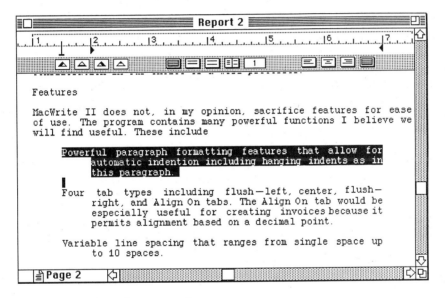

Fig. 3.8. *A selected paragraph.*

Obviously, you do not want to replace the selected text with a *z*. The Undo command provides a quick, easy method of reversing the last command executed. To reverse the action, select Undo Typing in the Edit menu (see fig. 3.10).

Remember one important rule: You can undo only the latest text-changing operation. After you make another change in your text, you cannot use the Undo command to restore the preceding change. MacWrite II remembers only the latest text-changing operation.

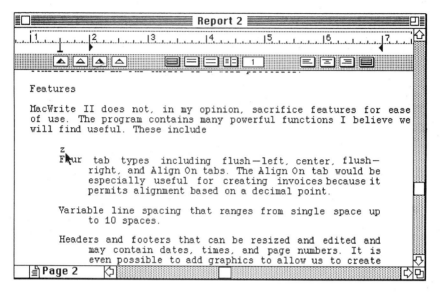

Fig. 3.9. *An accidental replacement.*

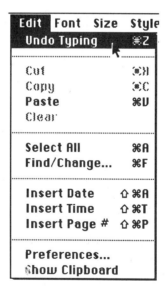

Fig. 3.10. *Selecting Undo Typing.*

This fact leads to some interesting variations in the Undo command's entry in the Edit menu. After a cut operation, for example, the Undo command reads Undo Cut. Following a paste operation, the command reads Undo

Paste. After you use the Undo command, the command usually changes to Redo. For example, if you cut a selection of text, the Undo command reads Undo Cut. If you select Undo Cut, the Undo command shows Redo Cut. In other words, you can undo an Undo command.

The keyboard equivalent for the Undo command is Command-Z (on extended keyboards you can press the F1 key).

Saving a Selection to Disk

At times, you may want to save your text selection to a separate file. This operation creates a new disk file that contains only the text selection, not the entire document. Suppose, for example, that you have created a table or other formatting-intense text and want to use it in another document. Instead of re-creating the text in the second document, you can save the selected text as a separate file, and then insert it by using the Insert File command (see Chapter 6 for more information).

To save a selection, do the following:

1. Select the text you want saved to disk.

2. Choose Save As from the File menu.

3. In the Save As dialog box that appears, choose the Selection Only option (see fig. 3.11).

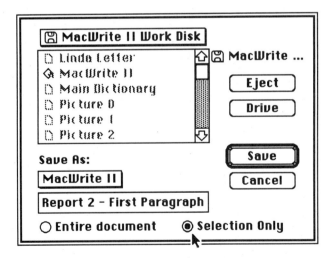

Fig. 3.11. Saving a selection of a document.

4. Type a name for the file that is to contain the text selection.

5. Click the Save button (or press Return).

The text selection is then saved to the new file and also remains in the current document.

Editing Paragraphs

The paragraph is the basic document element in any word processor. You spend most of your time working with paragraphs: typing, formatting, deleting, and moving paragraphs.

You do most paragraph editing by selecting the paragraph's text and performing any of the operations described for selected text. You can delete, replace, move, and copy a paragraph. Remember that to select a paragraph quickly, you place the mouse pointer anywhere in the paragraph and then click the mouse button four times in rapid succession.

Some editing procedures are specific to paragraphs: changing paragraph indents, spacing, tabs, and text alignment. You can take different approaches for editing paragraph formats. The first approach is to use the ruler settings. Changing a ruler setting while the cursor is in a paragraph alters that paragraph's formatting. Another approach is to use the Paragraph dialog box to make the change to the paragraph formatting. Again, the cursor must be in the paragraph being edited.

Joining and Splitting Paragraphs

The simplest paragraph operations involve joining two paragraphs or splitting one paragraph into two. Both these operations are easy to perform.

The carriage return character is the invisible formatting character used by MacWrite II to mark the end of a paragraph. Invisibles are explored in depth at the end of this chapter. For now, note that each time you press Return, the program inserts a carriage return character, marking the end of the paragraph. Consider the two paragraphs in figure 3.12.

To join two paragraphs, follow these steps:

1. Position the mouse pointer before the first word of the second paragraph.

2. Click the mouse button to place the cursor at that position.

3. Press the Backspace key (Delete on some keyboards) until the paragraphs join.

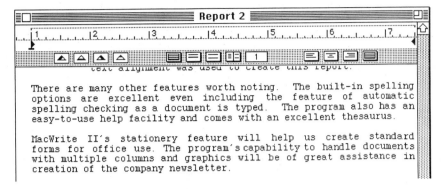

Fig. 3.12. Two paragraphs to be joined.

Keep in mind that looks can be deceiving. In the example, after you press Backspace, the second paragraph moves up against the first. You must press Backspace again to delete the second carriage return (entered to create the blank line between the two paragraphs).

To be certain that you are actually joining the paragraphs, you may want to show the invisibles—the hidden formatting characters in your document. Choose Show Invisibles from the View menu.

In figure 3.13, you see the carriage return character in several places: at the ends of the two paragraphs as well as on the blank lines between them. The character looks like a bent arrow.

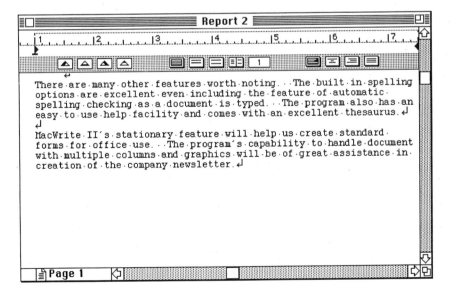

***Fig. 3.13. Showing the invisible carriage return character and
other hidden characters.***

With the carriage return characters visible, you can backspace over them or select and delete them, as discussed earlier in this chapter.

When you join two paragraphs, the second paragraph takes on the formatting characteristics of the first. The formatting that had been applied to the second paragraph is lost.

To hide the formatting characters and return to an uncluttered display, select Hide Invisibles from the View menu.

Splitting a paragraph into two paragraphs is even easier. Simply insert a carriage return character at the point where you want the paragraph to split. Use the following steps:

1. Place the mouse pointer at the location where you want the paragraph to split.

2. Press the mouse button to position the cursor.

3. Press the Return key.

4. Optionally, press the Return key again to insert a blank line to separate the paragraphs.

The paragraph splits, forming two separate ones. The two paragraphs have the same formatting settings as the original paragraph from which they were formed. You can format them separately after they have been split.

Changing Paragraph Indents

You can change any of the three indent settings in a paragraph. The procedure is similar to that of setting indents (see Chapter 2). You can use the ruler or the Paragraph dialog box to change indent settings.

Consider the paragraph in figure 3.14. You can see that the indent settings for this paragraph are basic—all three indents are set to the page margins.

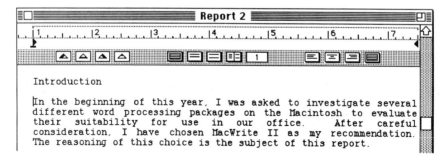

Fig. 3.14. The paragraph before indents are changed.

Using the Ruler

Assume that you have want to indent the first line of the paragraph by .5 inch. Follow these steps:

1. Place the cursor in the paragraph to be edited.

   The cursor must be in the paragraph whose formatting is to be changed. The exact location of the cursor within the paragraph is not important.

2. Drag the first-line indent marker to the new spot—the 1.5 mark on the ruler if the left margin is 1.

The paragraph's formatting changes immediately (see fig. 3.15).

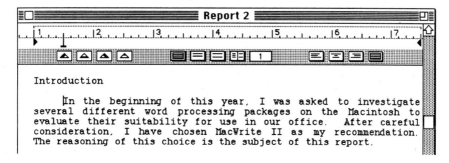

Fig. 3.15. *The paragraph after the first-line indent has been changed.*

You also can move the left and right indents to change the width of the paragraph. For example, to indent the paragraph by .5 inch on each side, drag the left indent marker to the 1.5 position on the ruler, and then drag the right indent marker to the 7 position.

To restore the paragraph's previous formatting, drag the indent markers to their original position. Using the Undo command also reverses the effect of the indent settings changes you make to the paragraph, restoring the paragraph to its original settings.

Using the Paragraph Dialog Box

You also can change the indent settings by using the Paragraph dialog box. With the cursor in the paragraph to be altered, choose the Paragraph command from the Format menu. The dialog box that appears shows the current settings of the paragraph (see fig. 3.16).

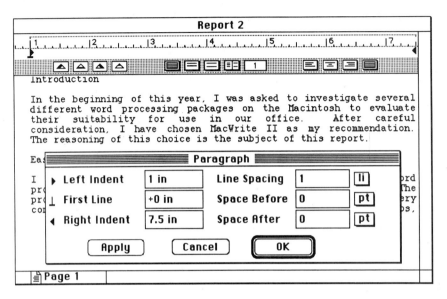

Fig. 3.16. *The Paragraph dialog box showing the current
paragraph settings.*

To alter any indent setting, type the new setting in the appropriate field. In the example, the first-line indent is .5 inch to the right of the left indent setting. To change the first-line indent, do the following:

1. Place the cursor in the paragraph.

2. Select Paragraph from the Format menu.

3. Enter the new value (+ 0.5) in the First Line field.

4. Click the OK button (or press Return).

The results are the same as in figure 3.15. You also can set the other two indent settings—Left Indent and Right Indent—this way.

The Undo command has changed to read Undo Format Change; select this command to restore the paragraph to its original formatting. When you use the Paragraph dialog box, however, the Undo command restores the paragraph to the last setting made with the dialog box. If you make more than one change using the Paragraph dialog box, you cannot use the Undo command to return to the original formatting.

If you want to view a change to the paragraph indents, click the Apply button. The indents change and the Paragraph dialog box remains on-screen so that you can experiment with different settings. You can enter a number in any of the indent fields and click Apply to see the effect. After you find the settings you want to use, click OK to confirm your choice.

Changing a Paragraph's Line Spacing

Changing the line spacing of a paragraph is similar to changing the indents. You can use the ruler or the Paragraph dialog box to make the change. Again, the cursor must be in the paragraph you want to change.

Using the Ruler

Suppose, for example, that you want to change a paragraph from single-spacing to one-and-one-half spacing. Using the ruler, follow these steps:

1. Place the cursor in the paragraph (place the mouse pointer anywhere in the paragraph and click the button).

2. Click the 1.5 spacing icon (see fig. 3.17).

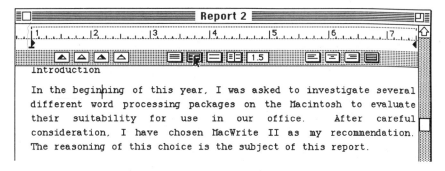

Fig. 3.17. Changing the paragraph's line spacing.

As soon as you click the 1.5 spacing icon, the paragraph's line spacing changes. Other paragraphs are unaffected. You can use any line spacing icon, including the fine-tuning icon (refer to Chapter 2 for a discussion of these icons).

The Undo command restores the paragraph to its original line spacing regardless of how many changes have been made in the ruler, as long as you have not entered any other type of command (such as Cut, Copy, and so on).

Using the Paragraph Dialog Box

Using the Paragraph dialog box to make line spacing changes for a paragraph is similar to changing indents. Use the following steps:

1. Place the cursor in the paragraph you want to change.

2. Select Paragraph from the Format menu.

3. Type the new line spacing in the Line Spacing field.

4. Click the OK button (or press Return).

The paragraph's line spacing is changed, and the line spacing indicator shows the new setting. The Undo command restores the paragraph to the last setting made with the dialog box (or ruler).

To view the effect of a line-spacing change on a paragraph, click the Apply button. The paragraph line spacing changes, but the Paragraph dialog box remains on-screen so that you can experiment with different settings. You can continue entering numbers in the Line Spacing field and clicking Apply to see the effect until you find the correct spacing. Click OK to confirm your choice.

Adding Space before and after Paragraphs

Although you can add blank lines between paragraphs by pressing Return, MacWrite II provides a method of automatically inserting space before and after paragraphs. This automatic spacing can be activated only through the Paragraph dialog box. (No ruler setting for this option exists.) Figure 3.18 shows two paragraphs that have been typed without a blank line between them. Assume that you have decided that these paragraphs should be separated by one blank line. To accomplish this, set the first paragraph to be followed by one line with these steps:

1. Place the cursor in the paragraph you want to change (here, the first one).

2. Select Paragraph from the Format menu.

3. In the Paragraph dialog box that appears, place the mouse pointer on the pt that follows the Space After field.

4. Press and hold the mouse button to pop up the Unit of Measure menu (see fig. 3.19).

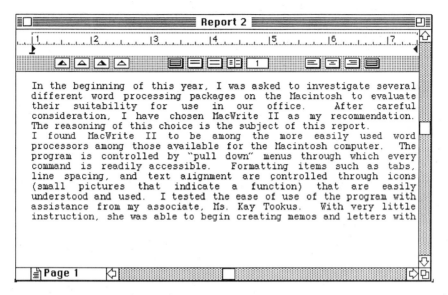

Fig. 3.18. *Paragraphs without blank lines between them.*

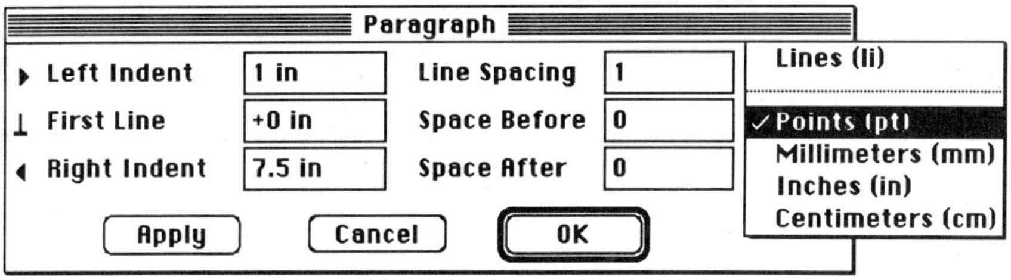

Fig. 3.19. *The Unit of Measure pop-up menu.*

5. Slide the mouse pointer up the menu until the unit you want is highlighted—for instance, Lines (li).

6. Release the mouse button. The unit of measure is now lines.

7. Type the new spacing interval (*1*) in the Space After field.

8. Click the OK button (or press Return).

The resulting spacing of the paragraphs is shown in figure 3.20. As you see, the paragraphs are separated by one blank line. You can enter the Space Before or After in any unit of measure you want. Keep in mind, however, that the Lines unit is adjusted according to the font size, but the other units are not. For more information on changing the unit of measurement, see Chapter 2.

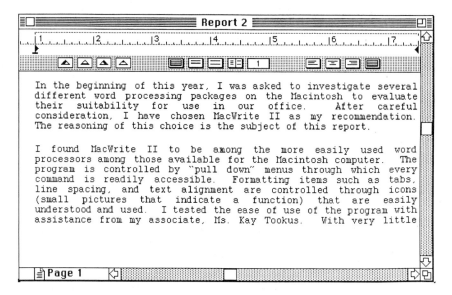

Fig. 3.20. *The paragraphs separated by a blank line.*

Changing Paragraph Tabs

You can add or modify tabs by using the tab icons on the ruler (see Chapter 2). To change the type or position of tab, use the Tab dialog box.

Using the Ruler

To change paragraph tabs by using the tab icons in the ruler, place the cursor in the paragraph where you want to change tabs. (Place the mouse pointer anywhere in the paragraph and click the mouse button.) Then simply drag the tab to the new location with the following steps:

1. Place the mouse pointer on the tab icon in the ruler (see fig. 3.21).

2. Press and hold the mouse button.

3. Slide the mouse pointer along the ruler until it reaches the new tab position.

4. Release the mouse button.

Figure 3.22 shows the paragraph from figure 3.21 after the tab icon has been moved from the 1.25 position to the 1.5 position.

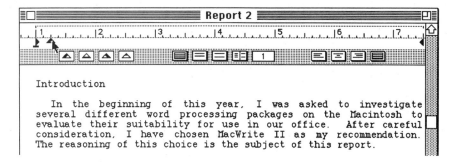

Fig. 3.21. Preparing to move a tab.

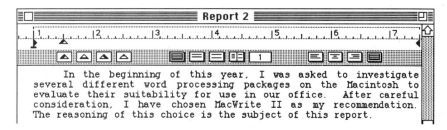

Fig. 3.22. The new tab position.

Removing a tab is a similar procedure. Select the tab icon and drag it down off the ruler until the icon disappears. The tab is then eliminated.

If you remove a tab, the paragraph shifts to conform to the remaining tabs. For example, figure 3.23 shows a paragraph with two tabs, one set at 1.25 and one at 2. If the tab at 1.25 is removed, the paragraph adjusts to the second tab as in figure 3.24.

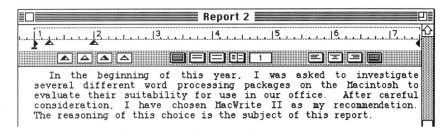

Fig. 3.23. A paragraph with two tabs.

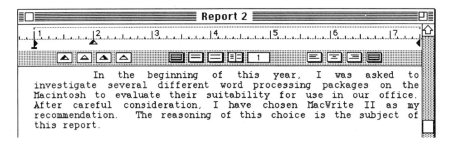

***Fig. 3.24.** The paragraph after one tab is removed.*

If no other tabs are defined for the paragraph, the paragraph adjusts to the nearest default tab (see Chapter 2).

Using the Tab Dialog Box

You access the Tab dialog box by selecting Tab from the Format menu or by double-clicking any tab icon in the ruler (see fig. 3.25). Using this dialog box, you can add or modify tabs. You can change the type of a tab—from a Left tab to a Center tab, for example—or reposition a tab. You also can change the tab fill character and the Align On tab's aligning character.

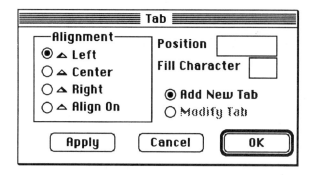

***Fig. 3.25.** The Tab dialog box.*

The parts of this dialog box include

- *Alignment.* These four buttons enable you to choose the type of tab you want to use.

- *Position.* This option enables you to specify the location of the tab on the ruler.

- *Fill Character.* This option defines the character that fills the space preceding the tab (covered in this chapter).

- *Add New Tab.* When this option is selected, you can add a new tab to the paragraph.

- *Modify Tab.* Choosing this option indicates that you want to alter an existing tab. This option is unavailable until a tab is selected.

- *Apply.* This button enables you to see the results of your changes without making them permanent; the Tab dialog box stays on-screen.

- *Cancel.* Choosing Cancel closes the Tab dialog box and returns you to your document without making changes.

- *OK.* This button closes the Tab dialog box and applies your changes to the document. Pressing the Return key performs the same function.

Adding a Tab

To add a new tab to a paragraph through the Tab dialog box, you first must decide on the type of tab you want to use: a Left, Center, Right, or Align On tab.

To choose a tab type, click the circle next to the type you want to use. The Left tab type is the default selected by the program.

To add a new tab to the paragraph, follow these steps:

1. Place the cursor in the paragraph by clicking anywhere within it.

2. Choose Tab from the Format menu.

3. Click the tab type you want to use.

4. Click the ruler at the location where you want the tab.

   or

   Type the number representing the location on the ruler where you want the tab.

When you click the ruler, a tab icon of the selected type appears. The location of the tab appears in the Position field in the Tab dialog box. Typing a position in the field places a tab icon at the entered location, just as if you had clicked that point on the ruler.

Specifying the Fill Character

At times you may want a tab to be preceded by a line of characters. An example of this style is a table of contents (see fig. 3.26). In the figure, the tab at the 6-inch position has a period as a fill character.

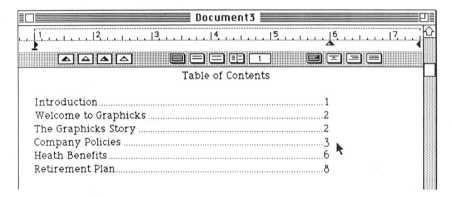

Fig. 3.26. Using a fill character.

Any tab type can have a fill character. You can use any fill character you want. The fill character fills the space between the preceding text and the tab position. To specify a fill character, perform the following steps in the Tab dialog box:

1. Press the Tab key until the highlighting reaches the Fill Character field. (Alternatively, you can place the mouse pointer in the field and click the mouse button.)

2. Type the fill character.

3. Click OK or press Return.

Any tab positioned while the Tab dialog box is on the screen uses the fill character. You can change the fill character at any time.

Using the Align On Tab

The primary use of the Align On tab type is the creation of columns of numbers. By aligning the numbers according to the location of the decimal point, the column appears in your text as a table (see fig. 3.27).

```
┌──────────────────── Document3 ────────────────────┐
│  |1........|2........|3........|4........|5........|6........|7........|
│                                                              │
│   ▲  ▲  ▲  ▲      ▭ ▭ ▭ ▭ ┊1┊        ▭ ▭ ▭ ▭        │
│                     Sales to Date                            │
│                                                              │
│   Widget Department _____$595.55         │
│   Neat Stuff Department _____$4,050.00       │
│   Pretty Picture Department_____$5,679.05       │
│   Supplies Department_____$3,345.99       │
│   Everybody Else Department _____$768.00         │
│   ---------------------------------------------------------  │
│   Total_____$14438.59     │
└──────────────────────────────────────────────────┘
```

Fig. 3.27. *A column of numbers using the Align On tab.*

When the column of numbers in figure 3.27 was typed, the Align On tab positioned the numbers so that the decimal points are in a vertical line. With an Align On tab, you press the Tab key and type the text. The program positions the text so that the Align On character is at the tab location.

You place the Align On tab type in the same way you do any other tab type. An additional consideration is the character to be used to align the text. When you choose the Align On tab type in the Tab dialog box, the Align On character field appears next to the Align On tab option (see fig. 3.28).

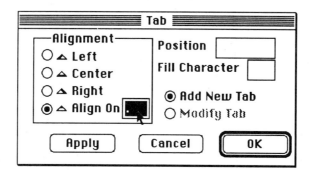

Fig. 3.28. *The Align On character field.*

The program assumes that you want to use the decimal point as the Align On character and has placed one in the field for you. You can, however, choose another character by simply typing the character.

Moving a Tab

You can move a tab with the Tab dialog box by specifying a new position for the tab. In the Position field, enter a number with up to 3 decimal places. You can place a tab, for example, at the 2 1/8th-inch position by entering *2.125*.

To change a tab's position, follow these steps:

1. Select Tab from the Format menu.

2. On the ruler, click the tab icon that is to be moved.

3. Type the tab's new position in the Position field.

    or

    Place the mouse pointer on the tab icon to be moved, press and hold down the mouse button, and drag the icon to the new spot on the ruler.

4. Click the OK button to confirm your choice.

You can open the Tab dialog box and select the tab icon to be modified by double-clicking the tab icon you want to modify. The Tab dialog box opens with that tab icon already selected. You then can reposition the icon.

Keep in mind that, as with any other formatting change, the cursor must be in the paragraph you want to change.

Changing a Tab's Type

You can change a tab on the ruler to any of the four types of tabs. For example, you may decide to change a Left tab to a Center tab. Using the ruler alone requires removing the Left tab icon and placing a new Center tab icon in its place. The Tab dialog box changes the tab type more quickly.

To change a tab's type, follow these steps:

1. Double-click the tab icon you want to change. The Tab dialog box appears.

2. Click the tab type you want.

3. Click the OK button to confirm your choice.

You see the tab icon in the ruler change into the icon you chose from the Alignment section of the Tab dialog box. The text of the paragraph the cursor is in adjusts to the new tab type.

Changing Paragraph Text Alignment

You change the text alignment of a paragraph by using the ruler text alignment icons. No dialog box has corresponding settings.

To change a paragraph's text alignment, follow these steps:

1. Place the cursor in the paragraph (move the mouse pointer to any position within the paragraph and click the mouse button).

2. Click the text alignment icon that represents the alignment of your choice.

The paragraph's alignment changes immediately. You can click any alignment icon any number of times to view the different effects on the paragraph. The Undo command (which reads Undo Format Change) restores the paragraph to its initial alignment setting.

Editing Several Paragraphs Together

At times, you may need to change the formatting of several paragraphs to the same settings. You can change each paragraph individually, but that approach takes time. The quickest way to change several paragraphs is to make all the changes at one time. Suppose that you want to change the paragraphs shown in figure 3.29.

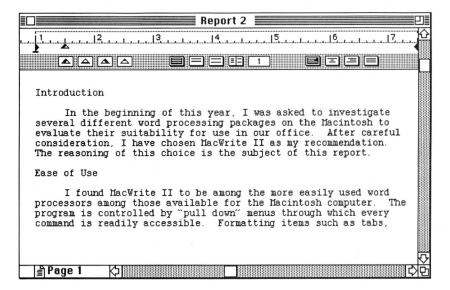

Fig. 3.29. *The paragraphs to be changed.*

These paragraphs have been formatted with a text alignment of justified text and have a tab set at the 1.5 position. Assume that you have decided to use flush-left alignment for these paragraphs and to move the tab to the 1.25 position. To make these changes, follow these steps:

1. Place the mouse pointer just before the word *Introduction*.

2. Press and hold the mouse button.

3. Drag the mouse through the paragraphs until the dark highlighting encompasses them entirely (see fig. 3.30).

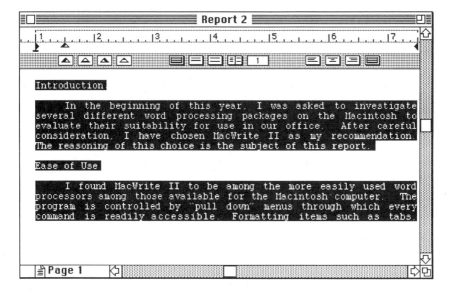

Fig. 3.30. *The paragraphs selected for changing.*

4. Click the flush-left icon in the ruler.

5. Move the mouse pointer to the tab icon at the 1.5 position.

6. Press and hold the mouse button.

7. Move the mouse, dragging the tab icon until it reaches the 1.25 position in the ruler.

8. Release the mouse button.

To eliminate the highlighting, click anywhere in the document. As you can see in figure 3.31, the paragraphs have adjusted to the new formatting settings.

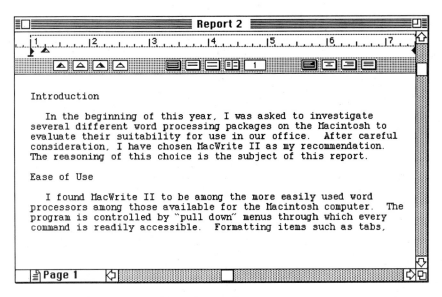

Fig. 3.31. The paragraphs with new formats.

By using the selection techniques discussed in the first part of this chapter, you can select any number of paragraphs. You then can change the paragraphs with these formatting methods:

- *Paragraph indents*. After selecting the paragraphs, use the ruler or Paragraph dialog box to change the indent settings of the selected paragraphs.

- *Paragraph line spacing*. After the paragraphs have been highlighted, use the ruler or Paragraph dialog box to change the line spacing of the paragraphs.

- *Space before and after*. Use the Paragraph dialog box to increase or decrease the space between the paragraphs. Remember that each paragraph selected will be preceded by the amount of space entered in the Space Before field and followed by the amount in the Space After field.

- *Paragraph tabs*. You can add tabs to selected paragraphs. Note that only the tabs the paragraphs have in common can be modified by this method. For example, if one paragraph has tabs at the 2-inch position and the 3-inch position and a second paragraph has only a tab at the 3-inch position, only the tab at the 3-inch position appears in the ruler when both paragraphs are selected together.

- *Paragraph text alignment.* After selecting a group of paragraphs, you can change the text alignments by clicking the desired text-alignment icon.

You can select any number of paragraphs and use the previously discussed paragraph editing methods to change the formatting.

The Edit menu contains a Select All command that selects (and highlights) the entire document. After selecting this command, you can make format changes that apply to the entire document. This technique is particularly helpful if you find, for example, that you have used justified text alignment in creating the document and you need flush-left alignment.

To make this change, follow these steps:

1. Choose Select All from the Edit menu.

2. Click the flush-left text alignment icon.

The entire document converts to flush-left alignment. You should be careful about making changes to an entire document. If you have a centered paragraph or two in the document, for example, they also change to flush left.

Copying Paragraph Formatting

After you have gone to all the trouble of formatting a paragraph, you may want to duplicate the formatting. You may have spent some time setting up a special paragraph only to find that another paragraph later in your document needs the same formatting.

You can go through the same process to format the second paragraph, but a much better method exists. MacWrite II provides two commands you can use to copy the formatting of a paragraph and transfer the formatting to another paragraph: Copy Ruler and Apply Ruler in the Format menu (see fig. 3.32).

To copy the formatting of one paragraph to another, do the following:

1. Place the cursor in the paragraph that has the formatting you want to copy.

2. Select Copy Ruler from the Format menu (or press Shift-Command-C).

3. Place the cursor in the paragraph that is to receive the formatting.

4. Select Apply Ruler from the Format menu (or press Shift-Command-V).

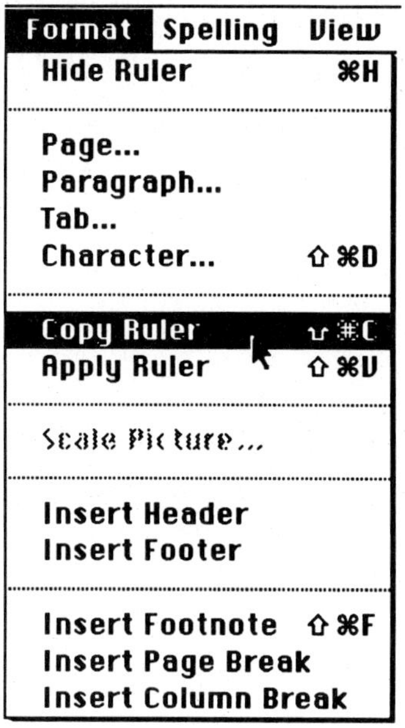

Format	Spelling	View
Hide Ruler		⌘H
Page...		
Paragraph...		
Tab...		
Character...		⇧⌘D
Copy Ruler		⌥⌘C
Apply Ruler		⇧⌘U
Scale Picture...		
Insert Header		
Insert Footer		
Insert Footnote		⇧⌘F
Insert Page Break		
Insert Column Break		

Fig. 3.32. The Copy Ruler and Apply Ruler commands.

The second paragraph's format now matches the first paragraph's format. These commands copy the indent settings, spacing, tabs, text alignment, and other formatting from the first paragraph to the second. The text of the paragraph is not copied.

After you copy a paragraph's formatting with the Copy Ruler command, the program remembers the formatting. You can apply the same format to as many other paragraphs as you want by repeating steps 3 and 4. The program remembers the formatting until you use the Copy Ruler command again or quit the program.

Editing the Invisibles

Every keystroke entered into a document is considered a character. The most obvious examples of characters are letters, numbers, and punctuation marks. Several characters are not normally visible in your document. These invisible characters concern the formatting of pages and paragraphs. They consist of such things as spaces, tabs, carriage returns, and page breaks.

You can edit invisible characters. You can, for example, add or eliminate spaces by using the space bar or Backspace key. At times, however, editing can be made easier by making these characters visible.

Showing the Invisibles

You show the invisibles by using the Show Invisibles command in the
View menu. Figure 3.33 shows some invisible characters.

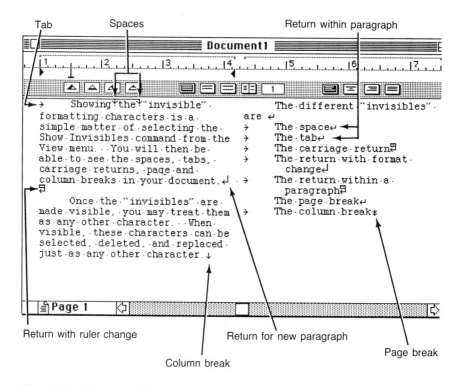

Fig. 3.33. *The invisible formatting characters.*

In the figure, the different invisible characters are labeled. Each invisible is
considered a single character, although some perform several functions.
After you have displayed the invisible characters, you can edit them as if
they were normal characters.

The first and simplest invisible character is the space, represented by a dot.
Although this dot looks similar to a period, a closer inspection shows that
the dot is higher than a period. Each dot represents a single space.

The tab is represented by an arrow pointing to the right. Each arrow
represents a single press of the Tab key. The character is placed in the text
at the point where the Tab key is pressed.

At the end of the first paragraph is the bent arrow representing the carriage return, an indication that the Return key was pressed at this point to end a paragraph. This character is also referred to as a return for new paragraph.

Immediately following the first carriage return character is the return with ruler change. This character is shown as a carriage return with a tiny ruler attached. The return with ruler change character marks the point where the paragraph formatting settings are changed.

At the end of the second paragraph of the figure is a small arrow pointing down. This character indicates a column break, where the Insert Column Break command in the Format menu was chosen (multicolumn documents are discussed in Chapter 11).

In the second column of the figure, you see a return within paragraph symbol shown immediately after the words *are*, *space*, and *tab*. On the return within paragraph symbol, the tail of the arrow is shorter than the return for new paragraph symbol. The return within paragraph symbol indicates that the Shift key was held down as the Return key was pressed. This action begins a new line without ending the paragraph. In the figure, the first four lines of the second column are considered part of the first paragraph despite the characters following each line. A new paragraph does not begin until the return for new paragraph character following the word *change*.

The page break character that comes at the end of the second column is a double arrow pointing down. This symbol indicates where the Insert Page Break command was selected to force the end of a page. Text following the page break character is on another page.

Using the Invisibles

Sometimes a paragraph or other part of your document may behave in odd ways when you attempt to edit it. One reason for unusual occurrences in your formatting is the accidental pressing of a key or execution of a command that is not readily apparent.

As an example, consider the paragraph in figure 3.34. The paragraph appears to be fine, but it has several incorrect characters hidden within it. After choosing Show Invisibles from the View menu, the paragraph's hidden mistakes become apparent (see fig. 3.35).

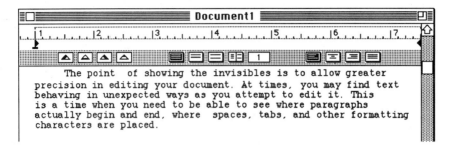

Fig. 3.34. *A paragraph with hidden problems.*

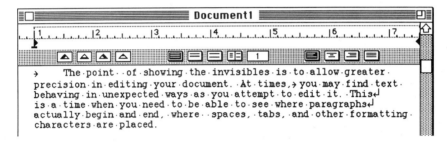

Fig. 3.35. *The hidden formatting characters revealed.*

Several errors are now apparent in this paragraph:

- Two spaces instead of one after the word *point* in the first line

- A single space instead of two between the first two sentences

- A stray tab in the second sentence after the phrase *At times*

- Two returns for new paragraph within the single paragraph—probably caused by pressing Return at the end of the line instead of at the end of the paragraph

You can correct these problems. For example, to eliminate the extra space between the word *point* and the word *of* in the first line, do the following:

1. Position the mouse pointer before the word *of*.

2. Click the mouse button to place the cursor.

3. Press the Backspace key to delete the extra space.

You can use this procedure to eliminate any stray formatting characters. You also can use the techniques discussed in the section "Deleting and Replacing Text Selections," earlier in this chapter.

The carriage return characters and the two page break characters cannot be replaced by use of the select-and-type method described in the "Deleting and Replacing Text Selections." After you delete carriage return or page break characters, you must retype them to replace them.

Hiding the Invisibles

You will not want the formatting characters visible at all times because they are distracting. To make them invisible again, select the Hide Invisibles command from the View menu. This command takes the place of the Show Invisibles command when the formatting characters are visible. The keyboard shortcut for the Show Invisibles and Hide Invisibles commands is the same. You hold down the command key and press the semicolon (;).

Summing Up

This chapter covers the basics of editing MacWrite II documents. You should now have an understanding of the methods of selecting and working with selected text.

The various paragraph-specific formatting features are also covered. You have seen how to set paragraph indents, spacing, text alignment, and tabs, and how to add space before and after paragraphs.

You also have seen how MacWrite II inserts invisible formatting characters and learned how to use the command that shows these characters so that you can edit them.

You are now ready to turn to some of the more advanced editing features of the program: checking spelling, searching and replacing text, using the Word Finder thesaurus, hyphenation, and working with special characters.

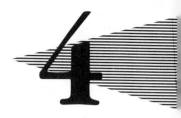

Correcting Spelling

Chapter 3 covers the basic editing of documents in MacWrite II, explaining how you select and edit text and alter the formatting of paragraphs. These editing features form the core of the program, but several advanced features help you speed the correction and revision of your document.

First among the more advanced editing features is the program's spelling-checking capability. MacWrite II has a dictionary of over 100,000 words against which it compares the spelling in your document in order to catch errors. The program is even capable of checking the spelling of your document as you type. This chapter explains the features of the spelling checker.

Installing Dictionaries

Before you can check the spelling of any word, you must provide the program with dictionaries against which to check the words. You may have any number of dictionaries, but at any one time you can use only one main dictionary and one user dictionary.

To install the dictionaries, place the Main Dictionary and the User Dictionary supplied with the program into the System Folder or the folder (or the disk) containing the MacWrite II program. With either method, MacWrite II automatically locates and loads the two dictionaries when the program starts.

If you use more than one main or user dictionary, however, you need to install the desired dictionaries before proceeding with the spelling check. If you are going to use more than one of either kind of dictionary, place the most frequently used main and user dictionaries where MacWrite II can find them automatically. Refer to Appendix A for this installation procedure.

Installing other dictionaries is a relatively simple procedure. Keep in mind, however, that the installation of another dictionary applies only to the current session. That is, if you install a dictionary and then quit the program, that dictionary is no longer installed. You have to install it again when you next begin using MacWrite II before you can use it to check your spelling.

To install a dictionary, follow these steps:

1. Select Install Dictionaries from the Spelling menu.

2. Click Main or User in the Select Dictionary dialog box, depending on the type of dictionary you are installing (see fig. 4.1).

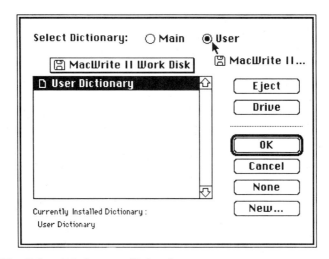

Fig. 4.1. *The Select Dictionary dialog box.*

3. Choose the dictionary to be installed by highlighting its name.

   Below the scroll box listing the dictionaries is the name of the currently installed dictionary. When Main is selected, the name of the installed main dictionary is displayed. When User is selected, the name of the installed user dictionary is shown. If no dictionary is installed, you see the notation ‹None›.

4. Click OK.

The Select Dictionary dialog box enables you to locate and choose a dictionary. As in the Open File dialog box, you select Eject to eject the disk, and you use Drive to switch to another drive on your system. Each time you click Drive, the program selects the next disk drive. To cancel the installation procedure and close the Select Dictionary dialog box, select Cancel.

Note two other options in the Select Dictionary dialog box:

- *None*. Appears only when the User option is selected. Clicking this button indicates that you want to use only a main dictionary and removes any user dictionary from the list of installed dictionaries. Clicking None does not delete any dictionary.

- *New*. Enables you to create a new user dictionary. This button appears only when you click the User option. When you click New, a dialog box appears, enabling you to name the new user dictionary (see the section "Creating User Dictionaries").

The best place to locate your dictionaries is in the folder or disk that contains your MacWrite II application program. This location makes them much easier to find. If you have trouble locating your dictionaries, refer to your Macintosh manual for further details on how to locate and open files.

Checking Spelling

After you have installed at least the main dictionary, you can check the spelling of your document. This section covers the first procedure of checking spelling, sometimes referred to as the *batch* process of checking spelling, which enables you to check the spelling of your entire document. The capability of checking your spelling as you type, called the *on-line* spelling-checking-option, is discussed in a later section of this chapter.

Understanding the Spelling Dialog Box

The Spelling dialog box is the control center for correcting spelling in your document. The Spelling dialog box is displayed whenever the program questions a word. You can retype the word, select from a list of alternative spellings, add the word to your user dictionary, or skip the word.

The Spelling dialog box, with its parts labeled, is shown in figure 4.2. Each part is described briefly in this section. The following sections explain in detail how to use the dialog box to correct your spelling.

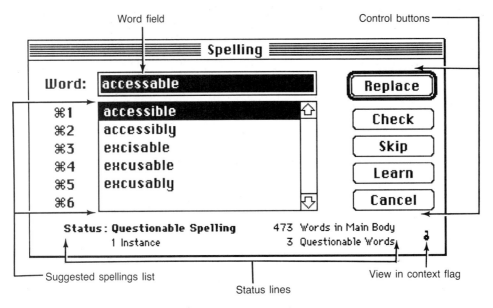

Fig. 4.2. *The Spelling dialog box.*

The Word field is located in the top left of the dialog box. Here MacWrite II displays the questioned word (which may be misspelled or simply not in the program's dictionaries). At any point, you can type in this field to modify a questioned word. Any typing you do when the Spelling dialog box is displayed is placed into this field.

Immediately below the Word field, MacWrite II lists possible correct spellings of the questioned word. Usually, only a few suggestions are given, and they are all visible in this box. If the program has found more than six alternative spellings, you can scroll to see the others by clicking the small arrows to the right of the box.

Along the left of the box containing the suggested spellings, you see a series of command symbols followed by numbers. These shortcut keys enable you to choose a suggested spelling from the keyboard. In figure 4.2, for example, the correct spelling of the questioned word is the first suggested spelling, accessible. To choose this spelling using the keyboard, hold down the Command key and press 1.

The five buttons on the right side of the dialog box function as follows:

- *Replace.* Replaces the questioned word with the highlighted alternative spelling or the spelling you have typed in the Word field. This button reads Done when all words have been processed or no misspellings are found.

- *Check*. Checks the word in the Word field against the words in the main dictionary and the user dictionary (if one is in use). Use Check when you type a correction to the questioned word and want to verify the spelling.

- *Skip*. Causes the program to ignore the questioned word and go on to the next

- *Learn*. Adds the questioned word to the user dictionary. Use Learn when the word is a proper name or some term MacWrite II does not have in its main dictionary. This button is available only if you have a user dictionary installed.

- *Cancel*. Ends the spelling-checking session and returns you to your document. Any changes you made before clicking this button are not affected.

At the bottom of the dialog box is a status line that tells you the number of occurrences of the questioned word MacWrite II has found, phrased as the number of *instances*. For example, in figure 4.2, the questioned word accessable was found in only one place, hence the displayed status of 1 Instance.

The status line also tells you how many words are in your document or selection (checking a selection is covered in a later section) and the number of questionable spellings found. In figure 4.2, the program has noted that the document contains 473 words in the main body, and 3 spellings are questionable.

In the bottom right corner is a small flag that enables you to see the questioned word in context. By clicking this flag, you expand the Spelling dialog box to include the line in which the questioned word is found. Seeing the word in context can help you determine whether the word is indeed misspelled.

Checking an Entire Document

Checking an entire document is by far the most common spelling-checking operation. At any point, you can check the spelling of your document and correct mistakes. Your document does not have to be complete before you check the spelling.

To initiate the spelling-checking process, select Check All from the Spelling menu. Alternatively, you can hold down the Command key and press the equal (=) key. The program proceeds to locate all questionable spellings in your document, and the Spelling dialog box appears, displaying the first word that MacWrite II does not recognize.

If the program finds no questionable words, the dialog box still appears, but does not list any questioned words. Instead, the Replace button reads Done. Select Done to close the Spelling dialog box (see the section "Completing Spelling Checking").

Replacing a Misspelled Word

When the Spelling dialog box appears, it displays the first word the program does not recognize. The questioned word is displayed in the Word field (see fig. 4.3).

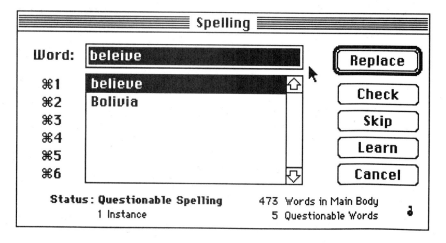

Fig. 4.3. *The questioned word.*

Below the Word field, a box lists alternative spellings. If the questioned word is misspelled and MacWrite II has suggested a correct alternative, you replace the word with the correct spelling as follows:

1. Highlight the correct spelling by clicking the word in the suggested spellings list.

2. Click Replace.

The program replaces every occurrence of the questioned word with the suggested spelling.

Alternatively, you can use shortcuts to reduce the two steps into one. If one suggested spelling is correct, you can hold down the Command key and press the number next to the suggested word. In figure 4.3, pressing Command-1 replaces the misspelled *beleive* with the correct spelling, *believe*.

Correcting a Misspelled Word

Sometimes the program does not suggest any alternative spellings, and at other times, none of the suggestions is correct. In these cases, you can edit the questioned word.

When the questioned word is surrounded by the dark highlighting band, whatever you type replaces the word. After typing a replacement, you can check it by clicking the Check button. MacWrite compares the new word against the main dictionary and the user dictionary, if one is installed. If the program does not recognize the new word, it again suggests alternative spellings.

A second method of editing a questioned word is to use MacWrite II's editing capabilities. You can click anywhere in the questioned word field to place the cursor and then add new letters to the word; you also can use the Backspace key (Delete on some keyboards) to remove letters.

To replace part of a word, complete the following steps:

1. Place the mouse pointer to the left of the first letter of the section to be replaced.

2. Press and hold the mouse button.

3. Drag across the word until the section to be replaced has been surrounded by the dark highlighting band.

4. Release the mouse button.

5. Type the new letters.

You can use this method to change a word such as *unfortunantly*, which should be spelled *unfortunately*, for instance. Select the letters *nt* in the misspelled word (see fig. 4.4). Then type *te* to replace them.

As with the first method, you can use the Check button to verify your new spelling. If your new spelling is correct, the status line at the bottom left of the dialog box reads Correct Spelling (see fig. 4.5).

When you are satisfied with the new spelling, click Replace to replace the incorrect spelling with the new one.

Skipping a Word

Sometimes the program questions a word that is not misspelled. This situation most commonly happens with proper names (names of people, cities, and so on) and technical terms not frequently used.

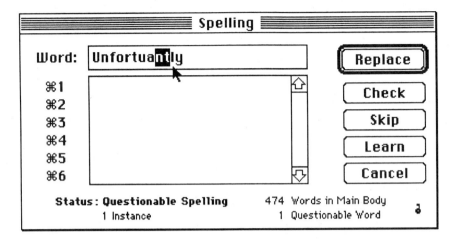

Fig. 4.4. *Selecting a section of a questioned word.*

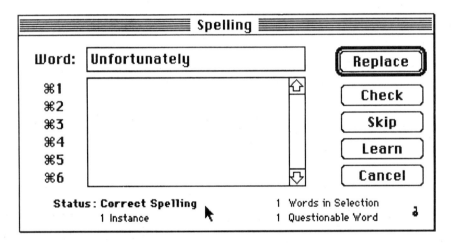

Fig. 4.5. *A spelling verified.*

Keep in mind that the program checks spelling against the main dictionary. If you are using the Main Dictionary supplied with MacWrite II, you have a dictionary of over 100,000 commonly used words. Although this dictionary is more than sufficient for most users, you still may encounter words that are not in the dictionary.

When this happens, you can add the word to your user dictionary by clicking the Learn button. (This procedure is covered in a later section.) You also can tell the program to ignore this word by clicking Skip.

Viewing a Word in Context

To help you decide what should be done with a word, the program enables you to view the word within the context of the line in which it occurs. When you want to view the word in context, click the small flag in the lower right corner of the Spelling dialog box. The box expands to include the line containing the word (see fig. 4.6). The questioned word is underlined.

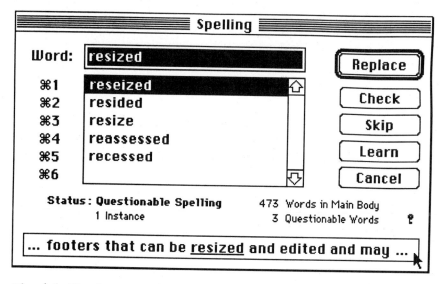

Fig. 4.6. *Viewing a word in context.*

Seeing the word in context may help you decide whether it is misspelled or is a word with which MacWrite II is unfamiliar.

Click the small flag again to restore the Spelling dialog box to its former size. You also can leave the dialog box in this state so that each questioned word is displayed in context and continue editing, replacing, skipping, and so on.

Completing Spelling Checking

The spelling checking continues with each word the program finds questionable. In each instance, MacWrite II expects you to replace, edit, or skip the word or add the word to the user dictionary (covered in a later section of this chapter).

After you take care of every questioned word, the Spelling dialog box changes. Replace becomes Done, and the status line reads Finished Spelling (see fig. 4.7).

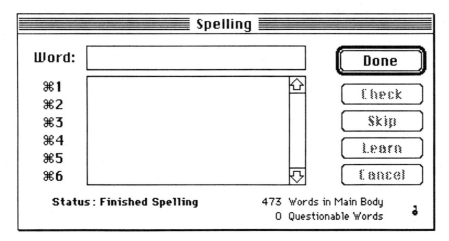

Fig. 4.7. *The completed spelling check.*

You can discontinue the spelling checking at any time by clicking the Cancel button. The Done button appears only when MacWrite II finds no more questioned spellings. To complete the spelling-checking process, click Done or press Return (Enter on some keyboards).

Keep in mind one point concerning the spelling-checking process. Although the program is excellent at finding misspelled words, it cannot "proof" your document. That is, a word can be correctly spelled but incorrectly used. For example, a common mistake is to type *from* instead of *form* or vice versa. A phrase such as "After we returned form Chicago . . ." is not questioned by the program. No matter how good a spelling checker is, it is no substitute for a careful reading of your document.

Checking Parts of Documents

Sometimes you may want to check the spelling of only a part of your document. MacWrite II provides the capability of checking a selection, a page element, or a word.

To check a selection, you use the text selection techniques covered in Chapter 3. If you are unfamiliar with selecting text, refer to that chapter.

Page elements are the building blocks of a document. In MacWrite II, page elements include the main body of text, the headers and footers, and the footnotes. Because you can check the spelling of these elements separately, you can save time by checking only particular elements of a document rather than the entire document.

Checking a Selection

If you are working on a document and have checked the spelling of the document before, you may want to check only the spelling of text you have added or edited. To check the spelling of a selection, you first select the text. (See Chapter 3 for information on selecting text.)

After you have selected text, the Check Selection command becomes available in the Spelling menu (see fig. 4.8). When no text is selected, this command is grayed out and cannot be used.

Fig. 4.8. Choosing Check Selection from the Spelling menu.

You also can use a keyboard shortcut for the Check Selection command. Figure 4.8 shows the Command symbol (the four-leaf clover) next to the letter K, indicating that you can select this command from the keyboard by pressing Command-K (holding down the Command key while you press K).

Executing the Check Selection command begins the spelling-checking process, which is the same as the procedure for checking an entire document. You are presented with the Spelling dialog box and expected to decide on each questioned word. The only difference is that the program checks only the words in the selection rather than the entire document.

Checking a Page Element

An alternative to checking the spelling of selected text is to check individual elements of your document. For instance, you can check the spelling of the main body of text, the header, footer, or footnotes by using a command that checks individual page elements.

This command checks the elements according to the location of the cursor. If the cursor is located in the header of the document, the program checks only the spelling of the header. If the cursor is in the main body of text, the program checks the spelling of the text but not the header, footer, or footnotes.

Chapter 9 covers creating and editing headers, footers, and footnotes. This section discusses only checking the spelling of these elements.

The page-element spelling-checking command changes according to the element in which the cursor is located. When the cursor is in the main body of text, the command in the Spelling menu reads Check Main Body. When the cursor is located in the header, the command is Check Header.

The variations of the command and the areas that are affected are as follows:

- *Check Main Body.* Checks the spelling of all text except the header, footer, and footnotes

- *Check Header.* Checks only the text in the header

- *Check Footer.* Checks only the text in the footer

- *Check Footnotes.* Checks all the footnotes in the document

After you select the command, the program proceeds in the same manner as with the Check All command. The Spelling dialog box appears with the first questioned word (if any). For a detailed description of the use of the Spelling dialog box, refer to the earlier section, "Checking an Entire Document."

Checking a Word

MacWrite II also enables you to check the spelling of an individual word. This capability comes in handy when you are uncertain how a word is spelled and want to verify it quickly.

To check the spelling of an individual word, follow these steps:

1. Select the word.

2. Choose Check Selection from the Spelling menu or press Command-K.

The Spelling dialog box appears. If the word is spelled correctly, nothing appears in the Word field, the Replace button reads Done, and the status line reads Finished Spelling. Click Done or press Return to close the dialog box and return to the document.

If MacWrite II does not recognize the word, it displays the word in the Word field with alternative spellings in the box below. You choose an alternative spelling by clicking it once and then clicking Replace (or pressing Return).

For a more detailed description of the operation of the Spelling dialog box, refer to "Checking an Entire Document."

Using User Dictionaries

Although the Main Dictionary supplied with MacWrite II has over 100,000 words, you may find that the program does not recognize many proper names and technical terms. You can place these words in a user dictionary so that you do not have to use the Skip option each time they are encountered. Also, when you place these words in a user dictionary, MacWrite indicates when they are misspelled.

A user dictionary is simply another dictionary. The difference between a main dictionary and a user dictionary is that you can add and remove words from the latter.

One user dictionary, User Dictionary, is supplied with the program. This dictionary contains no words—it awaits your additions. You can install this dictionary with the Main Dictionary, as described in Appendix A. If you follow this procedure, the dictionary is installed automatically each time you run MacWrite II.

You can have many user dictionaries, each with words specific to a particular kind of document you work with regularly. You can separate the proper names and words used in letters to friends and relatives from the terms used in technical writing. Fiction writers may want a separate user dictionary for a major work, especially those who write fantasy and science fiction in which many invented or unusual words are used.

The organization of user dictionaries is entirely up to you. You can have as many or as few as you want, and you can add words to or remove words from any user dictionary at will. The only restriction is that you can have only one user dictionary installed at any one time.

Creating User Dictionaries

If you install the supplied User Dictionary as described in Appendix A, the dictionary is installed in the program automatically and is ready to use. This dictionary may best be used for the words—such as proper names—you use most frequently.

You can create user dictionaries containing words specific to a document or type of document at any time. To create a new, empty user dictionary, follow these steps:

1. Select Install Dictionaries from the Spelling menu.

2. In the dialog box that appears, click the small button to the left of User in the Select Dictionary option (see fig. 4.9).

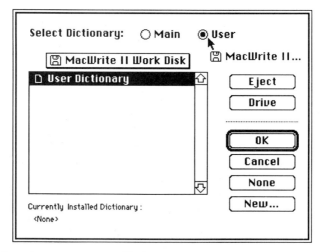

Fig. 4.9. *Creating a new user dictionary.*

3. Click New.

4. In the dialog box that appears, type the name of the dictionary (see fig. 4.10). Use any name that will help you remember the contents of the dictionary.

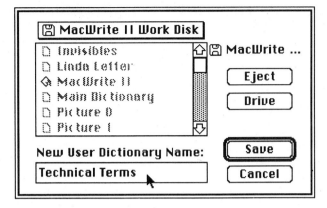

Fig. 4.10. *Naming the new user dictionary.*

5. Click Save.

You have now created and saved the new dictionary. When you quit MacWrite II, the dictionary is no longer installed. In order to use this dictionary during a spelling check, you have to install it again before using any of the spelling-checking commands. To install the dictionary, refer to "Installing Dictionaries" at the beginning of this chapter.

If you find that you are installing a particular user dictionary frequently, you may want to make that dictionary your primary user dictionary so that it is installed automatically. You can do this by changing its name to User Dictionary and installing it as described in Appendix A. Remember to rename the existing User Dictionary first.

You rename dictionaries—as you rename any file—through the Macintosh System software, not in MacWrite II. If you are unfamiliar with this procedure, check the manual that accompanied your computer.

Adding a Word to a User Dictionary

You can add words to an installed user dictionary in two ways. The first is through the Spelling dialog box during the spelling-checking process. The second method uses the User Dictionary command in the Spelling menu.

During the spelling-checking process, you may encounter a proper name or other word that the program does not recognize. This word may be a name or term that is spelled correctly. In figure 4.11, the program has questioned a proper name.

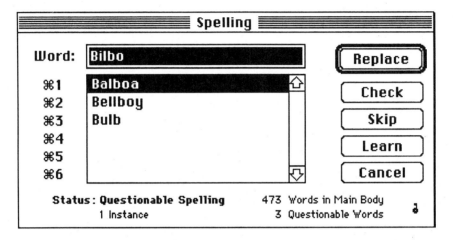

Fig. 4.11. *A proper name questioned.*

After verifying that the name is indeed spelled correctly, you can add the word to your user dictionary. Simply click Learn.

Learn adds the questioned word to the currently installed user dictionary. Be sure that the correct user dictionary is installed before you use Learn. If you are uncertain, click Skip. Then you can add the word with the User Dictionary command (discussed later in this section) after verifying that the correct user dictionary is installed.

Do not be too hasty in using Learn. If you install a misspelled word into a user dictionary, you defeat the purpose of the spelling-checking process. Although you can remove the word (this procedure is covered in the next section), you may not be aware of the error until long after many misspellings of the word have slipped by. Making certain of a word's spelling before adding it to a user dictionary can save you many headaches later.

You also can add words with the User Dictionary command in the Spelling menu. After you select this command, you are presented with the dialog box shown in figure 4.12.

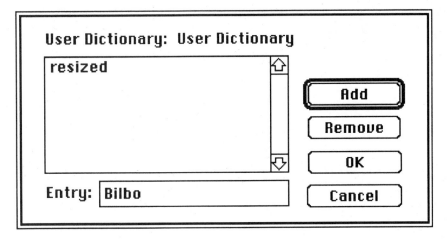

Fig. 4.12. *The User Dictionary dialog box.*

This dialog box acts as a window into the installed user dictionary. The name of the installed dictionary is at the top of the dialog box. Below the name is a scroll box that enables you to see the words in the dictionary.

You can scroll through the list of words by clicking one of the small arrows to the right of the box. Clicking once moves the list up or down one word. Holding down the mouse button while the mouse pointer is on the up or down arrow scrolls the list through the box up or down, respectively.

To add a word to the user dictionary, follow these steps:

1. Select User Dictionary from the Spelling menu.

2. Type the word in the Entry field.

3. Click Add (or press Return).

4. Click OK to close the dialog box and return to your document.

If you have more than one word to add to the user dictionary, repeat steps 2 and 3 as many times as necessary before performing step 4. Clicking OK confirms your additions and closes the dialog box.

A word that is already in the user dictionary cannot be added a second time (although it can be removed). If you attempt to add a word twice, the program notifies you of the error.

If you change your mind about the additions you have made, clicking Cancel aborts the changes and leaves the user dictionary as it was before. The program asks you to confirm the cancel order (see fig. 4.13).

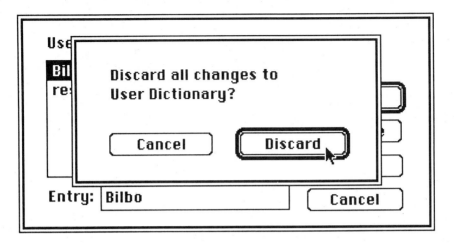

Fig. 4.13. *Confirming a cancel command.*

If you click Discard in this dialog box, any changes you have made are lost, and the user dictionary reverts to its previous contents. Clicking Cancel returns you to the User Dictionary dialog box with your changes intact.

Removing a Word from a User Dictionary

If you need to remove a word from an installed user dictionary, you use the User Dictionary command in the Spelling menu. After you select this command from the menu, the User Dictionary dialog box appears. To remove a word, follow these steps:

1. Scroll the list of words until the word you want to delete appears in the window (if it is not already visible).

2. Highlight the word to be removed by clicking it once.

3. Click Remove or press Command-R.

4. Click OK to close the User Dictionary dialog box and return to your document.

The word is removed from the installed user dictionary. You can repeat the steps to remove many words before clicking OK to confirm your actions. Clicking the Cancel button restores the user dictionary to its previous state.

If you have a large user dictionary and do not want to search for the word you want to remove, you can simply type the word and then click

Remove. The program searches for the word and removes it. If MacWrite II does not find the word, it displays a message notifying you to that effect. If you receive this message, your only recourse is to click OK (or press Return) and then scroll through the list for the word you are attempting to remove.

Controlling Spelling Options

Two options related to spelling checking determine whether the program pauses between document elements while checking spelling and where the Spelling dialog box appears on the screen.

Remember that a page element is a building block of a document; a page element may be the main body text, the header, the footer, or the footnotes. Page elements are important when dealing with the Auto Continue option.

The Auto Continue Option

When you select Check All from the Spelling menu, the program begins to check spelling from the current location of the cursor. The program continues through the main body text, the header, the footer, and the footnotes; then it loops around to the beginning of the document until it returns to the cursor position.

The program pauses only when it locates a word that it does not recognize. Because MacWrite II automatically turns on the Auto Continue option, the program works in this manner unless you turn off the option.

If you turn off the Auto Continue option, the program pauses between the different page elements during the spelling-checking procedure. For example, in figure 4.14, the program has finished checking the header of the document and now awaits the order to continue checking.

The status line at the bottom left of the dialog box indicates the element that has been checked. You can, at this point, cancel spelling checking by clicking Cancel. To continue to the next page element, click Continue or press Return.

You access the Auto Continue option by selecting Spelling Options from the Spelling menu. The Spelling Options dialog box appears (see fig. 4.15).

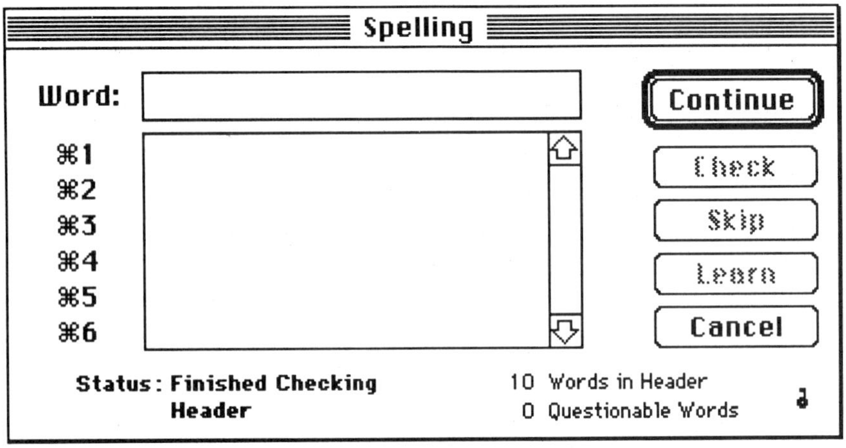

Fig. 4.14. *A spelling-checking pause.*

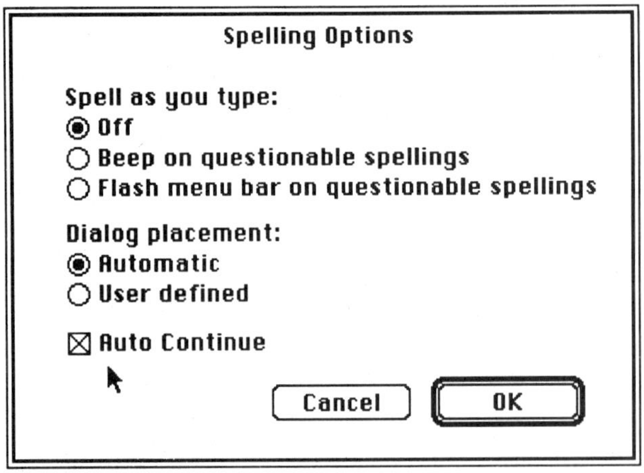

Fig. 4.15. *The Spelling Options dialog box.*

In figure 4.15, an X appears in the box to the left of the Auto Continue option, indicating that the option is on and that the program will not pause during the spelling-checking process.

To turn off this option, do the following:

1. Click the small box to the left of the Auto Continue option.

2. Click OK to close the dialog box and return to your document.

Use the same procedure to turn on the option.

The Spelling Dialog Placement Option

When you select any function that initiates spelling checking, the Spelling dialog box appears on-screen. If you want, you can change the location on the screen where the dialog box appears.

In the Spelling Options dialog box, you see a Dialog Placement option. This option is set initially to Automatic, which causes the program to place the Spelling dialog box at the bottom of the MacWrite II window.

To position the dialog box yourself, follow these steps:

1. Select Spelling Options from the Spelling menu.

2. Click the round button next to the User Defined option.

3. Click OK or press Return.

When the Spelling dialog box next appears on the screen, continue with the following steps:

4. Place the mouse pointer anywhere in the title bar of the Spelling dialog box (the top part where the word Spelling is displayed).

5. Press and hold the mouse button.

6. Move the mouse until the Spelling dialog box is in the desired location.

7. Release the mouse button.

The program remembers this location, and the Spelling dialog box now appears where you have positioned it. As long as the User Defined option is selected in the Spelling Options dialog box, you can reposition the Spelling dialog box by following steps 4 through 7. The program remembers the last location of the dialog box and places it on the screen where you last moved it.

To return to automatic placement of the dialog box, open the Spelling Options diaglog box, and click the round button next to the Automatic option.

Using the On-Line Spelling Option

As an alternative to checking all spelling at one time, you can have the program check each word as you type it. The program beeps or flashes the menu bar as soon as you type an unrecognized word. This section discusses using this on-line feature.

Activating On-Line Spelling Checking

The on-line spelling-checking option is activated in the Spelling Options dialog box. If you want the program to check each word as you type it, you must first choose the Spelling Options command from the Spelling menu to display the Spelling Options dialog box.

You then choose the way you want the program to notify you that the word you have typed is of questionable spelling—by beeping or by flashing the menu bar. If you want the program to beep, click the round button next to the Beep on Questionable Spellings option. If you want the program to flash the menu bar across the top of the screen, click the round button next to the Flash Menu Bar on Questionable Spellings option.

After choosing one of the methods of notification, click OK or press Return. On-line spelling checking is now active.

To turn off the on-line spelling checking, follow these steps:

1. Select Spelling Options from the Spelling menu.

2. Click the round button next to the Off option.

3. Click OK or press Return.

The program no longer checks each word as you type. Instead, it waits until you choose one of the Check commands in the Spelling menu.

You also can switch the method of notification at any time by using the same steps with one change. For step 2, you click whichever notification—a beep or a menu bar flash—you want to use.

Requesting a Word Spelling

When on-line spelling checking is active, the program beeps or flashes the menu bar when it questions a word. At that time, you can ask the program to provide possible alternative spellings for the word.

You request alternative spellings by selecting the Spell Word command from the Spell menu after the beep or menu flash. This command is available only when on-line spelling checking is active and the program has notified you of a possible misspelling. When you choose the Spell Word command (or press Command-Y), the Spelling dialog box, appears on the screen, displaying the questioned word and possible alternative spellings.

You then can choose an alternative spelling, add the word to the user dictionary, skip the word, or retype or edit the word. That is, you can use any of the options available in the Spelling dialog box, as described in the sections "Checking an Entire Document" and "Adding a Word to a User Dictionary."

Getting a Word Count

At times, you may want to know the number of words in your document. This feature is of special importance to those who sell their writing because many markets pay according to the number of words in a piece. Students who must write papers of certain lengths also will find this feature useful.

MacWrite II can provide you with the exact number of the words in your document without your having to count anything. You also can obtain a count of words in the main body, the header, the footer, or the footnotes. In addition, you can have the program count the number of words in any selection.

To get a word count, use the same procedures as for checking spelling. For example, for a word count of the entire document, select Check All from the Spelling menu. The Spelling dialog box appears with the number of words in your document displayed in the lower right corner (see fig. 4.16).

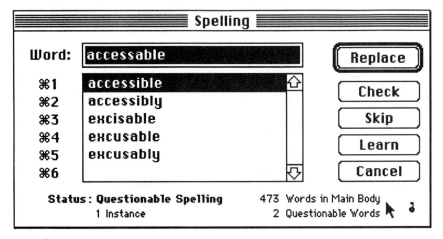

Fig. 4.16. The word count.

You do not have to proceed through the entire spelling-checking process at this time. If you want only a word count and do not want to check spelling, click Cancel to return to your document.

You also can use the techniques described in the preceding sections "Checking a Selection" and "Checking a Page Element" to obtain a word count of a selection of text or a particular page element. Again, use the procedures for checking the spelling of those items, but click Cancel to close the Spelling dialog box without proceeding through the entire spelling-checking procedure.

Summing Up

This chapter covers the spelling-checking capabilities of MacWrite II. You have seen how to install dictionaries, check the spelling of documents or parts of documents, work with user dictionaries, and use the spelling options.

The on-line spelling-checking capability of the program also has been covered. You now know that you have the option of checking spelling all at one time or as you type. The approach you use will depend on your work habits. If you write first drafts quickly and hold off on revisions, you will want to use the first approach. If you are creating a finished document needing few revisions, you probably want to know the moment a word is misspelled and thus will want to use the second approach.

In either case, you now know the available options and how they are put to use. You should be ready to learn about additional MacWrite II editing capabilities, which are discussed in the following chapter.

Advanced Document Editing

This chapter covers some of the more advanced editing features offered by MacWrite II. First among these features is the capability of searching for and replacing text and special formatting characters.

Also covered in this chapter is the Word Finder thesaurus, supplied with MacWrite II. This desk accessory provides an electronic thesaurus of over 220,000 words, available at any time during the creation or editing of a document. With this feature, you can find the word with just the right shade of meaning.

Hyphenation, the breaking of words between syllables, also is covered. You learn how to use and control hyphenation and the automatic hyphenation feature.

Finally, some special characters that you may need are covered, including long (em) dashes, short (en) dashes, nonbreaking spaces, and smart quotes.

Editing by Searching and Replacing

The capability of searching for and replacing text is one of the most powerful editing features of any word processing program. Here again, MacWrite II offers many options and features to help you locate and make changes to the text of your document.

Using the Find/Change command in the Edit menu, you can search for a word, phrase, or invisible editing character (*invisibles* are covered in Chapter 3). You also can search for text by using a pattern in order to locate different variations of a word or phrase.

Searching for a Word or Phrase

The simplest use of the Find/Change command is to locate a word or phrase. To find a word or phrase, follow these steps:

1. Select the Find/Change command from the Edit menu (or press Command-F).

2. The Find/Change dialog box appears (see fig. 5.1). Type the word or phrase you want to find in the Find What field. (You can enter up to 80 characters including spaces and punctuation.) For instance, type *time*.

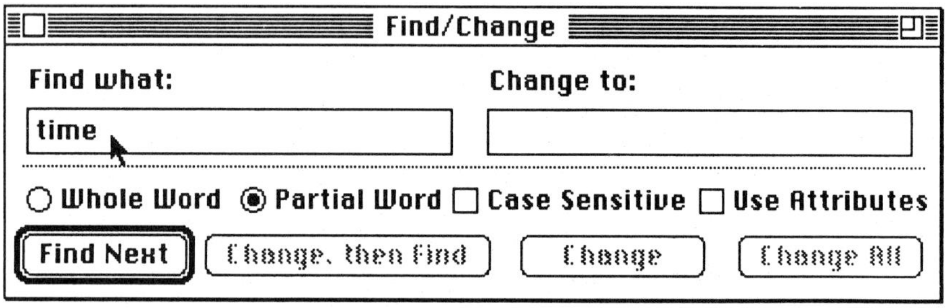

Fig. 5.1. *The Find/Change dialog box.*

3. Click Find Next or press Return.

The program locates and highlights the first occurrence of the word or phrase after the current position of the cursor (see fig. 5.2).

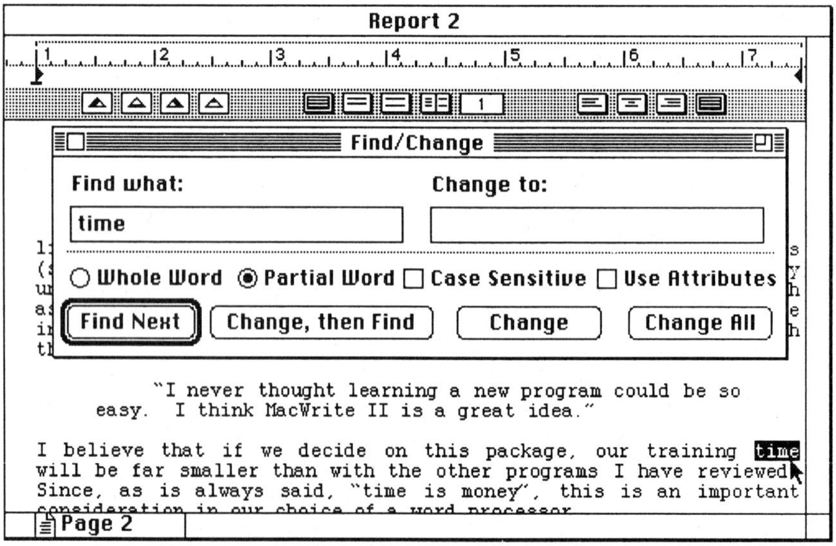

Fig. 5.2. *The first occurrence of the word you are finding.*

As you can see in figure 5.2, the word *time* has been found and highlighted by the program. To find the next occurrence of the word, simply click Find Next again (or press Return). The program locates and highlights the next occurrence of the word or phrase.

After you have found the word or phrase you are looking for, you can close the Find/Change dialog box by clicking the small close box in the upper left corner.

The program begins its search at the current location of the cursor in your document. When the search reaches the end of the document, the program begins again at the beginning of the document and continues the search. Unless the word or phrase is not present in your document, the search continues—starting again at the beginning after reaching the end—for as many times as you click Find Next.

If the program is unable to locate the word or phrase anywhere in your document, you see the dialog box shown in figure 5.3. Click OK to close the dialog box and return to the Find/Change dialog box.

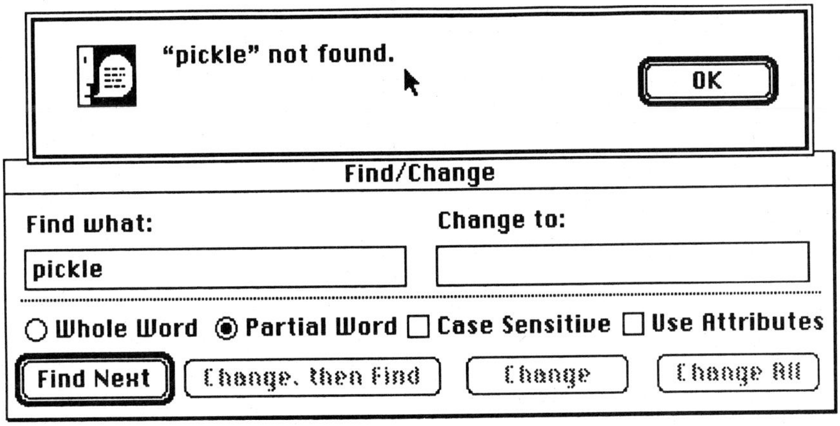

Fig. 5.3 The word was not found.

Searching for Whole and Partial Words

If you refer to figure 5.1, you see the Whole Word and Partial Word options below the Find What field. The program automatically selects the Partial Word option for you.

When the Partial Word option is selected, MacWrite finds the word or phrase you have typed in the Find What field even if the word is part of another word or phrase. For example, if you type *time* in the Find What field and select the Partial Word option, the program locates the words *time*, *times*, *anytime*, *sometime*, and so on.

Use this option when you are looking for words that have letters in common. For example, this book contains many references to figures, which take several different forms: "see fig. 5.1," "refer to figure 5.1," "Figure 5.1," and so on. To locate every figure reference, you consider what letters the references have in common. In this case, the letters in common are *fig*. To find the figure references, you can type *fig* in the Find What field, select the Partial Word option, and click Find Next (or press Return). Unless you also choose Case Sensitive, the program treats upper- and lowercase letters as exactly the same.

Each time you click Find Next (or press Return), the program finds the next occurrence of the letters *fig*, locating every figure reference in the document. Unfortunately, the search also locates such words as *configuration* and *disfigurement*.

To restrict the search, you must find some other common letter or character for the text you want. In the example, the only other character the figure references have in common is a space. That is, the three letters *fig* are always preceded by a space in a figure reference. To eliminate words such as *configuration* from your search, type a space and then the letters *fig*.

Likewise, if you to find the word *figure* only, you follow the word with a space as well as precede it with one. This method works, but the program provides an option that searches for whole words automatically.

To find a word that is not part of another word, use the Whole Word option in the Find/Change dialog box. This option recognizes that punctuation marks as well as spaces indicate the end of a word. To search for a whole word—*figure*, for instance—follow these steps:

1. Select Find/Change from the Edit menu (or press Command-F).

2. Type the word you want to find (*figure*) in the Find What field (leave no spaces before or after the word).

3. Select the Whole Word option.

4. Click Find Next (or press Return).

In this case, each time you click Find Next, the program locates the next occurrence of the whole word *figure*.

If you do a Whole Word search for the word *now*, the program does not find the words *nowhere* or *know* even though they contain the letters *now*. A Whole Word search locates *now*, *Now*, *NOW*, and so on.

Searching for Upper- and Lowercase Words

At times, you may want to narrow your search on the basis of a word's capitalization. You may be searching for a word at the beginning of a sentence or for a proper name.

The Case Sensitive option limits the search to only words or phrases that have the same case as the word or phrase you have entered. Normally, the program locates words by matching them to the words in the Find What field regardless of the case of the letters in the words. For example, if you type *now* in the Find what field, the program matches and locates *now*, *Now*, *NOW*, and so on. You get the same results if you type *NOW*, *Now*, or even *nOw*.

Suppose that you want to locate the name *Smith* in your document. You know that the word is capitalized because it is a proper name. At the same time, you want the program to ignore such words as *smith* or *blacksmith*. To restrict case in a search, follow these steps:

1. Select Find/Change from the Edit menu.

2. Type the text you want to find—in this case, the name *Smith*—in the Find What field.

3. Click the small box to the left of the Case Sensitive option. An X appears to indicate that the option is active (see fig. 5.4).

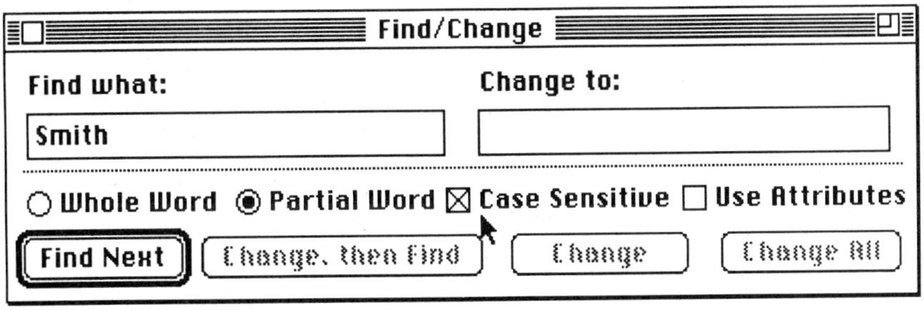

Fig. 5.4. *Selecting the Case Sensitive option.*

4. Click Find Next (or press Return).

The program locates the first occurrence of the proper name *Smith*. Because the Partial Word option is selected, the program also locates such words as *Smithers* and *Smithson*. To narrow the search to the word *Smith* only, use the Whole Word option (see the preceding section for a discussion of this option).

Note that this option indicates to the program that you want the case of the words located to match exactly what you have typed in the Find What field. If this option is on and you have typed *Now* in the Find What field, the program does not locate the word *now*, *know*, *NOW*, and so on, because the case of the letters does not match exactly.

Copying Text to the Find What Field

When you enter text in the Find What field, you can save some typing by using the Copy and Paste commands with the Find/Change dialog box to copy text into the Find What field.

For example, suppose that you need to locate a particular occurrence of a long word or phrase such as "The Department of Waste Management of The City of Hart." Although you can type the phrase, you also can use a shortcut by following these steps:

1. Place the mouse pointer at the beginning of the phrase in your text.

2. Click and hold the mouse button.

3. Move the mouse to select (and highlight) the phrase.

4. Release the mouse button.

5. Select Copy from the Edit menu (or press Command-C).

6. Select Find/Change from the Edit menu (or press Command-F).

7. Select Paste from the Edit menu (or press Command-V).

The selected phrase appears in the Find What field. You now can click Find Next to locate the next occurrence of the phrase.

You also can select the phrase by using the keyboard. If you are unfamiliar with the different text-selection techniques, see Chapter 3.

You may have noted that steps 5, 6, and 7 all have keyboard equivalents, which you can use to speed the process of copying the phrase into the Find What field of the Find/Change dialog box. In fact, you can combine these steps into one: hold down the Command key, and then press C, F, and V in sequence.

You can copy invisibles to the Find What field as well. You should use the Show Invisibles command in the View menu so that you can see what you are selecting. If you are not familiar with invisibles, refer to Chapter 3.

Searching by Word Patterns

If you are uncertain of the spelling of a word you are searching for, you can use what is called a *wild card* to help you in your search. A wild card is a character that matches any character: a letter, space, period, comma, and so on.

To insert a wild card into a word or phrase in the Find What field, press Command-8. This command places the symbol * in the word or phrase.

For example, suppose that you want to search for the word *field*. You aren't certain that you spelled the word consistently throughout the document; perhaps you accidentally spelled the word as *feild*. To search for every occurrence of the word, with either spelling, follow these steps:

1. Select Find/Change from the Edit menu.

2. Type the part of the word you want to find—up to where you want to insert the wild card. For this example, type *f*.

3. Press and hold the Command key.

4. Press 8 twice to insert two wild cards.

5. Type the remaining letters, *ld* (see fig. 5.5).

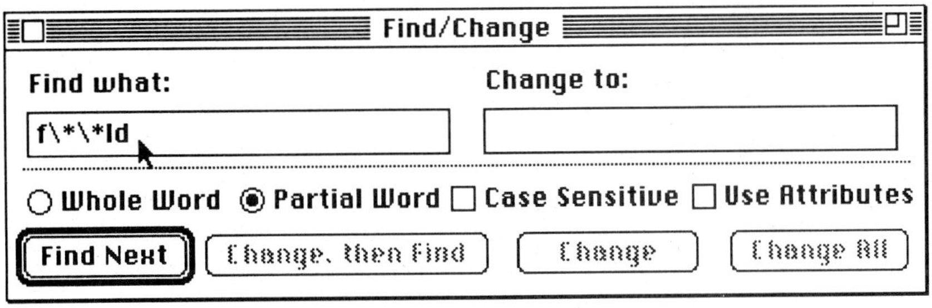

Find/Change

Find what: **Change to:**

`f\*\*ld`

○ Whole Word ● Partial Word ☐ Case Sensitive ☐ Use Attributes

[**Find Next**] [Change, then Find] [Change] [Change All]

***Fig. 5.5.** Searching for text by using wild cards.*

6. Click Find Next (or press Return).

The program finds the next occurrence of any group of five letters that begins with an *f* followed by any two characters and ends with the letters *ld*. In other words, the program finds the words *field*, *feild*, and so on.

Searching for Special Characters

The special characters in MacWrite II consist of the invisibles discussed in Chapter 3. At times you may want to locate words or phrases that are preceded or followed by a special character, such as a carriage return, tab, or page break.

Because you cannot type these characters in the Find What field, MacWrite II has provided a way to enter these characters by using special commands. Table 5.1 shows the commands for searching for the special characters.

Table 5.1
Commands for Entering Special Characters

To Enter	Press	Shows As
Carriage return	Command-Return	\p
Return within paragraph	Command-Shift-Return	\n
Tab	Command-Tab	\t
Nonbreaking em space	Command-Option-Space	\§
Column break	Command-Enter	\c
Page break	Command-Shift-Enter	\b
Merge break	Command-M	\m
Graphic	Command-G	\g
Footnote	Command-Option-F	\O
Time	Command-Option-T	\†
Short date	Command-S	\s
Abbreviated date	Command-A	\a
Long date	Command-L	\l
Discretionary hyphen	Command-hyphen	\-
Backslash (\)	\\	\\

Several characters in table 5.1 are part of features that are covered in later chapters. At this point, the important points to remember are

- To search for any of the invisibles or other characters listed in the table, you must use a command to enter them in the Find What field.

- The characters are represented in the Find What field by the backslash (\ ) and another character as listed in the Shows As column in Table 5.1.

For example, suppose that you need to locate a particular part of your text that you know comes at the end of a paragraph. You know that you ended the paragraph with the words *word processor* and a period. You also know that every paragraph ends with an invisible carriage return character. To locate this text, follow these steps:

1. Select Find/Change from the Edit menu (or press Command-F).

2. Type *word processor.* in the Find What field.

3. Press Command-Return.

4. Click Find Next.

In figure 5.6, you see how the text in the Find What field appears for this search. Note the \p characters at the end of the line.

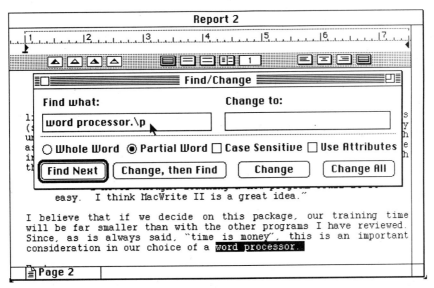

Fig. 5.6. Searching for text ending with a carriage return.

You also see in figure 5.6 that the program has found the words *word processor* at the end of a paragraph. The true power of the capability of searching for special characters becomes obvious in the later section "Editing by Searching and Replacing," where you learn how to search for and replace text. Using the special characters in a search and replace enables you to search for a formatting character in your text and replace it with another. Another feature—Use Attributes—enables you to search for and replace fonts and font attributes (see Chapter 10).

Viewing and Editing Located Words and Phrases

After a word or phrase has been located, you view it by closing, moving, or shrinking the Find/Change dialog box.

To close the Find/Change dialog box, click the close box in the upper left corner or press Command-W. The dialog box is closed and put away. You then can see the text that has been found. Located text is highlighted.

If you close the Find/Change dialog box, you must select Find/Change from the Edit menu (press Command-F) to reopen the dialog box and continue your search. The program does remember the last search; the dialog box opens with your last search settings still intact.

Alternatively, you can move the dialog box to give you a clear view of the located text. To move the window, place the mouse pointer in the title bar (near the words Find/Change). Hold down the mouse button and drag the box to a new spot.

At times, moving the dialog box still does not give you a clear view of your text. In this case, you can shrink the dialog box by clicking the zoom box in the upper right corner. The dialog box shrinks to only the option buttons (see fig. 5.7).

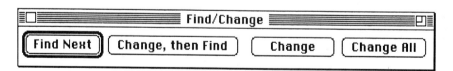

Fig. 5.7. *The dialog box shrinks.*

To expand the dialog box to its former size, click the zoom box. Each click switches the dialog box between the smaller size and its original size.

The dialog box does not have to be expanded to be useful. You can click Find Next (or press Return) to locate the next occurrence of what you typed in the Find What field even with the dialog box reduced in size. You must expand the dialog box, however, if you want to change any of the search settings or type new text in the Find What field.

When the program locates a word or phrase, it automatically selects the text. You can edit it after you close the box, or you can click anywhere in your document outside the Find/Change dialog box to bring the document window forward and make it the active window. Select Find/Change from the Edit menu or press Command-F to bring the Find/Change dialog box forward again.

Editing by Searching and Replacing

Although the capability of locating text is a helpful tool in editing, the capability of replacing the located text is of even greater benefit. With this capability, you can change individual occurrences of text, viewing each as the program locates it, or make changes throughout the document all at one time.

Using the Whole Word, Partial Word, and Case Sensitive options as well as the special characters and wild cards (all covered in preceding sections of this chapter), you can adjust and narrow your searches and replacements.

Replacing Words and Phrases

Instead of searching for text and then typing individual replacements, you can replace every occurrence of a word with another word. For instance, you can replace every occurrence of *Mr. Jones* with *Ms. Smith* in a document. Follow these steps:

1. Select Find/Change from the Edit menu (or press Command-F).

2. Type the text you want to replace—*Mr. Jones*—in the Find What field.

3. Press Tab.

4. Type the Text you want to insert as the replacement—*Ms. Smith*—in the Change To field.

5. Click Find Next to locate the first occurrence of *Mr. Jones*.

   When the program locates the first occurrence of the text in the Find What field, the three Change buttons become active (see fig. 5.8).

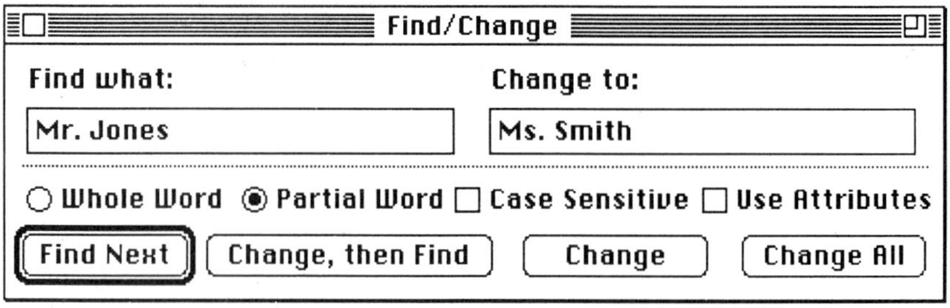

```
┌──────────────────────────────────────────────────────────┐
│ ▤▢▭══════════════ Find/Change ═══════════════▭▢▤          │
├──────────────────────────────────────────────────────────┤
│  Find what:                    Change to:                 │
│  ┌──────────────────────┐      ┌──────────────────────┐   │
│  │ Mr. Jones            │      │ Ms. Smith            │   │
│  └──────────────────────┘      └──────────────────────┘   │
│  ········································································· │
│  ○ Whole Word  ● Partial Word □ Case Sensitive □ Use Attributes │
│  ┌───────────┐ ┌──────────────────┐ ┌───────────┐ ┌────────────┐ │
│  │ Find Next │ │ Change, then Find │ │  Change   │ │ Change All │ │
│  └───────────┘ └──────────────────┘ └───────────┘ └────────────┘ │
└──────────────────────────────────────────────────────────┘
```

Fig. 5.8. The Change buttons.

6. Click Change, Then Find to replace the text and find the next occurrence.

    Or

    Click Change to change just this instance and not search any farther. The dialog box remains open on-screen.

    Or

    Click Find Next to leave this occurrence as is and find the next occurrence.

    Repeat step 6 until the program notifies you that no more occurrences of the text exist in your document.

7. Click OK to return to the Find/Change dialog box.

Replacing All Occurrences of a Word or Phrase

At times, you may want to replace a word or phrase with another throughout your entire document. You can go through the document and confirm each replacement. A quicker method, however, is to make all the changes throughout your document at one time by using Change All, as follows:

1. Select Find/Change from the Edit menu (or press Command-F).

2. Type the text to be replaced in the Find What field.

3. Press Tab.

4. Type the new text in the Change To field.

5. Click Find Next to locate the first occurrence of the text to be replaced.

6. Click Change All.

7. Click OK (or press Return) in the dialog box that appears (see fig. 5.9).

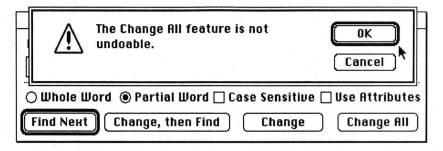

Fig. 5.9. *Confirming a Change All command.*

You cannot use the Undo command to restore your text after you execute a Change All command. The dialog box that appears when you select Change All enables you to cancel the Change All command by clicking Cancel.

When you click OK in the confirmation dialog box, the program proceeds to find and replace every occurrence of the text. When finished, the program displays the number of replacements made (see fig. 5.10). Click OK in this dialog box to return to the Find/Change dialog box.

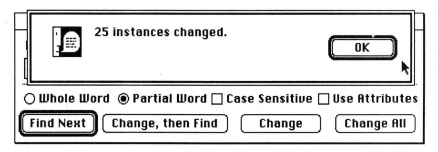

Fig. 5.10. *The completed Change All command.*

Keep in mind a few precautions when using the Change All command. You can damage your document with this command, and the damage can be difficult to fix. (Imagine accidentally replacing every occurrence of the word *the* in your document.) Here are a few tips to help you avoid such an accident:

- Narrow your search.

  Use the Whole Word and Case Sensitive options (described in preceding sections of this chapter) to limit the words and phrases that match the search text in the Find What field. For example, if you are replacing the name *Field*, use the Whole Word option to prevent replacement of the *field* part of other words (such as *Garfield*). You also can set the Case Sensitive option to prevent replacement of the word *field*. Be as specific as possible when using the Change All command.

- Verify your spelling.

  Make certain that the word or phrase in the Find What field is spelled correctly. If you are trying to replace every occurrence of the word *form* in your document, make sure that you don't enter *from* in the Find What field.

- Save the document to disk before using Change All.

  If the document has been saved to disk, you can restore it with the Revert to Saved command if your Change All command goes awry. (The Revert to Saved command is covered in Chapter 2.)

Undoing Replacements

With the exception of the Change All command, you can undo replacements of words and phrases. However, you can undo only the last change made. For example, if you have been using Change, Then Find to move through your document and have replaced six occurrences of *Mr. Jones* with *Ms. Smith*, only the last change can be undone. You have to change the other five replacements by using the Find/Change dialog box or by manually selecting and replacing.

Use the Undo command when you make a replacement and then realize you should not have. Suppose that you are replacing *Mr. Jones* with *Ms. Smith*, and when you make the first replacement, you notice that you have spelled the replacement name as *Ms. Smth*. To correct the problem, follow these steps:

1. Select Undo Find/Change from the Edit menu (or press Command-Z).

2. Double-click the misspelled name in the Change To field to select it.

3. Type the correct spelling.

In this operation, you have done two things. First, you have reversed the last replacement, restoring the text to its original state. Second, you have corrected the text in the Change To field so that future replacement operations are correct.

Editing with the Word Finder Thesaurus

Along with search and replace capabilities, a thesaurus also can be a useful tool when you are writing or editing a document. Many times you may realize you have used a word too many times, or you cannot recall a word with just the needed shade of meaning. A thesaurus can help by giving you alternative words with similar meanings. You are probably familiar with the printed versions of a thesaurus; if you are, you know that a thesaurus is essentially a list of synonyms.

MacWrite II comes with the Word Finder thesaurus from Microlytics, Inc. This thesaurus has over 220,000 synonyms contained in the WF Large Thesaurus file. Using Word Finder, you can request alternatives to any word in your text, and you can look up as many words as you want until you find one that suits you. You then can insert the new word into your document with the click of a button.

Word Finder is a desk accessory and must be installed using the Font/DA Mover provided by Apple. (Claris also provides a copy of the program on the MacWrite II Reference disk along with the Word Finder desk accessory and thesaurus.) For information on installing the thesaurus, refer to Appendix A.

Starting Word Finder

Because Word Finder is a desk accessory and not actually part of the MacWrite II program, you must start it separately each time you start MacWrite II in order to be able to use the thesaurus.

To start Word Finder, select Word Finder from the Apple menu (see fig. 5.11). This command installs the Word Finder menu at the far right of the menu bar (see fig. 5.12). As long as the Word Finder menu is in the menu bar, the thesaurus is available.

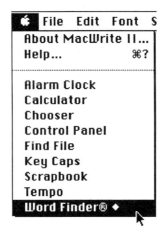

Fig. 5.11. Starting Word Finder.

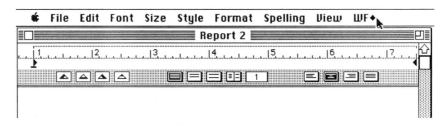

Fig. 5.12. Word Finder available on the menu bar.

If you have not installed the WF Large Thesaurus file in the same folder or disk as MacWrite II or in the System Folder, selecting Word Finder the first time brings up a dialog box asking you to locate the thesaurus file (see fig. 5.13).

Use the Open File dialog box that appears, to locate the thesaurus file (refer to the Macintosh manuals if you need information on locating files). When you have located the file, highlight it by clicking it once. Then click Open.

Now that you have told Word Finder where the thesaurus file is located, you do not need to repeat this step unless you move or rename the file.

If you are using MultiFinder, the Desk Accessory menu appears when you start Word Finder (after you have located the thesaurus file, if necessary). This menu is displayed because desk accessories are run under the program DA Handler in your System Folder. To install the Word Finder

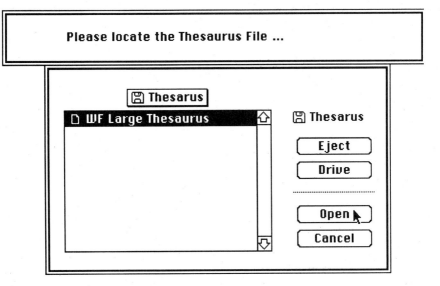

Fig. 5.13. *Locating the thesaurus file.*

menu in your MacWrite II menu bar, you must take one more step. Click the MacWrite II document window. The WF menu should then appear in the MacWrite II menu bar.

Looking Up a Word

You can use two different approaches when you want to look up a word, depending on whether you want to look up a synonym of a word already in your text or whether you are looking for a word to use.

If you want to find a synonym of a word already in your text, follow these steps:

1. Select the word (*investigate* in the example) by double-clicking it.

2. Select the Lookup command from the WF (Word Finder) menu (see fig. 5.14).

The program responds with a dialog box that displays the synonyms of the word you selected (see fig. 5.15).

Fig. 5.14. *Selecting Lookup from the WF menu.*

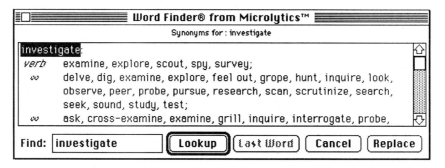

Fig. 5.15. *The Word Finder dialog box.*

To look up a word by using the second method, follow these steps:

1. Choose Lookup from the WF menu without selecting a word in your text. Word Finder beeps, and an empty dialog box appears. The cursor is in the Find field.

2. Type a word in the Find field and click Lookup (or press Return). Word Finder responds by locating and listing synonyms of the word.

If Word Finder does not find the word you selected or typed, it responds with a list of words closest to the spelling of the word you attempted to look up (see fig. 5.16). This list consists of the actual entries in the thesaurus. At this point, you can choose one of the words in the list to look up or attempt to look up a different word.

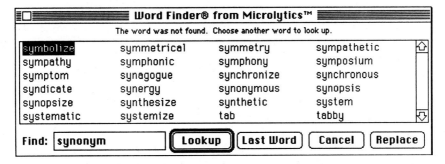

Fig. 5.16. Word Finder did not locate the word.

You can look up synonyms of one of the listed words as follows:

1. Click the word to select it.

2. Click Lookup (or press Return).

If none of the words Word Finder lists is what you want or if you want to look up another word, you can do one of the following:

- Click Cancel to return to your document.

- Select another word to look up by double-clicking it.

- Select Lookup again from the WF menu.

Or you can do the following:

1. Double-click the word in the Find field.

2. Type a new word.

3. Click Lookup (or press Return).

You can click Cancel and continue in your document at any time.

Choosing a Synonym

The primary part of the Word Finder dialog box is the scrolling list of synonyms. In figure 5.15, the word *investigate* was selected, and Word Finder responded with a list of synonyms.

Synonyms are divided by Word Finder according to parts of speech. That is, the synonyms are grouped depending on whether they are verbs, nouns, adjectives, and so on. In the case of the example, the word *investigate* can be used only as a verb. Therefore, only verbs are listed in the Word Finder dialog box.

The synonyms are further divided on the basis of meaning. In figure 5.15, the first line of synonyms (those following the word verb) are closest in meaning to the selected word *investigate*. The next group of words have a slightly different shade of meaning. Word Finder indicates a change in meaning with the infinity symbol (∞).

Suppose that, after looking over the synonyms, you decide to use the word *survey* instead of *investigate*. To insert the word into your text, you follow these steps:

1. Click the word you want to use—for instance, *survey*.

2. Click Replace.

A shortcut is to double-click the word of your choice. In either case, the Word Finder dialog box closes, and the word you choose is inserted into your document.

Because you have selected a word in the document, the new word replaces the selected word. If you look up a word by typing it into the Find field, selecting a new word inserts the word at the cursor position.

Looking Up Synonyms of Synonyms

After looking up the synonyms of a word, you may find that one of the synonyms is closer to the meaning you want but still isn't quite right. Word Finder provides a way to look up the synonyms of any of the synonyms listed.

In figure 5.15, the synonyms for the word *investigate* are displayed. Suppose that you decide that *survey* is close to what you are looking for but not exactly correct. You can look up synonyms of *survey* by following these steps:

1. Click the synonym for which you want to display additional synonyms—*survey* in this instance. (Do not double-click the word)

2. Click Lookup (or press Return).

The synonyms of the new word (*survey* in this case) are listed (see fig. 5.17). You can choose one of these words to be inserted into your document or to look up.

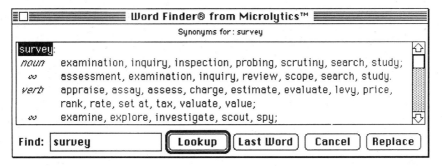

Fig. 5.17. *The synonyms for* survey.

Reviewing Previous Synonyms

The only problem with being able to look up synonyms of synonyms is that you can get "lost" after a while. Many times you find one word leading to another word that leads to yet another word until you begin to wonder what you were looking for in the first place.

Fortunately, Word Finder helps you keep track of the words you have looked up. The last 10 words you have looked up are kept and can be viewed by clicking Last Word. Word Finder responds with the dialog box shown in figure 5.18.

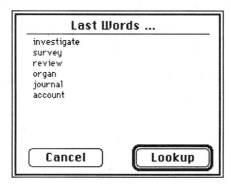

Fig. 5.18. *The last words looked up.*

You can return to any of these 10 words by performing the following steps:

1. Click the word to select it.

2. Click Lookup (or press Return).

The dialog box closes and the word and its synonyms are listed. You can, of course, simply review the list of words you have looked up. Click Cancel to close the dialog box without looking up any of the 10 listed words.

Undoing Synonym Substitutions

After choosing a synonym to replace the word you looked up, you may find that you prefer the original word after all. You do not have to retype the word. Instead, use the Undo command to restore the original word.

The Word Finder thesaurus "types" the synonym in your document when you click the Replace button. As in the case of any typing, the Undo Typing command "untypes" and restores the text to its original condition.

As is always the case with the Undo command, you can reverse only the latest command. If you perform any other command after a synonym substitution, you cannot use the Undo command to restore the original word. In this case, you must edit the word.

Positioning the Word Finder Window

The Word Finder window is positioned automatically when you select Lookup from the WF menu. You can change the window position from automatic to a user-defined location. In the WF menu, you see a check next to the Window Automatic option, indicating that the window is placed by Word Finder.

To position the dialog box yourself, follow these steps:

1. Select Window As Dragged from the WF menu.

2. Select Lookup. (Even if you are not looking up a word, you do this to position the window).

3. Place the mouse pointer in the title bar, the part of the dialog box that has the Word Finder name in it.

4. Press and hold the mouse button.

5. Drag the outline of the dialog box to the position you want.

6. Click Cancel (unless you are in the process of looking up a word, in which case you continue as usual).

Word Finder remembers the latest location of the window. When you next select Lookup, the Word Finder dialog box appears in the location where you last moved it—even if you quit Word Finder or MacWrite II. Word Finder returns to placing the dialog box automatically only if you select that option in the WF menu.

Leaving Word Finder

You can remove the WF menu from your menu bar if you want. Unless you use other desk accessories with menus that take up all the space on the menu bar, however, you probably will have no need to remove the WF menu.

To quit Word Finder and remove the WF menu from the menu bar, you choose the Close command from the WF menu.

Using Hyphenation

In addition to the thesaurus, MacWrite provides other editing tools, such as hyphenation. The primary use of hyphenation is in documents with justified text. Because justified text adjusts the spacing of the words within the document to achieve an even edge on both the left and right sides of the text, the spacing of the words sometimes turns out poorly. Large gaps between words occur because a long word is sometimes wrapped to the next line, leaving a large amount of space on the preceding line to be distributed among the words of that line.

To remedy this problem, word processing programs provide for hyphenation—breaking words into parts and separating them with hyphens. Hyphenation enables the program to distribute the space between words more evenly.

The best example of justified text that uses hyphenation is your daily newspaper. When you next read the morning paper, note how the spaces between the words are more or less even (although they are not identical in size). Longer words are broken between two lines. The overall effect is a smoothly flowing text with straight edges on both sides.

Although you can use hyphenation in any document, hyphenation is especially useful in multicolumn documents, which are covered in Chapter 12.

To use the Auto Hyphenate feature, you must install the MacWrite II Hyphenation file in the folder or disk with the MacWrite II program or in your System Folder. Otherwise, the program cannot perform hyphenation for you.

You do not need to install the Hyphenation file to use the discretionary hyphen, described in the following section. Not installing this file means that you must hyphenate manually, however.

Hyphenating a Word Manually

When you are typing and want to indicate to the program where you want a hyphen, you use a command to insert a discretionary hyphen. Inserting a discretionary hyphen tells the program, "Break the word here if it needs to be broken."

An inserted discretionary hyphen does not appear when you type it. Instead, MacWrite II remembers the location in case the word comes up against the margin and needs to be broken.

For example, consider the text of figure 5.19. This text is part of a fictional report that uses justified text alignment. In the sample text, note that the third line of the first paragraph contains an excessively large space. This line is a good example of a case where hyphenation is needed.

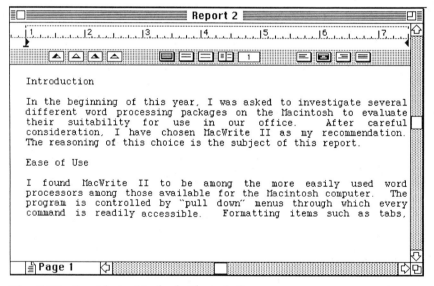

Fig. 5.19. Sample text to be hyphenated.

If you look to the fourth line of the paragraph, you can see that the word *consideration* is the cause of the spacing problem. Because the word is too long to fit on the third line, the program forces it to the fourth. Unfortunately, this movement leaves too much space in the third line.

To insert a discretionary hyphen, follow these steps:

1. Place the mouse pointer between the syllables where you want the break; in this case, between the *d* and the *e* of the word *consideration*.

2. Click the mouse button to place the cursor at that point.

3. Press and hold the Command key.

4. Press the hyphen key (-).

The program immediately hyphenates the word (see fig. 5.20).

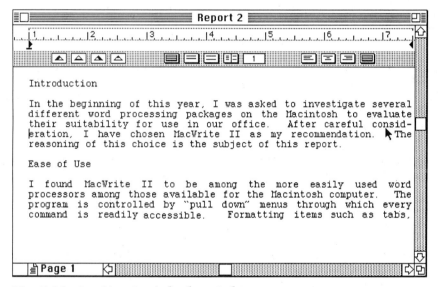

Fig. 5.20. *Consideration* **is hyphenated.**

You can insert more than one discretionary hyphen in one word. The word *consideration* has several syllables. You can, if you want, insert a discretionary hyphen between each pair of syllables so that the program can hyphenate the word as needed if you edit the paragraph and change the spacing.

You can perform these steps while you are typing a word or after the word has been typed. When you are typing the word, simply perform the steps just described at the point you want the word to be hyphenated (if necessary) and then continue typing the word. If the word is already typed, position the cursor at the syllable break and then insert the hyphen.

Using Automatic Hyphenation

Instead of typing a discretionary hyphen everywhere you need a word broken, you can have the program hyphenate for you. MacWrite II has a standard list of hyphenation rules stored in the MacWrite II Hyphenation file. When you request the program to hyphenate your document, MacWrite II processes your document according to those rules.

You can make exceptions to the rules. First, you can create a list of words that show MacWrite II exactly where to hyphenate the words, if at all. You also can use nonbreaking hyphens, hyphens that do not separate words.

Activating Automatic Hyphenation

To have MacWrite II hyphenate your document following the rules of the MacWrite II Hyphenation file, select Auto Hyphenate from the Spelling menu. The program immediately hyphenates your document (see fig. 5.21). Automatic hyphenation continues as long as the Auto Hyphenate option is selected (indicated by a check mark next to the option in the menu).

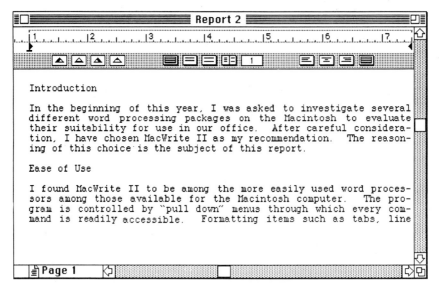

Fig. 5.21. *The document is hyphenated automatically.*

You also can choose this option before beginning to type a new document. The program hyphenates as you create the document.

To turn off the Auto Hyphenate option, select Auto Hyphenate from the Spelling menu again. The check mark disappears from next to the option in the menu, and your document is no longer hyphenated.

Remember that a discretionary hyphen overrides the Auto Hyphenate option. The program hyphenates the word where you place the discretionary hyphen (or hyphens) regardless of the rules the program normally follows.

Adding or Removing an Exception to Hyphenation

When using the Auto Hyphenate option, you may find that the program breaks a word that should not be broken or breaks a word in an incorrect location. In either case, you need to tell the program how to hyphenate the word by adding exceptions to the hyphenation rules with the Hyph. Exceptions command.

You can enter two types of exceptions in MacWrite II: words that you do not want hyphenated at all and words for which you want to specify the hyphenation.

To add exceptions, follow these steps:

1. Select Hyph. Exceptions from the Spelling menu.

2. In the Hyphenation Exceptions dialog box, type the word you do not want hyphenated in the Entry field (see fig. 5.22).

   Or

   Type the word, hyphenating it in the desired locations. For example, if you want MacWrite II to hyphenate the name *Shakespeare,* type *Shake-speare* in the Entry field of the Hyphenation Exceptions dialog box.

3. Click Add.

4. Click OK to confirm your entries, close the dialog box, and return to your document.

If you have several words to enter, repeat steps 2 and 3 until you have added all the words. Then perform step 4.

You do not have to enter proper names in this manner. MacWrite II does not hyphenate a proper name unless you insert a discretionary hyphen in the name or enter it as an exception.

A discretionary hyphen overrides the exceptions you enter as well as the rules MacWrite II normally uses.

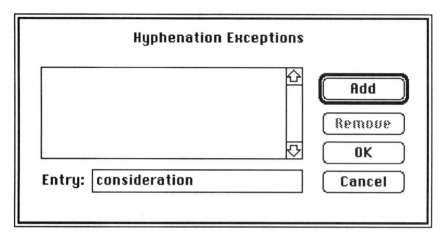

Fig. 5.22. *The Hyphenation Exceptions dialog box.*

Finally, if you change your mind about your entries, clicking Cancel in the Hyphenation Exceptions dialog box discards your additions. A dialog box appears asking you to confirm the cancellation (see fig. 5.23).

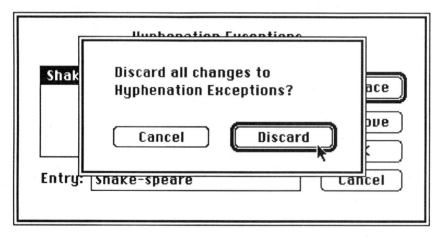

Fig. 5.23. *Confirming the cancellation.*

Click Discard to lose any additions you have made since selecting Hyph. Exceptions and restore the exceptions list to its original state. Previous additions that were confirmed by clicking OK are unaffected.

If you do not want to discard your changes, click Cancel, and you are returned to the Hyphenation Exceptions dialog box.

The procedure for removing one or more of the exceptions you have added to the exceptions list is similar to that for adding exceptions.

To remove an exception, follow these steps:

1. Select Hyph. Exceptions from the Spelling menu.

2. Click the word to be removed (or type the word in the Entry field).

3. Click Remove.

4. Click OK to confirm the removal and close the dialog box.

As with adding exceptions, you can remove several words in one session by repeating steps 2 and 3 as many times as you want before performing step 4.

Cancel discards any changes you have made to the exceptions list, restoring it to its original state. As with adding exceptions, the Cancel order is questioned by the program and you must confirm the order.

Preventing Word Division

Some words are normally hyphenated—for example, *x-ray* and proper names such as *Bilbo-Gordon*. Although these words contain hyphens, they should not be divided. To prevent the program from breaking these words, you must enter what is called a *nonbreaking* hyphen.

To enter a nonbreaking hyphen, follow these steps:

1. Type the part of the word that precedes the hyphen.

2. Hold down the Command and Option keys and press the hyphen key (-).

3. Type the remainder of the word.

This procedure inserts a hyphen in the word but does not permit MacWrite II to break the word.

Two types of dashes—the em and en dashes—are indirectly related to hyphenation. They are discussed in the following section.

Using Special Characters

Three special characters—the em dash (—), the en dash (–), and the nonbreaking space—are related to hyphenation in that they help you control how words are separated.

Em and en dashes are similar to hyphens in appearance but function differently. The em dash—which is the width of the capital letter M in the current font—is used to set off a parenthetical phrase. The en dash is one-half the width of the em dash and is used to indicate a range. For example, in the phrase "9 A.M.–11 A.M.," the dash between the two times is an en dash.

Nonbreaking spaces are used when you want to keep words together. Essentially, entering a nonbreaking space tells the program not to separate the words that have nonbreaking spaces between them.

The last special character discussed in this section is the *smart* quote. This option enables you to have opening and closing quotation marks rather than the standard straight quotation marks.

Entering Em Dashes

When you want to set off a parenthetical remark, you use an em dash. If you have experience with typewriters, you know that you use two hyphens to create a dash to set off parenthetical remarks. However, this method is not appropriate in MacWrite II because dashes consisting of two hyphens are treated as hyphens, which are used to divide words. The program does not separate words that have an em dash (—) between them.

For example, consider the phrase "...controlled through icons—small pictures that indicate a function—that are easily understood..." (see fig. 5.24).

To type this phrase with em dashes, follow these steps:

1. Type the words up through *icons*.

2. Instead of typing a space, hold down the Shift and Option keys and press the hyphen key (-).

3. Do not type a space; instead, continue with the rest of the text.

The Shift-Option-hyphen command inserts an em dash into your text. The words separated by the dash are not separated by the program; they will always be on the same line. The example has two em dashes (they usually come in pairs); you need to repeat steps 2 through 4 after you type the word *function*.

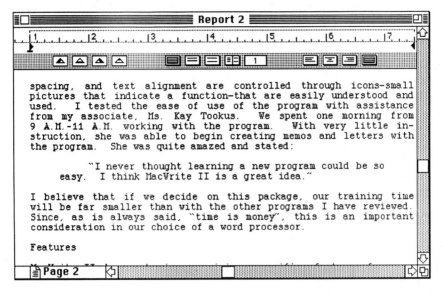

Fig. 5.24. *The sample text with em dashes.*

Entering En Dashes

When you need to enter a range, such as a range of dates or times, you need to use an en dash to indicate the range, but you do not want the numbers separated by the program. You cannot, therefore, use a hyphen.

To insert an en dash, follow these steps:

1. Hold down the Option key.

2. Press the hyphen key (-).

The en dash is inserted. An example of an en dash can be seen between 9 A.M. and 11 A.M in figure 5.24. The en dash keeps the two times together on the same line; the program does not separate them.

Entering Nonbreaking Spaces

At times, you may want words to be kept together on the same line (for example, when you are using a long proper name), but you do not have reason to use the dashes covered in the two preceding sections. In this case, you need to use a *nonbreaking* space (sometimes called a hard space). For example, "The City of Hart" should be separated by nonbreaking spaces to keep the full name together on one line.

Normally, MacWrite II separates (or wraps) words at the end of a line at spaces. You see this word wrap in operation as you type text. When you come to the margin, MacWrite II moves a word to the next line at the space between words.

To keep words together on the same line, insert a nonbreaking space in the following manner:

1. Hold down the Option key.

2. Press the space bar.

A nonbreaking space is entered. The space looks just like any other space. The only difference is that the program does not separate two words that have a nonbreaking space between them.

Using Smart Quotes

Smart quotes are a special character you should know about. With typewriters, you are limited to the standard quotation marks, which are straight. Typeset documents, such as books and newspapers, use opening quotation marks and closing quotation marks that are angled to indicate the start and end of a quotation. Consider the quotation in figure 5.24.

MacWrite II assumes that you want to use smart quotes, which are angled like the quotation marks in typeset documents. To use smart quotes, you do not have to do anything. Any quotation marks you type automatically appear as smart quotes.

If you want to control smart quotes, however, you can do so. To turn Smart Quotes on or off, do the following:

1. Select Preferences from the Edit menu.

2. In the Preferences dialog box, click the small box next to the Smart Quotes option (see fig. 5.25).

3. Click OK (or press Return).

The X in the box next to the Smart Quotes option indicates that the quotation marks are on.

Quotation marks entered before you change the Smart Quotes option are not affected by the change. If you want to change any quotation mark that was previously typed, you must select and replace it.

Preferences

Measure: [Inches]

☒ Smart Quotes (' '," ")
☐ Fractional Character Widths

┌─ Date Format ──────────
○ 6/25/89
○ Jun 25, 1989
◉ June 25, 1989
○ Sun, Jun 25, 1989
○ Sunday, June 25, 1989

┌─ Page Number ──────────
○ Current Page #
◉ Current [of] Total
Starting Page # [1]

┌─ Date & Time ──────────
○ Always Update
◉ Never Update

┌─ Footnotes ──────────
◉ End of Page
○ End of Document
☒ Auto Number Footnotes
Starting Number [1]

[Cancel] [OK]

Fig. 5.25. The Preferences dialog box.

Summing Up

In this chapter, you have learned how to search for and search and replace words, phrases, word patterns, and special characters in your document.

The chapter next explores the Word Finder thesaurus. You now should understand how you can locate synonyms of words and insert them into your text.

Hyphenation of words also has been covered. You now know how to hyphenate a word yourself or have the program do the hyphenation for you, and how to control the automatic hyphenation feature.

Finally, you have seen the purpose and use of the following special characters: em and en dashes, nonbreaking spaces, and smart quotes.

At this point, you are well on your way to putting MacWrite II to work to create a multitude of documents of your own design. You are now ready to consider working with multiple documents and document formats, and inserting text from other documents. These capabilities are the focus of the next chapter.

Working with Documents

In this chapter, you continue your exploration of MacWrite II by considering more of the program's document handling capabilities. You learn how to work with more than one document at a time—managing multiple windows, cutting and pasting between documents, and saving sections of documents to separate files.

MacWrite II is also capable of working with the formats of other programs. This chapter explains how to use translators that enable you to insert, open, and save document files created by other programs. Inserting text is given special attention. You learn how you can bring text into your document from different sources.

A special feature of MacWrite II enables you to create *stationery* files, templates of your most commonly used document formats. Basically, you learn how to use stationery files to save the settings of documents you use on a regular basis so that you do not have to specify each setting every time you create a similar document.

Working with Multiple Documents

MacWrite II is not limited to working with one document at time. You can, in fact, have up to seven documents open at any one time. Each document resides in its own document window, and you can move, resize, activate, or close any window at will. You also can cut, copy, and paste from one document to another.

Opening Multiple Documents

Before you can work with more than one document, you must open the documents. The procedure for opening multiple documents differs, depending on whether you have already started MacWrite II or are still at the desktop (that is, in the Macintosh System software).

Remember that you can have only seven documents open at one time. If you try to open more than seven, the program does not notify you; it simply does not open any more documents.

Opening Documents within MacWrite II

If you have already started the MacWrite II program, you open additional documents in the same way you open the first document.

To open a document, whether the first or the seventh, follow these steps:

1. Select Open from the File menu.

2. In the Open Document dialog box, highlight the document you want to open (see fig. 6.1).

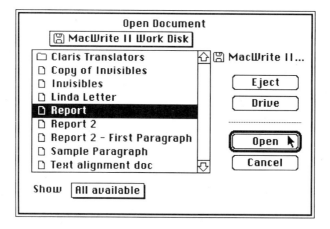

Fig. 6.1. The Open Document dialog box.

3. Click Open (or press Return).

The document is opened. To open another document, simply repeat these steps. When you have seven open documents, the Open command is no longer available in the File menu. You must close one or more of the open documents in order to open another document.

You cannot open a document twice. If you try, the program notifies you that the document is already open.

Opening Documents from the Desktop

You can start MacWrite II and open documents at the same time from the desktop, that is, from within the Macintosh System software. If you have been using the Macintosh, you may already be familiar with the method of double-clicking a document to open the document and start the program simultaneously. You may not be aware, however, that you can use a variation of this method to open more than one document at a time.

Figure 6.2 shows the MacWrite II icon and five document icons. Also shown are the User Dictionary and Main Dictionary and a folder for file translators (discussed in the next section of this chapter).

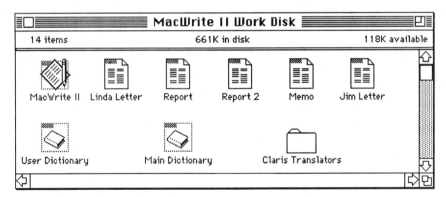

Fig. 6.2. *The MacWrite II and document icons.*

Suppose that you want to start MacWrite II and open the document Linda Letter. To open a document from the desktop, follow these steps:

1. Place the mouse pointer on the document icon—in this case, Linda Letter.

2. Double-click the mouse button.

The program starts. When the document window opens, it contains the text of Linda Letter instead of a blank new document.

You can extend this procedure to open several documents by selecting the group of documents. For example, suppose that you want to open the five documents shown in figure 6.2. To open multiple documents, follow these steps:

1. Place the mouse pointer near but not on the first document icon—in this case, Linda Letter.

2. Press and hold the mouse button.

3. Move the mouse pointer, dragging the dashed box across all the document icons you want to open (see fig. 6.3). Although the box must touch all the icons, it does not have to enclose them completely.

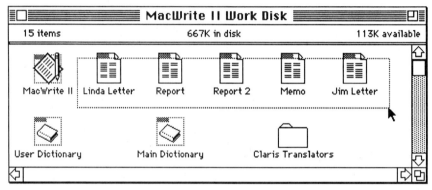

Fig. 6.3. *Selecting several documents to open.*

4. Release the mouse button.

The document icons darken to indicate that they have been selected. To open the selected documents, double-click one icon. (You can double-click any of the darkened icons.)

The program starts up and opens each document. If you select more than seven documents, the program opens only seven.

You may find an alternate method of selecting documents to be useful, especially if you are using the By Name, By Date, By Size, or By Kind option in the View menu of the desktop. This method enables you to select documents by *Shift-clicking*.

To select documents by Shift-clicking, follow these steps:

1. Click the first document icon. The icon darkens to indicate that it is selected.

2. Press and hold the Shift key.

3. Click each document icon you want to select.

As with the other selection method, after you have selected the documents to be opened, double-click any of them to start the program.

The selection methods described here are part of the Macintosh System software—not part of MacWrite II. You can find additional information on these methods in the manuals that accompanied your computer.

Closing All Open Documents

At some point, you may decide to close all the documents you have opened, without leaving MacWrite II. You can close a document window by clicking the close box in the upper left corner (see fig. 6.4). Other elements shown in this figure—the size and zoom boxes—are discussed in the following sections.

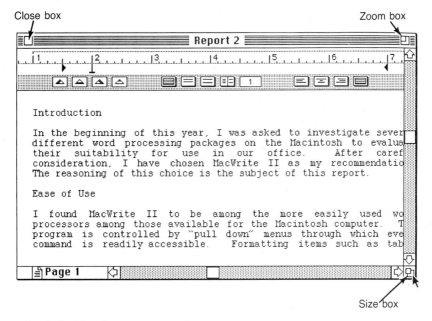

Close box

Zoom box

Size box

Fig. 6.4. The document window.

To close all open documents at one time, you do the following:

1. Press and hold the Option key.

2. Click the close box of any open document.

The program closes each document window in turn. If you have made changes in any document, the program pauses and asks whether you want to save the changes. If any document is new and has not yet been saved to disk, the program asks for a name. For further information on saving documents, refer to Chapter 2.

Managing Document Windows

After you have opened more than one document, an immediate problem is apparent. The program stacks the document windows one on top of another. To work with more than one document, you must learn how to manage more than one window.

Managing windows effectively requires that you be able to move and resize them as well as select the one you want to work with. Some of these functions are discussed in Chapter 2. Here, they are presented within the context of working with more than one window.

Resizing Document Windows

Unless you have a large-screen monitor (and sometimes even if you do), having several document windows open at one time leaves you with little room to work. Therefore, knowing how to change the size of a document window is important.

In the lower right corner of every document window is the size box (again see fig. 6.4). This box enables you to change the size of a document window.

To use the size box, do the following:

1. Place the mouse pointer in the size box.

2. Press and hold the mouse button.

3. Move the mouse, dragging the gray outline to the size you want the document window to be (see fig. 6.5).

4. Release the mouse button.

The document window shrinks or expands to fit the size of the gray outline.

After changing the size of a document window, you can restore it to its previous size quickly by using the zoom box, which is located in the upper right of every document window (again see fig. 6.4).

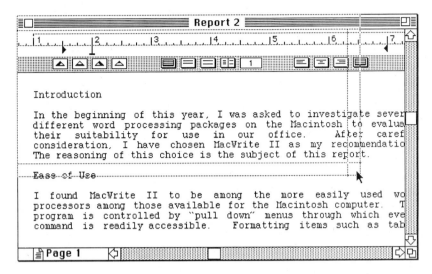

Fig. 6.5. *Resizing the document window.*

Clicking the zoom box once restores the document window to its previous size; another click changes the window to the size you set with the size box. Clicking the zoom box switches the window between its normal size and the size you last set using the size box.

Selecting a Document Window

Remember that MacWrite II commands operate on the front window, which is the active window. Only one window can be active at any one time. You can select (or make active) the document window in which you want to work in two ways. The method you use depends on whether you can see the window.

If a window is visible, even if it is behind another window, you can select and make it active with a simple click of the mouse. Follow these steps:

1. Place the mouse pointer on any part of the document window you want to make active.

2. Press the mouse button.

The window is brought forward and becomes the active window.

If the window you want to make active is not visible, you must select it from the View menu. As you open documents, the names of the documents are added to the end of the View menu. You can bring forward and make active any window by selecting it from this menu. For example, suppose that three documents are open. The names of the three documents—Linda Letter, Memo, and Report—have been added to the View menu (see fig. 6.6).

You can make any document window active by selecting its name from the menu. Simply open the View menu and highlight the document you want to make active.

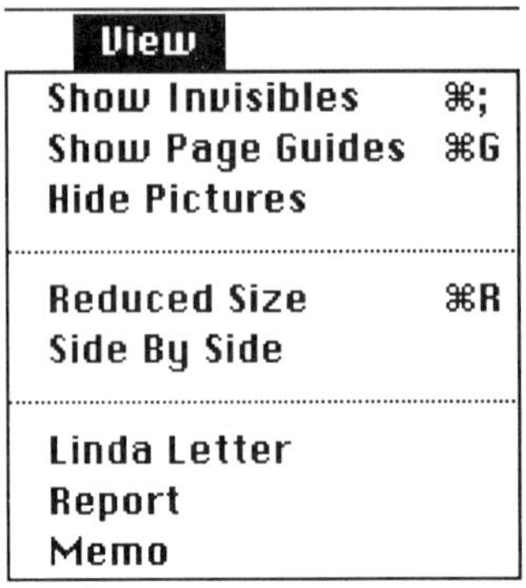

```
┌─────────────────────────────┐
│ ▐ View ▌                     │
├─────────────────────────────┤
│ Show Invisibles       ⌘;     │
│ Show Page Guides      ⌘G     │
│ Hide Pictures                │
├·····························─│
│ Reduced Size          ⌘R     │
│ Side By Side                 │
├·····························─│
│ Linda Letter                 │
│ Report                       │
│ Memo                         │
└─────────────────────────────┘
```

Fig. 6.6. Document names added to the View menu.

Moving Document Windows

Sometimes you may want to move a document window in order to see the window behind it. Or perhaps you want to move a window that is partially hidden behind another one to see more of the back window's contents.

To move the active window, follow these steps:

1. Place the mouse pointer in the title bar of the window.

2. Press and hold the mouse button.

3. Move the mouse, dragging the outline of the window to the location where you want the window to be.

4. Release the mouse button.

The window moves to the new location. Moving an inactive window involves the same steps with one addition. Before pressing the mouse button, press and hold the Command key. After moving the window, release the Command key and the mouse button.

Cutting, Copying, and Pasting between Documents

Chapter 3 deals with selecting, cutting, copying, and pasting text within a document. Many of the procedures explained in that chapter can be carried out between two (and sometimes more) documents.

This chapter assumes that you are familiar with the procedure of selecting text. If you are not, review Chapter 3.

Copying Text between Documents

Copying text between two documents is similar to the procedure of copying text within a document, with a few added steps to take you between documents.

For example, suppose that you have written a report about MacWrite II and the use of the program in your office. In the report, you quote a coworker. Before using the quotation, you are sending a draft of the report to the person quoted. You decide to include the quotation in the memo you are sending with the copy of the report. Instead of retyping the quotation, you can copy it from the draft of the report.

To copy text between documents, follow these steps:

1. Open both documents.

2. Select the first document—in this example, Report 2—from the View menu to make it the active document.

3. Select the text you want to copy—in this case, the quotation (see fig. 6.7).

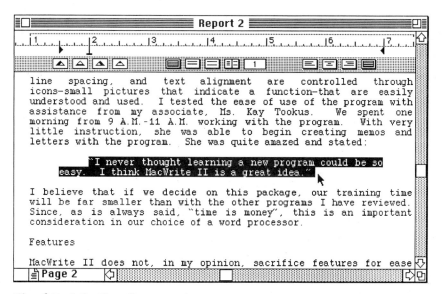

Fig. 6.7. Selecting the quotation.

4. Select Copy from the Edit menu (or press Command-C).

5. Select the second document—in this example, Memo—from the View menu to make it the active document.

6. Position the cursor where you want to insert the text.

7. Select Paste from the Edit menu (or press Command-V).

The quotation (which is a paragraph) and its formatting are inserted at the cursor in the document Memo (see fig. 6.8).

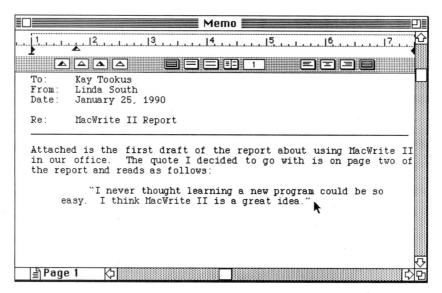

Fig. 6.8. *Pasting the quotation into the memo.*

You can use the same procedure to copy any amount of text from one document to another. The amount of text is determined by your selection.

Keep in mind that the Copy command places the text in a storage area called the Clipboard. Anything copied to the Clipboard remains there until you next use the Copy or Cut command. Therefore, if you want to copy the same text into several documents, you can do so by repeating steps 5 through 7 for each document.

Moving Text between Documents

At times, you may want to move text from one document to another. This operation is identical, except for one change, to the operation described for copying text.

To remove text from one document and place it in another, do the following (these steps assume that both documents are already open):

1. Select the document from which the text is to be moved (select it from the View menu, or click it if it is visible).

2. Select the text to be removed.

3. Select Cut from the Edit menu (or press Command-X).

4. Select the document into which the text is to be placed.

5. Position the cursor where the text is to be inserted.

6. Select Paste from the Edit menu (or press Command-V).

Keep in mind two things when using this procedure. First, before performing the Paste operation, make certain that the cursor position is where you want the text to appear in your document. You can move the cursor to place the text correctly.

Second, remember that the Clipboard holds only one selection of text at a time. Cutting text removes it from the document and places it in the Clipboard. If you then perform another Cut or Copy operation before pasting the text, you will lose this text.

Fortunately, if you accidentally lose the text in the Clipboard, you often can recover it by immediately performing the following steps:

1. Select the document from which the text was cut.

2. Select Revert to Saved from the File menu.

3. Click OK in the dialog box that appears (or press Return).

This procedure restores the document from which the text was cut to the last version saved to disk.

Keeping "Clippings"

One of the strange things about writing is that despite the sequential order of a book's paragraphs, pages, and chapters, the ideas, thoughts, and words rarely come in order. No matter how much you try to stick to an outline, you find your mind jumping from point to point with wild abandon. In the days of the typewriter, a new idea usually meant stopping, grabbing a pen and pad, and scribbling madly, hoping you could get the words down before you forgot them.

With MacWrite II's capability of having more than one document open at a time, you can have a "clippings" document, the electronic equivalent of a pen and paper, handy at all times.

Suppose that you are working on a paper and find yourself suddenly thinking of a point that is pages away. You know exactly how you want to word a later paragraph or two. To pull out your electronic pen and paper, do the following:

1. Select New from the File menu (or press Command-N).

2. Type the paragraph (or paragraphs).

3. Select your original document from the View menu.

Now you can continue, and your ideas are safe in the new document. When you are ready for those ideas, use the copy or move procedures outlined in the two preceding sections to place the paragraphs in your document.

Keeping a "clippings" document also can be handy during editing. You may need to move a section of text, but you're not sure where you should put it. Although the Clipboard can hold text for the duration of a cut-and-paste operation, the Clipboard is not suitable for longer storage.

A "clippings" document also can be a handy place to store notes and random thoughts related to the document on which you are working. And if you need to stop working for a while, you can save the document to disk and later reopen it along with your main document.

Using Other Document Formats

One major trend in personal computers today is the increasing capability that programs and computers have of sharing files. In the early days of microcomputers, if two people were working on two different word processors, the only way the two could share their files was by printing them and handing them to each other.

The differences among formats and computers were so great that in the days when the floppy drive was still relatively new, many times not even disks could be exchanged. Instead of the two major formats we have today (Macintosh and MS-DOS), more than a dozen were in use. Two different word processors not only were unable to read each other's files, but many times the disks were not recognized by the different computers.

In recent years, although the differences among computers and programs persist, transferring data among computers and programs has become much easier. Data transfer and conversion programs have become widespread. With the introduction of the Super Drive on the Mac II and now even the SE, Apple has given users the capability of using MS-DOS-formatted disks.

Claris supported this trend by providing MacWrite II with built-in translation capabilities. The program can translate other word processing program files directly when provided with a translator that describes those programs' file structures. You simply have to make sure that the correct file translator is in place; MacWrite II does the rest.

Reviewing Formats Available in MacWrite II

Without your having to do anything special, MacWrite II can translate files among four formats. The first two formats are specific to MacWrite II itself: the MacWrite II document file format and the MacWrite II stationery file format. The second two formats are Text and Text with Line Breaks; both formats are for files that contain only text with no formatting.

Additional translators are provided on the MacWrite II Reference disk in a folder called Claris Translators. These translator files give MacWrite II the capability of working with the files of the following programs:

Acta 3.0
AppleWorks
MacPaint
MacWrite (the earlier version)
Microsoft Word 3.0 and 4.0
Microsoft Works 1.1 and DB
WordPerfect
WriteNow

Additional translators are provided for the following IBM-compatible programs:

Microsoft Word 4.0 (also handles Version 5.0)
WordPerfect 4.2
WordPerfect 5.0

Two standard file types also are supported with translators:

PICT (for graphics)
RTF (for text)

Finally, on the MacWrite II Help disk, a translator called the MacLink Plus/ Bridge is provided. This translator enables you to use translators designed for the popular DataViz program MacLink Plus. This program is a file-transfer program that enables Macintosh and standard IBM PC users to transfer and translate one another's files. DataViz sells several file translators that MacWrite II users can take advantage of through the MacLink Plus/Bridge translator.

The information contained here concerning file translators applies to Version 1.1 of MacWrite II, which Claris released to replace the earlier V1.0 of the program. If you have V1.0, you should contact Claris about upgrading to the new version as soon as possible. At the time of this writing, the upgrade was free to any registered owner.

Installing Translators

To install translators, place the needed files in your System Folder or on the disk with MacWrite II. The program automatically recognizes the files.

If you have a hard disk and know that you frequently will be converting files of different formats, you may want to copy the entire Claris Translators folder from the MacWrite II reference disk into your System Folder or your MacWrite II folder. If you have any DataViz translators, you should place them in the same location and copy the MacLink Plus/Bridge file as well.

Opening Files in Other Formats

After the translator for a particular file format has been installed, you open a file in that format in the same way you open a MacWrite II file from within the program. Even with the translators installed, you cannot double-click a document file created by another program and have MacWrite II start.

To open a document file of another program, follow these steps:

1. Select Open from the File menu.

2. Select the file by clicking its name.

3. Click Open.

The program responds with a dialog box indicating that it is translating the file (see fig. 6.9). This process can take a while on large files. MacWrite II provides a Cancel button if you want to stop the translation process.

MacWrite II adds (Converted) to the name of the document when it opens. The document is then treated as a new document. When you close it, the program asks whether you want to save changes even if you have done no editing.

MacWrite II also can filter the files in the Open Document dialog box. Below the scrolling list of files in the dialog box is the Show menu. Normally, the Show menu contains the All Available option, and the

Converting: Report (MSW)

From: Microsoft Word 3.0

[Cancel]

Fig. 6.9. *Translating the file.*

scrolling list shows all files and folders that you can open. Any document files of the formats for which you have installed translators as well as the built-in formats are shown. If you select any other format by using the Show menu, only document files of that format are shown in the scrolling list of the dialog box.

To select one of the formats from the Show menu, follow these steps:

1. Place the mouse pointer on the All Available option.

2. Press and hold the mouse button; the menu pops up (see fig. 6.10).

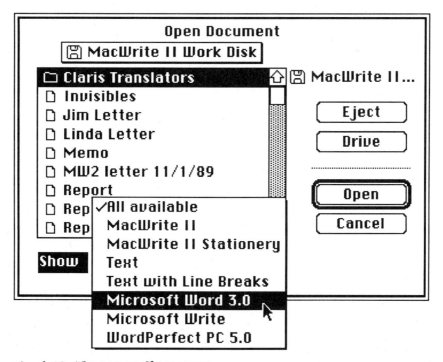

Open Document

MacWrite II Work Disk

Claris Translators   MacWrite II...

Invisibles

Jim Letter

Linda Letter

Memo

MW2 letter 11/1/89

Report

Rep   ✓All available

Rep   MacWrite II

Show   MacWrite II Stationery

   Text

   Text with Line Breaks

   Microsoft Word 3.0

   Microsoft Write

   WordPerfect PC 5.0

Eject

Drive

Open

Cancel

Fig. 6.10. *The pop-up Show menu.*

3. Move the mouse up or down to highlight the format of your choice.

4. Release the mouse button.

The Show menu then displays the format you have chosen, and the scrolling list of document files shows only files of that format (see fig. 6.11).

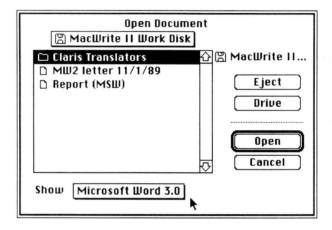

Fig. 6.11. *Showing only Microsoft Word 3.0 documents.*

The program resets the menu to All Available when you quit.

Saving Documents in Other Formats

MacWrite II is capable not only of opening document files in other formats but also of saving document files in any format for which you have installed a translator. To save a document in a format other than the standard MacWrite II format, you use the Save As command. You also must select a format from the Save As dialog box.

For example, suppose that after completing a report, you want to give it to a coworker who uses Microsoft Word. To save the document in Microsoft Word format, follow these steps:

1. Open the document.

2. Select Save As from the File menu.

3. In the dialog box that appears, place the mouse pointer on MacWrite II in the Save As field.

4. Press and hold the mouse button; the Format menu pops up (see fig. 6.12).

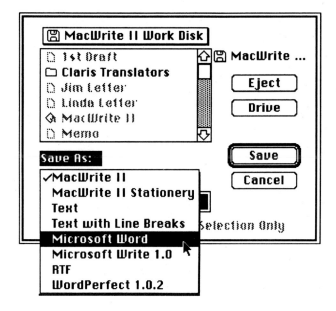

Fig. 6.12. The Format menu in the Save As dialog box.

5. Move the mouse down until the new format—in this case, Microsoft Word—is selected.

6. Release the mouse button.

7. Click Save.

The program notifies you that it is converting the document into the new format. You can stop the conversion process by clicking Cancel.

If you are saving the new converted document on the same disk as the original, you should type a new name in the Save As dialog box before clicking Save. Otherwise, the original will be replaced.

Inserting Text

You can insert text into your document from a variety of sources. Earlier sections of this chapter deal with inserting text from other parts of your documents and from other open MacWrite II documents. This section is concerned primarily with inserting text from documents that have not been opened or are of a format other than MacWrite II.

Inserting Text with the Clipboard

One little-known aspect of the Macintosh Clipboard may be useful to you, especially if you are using MultiFinder. The Clipboard is part of the System software and independent of MacWrite II or other programs. The actual use of the Clipboard is up to the author of the software, however. The following procedure may not work with every program, so you may need to experiment with it.

When you are working in a word processing program (or other program) and use the Copy or Cut command, the text (or graphic) you have selected is copied to the Clipboard. The Clipboard is part of the System, not the application program, and only one Clipboard exists (although later releases of the Macintosh System software may have more than one).

Because only one Clipboard exists, text (or graphics) copied or cut from a document in a program often can be pasted into a document of a different program.

To illustrate, consider the following example. You are working in another Macintosh word processing program, and you do the following:

1. Select a paragraph.

2. Choose Copy from the Edit menu.

3. Select Quit from the File menu.

4. Double-click the MacWrite II icon to start the program.

5. After the new blank document appears, select Paste from the Edit menu.

The text you copied from the other document appears in the MacWrite II document.

Users of MultiFinder (another part of the Macintosh System software) can perform these steps without having to quit one program before starting another. Assuming that both MacWrite II and Microsoft Word are running under MultiFinder, you can perform these steps:

1. Select the text.

2. Choose Copy from the Edit menu.

3. Switch to MacWrite II.

4. Select Paste from the Edit menu.

If you are unfamiliar with MultiFinder, refer to the manuals that accompanied your computer.

The point here is that the Clipboard does not necessarily vanish when you quit a program (or with MultiFinder, switch to another program). Many programs permit transfers by use of the Clipboard, and these transfers are not one-way. Often, you can copy, cut, and paste text from MacWrite II into another program.

You typically lose any formatting when performing such a transfer of text. Also, you cannot transfer all graphics in this manner.

The Clipboard is intended as temporary storage. Do not expect the data to be saved when you turn off the computer. A more permanent alternative to the Clipboard is the Scrapbook, which is discussed in the following section.

Inserting Text with the Scrapbook

The Scrapbook is an alternative to the Clipboard method of transferring text (and graphics) between programs. The Scrapbook is a desk accessory, which you must install in your System file before the program is available for use. The Scrapbook is also a part of the Macintosh System software and not part of MacWrite II. The installation of desk accessories is beyond the scope of this book but is covered well in the manuals that come with the Macintosh.

The Scrapbook is exactly what its name indicates, a place where you can paste odds and ends to be kept as you work. You can use the Scrapbook in a manner similar to the way you use the "clippings" document discussed earlier in this chapter.

Because the Scrapbook desk accessory creates a file that is stored in your System Folder, the Scrapbook is better than the Clipboard for storing text and graphics you use frequently in many documents. A good example of such a use may be a company letter head or logo.

To save text to the Scrapbook, do the following:

1. Select the text.

2. Choose Copy from the Edit menu.

3. Select Scrapbook from the Apple menu (see fig. 6.13).

Fig. 6.13. Selecting the Scrapbook.

4. Select Paste from the Edit menu. The text is pasted into the Scrapbook.

In figure 6.14, you see the Scrapbook containing some text pasted from a MacWrite II document. To understand the Scrapbook, think of a pad of paper. Each item pasted into the Scrapbook is like a page of the pad. You "flip" the pages by clicking the small left or right arrow near the bottom of the Scrapbook window.

The numbers in the lower left corner indicate the current page and the total pages in the Scrapbook. The numbers 1/24 mean that you are viewing the first of 24 pages.

Close the Scrapbook by clicking the small close box in the upper left corner of the window. The items you paste into the Scrapbook are stored in a file and are not lost when you close the Scrapbook or even when you quit the program. Items can be removed only by using the Cut or Clear command.

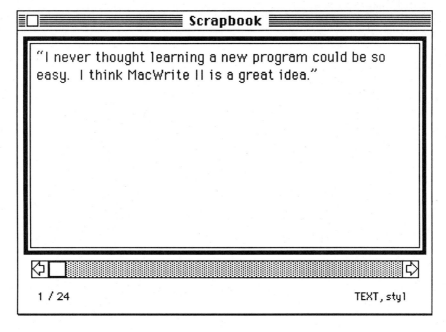

Scrapbook

"I never thought learning a new program could be so easy. I think MacWrite II is a great idea."

1 / 24   TEXT, styl

Fig. 6.14. *Text pasted into the Scrapbook.*

When you want to paste something from the Scrapbook into your document, follow these steps:

1. Select Scrapbook from the Apple menu.

2. Click the left or right arrow until you find the item you want to use.

3. Select Copy from the Edit menu.

4. Click the close box of the Scrapbook.

5. Select Paste from the Edit menu.

The Scrapbook item is pasted into your document at the current location of the cursor. You are not limited to storing items from MacWrite II documents in the Scrapbook. You can paste items into the Scrapbook from various programs and then paste the items into your MacWrite II documents.

Your only limitation concerns disk space. Items pasted into the Scrapbook are stored in a Scrapbook file in your System Folder. If you are using a hard drive, space is probably not a problem. Floppy disk users, however, may not be able to store many items before running out of room.

Inserting Another Document File

You can insert text from any document in a format recognized by MacWrite II: any MacWrite II file, any text file, and any file for which you have installed a translator. The capability of inserting documents into other documents can be of great benefit if you create many forms and letters of a similar nature. Law offices, for example, have carefully worded sections of legal documents that can be stored separately and assembled as needed. With MacWrite II, each section can be kept in a different file and inserted when needed.

Saving a Selection of a Document

Before you learn how to insert a document into another document, you should understand the process of saving parts of documents, which enables you to create document files that serve as building blocks. In other words, you can save parts of documents that you want to insert into other documents later.

To save a selection of a document, follow these steps:

1. Select the text to be saved.

2. Select the Save As command from the File menu.

3. Click the Selection Only option in the lower right of the Save As dialog box (see fig. 6.15).

4. Type a name for the new file that is to contain the selected text.

5. Click Save (or press Return).

MacWrite creates a new document file that contains only the selected text. In this way, you can create various document files containing sections of documents that you can use later to build new documents.

Using the Insert File Command

The Insert File command in the File menu enables you to insert another document file into your current document. The Insert File command, like the Open command, can translate the formats of documents created with other programs. The formats available depend, of course, on translators you have installed.

Keep in mind that when you insert another document into your current document, the entire document is inserted at the current position of the cursor. You should make certain that the cursor is in the proper location

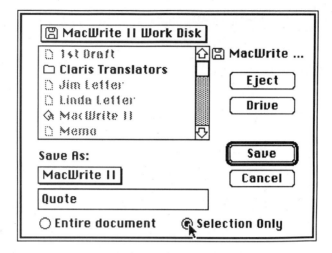

Fig. 6.15. *Choosing the Selection Only option.*

before selecting Insert File. If you make a mistake, however, you can use the Undo command to restore your text.

To insert a document file on disk into your current document, follow these steps:

1. Make certain that the cursor is located where you want to insert the text.

2. Select Insert File from the File menu (or press Shift-Command-I).

3. Select the document file you want to insert by clicking its name in the Insert File dialog box.

4. Click Open (or press Return).

If the document file is in a format other than MacWrite II, the program notifies you that the file is being converted. The contents of the document file are inserted at the current cursor position. If the document is in MacWrite II format, the insertion occurs immediately because the file does not have to be converted.

After inserting a document, you often have to edit the format of the new text, especially if the document was originally created using a program other than MacWrite II on another Macintosh (or on an IBM PC or compatible). This editing is most often necessary when the document was created using formatting not available in MacWrite II or fonts that are not in your System file. MacWrite II attempts to match the formatting and fonts as closely as possible. Sometimes, however, some formatting or fonts in a document do not translate.

Immediately after using the Insert File command, you can restore your text by choosing Undo Insert File from the Edit menu or by pressing Command-Z.

Using Stationery

After you have gone to all the trouble of formatting and editing a memo, letter, report, or other document, you may wonder whether you must go through the entire procedure each time you want to produce a similar document. The good news is that you do not.

MacWrite II provides a built-in format called MacWrite II Stationery that enables you to store the format of a document, which then can act as a *stationery* file. That is, when you open the file, you "tear off" a copy as if you were working with a pad of paper stationery.

The program also offers automatic stationery, which enables you to configure the format of the new, blank document MacWrite II opens when you start the program or select the New command from the File menu. By using automatic stationery, you can set the program to offer blank documents in the format you use most often.

Creating and Using Stationery

The major part of creating stationery is setting the format you want to use. You create stationery the same way you create a regular document. A document becomes stationery when you choose the MacWrite II Stationery format before saving the file.

For example, consider the memo format in figure 6.16. This memo was created mostly by typing the items in the appropriate locations. In other words, the memo format was created, but the names and the subject were not filled in.

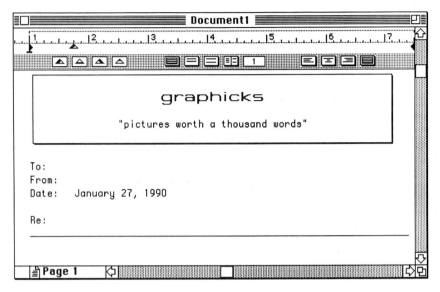

Fig. 6.16. *A memo to be made stationery.*

The logo at the top was created in another program and then pasted into MacWrite II by using the Clipboard (graphics are covered in Chapter 12). The date was inserted using the Insert Date command in the Edit menu (see Chapter 9). With this command, dates are updated automatically. Therefore, each time the memo stationery is accessed, it always has the current date. Finally, the line that divides the memo header information from the memo body is simply a series of underscores.

More important, however, is the process of turning the document into stationery. To create stationery, follow these steps:

1. Create and format the document.

2. Select Save As from the File menu.

3. In the Save As dialog box, place the mouse pointer on the Format menu beneath the words Save As.

4. Press and hold the mouse pointer; the Format menu pops up.

5. Move the mouse down until the format MacWrite II Stationery is highlighted.

6. Release the mouse button.

7. Type a name for the stationery document.

8. Click Save (or press Return).

The document is saved to disk and becomes a stationery file.

The icon for a stationery file is different from the normal MacWrite II document icon (see fig. 6.17). The icon looks like a pad of paper, indicating its function. When you double-click the icon or open the document within the program, you are given a copy of the document, not the original. You can add text, edit, or change the document in any way. When you close the document or attempt to save it, you are presented with a dialog box asking you to name the document (see fig. 6.18).

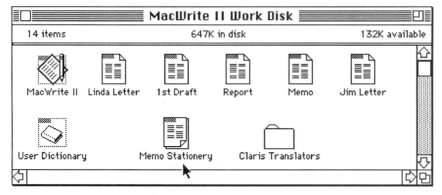

Fig. 6.17. *The stationery document icon.*

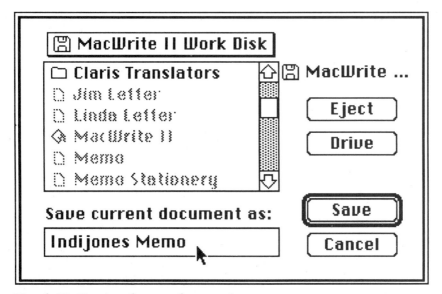

Fig. 6.18. *Naming the new document.*

Normally, when you choose Save from the File menu or indicate to the program that you want to save changes made to a document, the program writes the document to disk over the original copy. In the case of stationery, the program assumes that you do not want to save your document over the stationery file. Therefore, MacWrite asks for a name for the new document. In this way, the stationery file remains available for future use.

To change a stationery file, you open the file and make whatever changes you want. You then use the Save As command, making sure to specify the format as MacWrite II Stationery as you did the first time you saved it. If you enter the same name, the program responds with a dialog box asking whether you want to replace the existing file. Click Yes. Make certain that you choose the MacWrite II Stationery format before clicking Save to indicate to the program that you want to save the document as stationery. Otherwise, the new document is saved as a regular MacWrite II document.

Using Ready-Made Stationery

Claris has provided four stationery *templates* for your use. These templates are stored on the MacWrite II program disk in a folder named Stationery Templates and include Letter Stationery, Memo Stationery, Newsletter Stationery, and Resume Stationery.

Each stationery document has a standard format for the kind of document for which the template is named. You can use these documents as a starting point for creating documents or stationery of your own.

To use any stationery document, simply copy the document to your MacWrite II disk (or folder). To start MacWrite II and obtain a copy of the stationery file, double-click the icon of the template you want to use.

You then can edit the file as needed, save, and print the document. By following the steps outlined in the preceding section for altering existing stationery, you can use these ready-made documents as starting points to create stationery tailored to your needs.

Using Automatic Stationery

If you find that you use one particular format for most of your documents, you can make this document format automatic stationery. After you have created the automatic stationery, any time you start MacWrite II (without opening any document) or select New from the File menu, the new document is in the format you set in the automatic stationery file, unless you direct the program otherwise.

Creating Automatic Stationery

Creating automatic stationery is a process similar to creating standard stationery. The only differences are that the stationery file must have a particular name and must be located in the System Folder. To create automatic stationery, follow these steps:

1. Create the document.

2. Choose Save As from the File menu.

3. Choose the MacWrite II Stationery format.

4. Type the name *MacWrite II Options* for the document.

5. Select and open your System Folder. (If you are unfamiliar with how to do this, check your Macintosh manuals for further information.)

6. Click Save (or press Return).

Now all new blank documents are created in the format you have set in the MacWrite II Options document.

Creating a Document with the Standard Format

If you have created automatic stationery, all new documents are given the format of the automatic stationery. If you need a new blank document without the formatting contained in the automatic stationery, you can do the following:

1. Press and hold the Option key.

2. Select New from the File menu.

A new blank document is created without the formatting of the automatic stationery. You are then free to format the document as needed.

If you find yourself using the Option-New command frequently, you may want to remove the MacWrite II Options file from your System Folder and use it as a regular stationery file.

Summing Up

In this chapter, you have seen how to work with documents in various ways. You have learned how to work with more than one document open at a time, and you have explored the various functions for moving and copying text between documents.

MacWrite II's capability of working with the formats of other programs has also been explored. You have seen how to install translators, open document files of other program formats, save in other formats, and insert text saved in other formats.

Inserting text from various sources also has been covered; you now should be more familiar with the operation of the Macintosh System Clipboard and the desk accessory Scrapbook.

In addition, you now should understand and be able to use stationery to speed creation of similar documents and know how to use automatic stationery for default formatting of new documents.

This chapter ends the first part of this book. You now should be well grounded in the basics of the MacWrite II program and ready to move on to the topic of page layout and design, which is the subject of Part II.

Part II

Document Design

Quick Start: Creating a Booklet

Part I of this book introduces you to MacWrite II's basic features. Part II adds to the tools introduced so far, focusing on designing and creating documents.

To begin this part of the book, this chapter leads you through the design and creation of a booklet—an employee handbook for a fictional company. As you work through this chapter, you see how pages are laid out and left and right pages created. You create a title page, headers, footers, and a footnote. Finally, fonts and styles are introduced, and using the View menu with left and right pages is covered.

Determining the Page Layout

Page layout concerns the overall format of the pages of a document. As such, page layout consists of margin settings, left and right page settings, title page settings, number of columns, paper size, page orientation, and so on. Page layout is controlled primarily through the Page command in the Format menu; however, the Page Setup command of the File menu also comes into play.

To begin this quick start, you start MacWrite II by double-clicking on the program's icon. You are presented with a new blank document. If you have automatic stationery set up, you need to close this document and open a new one by holding down the Option key and selecting New from the File menu.

Setting the Page Size and Orientation

In all probability, the page size setting is already correct, but you should check it to make sure. To set the page size, do the following:

1. Select Page Setup from the File menu.

2. In the Page Setup dialog box, click the US Letter Paper option (see fig. 7.1).

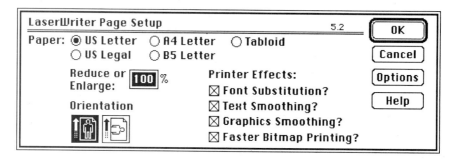

Fig. 7.1. *The Page Setup dialog box for LaserWriters.*

The exact Page Setup dialog box you see depends on your printer. All Page Setup dialog boxes, however, have a US Letter setting.

You can choose one of two settings for page orientation: portrait or landscape. In this quick start, you should use the portrait setting. To set the orientation, do the following:

1. Click the left Orientation icon; the selected icon darkens (again see fig. 7.1).

   Even though some printers may use a different Page Setup dialog box, most have the same orientation icons. If you do not see a similar icon or a portrait option, consult your printer manual.

2. Click OK to confirm your choices.

The dialog box closes, and you are returned to your document.

Setting Left and Right Pages and Margins

Because this document is to be a booklet, you need to have margin settings that accommodate left and right pages and leave room for binding. You must notify MacWrite II that you are using left and right pages and set the margins, as follows:

1. Select the Page command from the Format menu.

2. In the Page dialog box, click the box next to the Left/Right Pages option (see fig. 7.2).

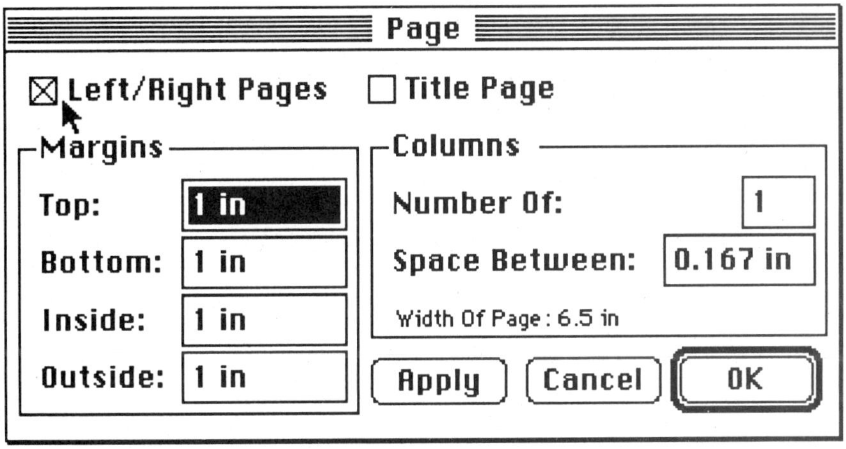

Fig. 7.2. Choosing left and right pages in the Page dialog box.

When you click the box next to this option, an X appears to indicate that the option is selected. The Left and Right Margins settings change to Inside and Outside.

Before setting the margins, make sure that the Top Margins field is highlighted. If it is not highlighted, press the Tab key until the highlighting moves into this field. Then continue.

3. Type *0.75* in the Top Margins field.

4. Press Tab.

5. Type *0.75* in the Bottom Margins field.

6. Press Tab.

7. Type *1.25* in the Inside Margins field.

8. Press Tab.

9. Type *0.75* in the Outside Margins field.

Notice that the Width Of Page indicator changes as you type the Inside and Outside Margins settings. When you have finished, the reading returns to 6.5 in. Although you have changed the margins, you have maintained the original width of the page. Essentially, you have moved the text over to allow room for binding the pages.

10. Click OK.

Adding the Title Page

The booklet requires a title page to identify its subject, author, and so on. At this point, the Font, Size, and Style menus are introduced to show you how you can use them to change the appearance of text.

Creating the Title Page

The title page is the first page in your document. Title pages usually do not have page numbers, headers, or footers. To indicate to MacWrite II that you want the first page of the document to be a title page, follow these steps:

1. Select Page from the Format menu.

2. Click the small box next to the Title Page option (see fig. 7.3). An X appears to indicate that the option has been chosen.

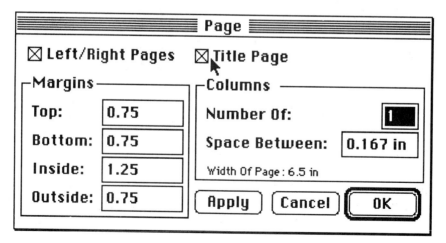

Fig. 7.3. Choosing the Title Page option.

3. Click OK to confirm your choice and close the Page dialog box.

You are returned to the document, and you are now looking at the title page of your document. The title page is going to consist of five centered lines. To enter the title page, follow these steps:

1. Click the center text alignment icon.

2. Press Return 20 times.

3. Type the company name *Graphicks* and press Return twice.

4. Type the phrase *Employee Handbook* and press Return twice.

5. Select Preferences from the Edit menu.

6. Click the June 25, 1989 Date Format option (see fig. 7.4).

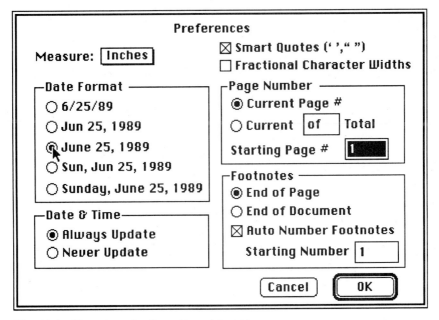

Fig. 7.4. Choosing the Date Format option.

7. Click OK.

8. Select Insert Date from the Edit menu (or press Shift-Command-A).

You have now entered the text for the title page.

Selecting the Text Style

Although you have entered the text for the title page, the type is rather plain. Usually, you want a title page to show some style—that is, to be catchy and appealing. The Font, Size, and Style menus can be helpful for achieving this goal.

In this example, you may see some fonts that do not appear in your Font menu because of the configuration of your System file. You can find instructions for adding or removing fonts in your Macintosh manuals in the section where the Font/DA Mover is discussed.

If a font used in this example does not appear in your Font menu, substitute another choice. To help you choose, the fonts are displayed in the menu as they will appear in your text.

To increase the size of the company name, follow these steps:

1. Place the mouse pointer (which turns into the I-beam as you move into the text area) on the word *Graphicks*.

2. Double-click to select and highlight the word.

3. Select 24 pt from the Size menu (see fig. 7.5).

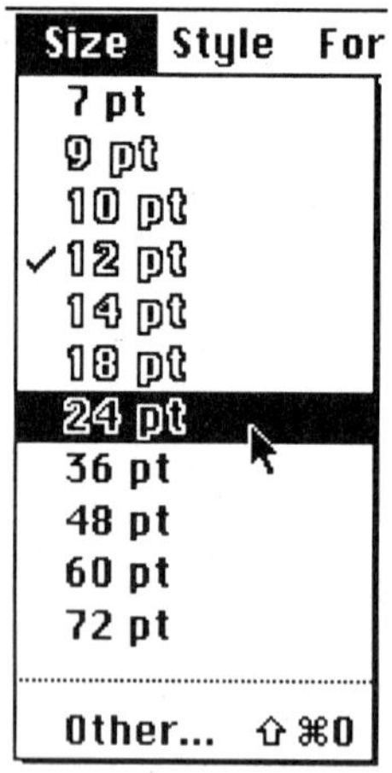

Fig. 7.5. The Size menu.

The company name immediately becomes larger. The name is still surrounded by the dark highlighting, so you know that it is still selected. To emphasize the name still more, boldface the word by following these steps:

1. Select Bold from the Style menu, or press Command-B (see fig. 7.6).

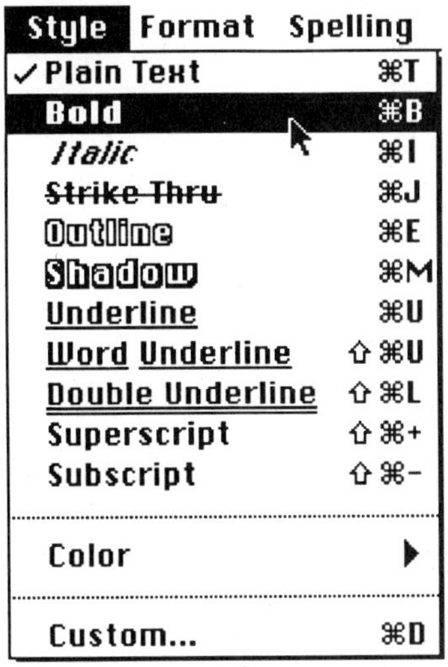

Style	Format	Spelling
✓ Plain Text		⌘T
Bold		⌘B
Italic		⌘I
~~Strike Thru~~		⌘J
Outline		⌘E
Shadow		⌘M
Underline		⌘U
Word Underline		⇧⌘U
Double Underline		⇧⌘L
Superscript		⇧⌘+
Subscript		⇧⌘−
Color		▶
Custom...		⌘D

Fig. 7.6. The Style menu.

2. Click anywhere in the document to remove the highlighting from the word.

You now see that the company name has been boldfaced to make the letters darker than normal.

To continue enhancing the appearance of the cover page, you can alter the style of the second line, *Employee Handbook*. Follow these steps:

1. Select the words *Employee Handbook* by triple-clicking *Employee*.

2. Select 14 pt from the Size menu.

3. Select Italic from the Style menu (or press Command-I).

4. Select Underline from the Style menu (or press Command-U).

5. Click anywhere in the text area to remove the highlighting from the line *Employee Handbook*.

Your title page should look like figure 7.7. Don't be concerned with slight variations. The Helvetica font was used in the example, but you may have used another.

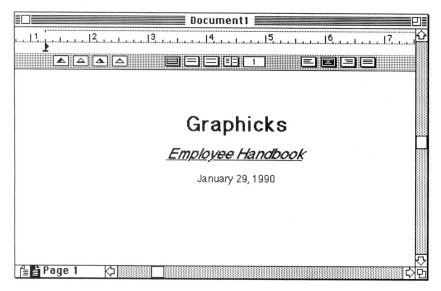

Fig. 7.7. *The finished title page.*

Adding Headers and Footers

Headers and footers are the text you see at the tops and bottoms, respectively, of pages throughout a document. Headers and footers are used for book names, chapter titles, page numbers, and similar repeated information.

Because this document consists of left and right pages, you can define separate headers and footers for those pages. That is, you may have one set of headers and footers for left pages and another set for right pages.

Adding a Header to the Left Page

Before you add a header or footer, the cursor must be on the first page of your document after the title page. Therefore, do the following:

1. Click the mouse pointer just after the last line of the title page, that is, after the year.

2. Press Return until the next page appears in the window, and the cursor moves to that page.

Notice that the small page icon in the bottom left of the screen has changed. The left side of this icon is now darkened. This shading means that you are now on a left page rather than a right page.

This change also is the reason the margins shifted. The margin settings for left and right pages are not the same despite the fact that they produce the same text width.

Now, to add a header, do the following:

1. Select Insert Header from the Format menu, but this time, do not release the mouse button.

   As you make this selection, you notice that another menu appears to the right of the current menu (see fig. 7.8). In this menu, two selections are available: All and Left.

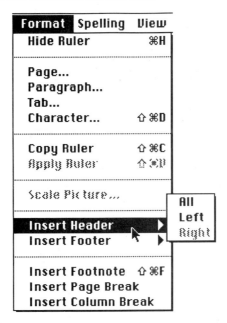

Fig. 7.8. *The second header menu.*

2. Holding the mouse button down, move the mouse to the right until Left is selected.

3. Release the mouse button.

The header box appears on the page with the cursor placed in the box (see fig. 7.9).

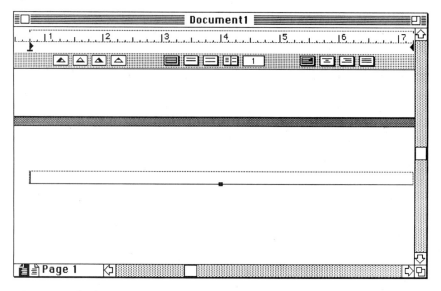

Fig. 7.9. *The header in place on the page.*

Adding the Page Number

Now you are ready to place the page number in the header. Because this page is a left page, you should place the page number at the left so that it will be clearly visible. Follow these steps:

1. Select Paragraph from the Format menu.

2. Change the Line Spacing measure from lines to points by selecting Points from the Unit of Measure menu (see fig. 7.10).

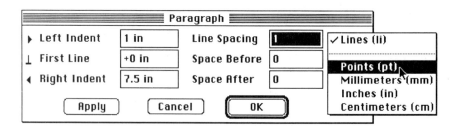

Fig. 7.10. *Changing the line spacing measure.*

3. Enter *4* in the Line Spacing field.

4. Click OK.

   The reason for the line spacing change becomes apparent later in the example.

5. Select the Helvetica font from the Font menu (see fig. 7.11).

Fig. 7.11. The Font menu.

6. Select 24 pt from the Size menu.

7. Select Bold from the Style menu (or press Command-B).

8. Select Insert Page # from the Edit menu (or press Command-Shift-P).

The page number is inserted by the program in a large boldface font.

Adding the Header Text

You are now ready to place the company name in the header. You want to center the name in the header. Follow these steps:

1. Place a Center tab at the 4-inch position by dragging the Center tab icon onto the ruler.

2. Press Tab.

3. Select 18 pt from the Size menu.

4. Select Plain Text from the Style menu.

5. Type the name *Graphicks*.

The header is now almost complete. All that remains is to add a rule to set off the header from the main text. Follow these steps:

1. Press Return.

2. While holding down the Shift key, press and hold the underscore key (usually to the immediate right of the 0 key on the main keyboard).

You want the rule to go completely across the header but not into the next line. If some of the rule ends up on the next line, however, simply backspace until the rule disappears from the second line. After you have drawn the rule, click below the header in the text area to eliminate the dashed line around the header so that you can see your work. The header should appear as in figure 7.12.

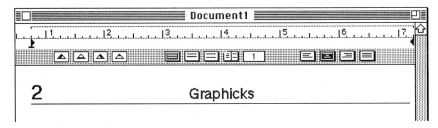

Fig. 7.12. *The completed left-page header.*

As you can see, the separating line in the header is close to the header text because the line spacing is set at only four points. Using a standard line spacing of one line would leave a great deal more space between the text and the separating line. The Underline command on the Style menu does not work in this case because the blank spaces of the header would not be underlined.

The left-page header is complete. When you move to a right page, you can create a right-page header in the same manner.

Adding a Footer

Because company handbooks are revised periodically, a good item for the footer is the date of the handbook. In this case, instead of having a left or right footer, the footer will be the same on all pages.

To add the footer, do the following:

1. Select Insert Footer from the Format menu, holding the mouse down so that the submenu for selecting the footer position appears.

2. Select the All option.

3. Release the mouse button.

Now, add the text to the footer:

1. Select the center text alignment.

2. Select 9 pt from the Size menu.

3. Type *Date of last revision:* followed by a space.

4. Select Insert Date from the Edit menu.

The footer is complete and should appear as in figure 7.13.

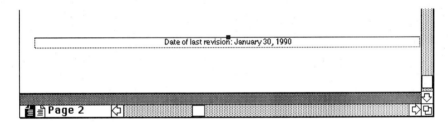

Fig. 7.13. *The completed footer.*

Now is a good time to save the document to disk, if you have not already, by selecting Save from the File menu. When the Save dialog box appears, type the name *Handbook* for the document and click OK (see fig. 7.14).

Typing the Booklet Text

You now are ready to create the main body of the document. You learn more about the text style features of the MacWrite II program as you work through this example.

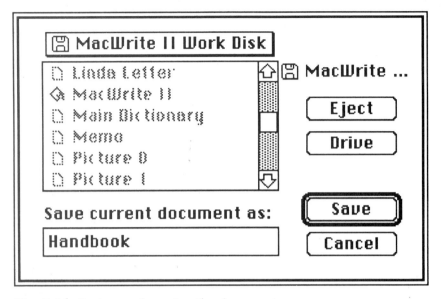

Fig. 7.14. *Saving and naming the document.*

Selecting the Text Alignment and Paragraph Settings

Because much of the text you have worked with up to this point has been centered, the text alignment setting may be set to centered text. For the main body text, you need a different alignment.

You have the choice of flush-left alignment or justified. In this example, you use justified text to give the document a professional, blocked look. To select the alignment, click the justified text icon in the ruler.

After you have set the text alignment, consider the width of the document's paragraphs. Instead of having them reach from one end of the header to the next, indent them slightly. At the same time, use the Space After option to separate paragraphs from each other.

To select these options, follow these steps:

1. Place the cursor after the header, and press Return to add a blank line between the header and the first paragraph.

2. Select Paragraph from the Format menu.

3. Enter *1* in the Left Indent field.

4. Press Tab twice to skip the First Line indent field.

5. Enter 7 in the Right Indent field.

6. Press Tab three times to reach the Space After field.

7. Select the Lines unit of measure.

8. Enter *1* in the Space After field.

9. Click OK to confirm your choices.

You have now set the paragraphs of your document to be justified (that is, have a smooth right edge), indented by one-quarter inch from either side of the header, and separated by one line of space.

Selecting a Font and Font Style

As you become more experienced in using MacWrite II, selecting a font can be a difficult decision because the Macintosh provides a tremendous variety of fonts. Only a certain number of fonts actually come with the machine, however. In this example, you need to use only the fonts provided by Apple on the disks that came with your machine. For information on installing or changing fonts, check the manuals that accompanied your Macintosh.

To set the font and font style for the first line of the document, do the following:

1. Select the New York font from the Font menu.

2. Select 12 pt from the Size menu.

3. Select Plain Text from the Style menu (or press Command-T).

Now type the text shown in figure 7.15. Remember to press Return only once after each paragraph—the program adds the extra line for you.

As you type, you see that the font is different from the one used in the header. New York is a good font to use for professional-looking documents.

Adding a Quotation and a Footnote

The handbook includes a statement by the founder, which is to be set off from the rest of the text with different indent settings. You also will create a footnote referencing the source of the quotation.

First, however, type the text shown in figure 7.16, using the same format as before. This text introduces the quotation.

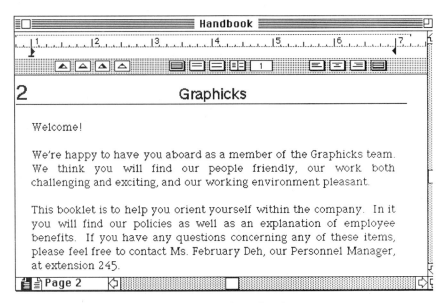

Fig. 7.15. *The welcoming text of the handbook.*

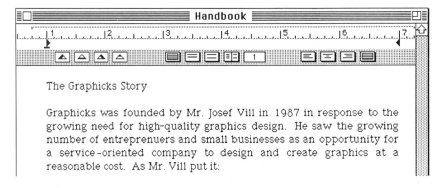

Fig. 7.16. *More handbook text.*

The quotation is to be set off from the rest of the handbook text by indenting it one-half inch on either side:

1. Place the mouse pointer on the left indent marker.

2. Press and hold the mouse button.

3. Drag the left indent marker to the 1.5-inch mark on the ruler.

4. Release the mouse button.

Use the same steps to move the right indent marker. The location for the right indent marker is the 6.5-inch mark on the ruler.

You are now ready to type the text of the quotation (see fig. 7.17). Do not press Return after typing this paragraph.

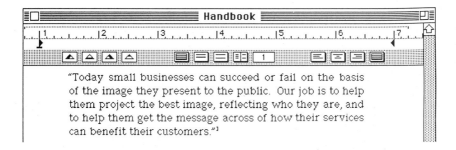

Fig. 7.17. *The founder's quotation.*

You now add a footnote to identify the source of the quotation. To add the footnote, follow these steps:

1. Select Insert Footnote from the Format menu (or press Command-Shift-F).

   The cursor is moved to the bottom of the page to the footnote location (changing this location is covered in Chapter 9).

2. Type the footnote text, *From the meeting of the board, January 13, 1988* (see fig. 7.18).

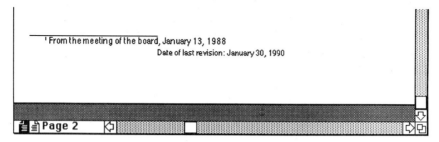

Fig. 7.18. *The footnote.*

3. Press Command-Return to move the cursor back to the main body of text.

You see a small superscript number where the footnote has been inserted. This number may be hard to read on-screen but should print clearly on your printer.

Adding the Right-Page Header

Before you can add the right-page header, you must complete the current page and move to a right-hand page. Before you can type the text, however, you must reset the formatting from the quotation settings.

Follow these steps to reset the formatting:

1. Click once in the paragraph preceding the quotation (the paragraph that begins "Graphicks was founded by . . . .")

2. Select Copy Ruler from the Format menu (or press Command-Shift-C).

3. Press Ctrl-D (or the End key) to move the cursor back to the end of the document.

   If you do not have an extended keyboard, you need to use the mouse to position the cursor by clicking at the end of the document.

4. Select Paste Ruler from the Format menu (or press Command-Shift-V).

This command copies the formatting of the first paragraph of the document to the paragraph that will follow the quotation. In this way, a few simple steps replace several steps.

Type the text shown in figure 7.19. When you reach page 3, you will be on a right-hand page. You can verify this position by looking at the page icons in the lower left corner of the document window.

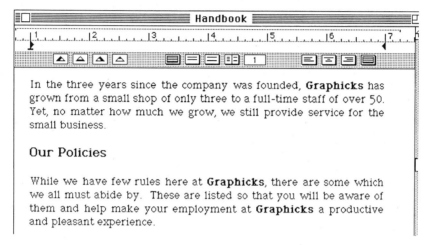

Fig. 7.19. *The remaining text for page 2.*

Creating the Header

Adding a header to a right-hand page is a process similar to adding a header to a left page. The only real difference you see in this example is that the page number is placed on the right side of the page so that the number is toward the outside of the booklet.

To add the right-page header, do the following:

1. Select Insert Header from the Format menu, holding down the mouse button until the header position submenu appears.

2. Move the mouse to the right into the second menu and select the Right option.

3. Release the mouse button.

The header appears on the page.

Adding the Header Text

The process of adding the header text is almost the same for the right-hand page as for the left; however, the header text must be positioned one-half inch to the right to accommodate the shifted margins of the right page.

Follow these steps:

1. Select Paragraph from the Format menu.

2. Change the Line Spacing measure from lines to points.

3. Enter *4* in the Line Spacing field.

4. Click OK.

    These steps place the underlining close to the header text.

5. Drag a Center tab icon onto the ruler and place the icon at the 4.5-inch position.

6. Press Tab.

7. Select Helvetica font from the Font menu.

8. Select 18 pt from the Size menu.

9. Select Plain Text from the Style menu (or press Command-T).

10. Type the phrase *Employee Handbook*.

Adding the Page Number

The page number must be to the right of the page in order to be on the outside. To add the number, follow these steps:

1. Drag a Right tab icon onto the ruler and place it at the 7.75-inch position.

    The right indent marker and Right tab marker are superimposed on each other.

2. Press Tab.

3. Select 24 pt from the Size menu.

4. Select Bold from the Style menu (or press Command-B).

5. Select Insert Page # from the Edit menu (or press Command-Shift-P).

The page number is inserted by the program in a large, boldfaced font.

Finally, as with the left-page header, the right-page header is to be set off using an underscore that runs the length of the header.

Follow these steps:

1. Press Return.

2. Select 18 pt from the Size menu.

3. Hold down the Shift key and press the underscore key (the hyphen key).

4. Hold both keys down until the underscore stretches across the entire header; then release the keys.

   If you accidentally cross into the next line, simply backspace until the underscores on the second line are eliminated.

5. Press Command-Return to move the cursor back into the main text area.

The completed header should appear as in figure 7.20

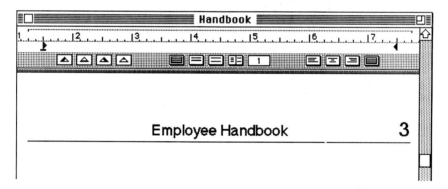

Fig. 7.20. *The completed right-page header.*

Using Styles for Emphasis

The Style menu contains many features you can use to enhance your text. Boldface can bring out a word; underlining or italic can emphasize the importance of a word or phrase. You use examples of each of these features in the following sections.

Using Boldface

Boldface emphasizes a word by making it darker. As you type this part of the sample document, you use boldface to emphasize the section headings.

Consider the text in figure 7.21. In this figure, you can see examples of boldface in the section headings: **Tardiness** and **Absenteeism**.

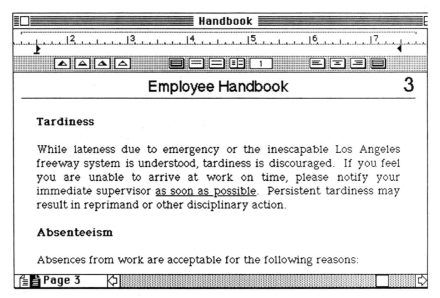

Fig. 7.21. Examples of boldface.

To boldface *Tardiness*, do the following:

1. Select Bold from the Style menu.

2. Type the word.

3. Select Plain Text from the Style menu to turn off the Bold style.

Now type the remaining text of figure 7.21 up to the point at which you encounter the underlined phrase "as soon as possible".

Using Underlining

After typing the phrase "your immediate supervisor", you are ready to type the underlined phrase in the paragraph. To underline the phrase, do the following:

1. If you have not already done so, space after the word *supervisor*.

2. Select Underline from the Style menu.

3. Type the phrase, but do not type the period.

4. Select Plain Text from the Style menu to turn off underlining.

5. Type the period.

6. Type the remainder of the paragraph shown in figure 7.21.

Using Italic

Figure 7.22 shows more of the text of the Employee Handbook. In the paragraph that discusses illness, you see that the word *may* is italicized for emphasis.

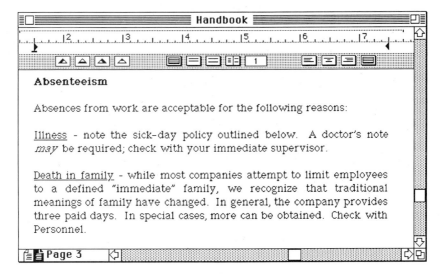

Fig. 7.22. *An example of italic.*

To make this word italic, follow these steps:

1. Select Italic from the Style menu.

2. Type the word.

3. Select Plain Text from the Style menu.

Although italic words may not be clear on-screen, when they are printed, the quality is much improved, especially with laser printers.

Continue with the example by typing the remainder of the text in figure 7.22. Obviously, this example could go on for many pages, but then so would this chapter. Instead, consider how you can change the style of words you have already typed.

Editing Styles

The process of editing styles consists of two major steps:

1. Select the text.

2. Select the style (or styles).

Consider the text from page 2 shown in figure 7.23. After typing this text, you have decided to use different styles to emphasize different parts.

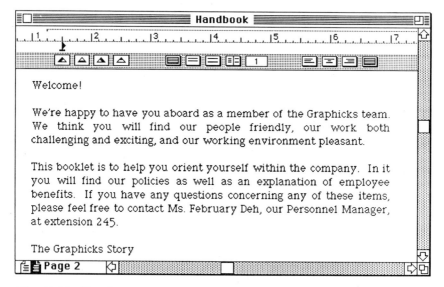

Fig. 7.23. Text from page 2.

First, the word *Welcome!* could be enlarged and boldfaced similar to the headings of the policy section of the handbook. To enlarge and boldface *Welcome!* do the following:

1. Place the mouse pointer on *Welcome*.

2. Triple-click (press the mouse button three times quickly) to select the entire line, including the exclamation mark.

3. Select 14 pt from the Size menu.

4. Select Bold from the Style menu (or press Command-B).

5. Click anywhere in the document to remove the highlighting from the word *Welcome*.

Welcome! has now been enlarged to the next font size and boldfaced for greater emphasis. Boldfacing a word without changing the font size is a similar process. For example, to boldface the company name in the first paragraph, follow these steps:

1. Place the mouse pointer on the word *Graphicks*.

2. Double-click (press the mouse button twice quickly).

3. Select Bold from the Style menu (or press Command-B).

Graphicks is then boldfaced. Underlining a word is just as easy. For example, you can underline the word *any* in the phrase "If you have any questions..." (in the second paragraph) with the following steps:

1. Place the mouse pointer on *any*.

2. Double-click.

3. Select Underline from the Style menu (or press Command-U).

In figure 7.24, the name of the personnel manager has been boldfaced.

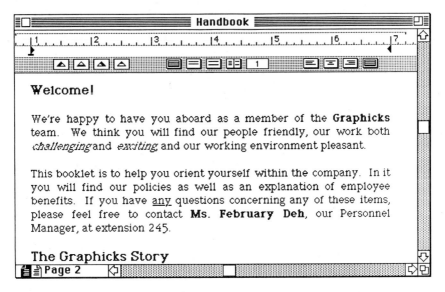

Fig. 7.24. The text with new styles applied.

To boldface the personnel manager's name, which consists of three words, you cannot double-click or triple-click to select the three words. Instead you must use the following steps:

1. Place the mouse pointer so that it immediately precedes *Ms.*

2. Press and hold the mouse button.

3. Move the mouse pointer across the text, highlighting it.

4. Release the mouse button when the highlighting includes the name *Deb*.

5. Select Bold from the Style menu (or press Command-B).

By using the various selection techniques (discussed in Chapter 3), you can apply any style to any amount of text.

Viewing the Booklet

Before printing the booklet, you may want to view its overall appearance. To do so, use the View menu, following these steps:

1. Select Reduced Size from the View menu.

2. Select Side By Side from the View menu.

Unless you have a large-screen monitor, you have to scroll the document up or down to view it completely. In any case, you should see a display similar to figure 7.25.

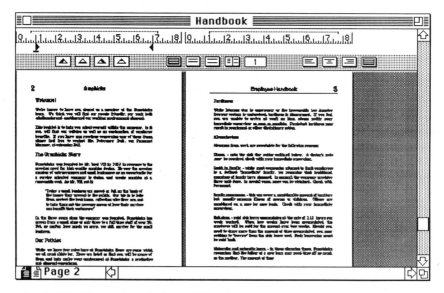

Fig. 7.25. *The reduced view of the document.*

Remember that the reduced view of a document is designed only to enable you to look over the document before printing. Because of the limits to the Macintosh computer's screen, the characters of the words do not appear as clear and crisp as at the normal size. However, you still can get a good feel for the appearance of your document.

To restore the normal view of the document, select Actual Size from the View menu.

Saving and Printing the Document

Although you have already saved and named the document, select Save again to save to disk the changes you have made since the last Save command.

To print the handbook document, do the following:

1. Select Print from the File menu (or press Command-P).

2. Click OK in the dialog box that appears.

The program then prints the document. When the printing has finished, leave MacWrite II by selecting Quit from the File menu.

Designing the Page Layout

This chapter explores the basics of laying out the document pages. The topics include selecting the paper size and orientation, reducing and enlarging your document, and creating and working with left and right pages.

Setting Page Size

Although some information about selecting paper type and page sizes has been covered in an earlier chapter, the relationship between a page size setting and the document's page settings is yet to be discussed. Choosing a paper size, enlarging or reducing a document, and setting a page orientation affect the page margins and document ruler.

Selecting Paper Size

Selecting paper size is a difficult subject to cover because of the wide variety of printers available for the Macintosh computer. This book cannot cover every possible printer combination. Consequently, the discussion is limited to the four major Apple printers: the LaserWriter (I, Plus, and II series); the LaserWriter IISC; the Imagewriter (I and II); and the ImageWriter LQ.

Because of the standardization among printers for the Macintosh, even if your printer is not made by Apple, most of the information in this chapter still is applicable to your printer. Read your printer manual to determine the differences between Apple printers and your printer.

Although different printers have different paper sizes from which to choose, the basic procedure for selecting a paper size is the same for all printers. To choose a paper size, do the following:

1. Select Page Setup from the File menu. A dialog box specific to your printer appears (see fig. 8.1).

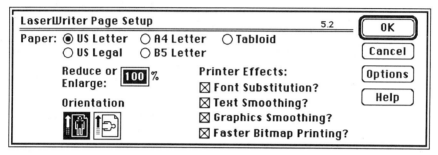

Fig. 8.1. The LaserWriter Page Setup dialog box.

2. Click the button next to the paper size of your choice.

3. Click the OK button to confirm your choice and return to the document.

All Page Setup dialog boxes have a section for selecting paper sizes similar to that shown in figure 8.1. Although you can select paper size at any time, you should select a paper size before creating a document. If you change paper size after beginning a document, the program reformats the document to fit the new paper size, and you may need to edit the document.

Paper Size on the LaserWriter

The LaserWriter series of printers can use five different sizes of paper. As shown in figure 8.1, the different sizes are

- *US Letter.* Standard 8.5-by-11-inch paper

- *US Legal.* 8.5-by-14-inch paper

- *A4 Letter.* The European equivalent of US Letter, 8.25-by-11.66-inch paper

- *B5 Letter.* The international standard letter size, approximately 7-by-10-inch paper (6.93-by-9.83)

- *Tabloid.* The largest size, 11-by-17-inch paper. This option was added with the Macintosh System 6.0.2.

Because MacWrite II tries to show the document as it will appear when printed, the paper size you choose in the Page Setup dialog box affects the ruler and the locations of page breaks. Figure 8.2 shows a reduced view of a document using letter-size paper.

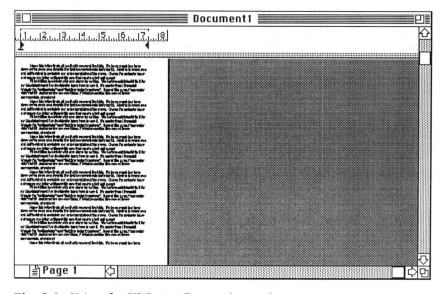

Fig. 8.2. *Using the US Letter Paper size option.*

The ruler across the top of the page displays 0 through 8.5 inches, the width of letter-size paper. To see the change in the ruler according to paper size, consider figure 8.3. This figure shows a smaller view of a document using the Tabloid Paper size option. Note that the ruler is now 11 inches wide.

Paper Size on the LaserWriter IISC

The paper sizes for the LaserWriter IISC are similar to paper sizes of other LaserWriters, except that the No. 10 Envelope size has been added, and the Tabloid size has been dropped (see fig. 8.4).

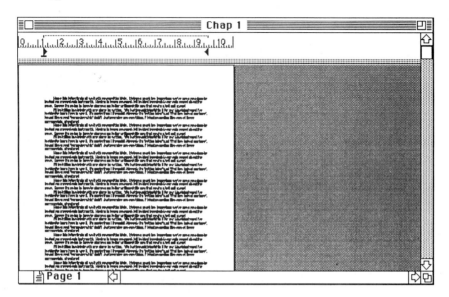

Fig. 8.3. *Using the Tabloid Paper size option.*

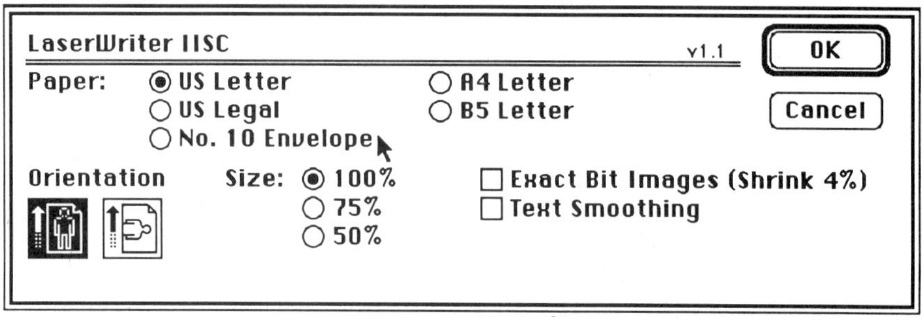

Fig. 8.4. *Paper sizes on the LaserWriter IISC.*

The No. 10 Envelope size enables you to print on the standard 9.5-by-4.25-inch envelope. When you use this paper size, the screen display of the envelope is turned sideways when you first select the option (see fig. 8.5). Obviously, this orientation is not the way you address an envelope. You have to use the landscape orientation (covered later this section) to print the document in the correct direction.

Paper Size on the ImageWriter

The ImageWriter I and II printers have five different paper sizes available through the Page Setup dialog box (see fig. 8.6).

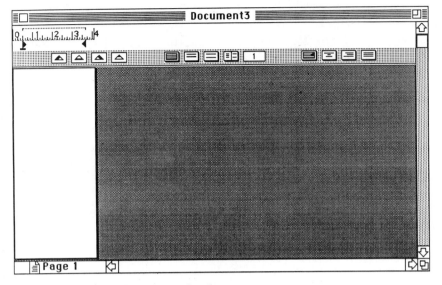

Fig. 8.5. *The envelope turned sideways.*

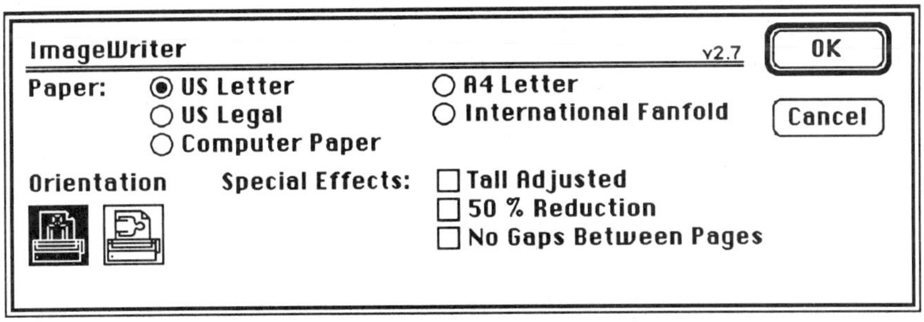

Fig. 8.6. *The ImageWriter Page Setup dialog box.*

Three options are the same as the options for the LaserWriter series. US Letter, US Legal, and A4 Letter are used for single sheets of paper and tractor-fed fanfold paper. For the sizes of these paper types, see the section, "Paper Size on the LaserWriter."

The other two options are used for tractor-fed fanfold paper:

- *Computer Paper.* Used for the 14-by-11-inch continuous sheets of paper

- *International Fanfold.* Used for 8.25-by-12-inch continuous sheets of paper

Paper Size on the ImageWriter LQ

The newest addition to the ImageWriter series has six paper options, five of which are shared with previous ImageWriters: US Letter, US Legal, Computer Paper, A4 Letter, and International Fanfold. The Envelope (#10) size has been added (see fig. 8.7).

```
┌─────────────────────────────────────────────────────────┐
│ ImageWriter LQ                          v2.0    ┌──────┐  │
│                                                 │  OK  │  │
│ Paper:    ◉ US Letter      ○ A4 Letter          └──────┘  │
│           ○ US Legal       ○ International Fanfold        │
│           ○ Computer Paper ○ Envelope (#10)     ┌────────┐│
│                                                 │ Cancel ││
│ Orientation   Special Effects: □ No Gaps Between Pages    │
│  ▣ ▣                             ◉ Full Size             │
│                         Reductions: ○ 33 % Reduction      │
│                                     ○ 66 % Reduction      │
└─────────────────────────────────────────────────────────┘
```

Fig. 8.7. *The ImageWriter LQ Page Setup dialog box.*

As in the other Page Setup dialog boxes, you select a paper size by clicking the small button next to the paper size and then clicking the OK button. The document shown in the window adjusts to the new paper size. The Envelope (#10) option is shown in figure 8.8. To show the entire document, the document has been reduced in size. Note that the program shows the envelope oriented as it is inserted into the printer.

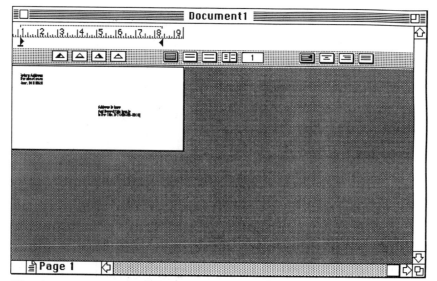

Fig. 8.8. *An envelope document for the ImageWriter LQ.*

Reducing and Enlarging Documents

If you have used a copy machine with reducing and enlarging capabilities, you are familiar with the basic concepts of changing document sizes with printer options. The enlargement and reduction features offered by many printers increase or decrease, respectively, the size of the printed document as do many copy machines.

You may want to reduce the size of a document in order to include more information on each page. For example, you can reduce a phone-number list so that you can put it in one of the small, loose-leaf schedulers carried by many business people today. In another instance, you may want to increase the size of the text and graphics in a flier for emphasis.

An important principle is that the reduction and enlargement options change the size of the text and graphics during printing. Text and graphics do not appear larger in the document window.

Because the size of the text and graphics is changed, the layout of your page is changed. When you use the reduction option, the text and graphics of the document decrease in size. This change leaves more space on the paper page. Enlarging the text and graphics reduces the amount of space with which you have to work.

MacWrite II shows you these changes by adjusting the size of the page in the document window rather than by changing the size of the text and graphics of the document. This method may seem odd at first but consider an example. Figure 8.9 shows a document of the standard 8.5-by-11-inch US Letter size. The document is shown reduced in size by the Reduced Size command in the View menu so that you can see the document better. The Reduced Size/Actual Size command of the View menu changes the size of the document only in the window. The command has *no* effect on the printed document.

Suppose that you decide to reduce this document to one-half its normal size. Also suppose that you are using a LaserWriter printer. Follow these steps:

1. Select Page Setup from the File menu.

2. Type *50* in the Reduce or Enlarge field.

3. Click the OK button.

The document now appears as in figure 8.10.

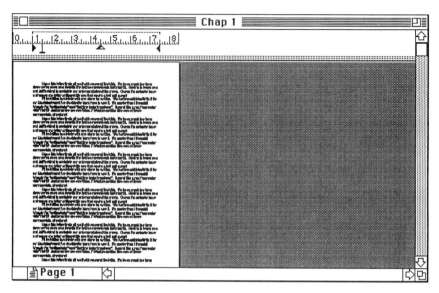

Fig. 8.9. *A sample US Letter size document.*

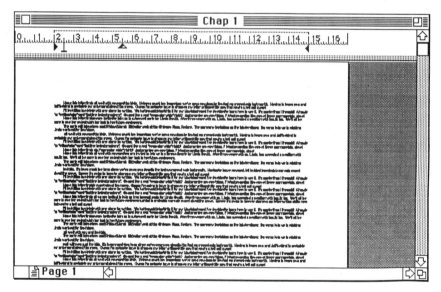

Fig. 8.10. *The document reduced by 50 percent.*

Oddly enough, the document appears to have *increased* in size rather than decreased. Steps 1 through 3 instructed the *printer* to reduce the document size by 50 percent (one-half). MacWrite II responds by showing a document that is twice as big because the text and graphics in the document will be reduced to one-half their normal size during the *printing* process. As a result, you can print twice as much on a single sheet of paper; therefore, the program shows that you have twice as much room with which to work.

If your goal is to print a document that is literally one-half the size of a regular US Letter size document, you must adjust the page margins and other page layout settings. To adjust the document of figure 8.10 to print at one-half size, you perform the following steps:

1. Select Page from the Format menu.

2. Enter *1* in the Top Margins field.

3. Enter *12* in the Bottom Margins field.

4. Enter *1* in the Left Margins field.

5. Enter *9.5* in the Right Margins field.

6. Click the OK button.

Figure 8.11 shows the resulting page margins.

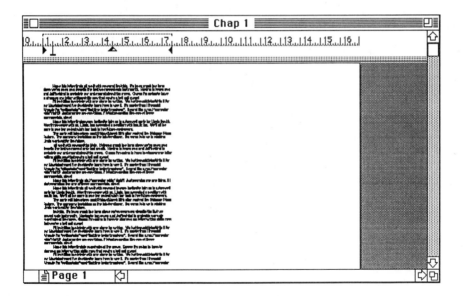

Fig. 8.11. *The reduced document with margins adjusted to make the page smaller.*

Essentially, you now have an 8.5-inch-wide document on a 17-inch-wide page. The margins, as you see in the figure, leave 1 inch of space on either side of the text and graphic area. The printed document will be a 4.75-inch-wide document (with 0.5-inch margins). This change occurs because the document in the document window is reduced by the printer to one-half size.

A similar change occurs when you use the enlargement option. Figure 8.12 shows the sample document with a 400 percent enlargement (specified by entering *400* in the Reduce or Enlarge field of the Page Setup dialog box). This figure is shown at actual size in the window rather than reduced size. Because the text has been increased to four times its normal size, the amount of space you have to work with on the page has been decreased.

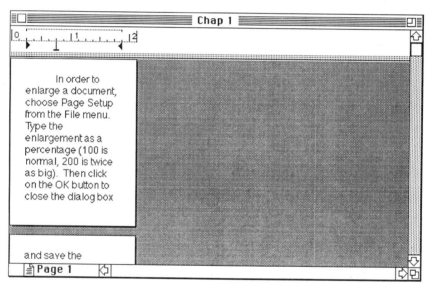

Fig. 8.12. *A document with 400 percent enlargement.*

Different printers have different enlargement and reduction settings. The LaserWriters (except the SC) produce a range from a 25 percent reduction to a 400 percent enlargement. You must use whole numbers when you enter these percentages.

The LaserWriter IISC has three choices. You can have 100 percent (normal size), 75 percent (three-quarters size), or 50 percent (half size). You cannot enlarge a document with the LaserWriter SC.

The ImageWriter I and II have only 100 percent and 50 percent reduction. The ImageWriter LQ has 100 percent, 33 percent reduction, and 66 percent reduction. A 33 percent reduction, for example, means that the document will shrink by one-third when printed. Consequently, the document size in the window is increased by one-third, from 8.5 inches to 12.75 inches. The ImageWriter LQ cannot enlarge documents.

To select a reduction option, follow these steps:

1. Choose Page Setup.

2. Click the reduction of your choice.

3. Click the OK button.

Setting Page Orientation

The section "Paper Size on the LaserWriter IISC" shows the envelope turned the wrong direction. The short sides are at the top and bottom rather than the left and right. You must change the orientation of the page to match the orientation of the envelope.

In portrait orientation (normal orientation), the document prints on the page with the short edges of the paper at the top and bottom. Landscape orientation is sideways, with the long edge of the paper at the top.

The icons used in the various Page Setup dialog boxes illustrate this point. Figure 8.13 shows the two versions of the icons used to select the orientation.

Fig. 8.13. The Orientation icons.

The procedure for choosing an orientation is the same for all the printer types:

1. Select Page Setup.

2. Click the Orientation icon.

3. Click the OK button.

As with selecting paper size, you should choose the page orientation before you begin creating the document. Although you can change the orientation at any point, if you have already entered text into a document when you make the orientation change, you may have to do major editing.

Using Page Guides

When you are first laying out your document, the Show Page Guides command in the View menu can be helpful. This command places a dotted box on the document to show you the margins (see fig. 8.14).

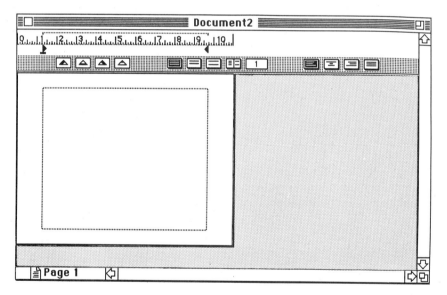

Fig. 8.14. *The dotted box forming the page guides.*

This command can help you determine the location of page margins after you have changed paper size, reduced or enlarged your document, or changed the orientation. Page margins are set in the Page dialog box (discussed in Chapter 2).

Seeing the page margins can help you decide paper size, orientation, and so on, because the guides indicate the limits of your text on the page. You can see the exact location and size of the text area of your document.

To turn on page guides, select Show Page Guides from the View menu or press Command-G. To turn off the page guides, select Hide Page Guides from the View menu or press Command-G again.

Setting Left and Right Pages

In the quick start in Chapter 7, you created a document with left and right pages. You must set inside and outside page margins instead of left and right page margins because a document created with left and right pages is meant to be bound. Consider the handbook in figure 8.15. The document is displayed using the Side By Side and Reduced Size commands in the View menu. The page guides have been turned on so that you can see the page margins.

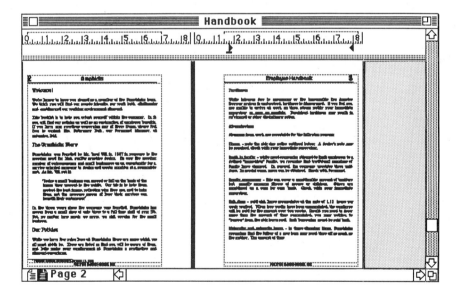

Fig. 8.15. *A document with left and right pages.*

As you can see in the figure, the text on the left page is shifted to the left, and the text on the right page is shifted to the right. The printed pages will have ample room to bind the pages to form a booklet.

When laying out pages that are to be bound into book form, you should consider the amount of the page that will be taken up by the binding so that you can determine the inside margin setting.

Creating Left and Right Pages

You create left and right pages with the Page dialog box by following these steps:

1. Select Page from the Format menu.

2. Click the box next to the Left/Right Pages option, placing an X in the box (see fig. 8.16).

3. Click the OK button to confirm the setting and close the dialog box.

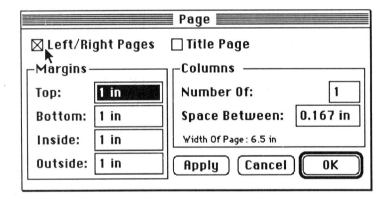

Fig. 8.16. *Selecting the Left/Right Pages option.*

The X in the box indicates that the document has left and right pages. To eliminate left and right pages, follow the same steps. This time, clicking the box next to the Left/Right Pages option removes the X.

Setting Page Margins for Left and Right Pages

After you have set a document to contain left and right pages, setting the page margins is different from the usual method (see Chapter 2). A document with left and right pages does not have left or right margins—the margins are inside and outside.

The inside margin is placed on the right side of left pages and the left side of right pages. Therefore, the inside margin determines the amount of space that is allowed for binding. The outside margin determines the distance from the text to the outside edge of the paper—left on left pages, right on right pages.

As you lay out the pages for a booklet like the one created in the Chapter 7 quick start, for example, suppose that you decide on a 0.75-inch margin on all sides of the text. The problem is that the binding takes up some of the paper. After checking, you find that binding uses 0.5 inch. Three of the page margin settings are simple enough: 0.75 inch for the top, bottom, and outside page margins. The inside margin, however, is not so simple. Add the inside margin you want (0.75 inch) and the binding (0.5 inch) to calculate the inside margin setting. In this case, the inside margin setting is 1.25 inches.

To enter these margin settings, perform the following steps:

1. Select Page from the Format menu.

2. Type *0.75* in the Top Margins field and press Tab.

3. Type *0.75* in the Bottom Margins field and press Tab.

4. Type *1.25* in the Inside Margins field and press Tab.

5. Type *0.75* in the Outside Margins field.

6. Click the OK button to confirm the settings and close the dialog box.

Note that the Width Of Page setting is 6.5 inches. The Width Of Page setting is the document width minus the Inside and Outside margin settings. Because this document is using the US Letter setting, the paper width is 8.5 inches. A paper width of 8.5 inches minus the Inside and Outside settings of 1.25 and 0.75 inches yields a text width of 6.5 inches.

To see the effect of the page margin settings, you perform the following steps:

1. Select Reduced Size from the View menu.

2. Select Show Page Guides from the View menu.

You then see the dotted box of the page guides showing you where the margins are (see fig. 8.17).

Fig. 8.17. The page guides showing the margin locations for a right-hand page.

In the figure, you see that the text area of the document is shifted toward the right. The first page is shifted because the first page of any document with left and right pages is a right page unless you select the Title Page option (covered in Chapter 9).

To restore the document to normal view, select Hide Page Guides from the View menu. Then select Actual Size from the View menu. Although you can edit a reduced-size document, the text is so small that editing is difficult. If you want, you can leave the page guides on when the document is at normal size so that you can see the edge of the text area as you work.

Working with Left and Right Pages

Now that you know how left and right pages are created, consider these points when working with them. First, you can determine whether the page you are working on is a left or right page. Second, you can use two-page displays so that you can work with two pages side by side.

Understanding the Left/Right Page Icons

With your document in actual size, you may have difficulty telling whether the current page is a left page or a right page. Fortunately, MacWrite II provides an indicator.

After you indicate that you want your document to consist of left and right pages, the page number indicator in the lower left corner adds a second page icon (see fig. 8.18). The two icons indicate whether the current page is a left page or a right page.

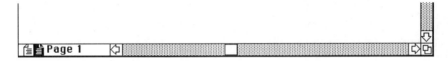

Fig. 8.18. *The left/right page indicator.*

In the figure, the current page (Page 1) is a right-hand page. You know this because the right page in the page icon is dark. The *current page* is the page where the cursor is. If you are simply scrolling through your document, the left/right page icons do not change even though the page number indicator changes.

Working with Pages Side by Side

If you are using a two-page display, you can work with two pages side by side—even if the document does not have left and right pages.

To work with two pages side by side, do the following:

1. Select the Side By Side command from the View menu.

2. Adjust the size of the document window to fit your display.

Odd pages are on the right while even pages are on the left, regardless of whether a document has left and right pages.

To return the display to one page at a time, select the Side By Side command in the View menu again.

Summing Up

This chapter is concerned with features of MacWrite II that relate to page layout. You should now understand some of the primary considerations for creating a document.

The selection of paper size and the effect of that selection on the working space of the document is explored in this chapter. You also see how enlarging, reducing, and changing the orientation of a page changes the pages in the document window. Because of these changes, the pages in your document window appear similar to the printed copy.

Left and right pages are covered in this chapter. You now know how to create a document with left and right pages, and set the inside and outside margins to accommodate document binding. The left/right page icons are discussed. You also see how to work on two side-by-side pages.

Now that you understand the basics of laying out a new document, you are ready to turn to Chapter 9's discussion of other document elements: title pages, headers and footers, dates and times, and page numbers.

Adding Other Document Elements

Up to this point, this book has dealt with only two document elements—the page and the paragraph. Although these two are the most important, other useful elements exist.

This chapter explores the other document elements available in MacWrite II. These elements, which you use to enhance documents, are title pages, headers and footers, footnotes, dates and times, and page numbers.

Creating Title Pages

If you have worked with reports or term papers, you already know that title pages contain elements like the title of a document, the author, date, and so on. In MacWrite II, however, these items do not distinguish a title page from a regular page. MacWrite II defines a title page as a page that is first in a document, does not have a header or footer, and has one column of text.

Adding a Title Page

The process of adding the title page to your document is simple. Follow these steps:

1. Select Page from the Format menu.

2. In the Page dialog box, click the box next to the Title Page option, causing the X to appear (see fig. 9.1).

3. Click the OK button to close the dialog box and return to your document.

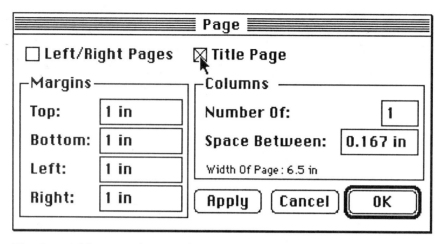

Fig. 9.1. *Adding a title page through the Page dialog box.*

An X in the box next to the Title Page option indicates that the first page in your document is a title page.

After you have added a title page to your document, you can format and create the text for the title page. While the cursor is in the title page, the Insert Header and Insert Footer commands are unavailable; and regardless of how many columns you have defined for your document, the title page has one column. Within these restrictions, you can format the title page any way you want.

Removing a Title Page

Removing a title page is also a simple operation. This operation, however, does not actually remove the page; instead, the restrictions that define a title page are removed. You are changing the first page of your document from a title page to simply another page. In other words, any text that was on the title page becomes text on page 1 of your document.

To remove a title page, follow these steps:

1. Select Page from the Format menu.

2. In the Page dialog box, click the box next to the Title Page option, causing the X to disappear.

3. Click the OK button to confirm your choice and return to your document.

If you remove a title page after adding text to your document, you may notice some interesting changes. The header and footer now appear on the first page of the document. The former title page conforms to the number of columns defined for the document. As with other formatting, you should plan ahead for title pages in order to avoid major editing.

Using Headers and Footers

Headers and footers are used in documents to carry information you want on each page of the document (except for the title page). *Headers* are text printed at the tops of pages. *Footers* are text printed at the bottoms of pages. In general, headers and footers are used for document titles, page numbers, and other information that is to be repeated on each page (see the Chapter 7 quick start).

In MacWrite II, a document can have text for one header and one footer. In documents that have left and right pages, however, you can have one header and footer for left pages and a different header and footer for right pages.

Headers and footers are considered document elements and are separate from the page and its paragraphs despite the fact that they reside on the page. You format headers and footers separately and spell check them separately.

Creating a Header

To add a single header to a document without left and right pages, follow these steps:

1. Select Insert Header from the Format menu.

   Selecting this command adds a header to the document and places the cursor in the header area. A dotted box guide—similar to the page guides of the View menu—shows the location and size of the header (see fig. 9.2).

2. Type and format the header text. You can use any formatting option the program offers. You can place tabs, change fonts, change styles, use a different line spacing, and so on.

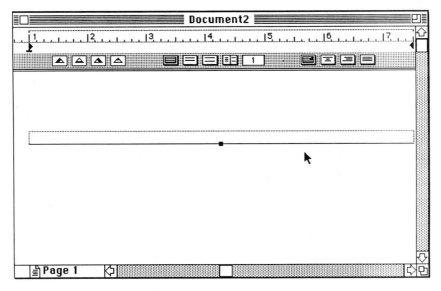

Fig. 9.2. *Adding a header to a document.*

In figure 9.3, the text of the header is centered over the page. The header will appear on every page except the title page (if the document has a title page).

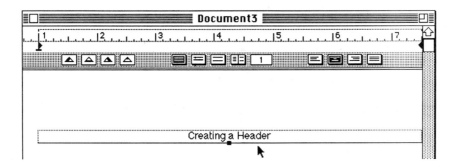

Fig. 9.3. *A sample header.*

After creating a header, you can return to the point where you left off in your main text by holding down the Command key and pressing the Return key (Enter on some keyboards).

Creating Headers on Left and Right Pages

With a document that has left and right pages, MacWrite II permits one header for left pages and a different header for right pages. You also can define one header to appear on all pages. Another alternative is to define a header for left pages only or right pages only, with no header on the facing pages.

You can add a header to left pages only if the cursor is on a left page when you create the header. Similarly, you can add a header to right pages only if the cursor is on a right page. The left/right page icons tell you whether the cursor is on a left or right page (see Chapter 8 for a discussion of these icons).

When you have left and right pages, the Insert Header menu selection changes. The command now has an arrow to its right. This arrow indicates that another menu is contained in the command (see fig. 9.4).

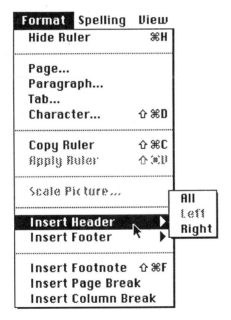

Fig. 9.4. *The second header menu.*

This second menu appears when you select the Insert Header command. When you hold down the mouse button and move the mouse to highlight the Insert Header command, the second menu appears.

This menu contains three options, only two of which are available at one time. The All option (always available) inserts a header that appears on all pages of the document. The other two options are available depending on whether the cursor is currently on a left or right page. When the cursor is on a left page, the Left option is available. When the cursor is on a right page, the Right option is available. Selecting the Left option adds a header to left-hand pages; selecting the Right option adds a header to the right-hand pages of the document.

Suppose that you want to add a header to only the right-hand pages of your document. Work through the following steps:

1. Select Insert Header from the format menu but *do not* release the mouse button.

2. Hold down the mouse button and move the mouse to the right until the Right option is highlighted.

3. Release the mouse button.

4. Type and format the header text.

The header you create will appear on only the right-hand pages of your document. Headers for all or left-hand pages are created in the same manner; simply choose the appropriate option from the Insert Header command.

Resizing Headers

The header is created one line in height, but you can adjust the height. Headers are not limited to their default size—they can be almost as large as the page. The actual limit is the size of the page minus two lines, one for the footer and one for the main body text. Of course, most headers are considerably smaller.

You can use one of two ways to change a header's size. The first method is simply to press Return and type another line of text. The header expands to accommodate the new text. The second method enables you to create space between the header and the main body text. Move the header's handle to change the size of the header without typing text.

In figure 9.5, the header text and the main body text are close together. To separate the header text from the main body text, increase the size of the header with the following steps:

1. Click anywhere in the header to make it active (an active header is surrounded by a dotted box).

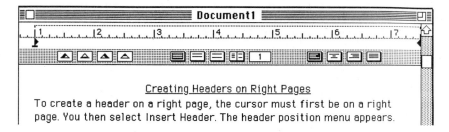

Fig. 9.5. *A sample header and main text.*

2. Place the mouse pointer on the small black square centered below the header—the header's handle.

3. Press and hold the mouse button.

4. Move the mouse, dragging the header outline to the desired position (see fig. 9.6).

5. Release the mouse button.

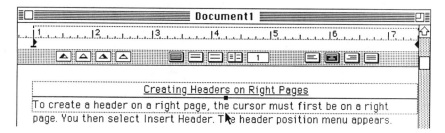

Fig. 9.6. *Resizing the header.*

The header increases in size. You can, at this point, return to your main body text by holding down the Command key and pressing the Return key. The resulting header, set off from the main body text, is shown in figure 9.7.

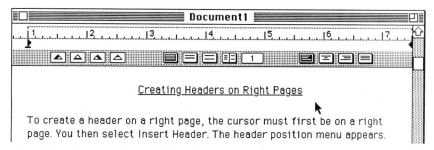

Fig. 9.7. *The header set off from the main text.*

A header that has been expanded by this procedure can be reduced in size by the same procedure. Drag the header outline up instead of down. You cannot shrink a header to a size smaller than its contents. If the header contains two lines of text, for example, you cannot shrink it to one line.

After resizing a header, you can restore it to its previous size by selecting the Undo Header Change command from the Edit menu. You must use this command immediately after the change, however. If the cursor leaves the header, the Undo command will not undo the header change—you must resize the header to restore it to its previous size.

Removing Headers

You may find that you do not want the header you have created, after all. MacWrite II provides a quick, easy way to remove a header.

After you add a header, the Insert Header command changes to the Remove Header command. In a document that does not have left and right pages, follow these steps to remove a header:

1. Select Remove Header from the Format menu.

2. In the warning dialog box that appears, click the OK button (see fig. 9.8).

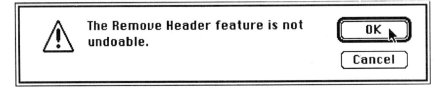

Fig. 9.8. Confirming a Remove Header command.

The header is removed from the document. You cannot use the Undo command to restore the header after you remove it. To restore the header, you have to recreate it.

The warning dialog box provides a Cancel button (again see fig. 9.8). If you change your mind about removing the header, click the Cancel button.

When you are dealing with a document that has left and right pages, the Remove Header command, like the Insert Header command, has a second menu attached. This menu operates exactly as the Insert Header command's secondary menu operates. That is, to remove a header, select Remove Header, but before releasing the mouse, select the Left, Right, or

All option. To remove a right-page header, the cursor must be on a right page. The same rule applies for left-page headers. The All option is available if you have both left and right headers.

Creating Footers

A footer is text you place at the bottoms of pages. As with headers, footers can contain a variety of information, including page numbers, dates, and times. Documents with left and right pages can have one footer for all pages or one for left pages and another for right pages.

Creating a footer is so similar to creating headers that creating footers is discussed only briefly here. Consider the footer shown in figure 9.9.

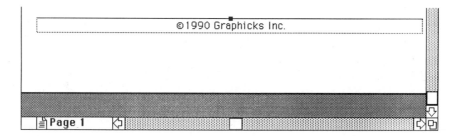

© 1990 Graphicks Inc.

Page 1

Fig. 9.9. A sample footer.

To create a footer, follow these steps:

1. Select Insert Footer from the Format menu.

2. Select any formatting. For the sample, click the center text alignment icon.

3. Type the text.

As with headers, you can use text alignment, tabs, fonts, and other formatting in a footer. (By the way, the copyright symbol shown in the figure is usually generated by holding down the Option key and pressing the letter G.)

For documents with left and right pages, the same rules that apply to headers apply to footers. That is, the cursor must be in a left page to create a left-page footer and in a right page to create a right-page footer. If you use the All option to place footers on all pages, the cursor can be on either page. To resize a footer, follow the same steps you follow to resize a header.

A footer can be as large as the page minus the size of the header and minus one line of main body text. If the page lacks a header, the footer can be as large as the size of the page minus two lines.

Removing Footers

To remove a footer from a document that does not have left and right pages, do the following:

1. Select Remove Footer from the Format menu.

2. In the dialog box that appears, click in the OK button (or press Return). Click Cancel if you change your mind.

After a footer is removed, it can be restored only by recreating it.

In documents that have left and right pages, the process of footer removal mirrors that of header removal. To remove a footer from a left page, the cursor must be on a left page; and to remove a right-page footer, the cursor must be on a right page. If you have footers on both left and right pages, the All option becomes available.

Editing Headers and Footers

In headers and footers, you can use all the MacWrite II editing and formatting features that are available for use in the main body of text. You can cut, copy, and paste text. You can check the spelling of a header or footer separately from the main text. You can select and edit text. You even can search for and replace text in headers and footers.

In order to do any formatting or editing (other than using the Find/Change command), you must make the header or footer active. An active header or footer is surrounded by the dotted box with the resizing handle. To make a header or footer active, click inside it.

After a header or footer is active, you can check its spelling by selecting the second command on the Spelling menu. This command changes according to the location of the cursor. For example, with the cursor in a left header, the spelling-checking command appears as in figure 9.10.

The only time you do not have to make a header or footer active is when you use the Find/Change command (covered in Chapter 5). This command searches headers and footers for the text you specify without your having to activate the header or footer.

Fig. 9.10. *The Check Left Header spelling-checking command.*

When searching a document, the Find/Change command follows a fixed order: main body text followed by headers, then footers, then footnotes. This order is circular. That is, after searching the document's footnotes for the search text, the program again searches the main body text and continues in the same order until the program locates the designated text or determines that the text is not in the document.

The cursor position determines where in the order list the program begins searching. If the cursor is in a header, the header is searched first. The program proceeds to search the footers and the footnotes before searching the main body text.

When you have finished editing a header or footer, you can use a single command to return to the last cursor position in your document's main body text. Hold down the Command key and press the Return key. The cursor immediately jumps to its last position within the main body.

Creating Footnotes

Footnotes are short notes at the bottom of a page or the end of a document. They provide additional information or references to information sources. Footnotes are most commonly used in reports for business or school.

In the quick start in Chapter 7, you saw how easy inserting a footnote is in MacWrite II. You should, however, know about other options involved in footnotes, including choosing the location of and numbering footnotes.

Setting the Footnote Location

Although footnote references occur throughout text, the footnotes themselves can be located at the end of each page or at the end of the document.

When footnotes are printed at the bottom of the page, only footnotes that are referenced on a page are printed at the bottom of that page. This method saves the reader from having to flip back and forth between the text and the footnotes. If your footnotes are long, however, you may want to print them at the end of the document.

The footnote location is controlled through the Preferences dialog box. As an example, if you want all footnotes to print at the end of the document, do the following steps:

1. Select Preferences from the Edit menu.

2. Click the circle (called a radio button) next to the End of Document option (see fig. 9.11).

3. Click the OK button or press the Return key.

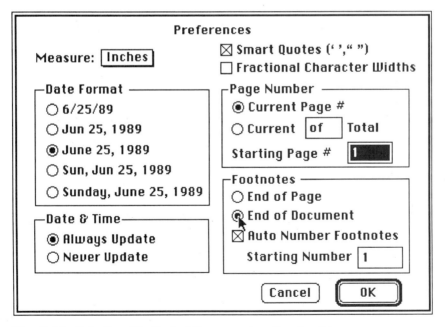

Fig. 9.11. *Selecting the End of Document option for footnotes.*

The dialog box closes, and you are returned to your document. You do not have to set this option before entering text, although you may. At any time, regardless of how many footnotes you have entered, you can choose either option. The program moves footnotes to their proper places.

Inserting Footnotes

You can insert a footnote as you type by working through the following steps. This technique inserts a footnote reference at the point where the cursor is located when you select the Insert Footnote command.

To insert a footnote,

1. Select Insert Footnote from the Format menu (or hold down the Shift and Command keys and press F).

   The program inserts the footnote number at the cursor location and immediately moves the cursor into the footnote area (see fig. 9.12).

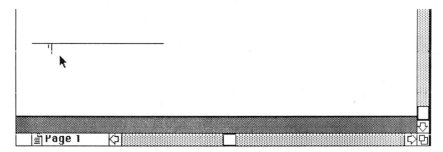

Fig. 9.12. *Preparing to type a footnote.*

2. Type the footnote.

3. Hold down the Command key and press the Return key to move the cursor back into the main body of text.

Figure 9.13 shows the footnote reference in the main body. The number may be hard to see because of its size, but it follows the word *customers* at the end of the paragraph.

You then continue typing text in your document. At any point, follow the steps outlined to insert a footnote. The program automatically numbers footnotes as they are inserted.

You also can insert footnotes after the text has been typed. As you know, footnote references are inserted at the location of the cursor when you

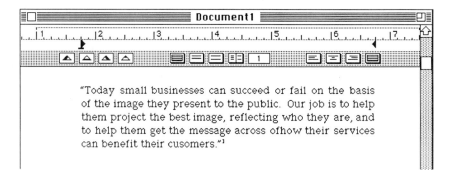

Fig. 9.13. The footnote reference.

choose the Insert Footnote command. To insert a footnote after text has been typed, you first place the cursor where you want the footnote reference to appear. Place the mouse pointer at the desired location in text and click the mouse button once. Then follow the steps to insert a footnote.

The program renumbers footnotes and footnote references for you. If you insert a footnote reference between footnote reference number 1 and footnote reference number 2, for example, the inserted footnote reference becomes number 2. The previous number 2 becomes number 3. The following footnote references are renumbered accordingly.

Remember that automatic renumbering occurs only if you are using the Auto Number Footnotes option set in the Preferences dialog box. For more information on this option, see the following section, "Numbering Footnotes."

Numbering Footnotes

The program numbers footnotes beginning with 1 and proceeding sequentially—2, 3, 4, and so on. When you delete or insert a footnote, the program automatically renumbers the footnotes.

You are not limited to this numbering scheme. In fact, you can use any character or combination of characters (up to nine) for footnote references.

The Auto Number Footnotes option in the Preferences dialog box is set as a default by the program. In figure 9.14, you can see that the Auto Number Footnotes option is on because of the X in the box to the left of the option.

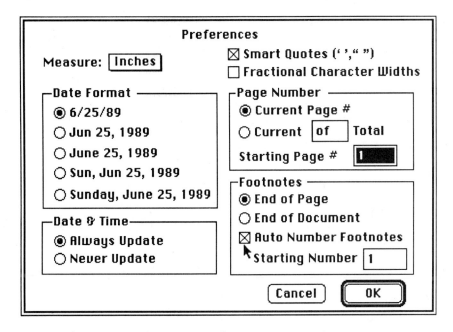

Fig. 9.14. *Choosing the Auto Number Footnotes option.*

To turn the Auto Number Footnotes option on or off, work through the following steps:

1. Select Preferences from the Edit menu.

2. Click the box next to the Auto Number Footnotes option.

3. Click the OK button (or press Return).

Note that if you have been entering footnotes with the Auto Number Footnotes option off and then turn on the option, the program does not renumber the previously entered footnotes.

Setting the Footnote Starting Number

When the Auto Number Footnotes option is on, the program numbers the footnotes starting at the number specified in the Starting Number field of the Preferences dialog box. The program initially sets this number to 1.

If you have a document that has been broken up into several files, you may want to change the footnote starting number. You can start with any number up to 32,000.

To set the footnote reference starting number, do the following:

1. Select Preferences from the Edit menu.

2. Press the Tab key or place the mouse pointer in the Starting Number field in the Footnotes section, and double-click.

3. Type the number with which you want footnote references to begin.

4. Click the OK button (or press Return).

You can change the starting number at any time, and the program will renumber your footnotes accordingly if you are using the Auto Number Footnotes option.

Using Other Symbols for Footnote References

You are not limited to using numbers for footnote references. You can use any character or characters (up to nine in a single footnote reference). To use other symbols, you first must turn off the automatic numbering of footnotes.

When you have turned off automatic footnote numbering, the process for inserting footnotes changes slightly. To insert a footnote, the program prompts you for the footnote reference symbol. To insert a footnote at the current cursor position with automatic numbering off, follow these steps:

1. Select Insert Footnote from the Format menu (or press Shift-Command-F).

2. In the dialog box that appears, type the character or characters you want to use for the footnote reference (see fig. 9.15).

3. Click the OK button (or press Return).

4. Type the footnote text.

5. Press and hold the Command key and press the Return key to return the cursor to its last position in the main body text.

Note that the dialog box in figure 9.15 has a Cancel button in case you change your mind about inserting the footnote. If you do, simply click Cancel.

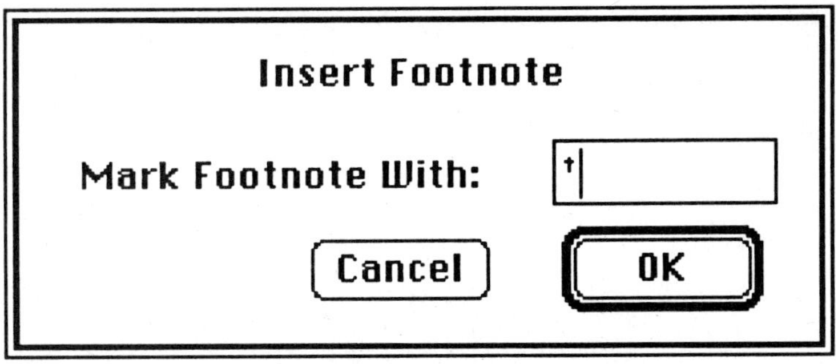

```
┌─────────────────────────────────────────┐
│                                         │
│            Insert Footnote              │
│                                         │
│                           ┌───────────┐ │
│   Mark Footnote With:     │ †│        │ │
│                           └───────────┘ │
│                                         │
│          ┌──────────┐   ╔══════════╗    │
│          │  Cancel  │   ║    OK    ║    │
│          └──────────┘   ╚══════════╝    │
│                                         │
└─────────────────────────────────────────┘
```

Fig. 9.15. *Entering the footnote reference character.*

Using the Key Caps Desk Accessory

The Key Caps desk accessory helps you locate the different symbols used for footnote references. To use Key Caps, select the command from the Apple menu (see fig. 9.16). An image of your keyboard appears (see fig. 9.17). A new menu called Key Caps is added to the menu bar.

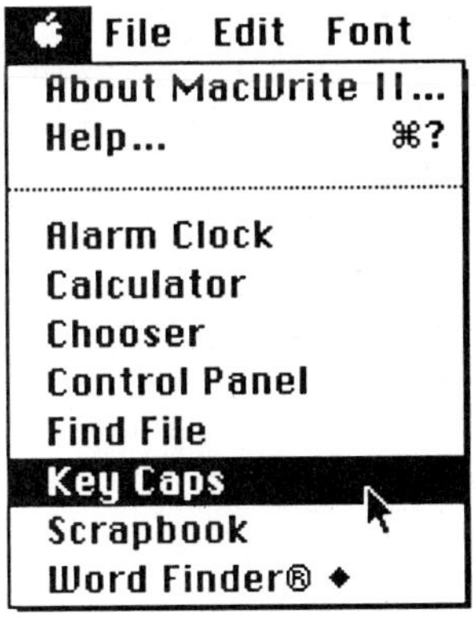

```
┌─────────────────────────────┐
│  🍎  File  Edit  Font        │
├─────────────────────────────┤
│  About MacWrite II...        │
│  Help...              ⌘?     │
│  ·························    │
│  Alarm Clock                 │
│  Calculator                  │
│  Chooser                     │
│  Control Panel               │
│  Find File                   │
│  ▓Key Caps▓▓▓▓▓▓▓▓▓▓         │
│  Scrapbook          ▶        │
│  Word Finder® ◆              │
└─────────────────────────────┘
```

Fig. 9.16. *Selecting Key Caps from the Apple menu.*

If Key Caps does not appear in your Apple menu or if you receive a warning message concerning the keyboard layout, refer to your Macintosh manuals (and keyboard manual if your keyboard is not from Apple). The procedure for installation of this desk accessory is outside the scope of this book.

To use Key Caps to locate footnote reference characters, you first select the font you are using from the Key Caps menu (see fig. 9.18).

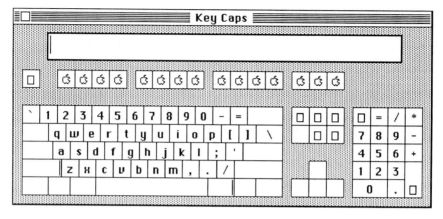

Fig. 9.17. *A keyboard image from Key Caps.*

Fig. 9.18. *Selecting a font from the Key Caps menu.*

When you select a font from the Key Caps menu, the keyboard display changes to show you the characters entered by each key on the keyboard. The initial character display is of the lowercase letters. You can view the other available characters by holding down one of the modifier keys (Shift, Option, Command, or Control) or a combination of keys (such as Shift and

Option). The keyboard image changes to show the characters that will be entered if you hold down the same modifier key (or combination of modifier keys) and then press the key that corresponds to the key shown on-screen.

As an example, assume that you have chosen the New York font, and hold down the Option key. The key caps in the keyboard image change to show you the characters now available. In figure 9.19, the letter *T* has been replaced with the small cross often used as a footnote reference symbol. This replacement tells you that if you hold down the Option key and press T, the cross symbol is entered.

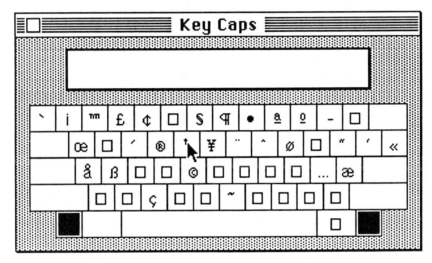

Fig. 9.19. *The Option-key characters available in the New York font.*

After you have found the symbol you want to use, close the Key Caps desk accessory by clicking the close box in the upper left corner of the Key Caps window. When the dialog box asks for the footnote reference symbol, press the key combination you learned from Key Caps in order to enter the symbol.

Editing Footnotes

Editing footnotes is like editing any other text in MacWrite II. As with headers and footers, you must move the cursor into the footnote area to edit the footnote.

As an example, consider the footnote in figure 9.20. Suppose that you have decided to add the company name between the words *the* and *meeting*.

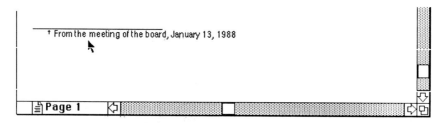

Fig. 9.20. *A sample footnote to be edited.*

To edit this footnote, follow these steps:

1. Place the mouse pointer where you want to begin editing—between *the* and *meeting*.

2. Click to place the cursor.

3. Type the next text—the company name.

All the editing techniques covered in Chapter 3 work in a footnote. You can select the text of only one footnote at a time, however.

You also can use the Find/Change command to alter footnote text (see "Editing Headers and Footers" for a discussion of the Find/Change search order). The Find/Change command is covered in Chapter 5.

To check the spelling of the document's footnotes, use the Check Footnotes command in the Spelling menu. This command appears only when the cursor is in a footnote.

The various formatting features of the program work with footnotes. The cursor must be in the footnote you want to change, or the footnote text must be selected. Then you can use such options as text alignment, paragraph indents, font changes, and so on, to change the appearance of your footnotes.

As a final note, if you want to have a particular style and format for your footnotes, set the formatting (font, indents, and so on) after inserting the first footnote reference but before typing the first footnote text. You also can select the footnote's number and change its font or style. Subsequent footnotes will have the same formatting and style.

Removing Footnotes

Removing a footnote is easier than inserting one. You simply remove the footnote reference (the small number). When the footnote reference is deleted, the footnote is removed also.

Follow these steps to delete a footnote:

1. Place the mouse pointer immediately following the footnote reference.

2. Click the mouse button.

3. Press the Backspace key (Delete on some keyboards).

When the footnote reference is gone, the footnote itself is removed. Any other footnotes in the document are renumbered (unless you have turned off the Auto Number Footnotes option).

If you delete a footnote and immediately realize that you need it, you can use the Undo Typing command in the Edit menu to restore the footnote.

Entering Dates and Times

MacWrite II takes advantage of the Macintosh's built-in clock and calendar to insert dates and times into your document. Not only can you insert dates and times, but you can instruct the program to update them. The purpose of automatic updating—called *time-stamping*—can be particularly useful in memo and letter stationery.

MacWrite II provides five different date formats. They run from the short version of dates—6/25/89—to the long version—Sunday, June 25, 1989. Times have two formats: the standard 12-hour format (8:30 PM) and the 24-hour format (20:30), also known as military time.

Setting the Date Format

Date formats are controlled through the Preferences dialog box. You must set the date format before you insert the date into the document. If you decide to use a different date format, you must select the format and reinsert the date.

To choose a date format, use the following steps:

1. Select Preferences from the Edit menu.

   The Preferences dialog box appears (see fig. 9.21). The date format options are in the upper left box.

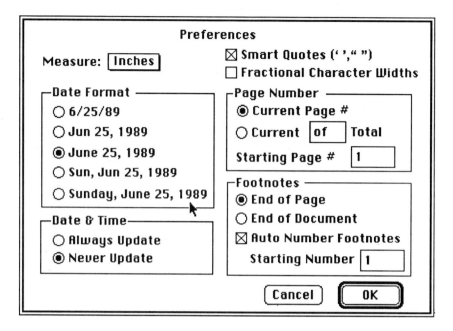

Fig. 9.21. *Choosing the date format in the Preferences dialog box.*

2. Click the circle (called a radio button) next to the date format you want to use.

3. Click the OK button (or press Return).

The date format is now set and is saved with the document. The program remembers the format chosen for that document, even after you quit the program.

If you make a change to the date format while you are working on a document, only dates inserted after the format change are affected. Previously inserted dates remain in their original format.

Setting the Update Option

In figure 9.21, you also see the Date & Time box in the Preferences dialog box. The Date & Time box contains two update options for dates and times. To choose an option, you click the small circle next to the option. You probably should set this option at the same time you choose a date format.

The update option you use depends on your needs. If you set the Always Update option and then insert a date into a document, the date is always current every time you open the document. You can use this option in such items as memo stationery (see Chapter 6 for a discussion of stationery).

In many documents, date changing is undesirable because you do not want the program to change the date each time you open the document. In these cases, choose the Never Update option before inserting the date.

Inserting and Removing Dates

After you have chosen the date format and update option, insert the date by selecting Insert Date from the Edit menu (or pressing Shift-Command-A). The date is inserted at the cursor position in the format you chose in the Preferences dialog box.

MacWrite II considers a date inserted by the Insert Date command to be a single character. When you backspace, the entire date—regardless of length—is deleted. To delete a date, follow these steps:

1. Place the mouse pointer at the point immediately following the date.

2. Press the mouse button to place the cursor.

3. Press the Backspace key.

or

1. Place the mouse pointer anywhere on the date.

2. Double-click the mouse button.

3. Press the Backspace (Delete on some keyboards) key.

To restore an accidentally deleted date, use the Undo Typing command in the Edit menu.

Setting the Time Format

The format of the time is not actually controlled by MacWrite II. The program derives the format from the Macintosh's built-in clock and the System software.

As mentioned, two time formats are available: the standard 12-hour time and the 24-hour military time. Times of the 12-hour format have AM or PM appended to them. Times of the 24-hour format do not.

To set the time format, you use the Control Panel. You access the Control Panel by selecting it from the Apple menu. If your Apple menu does not contain the Control Panel, consult your Macintosh System software manual. You also must have the General Control Panel device in your System Folder.

To select a time format, perform the following steps:

1. Select the Control Panel from the Apple menu.

2. Click the General icon if it is not already selected (see fig. 9.22).

3. Click the 12hr. or 24hr. option.

4. Click the close box of the Control Panel.

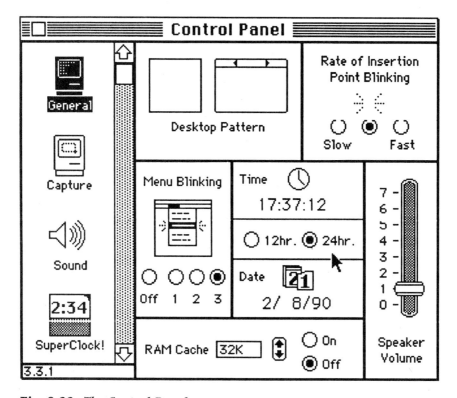

Fig. 9.22. *The Control Panel.*

You can change the time format any time, even if MacWrite II is not running.

Inserting and Removing Times

To insert a time at the current cursor position, select Insert Time from the Format menu (or press Shift-Command-T). The time is inserted. The format of the time is the selection you made in the Control Panel.

To remove a time, follow these steps:

1. Place the mouse pointer at a point immediately after the time.

2. Press the mouse button to place the cursor.

3. Press the Backspace (Delete on some keyboards) key.

or

1. Place the mouse pointer anywhere on the time.

2. Double-click the mouse button.

3. Press the Backspace (Delete on some keyboards) key.

Setting the Date and Time

Because MacWrite II relies on the Macintosh's built-in clock to provide the date and time, to set the date or time, you must resort to the System software. The date and time are controlled through the Control Panel.

To set the date, follow these steps:

1. Select the Control Panel from the Apple menu.

2. Click the General icon if it is not already selected.

   The Date section of the Control Panel shows a small calendar icon and a date.

3. Click the part of the date (the number for the month, day, or year) you want to change.

   The selected part of the date is highlighted, and a small control with two arrows (one up and one down) appears.

4. Click the up arrow to increase the date by one. Click the down arrow to decrease the date by one.

   Continue to click the appropriate arrow until the selected part of the date is correct.

   You then can select another part of the date (step 3) and use the arrows to change it.

   or

A quicker method is simply to type the number after you have selected the part of the date to be changed.

5. Click the close box of the Control Panel to accept your changes and close the Control Panel window.

The Time section of the Control Panel shows a small clock icon and the time. To set the time, follow the same procedure you use to set the date.

Using Page Numbering

The similarities between page numbers and dates and times are many. Page numbers also are considered single characters, are updated by the program, come in two formats set in the Preferences dialog box, and are inserted with a single command.

The biggest difference between these elements is that page numbers usually appear on every page of a document except the title pages. Placing a page number on a page, however, does not make page numbers appear on all pages. To make page numbers appear on all pages, you must insert page numbers into headers or footers.

Setting the Page Number Format

Two page number formats are available in MacWrite II. The first is the standard current page number. The second is a current-of-total page number (2 of 3, for example).

Page number formats are controlled through the Preferences dialog box. To select a format, follow these steps:

1. Select Preferences from the Edit menu.

2. Click the small circle next to the Current Page # or Current of Total option (see fig. 9.23).

3. Click the OK button (or press Return) to confirm your choice and close the dialog box.

Choosing the Current Page # format means that when you insert the page number, the number of the current page appears at the cursor position. If the Current of Total option is on, the number of the current page is followed by the word *of*, which is followed by the total number of pages in the document.

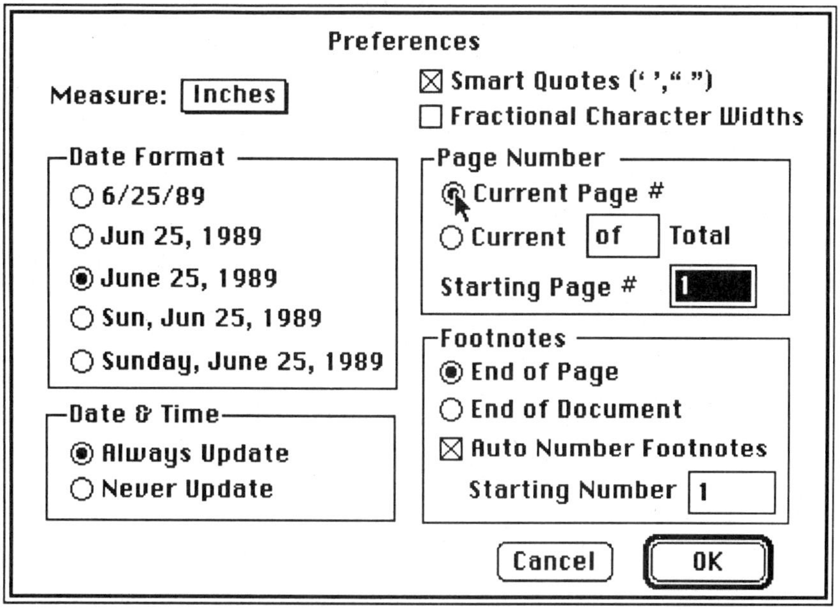

Fig. 9.23. *Choosing a page numbering format.*

As with dates and times, changing the format option does not affect page numbers that have already been inserted. The option set in the Preferences dialog box applies only to page numbers inserted after the option has been selected.

Setting the Starting Page Number

You may want to change the starting page number from its default setting of 1. Two common reasons for changing the starting page number are

- You have a title page that you do not want to be counted in the page numbering.

- You have broken a large document into separate document files and want the page numbering of each document file to pick up where the page numbering of the preceding document left off.

In some documents, the title page is considered page 1 even if the title page does not carry a page number. In this case, the default setting is correct—the page after the title page is page 2 although it is the first page to carry a page number. But in other cases, the title page is not considered page 1, and the page after the title page is where page numbering begins. To start page numbering there, you must do the following:

1. Select Preferences from the Edit menu.

   When the Preferences dialog box appears, the highlighting probably is in the Starting Page # field. If you have been setting other items in the dialog box, however, the highlighting band may be in another field. Simply press the Tab key until the band moves to the Starting Page # field.

2. Type the number *0* (zero) in the Starting Page # field.

3. Click the OK button (or press Return) to confirm the setting and close the dialog box.

Changing the starting page number affects page numbers that have already been inserted. Therefore, you can change the starting page number at any time without having to insert the page number again.

You may want to break up a large document into more than one document file. For example, you could save a novel in chapter-sized documents. In this case, you would have to enter a new starting page number for each chapter. The second chapter may begin with page 27, for example. Note that the maximum starting page number is 32,000.

Adding Page Numbering

After you have chosen the page numbering format and set the starting page number, you are ready to insert the page number itself. To insert the page number at the current cursor position, select Insert Page # from the Edit menu (or press Shift-Command-P).

The current page number in the chosen format appears. Because the page number is not a repeating element—it will not appear on following pages—you should put page numbers in headers or footers. In documents with left and right pages, if you have one header (or footer) for left pages and another for right pages, you can insert a page number on the left-page header (or footer) or the right-page header (or footer). Of course, you can insert page numbers in both so that you have page numbers on all the pages.

Creating Custom Page Numbering

Because MacWrite II treats page numbering as a character, you can create your own page numbering formats. You also can use the Current of Total text field to change the *of* to any seven-character (or fewer) word or string of symbols you desire.

As an example of one page numbering format, consider the header shown in figure 9.24.

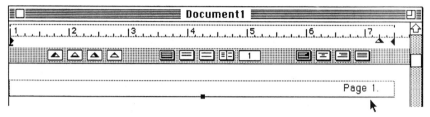

Fig. 9.24. *A sample page numbering scheme.*

Note the page numbering on the right side. This form—Page 1.—is created with the following steps. (If the default Current Page # option is already set, begin with step 4.)

1. Select Preferences from the Edit menu.

2. Choose the Current Page # option.

3. Click OK.

4. Place a Right tab at a position close to the right-hand page margin (in the example 7.25 inches).

5. Press Tab.

6. Type *Page* followed by a space.

7. Select Insert Page # from the Edit menu.

8. Type a period.

This example demonstrates how you can enclose a page number with other words and characters to produce a custom page-numbering scheme.

Another commonly used page-numbering format is to precede the page number with the chapter number. An example of this format is found in your MacWrite II manual (as well as many other computer manuals). This page numbering scheme can be accomplished with steps similar to those for the format outlined previously. You change step 6 to

Type the chapter number followed by a hyphen.

Omit step 8. The resulting page number is shown in figure 9.25.

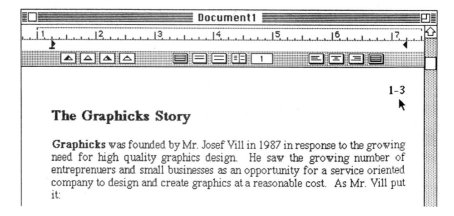

Fig. 9.25. *Using the chapter number as part of a page number.*

One option of the Current of Total page number format may be of use to you. Normally, page numbers of this format are the current page number, followed by the word *of*, followed by the total number of pages in the document (such as *2 of 3* or *1 of 6*). The *of* can be replaced by any word or string of characters, up to seven characters long.

To change the middle text of the Current of Total option, follow these steps:

1. Select Preferences from the Edit dialog.

2. Press Tab until the highlighting is in the text field between the words *Current* and *Total* in the Current of Total option.

3. Type the new text (up to seven characters).

4. Click the OK button (or press Return).

The text of the Current of Total option can be changed at any time. The program will update the previously inserted page numbers of that format.

Removing Page Numbering

As with dates and times, MacWrite II considers a page number a single character regardless of length. You can delete page numbering with the same techniques used for deleting a single character. Because headers and footers are repeating elements, deleting one page number in a header or footer deletes all page numbers.

To delete page numbering, select the page number and press Backspace.

Keep in mind that left and right headers (as well as footers) are separate elements. If you delete page numbering from a left header, page numbering is removed from all left headers, but the right headers are not affected.

Summing Up

Several different elements have been covered in this chapter. You should now know how to add and remove title pages, headers and footers, footnotes, dates and times, and page numbers. With these elements, you can create a variety of documents.

Remember to think of the items covered in this chapter as document elements—the building blocks of MacWrite II. One of the most important parts of document design is to start with the basics, such as page margins and paragraph indents, and then add other elements as needed.

You are now at a point where you can begin considering such things as fonts and text styles. Having the tools and elements to build your document, you are ready to enhance the document—the topic of the next chapter.

10

Enhancing Documents

One of the most revolutionary aspects of the Macintosh computer was the addition of font and text style capabilities—features that formerly had been reserved for typesetters. Mac users fell in love with their newfound capabilities to choose fonts and styles and create professional-looking documents right at their desks.

At first, only a handful of fonts were available, and the laser printer was something only large corporations purchased. Now, of course, an almost bewildering variety of fonts and text styles exists. Users can purchase whole libraries of fonts, and the competition to provide more sophisticated fonts continues. Laser printers are on the verge of becoming the printer of choice, and color printers are making rapid inroads. MacWrite II is ready to help you take advantage of these new capabilities. Three of the program's menus are dedicated to fonts and font styling; color and custom font styles are available.

This chapter explores the font-related capabilities of MacWrite II. The Macintosh has become famous for creating terrific-looking documents; fonts are an essential part of this reputation.

Using Fonts

A *font* is a set of letters with a unique appearance. Fonts have many technical aspects that are beyond the scope of this book. Discussing such things as serif, san serif, and kerning is best left to books and articles dedicated to that purpose. This chapter focuses on how to put different fonts to work in your document.

MacWrite II is not responsible for the number, type, and sizes of fonts available. Fonts reside in the System software of the Macintosh computer. They are removed and installed by using the Font/DA Mover utility, which is part of the System Utilities package provided by Apple. Although the installation of fonts is discussed briefly in this chapter, your best resources are the manuals that accompany your computer.

Using the Font Menu

Before you use a font, that font must be installed in the System file. Installing a font makes it available for selection in the Font menu.

The System software shipped with your Macintosh computer contains several fonts that are available for use in MacWrite II. Your Font menu—if you have not modified the fonts—looks like figure 10.1.

Fig. 10.1. A Font menu showing the standard Macintosh fonts.

Note that fonts appear in the menu as they appear in documents. Some older fonts, however, may appear in plain text. The currently selected font is indicated by a check mark next to the font's name in the menu. In figure 10.1, Helvetica is the current font.

To increase the variety of fonts available, many people use programs like Suitcase II, which permits quick and easy installation of a large number of fonts. When you have a great many fonts, the Font menu becomes a scrolling menu. An arrow at the bottom of the menu indicates that more fonts are available than can be displayed at one time (see fig. 10.2).

You access the remaining fonts in the menu by holding down the mouse button and moving the mouse pointer beyond the bottom of the menu. The remaining fonts scroll up. An arrow appears at the top of the menu, indicating that other fonts are listed above those displayed. You can access those fonts by holding down the mouse button and moving the pointer up the menu.

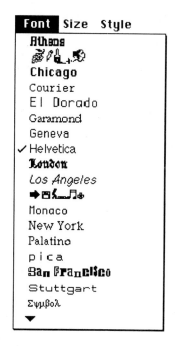

Fig. 10.2. A scrolling Font menu.

The Font menu is your first stop in choosing a style of text to use in your document. Other early steps include setting page margins, paragraph indents, and other page layout settings. Although the initial choice of the font for your document is important, remember that you can change and edit fonts.

Choosing a Font

When the MacWrite II program first starts, you are presented with a blank document. The program must select a font to be used if you do not specify a font; the default choice is Helvetica. If you do not have Helvetica in your System file (a rare event), the program chooses another font. Therefore, you do not have to select a font before beginning to type. The program automatically selects Helvetica (or another font), and you can work in that font.

When you do not want to use the default font, you need to consider two questions:

- How do you choose another font?

- Which font is best to use in a given situation?

You choose a font by following these steps:

1. Open the Font menu.

2. Continue to hold down the mouse button, and move the mouse pointer down the list of fonts until the font you want is highlighted.

3. Release the mouse button.

The currently selected font is indicated by a check mark to the left of its name.

Selecting a font is easy. Deciding which font to use is more difficult. Three factors influence the choice of a font:

- *Appearance*. This factor moves the decision into the realm of personal preference. You may want to use the Geneva font, for example, simply because you like the way it looks. Remember that the Font menu displays fonts as they appear in documents.

  A font is not displayed as it appears in the document if the font cannot be sized to fit in the Font menu. These fonts are shown in the same typeface as the Chicago font.

- *WYSIWYG*. Although Apple has gone to great lengths to create a what-you-see-is-what-you-get (WYSIWYG) environment in the Macintosh, what is printed by your printer may not be exactly what you see on-screen. This difference is not usually a problem with the ImageWriter or other dot-matrix printers. These printers print with the font installed in your System file. LaserWriters (except the SC, which uses fonts the way ImageWriters use fonts) and other laser printers print with fonts in their memory.

  Check your printer manual to determine what fonts are available in your printer. Those fonts produce the best results. You can use a font that is not available in your laser printer's memory, but the printed fronts may not look as sharp or as clear as the fonts in your printer. To help avoid confusion, laser printers are usually accompanied by disks containing fonts you can install in your System file. These fonts correspond to the fonts in the printer's memory.

  For users interested in printing with more than their printer's built-in fonts, most laser printers provide a method of storing additional fonts in the printer's memory. This process is called *downloading*. When you purchase a font, the company usually provides a utility to download the font to the printer's memory. To determine whether this option is available to you, check your printer manual.

- *Testing.* To determine the best font(s) for your document, you may need to experiment. You can create and print a test document that contains all the fonts available in the Font menu. Besides seeing how the fonts appear when printed, you can compare the fonts' printed appearance with their appearance on-screen.

Installing New Fonts

The actual procedure for font installation is beyond the scope of this book. This procedure is covered in your Macintosh manuals. You do, however, need to know that the content of the Font menu depends on the fonts installed in your System file.

Font installation requires a program called Font/DA Mover, which is on the System disks supplied by Apple. With Font/DA Mover, you can install or remove fonts from your System file. The fonts are in files on the disk supplied with your printer, the System disks supplied by Apple, or the disk supplied by the company from which you purchased the font. Font/DA Mover "moves" the fonts into your System file, making them available in your Font menu.

Font installation does have some restrictions. The number of fonts you can install in your System file is limited. Check your Macintosh System manuals for the current limit. Keep in mind that you should install only the fonts you are actually going to use. Fonts consume a considerable amount of disk space. Installing a large number of fonts can cause your System file to be quite large.

Certain fonts cannot be removed from the System file because they are used by the Macintosh itself for such things as menu names and system messages. The Chicago font, for example, is used for the menu bar and window titles. Your Macintosh manual lists the fonts that cannot be removed from your System file.

Finally, keep in mind that the upcoming System 7 release will change and simplify the entire font installation procedure.

Selecting the Font Size

Fonts sizes are measured in points. but unfortunately, the sizes do not correspond directly among fonts. As a result, one 12-point font may not be the same size as another 12-point font. Within a single font, however, the sizes can be compared. For example, 24-point Helvetica is twice as big as 12-point Helvetica.

The technical definition of font size does little to help the average user. For those interested, a font is measured from the tops of the ascenders on one line to the tops of the ascenders on the next line of single-spaced text. An *ascender* is the part of a lowercase letter that rises above the main body of the letter. A *point* is about 1/72nd inch.

Experience is more useful in judging the sizes of fonts. If you are involved with desktop publishing, however, you may want to consider reading a book or two about typestyles and fonts.

To select a font size in MacWrite II, follow these steps:

1. Open the Size menu.

2. Select a font size.

A check mark next to the font size shows the current selection.

Installed Font Sizes

In the Size menu, the sizes of the fonts currently installed in the System file are outlined. In figure 10.3, the installed sizes of the current font are 9, 10, 12, 14, 18, and 24 points. The 7-, 36-, 48-, 60-, and 72-point sizes of the current font are not installed in the System file. You still can use these fonts, but they will not appear as crisp or as clear as the installed sizes.

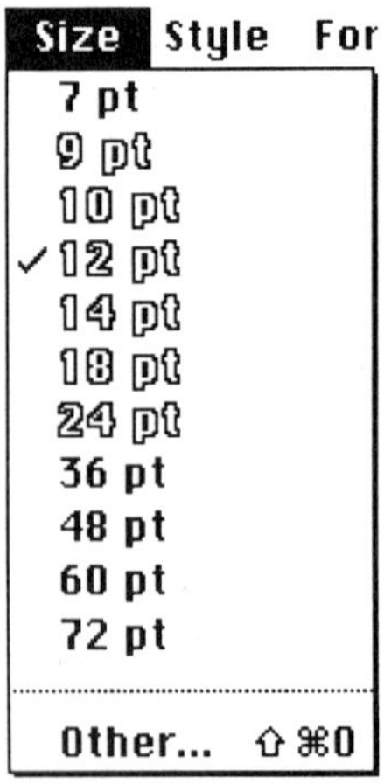

Size	Style	For
7 pt		
9 pt		
10 pt		
✓ 12 pt		
14 pt		
18 pt		
24 pt		
36 pt		
48 pt		
60 pt		
72 pt		
Other... ⇧⌘O		

Fig. 10.3. The Size menu, showing installed font sizes.

Figure 10.4 shows the Geneva font in several sizes. Because the font sizes from 9-point through 24-point are installed for this font, these sizes of the font appear best on-screen. The 7-, 36-, and 48-point sizes are not installed and have a jagged look.

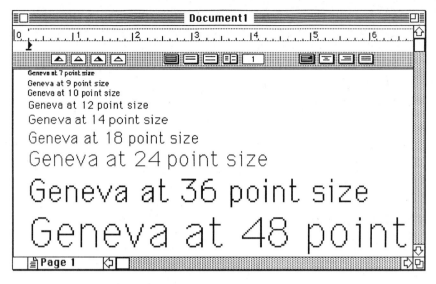

Fig. 10.4. *The Geneva font in various sizes.*

When you request a font in a size that is not installed, that font must be scaled to the size you request. The Macintosh takes the font in an installed size and increases or reduces the font to match your size request.

Keep in mind that different printers use different ways to get the fonts used in printing. ImageWriter printers (and similar dot-matrix printers) print with the fonts installed in your System file. If a font size is not installed in your System file, the Macintosh must adjust one of the installed sizes (increasing or decreasing the font) to match the requested size. This adjustment may result in a "jagged" appearance in the printed document. For printers of these types, use the installed font sizes for the best results in printing.

LaserWriter printers (except the SC) and other laser printers print with the fonts in their memories. If a font is installed in the printer's memory, the font can be scaled (adjusted) to any size with no loss in print quality. You are free to choose a font size regardless of whether that size is installed in your System file. Remember, however, that a font size which is not installed in your System file may appear "jagged" on the screen although the laser printer may print it quite satisfactorily.

You should check the printer's manual and do some experimenting to find the best font sizes for your system.

Custom Font Sizes

At times, you may need a font size that is not listed in the Size menu. For example, you might want to create a banner with a large font size. MacWrite II permits you to enter a font size directly through the Other option in the Size menu. When you choose Other from the Size menu, the dialog box shown in figure 10.5 appears. In this dialog box, you enter a number from 2 to 500, and the selected font is scaled to that size.

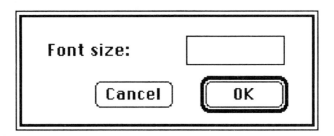

Fig. 10.5. The Font Size dialog box.

Enter the desired point size and click the OK button. The current font is scaled to the entered size. A Cancel button is provided in case you change your mind. When you use the Other option in the Size menu to create a font size that is not in the Size menu, the Other option has a check mark next to it.

Changing the Font and Font Size

You can change the font and font size for a selection of text at any time. This selection may be as small as a single letter or as large as the entire document. (The process of selecting text is covered in Chapter 3.)

After making a text selection, you change the font or font size of that selection by choosing the desired font or size from the menu. The text selection immediately changes to the new font or font size.

Because text stays selected until you click elsewhere in the document, you can make several experimental changes to the text selection without selecting the text again. You also can print the document with the text selected to see the printed results. Even if you click elsewhere in the document, you need only to select the text again to make more changes.

You can reverse font and font size changes immediately after they are made by selecting the Undo command from the Edit menu (or pressing Command-Z).

If you want to change the font or font size of an entire document, you can use the Select All command (Command-A) in the Edit menu and then choose the new font or font size. Note, however, that Select All selects only the document element in which the cursor currently resides. That is, if your cursor is in the main body, the Select All command selects all the main body; but the headers, footers, and footnotes must be selected separately.

Changing Text Styles

Besides choosing a font and its size, you can apply a style to text. Style includes such things as boldface, underlining, italic, and color.

You can apply more than one style to a section of text. A section of text may be boldface, italic, and underlined at the same time. You can create custom styles, which are not new styles, but combinations of the available styles into one group that may be applied with a single menu selection.

These functions are controlled through the Style menu (see fig. 10.6). Color is controlled through a second menu. The menu indicates with check marks which styles currently in effect. In the figure, the current style is Plain Text in Black.

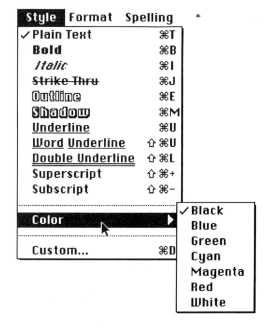

Fig. 10.6. *The Style menu and Color menu.*

Choosing a Style

Before typing your text, you can choose a style by making the appropriate menu selection or using the corresponding keyboard command. For example, before typing a word that you want to be in boldface, do the following:

1. Open the Style menu.

2. Select the style—Bold (or press Command-B).

3. Type the text.

To return to normal text, choose the Plain Text style from the menu or press Command-T.

You also can change the style of a part of your text by selecting the text and then choosing the desired style.

Suppose that you want to boldface the company name, *Graphicks*, in the first line of the first paragraph shown in figure 10.7. Follow these steps:

1. Select the word *Graphicks*.

2. Select the Bold style from the Style menu or press Command-B.

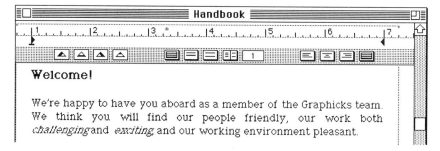

Fig. 10.7. Sample text to be boldfaced.

Figure 10.8 shows the results.

Fig. 10.8. *Graphicks in boldface style.*

The styles available in the Style menu and the keyboard commands that activate these styles are listed in table 10.1.

Table 10.1
Keyboard Commands for Styles

Style	Keyboard Command
Plain Text	Command-T
Bold	Command-B
Italic	Command-I
Strike Thru	Command-J
Outline	Command-E
Shadow	Command-M
Underline	Command-U
Word Underline	Shift-Command-U
Double Underline	Shift-Command-L
Superscript	Shift-Command-+ (plus)
Subscript	Shift-Command-− (minus)

Combining Styles

You can combine most of the styles in the Style menu. A section does not have to be boldface or italic; a section can be boldface and italic, or boldface, italic, and underlined. In many cases when you turn on a style, you do not turn off other styles.

The Style menu appears to have three groups of styles separated by dashed lines (again see fig. 10.6). Actually, the Style menu has six style groups:

- *Plain Text.* This command cancels all other styles except color and returns you to normal text. Plain Text, therefore, is not really a style—Plain Text is simply a quick way to turn off all styles in the selected text.

- *Toggled Styles.* This group of styles consists of Bold, Italic, Strike Thru, Outline, and Shadow. Each choice of the style turns it on or off. You can combine any of these styles.

- *Underlining.* You can combine any one of the three types of underlining with the other styles; choosing one of the types of underlining cancels any previous choice of underlining. The three types of underlining are Underline, which places a line under all characters and spaces; Word Underline, which underlines words and skips spaces; and Double Underline, which underlines words and spaces twice.

- *Superscript/Subscript*. Text may be superscript or subscript, but not both. Superscripting or subscripting can be combined with other styles.

- *Color*. In the secondary Color menu, one of the eight colors can be chosen at a time for a selection of text.

- *Custom*. This command brings up a dialog box that enables you to create custom styles. Styles created in this manner are listed below the Custom command. Choosing one of the custom styles overrides any other selected styles.

You can combine these options to produce hundreds of different styles of text. When you add the styles that are available in the Character and Custom dialog boxes (covered later this chapter), you have a tremendous variety of text styles from which to choose.

Choosing and Changing Colors

If you have a Macintosh capable of displaying color, you can use the secondary Color menu within the Style menu to choose one of eight colors for your text. Follow these steps:

1. Select Color from the Style menu. Hold down the mouse button to display the Color menu.

2. Move the pointer up or down until the desired color is highlighted (see fig. 10.9).

3. Release the mouse button.

4. Type the text.

To change the color of a selection of text, select the text, and then choose the desired color.

Using the Character Dialog Box To Set Text Styles

All the previously mentioned text attributes—fonts, font sizes, text styles, and color—can be controlled through the Character dialog box. A few styles can be accessed only through the Character dialog box and the Custom dialog box (covered later this chapter).

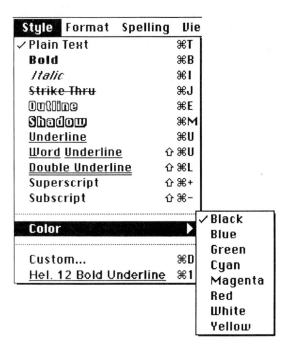

Fig. 10.9. *Choosing the color.*

The Character dialog box is best used when you want to change several settings at one time. To open this dialog box, select Character from the Format menu (or press Shift-Command-D). The Character dialog box contains five pop-up menus, eleven check boxes, and three buttons (see fig. 10.10).

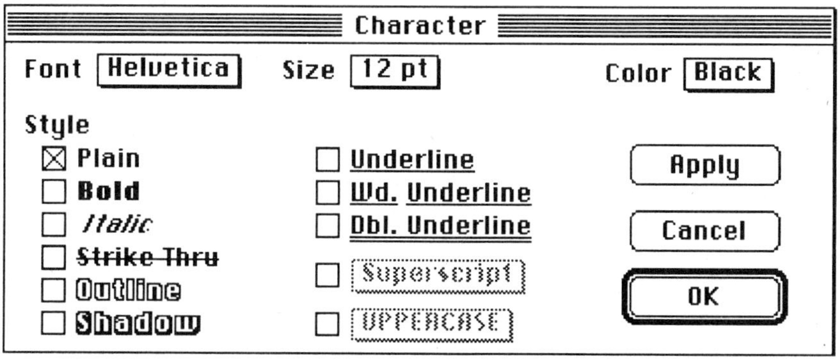

Fig. 10.10. *The Character dialog box.*

Setting Font, Font Size, and Color

The first two pop-up menus in the Character dialog box control the font and font size. You open these menus by placing the mouse pointer on the menu and then pressing and holding the mouse button.

To choose the New York font, for example, do the following steps:

1. Open the pop-up Font menu (see fig. 10.11).

2. Move the highlighting band to the New York font name.

3. Release the mouse button.

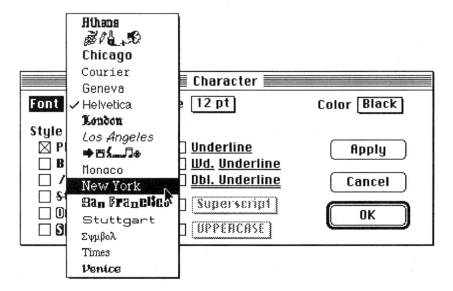

Fig. 10.11. The pop-up Font menu in the Character dialog box.

The dialog box displays New York, reflecting the font change. You use the same technique to choose a font size. The Size menu pops up to permit you to choose any of the available size selections, including the Other option.

If you choose the Other option, a field next to the menu permits you to enter the desired font size (see fig. 10.12). You can enter a number between 2 and 500 to size the font.

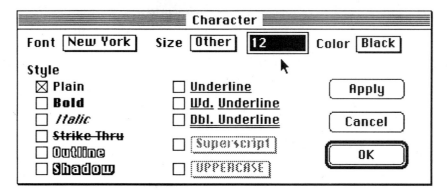

Fig. 10.12. *The Other Font Size field.*

You set text color the same way you set the font and font size. The Color menu in the Character dialog box is a pop-up menu. To choose a color for your text, open the Color menu and select a color (see fig. 10.13).

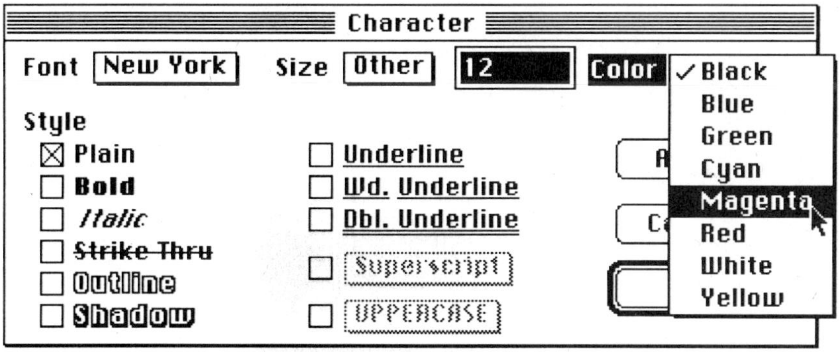

Fig. 10.13. *Choosing a color through the Character dialog box.*

The menu in the dialog box displays the chosen color's name.

Setting the Style

Eleven check boxes appear beneath the Style heading. To make a selection, click the box (or boxes) next to the style(s) you want to use. An X in a style's check box indicates that the style is on. An empty check box indicates that the style is off.

The same basic rules govern style choices in the Character dialog box as those that control style choices in the Style menu.

You select superscripts and subscripts differently than you do from the Style menu, however. From the Character dialog box, you click the box to turn on the Superscript/Subscript/Superior menu. Until you click the box next to the menu, the menu remains inactive. When active, the menu enables you to choose superscript, subscript, or superior (see fig. 10.14). Superior is not available from the Style menu. The program uses this style to enter footnote numbering. The Superior style is similar to Superscript, but the type is smaller.

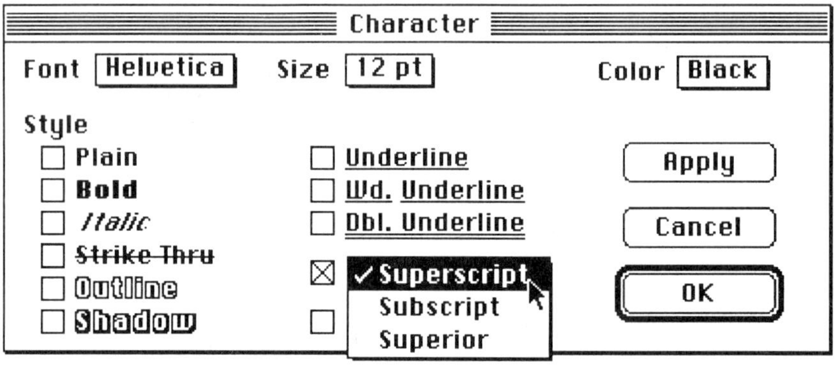

Fig. 10.14. *Selecting Superscript.*

The Uppercase, Lowercase, and Small Caps styles are available only through this dialog box and the Custom Style dialog box. The menu operates like the Superscript/Subscript/Superior menu. You click the box to turn on the option; then drag down to select the style. These three style options can be combined with other style options:

- *Uppercase.* All type in this style is in capital letters regardless of whether the Shift key or Caps Lock key is used.

- *Lowercase.* The reverse of Uppercase, all type is in lowercase letters regardless of the Shift key or Caps Lock key position.

- *Small Caps.* Produces for lowercase letters capital letters the size of lowercase letters and for uppercase letters uses regular capital letters.

Applying, Confirming, and Canceling Changes

If you are using the Character dialog box to change selected text, you can see the effect of the changes without closing the dialog box or making the changes permanent. Simply click the Apply button or press Command-A.

To confirm the changes and make them part of your document, you must click the OK button (or press the Return key). This action applies the changes and closes the dialog box.

Alternatively, you can use the Cancel button (or press Command-period) to return the text to its appearance before you opened the Character dialog box. Clicking the Cancel button also closes the dialog box.

Creating Custom Styles

You may find yourself using a particular set of styles frequently. This repetition can be a problem as you find yourself setting these same styles every time you need them. The Custom command in the Style menu saves a group of style settings as a custom style.

A custom style is not a new style. The Custom command gathers several style settings together under one style name. Then, you can choose the multiple settings by selecting a name from the Style menu.

To call up the Custom Style dialog box, choose Custom from the Style menu or press Command-D. The Custom Style dialog box is similar to the Character dialog box (see fig. 10.15).

You can add as many as 30 custom styles. The styles appear in the Style menu below the Custom command. MacWrite II assigns keyboard equivalents to the first 10 custom styles: Command-1, Command-2, and so on.

Choosing the Font, Size, Color, and Style

The Font, Size, and Color options are set using the three pop-up menus across the top of the Custom Style dialog box. To make a selection, open the menu and select the option.

When you choose the Other option from the Size menu, a field appears next to the menu to permit you to enter the desired font size. You enter a number between 2 and 500 to size the font.

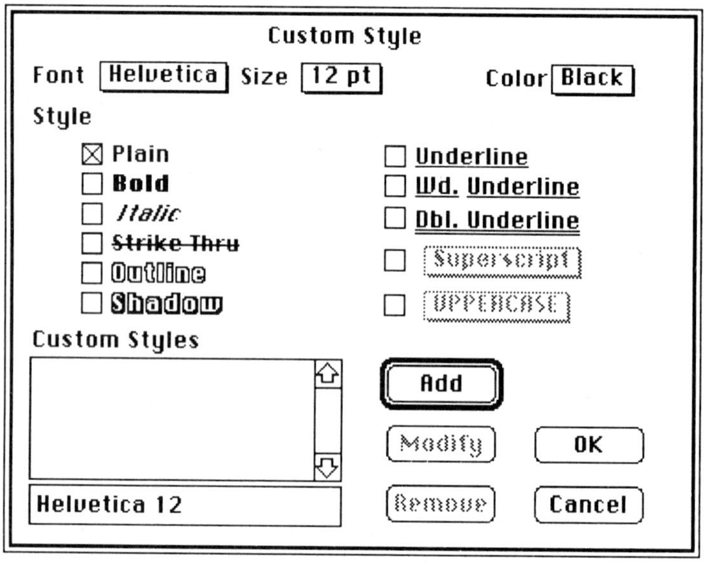

Fig. 10.15. *The Custom Style dialog box.*

You make style choices in the same manner as you do in the Character dialog box, and the same rules apply.

Adding and Removing Custom Styles

After you choose the font, font size, color, and text styles you want for your custom style, you must add the style to the Custom Styles list. The program automatically supplies a name made up of the font name and size. This name, however, does not take into account differences in text styles. That is, the program assigns the name *Helvetica 12-point* to both Helvetica 12-point Plain Text and Helvetica 12-point Bold. You should enter a name to help distinguish the custom style.

·To add the new style to the Custom Styles list, follow these steps:

1. Type a name for the style in the text box below the Custom Styles list (Hel. 12 Bold Underline, for example).

2. Click the Add button (or press Return).

   The style name appears in the Custom Style list box of the Custom Style dialog box (see fig. 10.16).

3. Click the OK button.

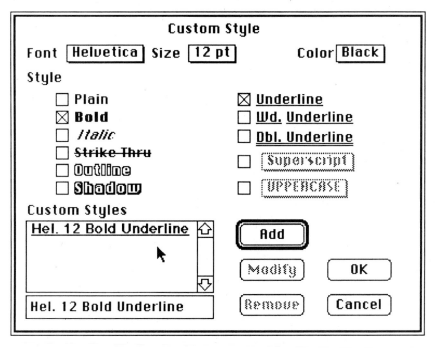

Fig. 10.16. *The custom style name in the Custom Styles list.*

The custom style name also appears in the Style menu below the Custom command (see fig. 10.17).

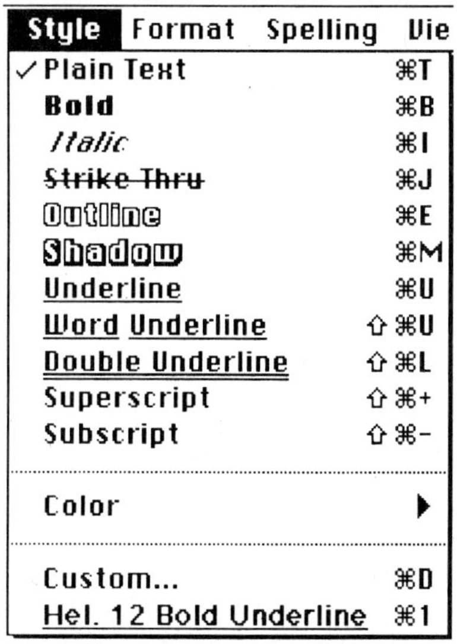

Fig. 10.17. *The custom style added to the Style menu.*

To remove a custom style, follow these steps:

1. Select Custom from the Style menu (or press Command-D).

2. Highlight the name of the style to be removed by clicking its name.

3. Click the Remove button (or press Command-R).

4. Click the OK button.

The style is removed from the Custom Styles list and the Style menu.

Modifying a Custom Style

After creating a custom style, you may find that some part of the style needs to be changed. You may have created a custom style, for example, that consists of all uppercase letters with word underlining. You decide that the custom style also needs to boldface the letters.

Use the following steps to change a style:

1. Select Custom from the Style menu.

2. Click the name of the custom style (see fig. 10.18).

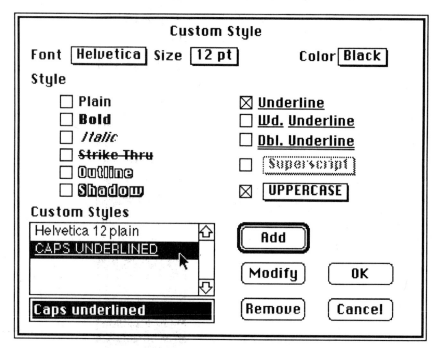

Fig. 10.18. Highlighting the style to be modified.

When the custom style is highlighted, the Custom Style dialog box changes to reflect the style's settings.

3. Make the desired changes to the style's settings.

4. Click the Modify button (or press Command-M).

5. Click the OK button.

The custom style is now changed, and its entry in the Style menu reflects the change.

Using a Custom Style

To use a custom style, you follow the same steps you use to apply any other style. That is, you can select the style before typing the text or after selecting previously typed text.

Custom styles are added to the Style menu below .the Custom command. Style names reflect the style attributes of that style. For example, the Helvetica 12 Bold Italic style shown at the bottom of the Style menu is shown in the Helvetica font—boldfaced and italicized (see fig. 10.19).

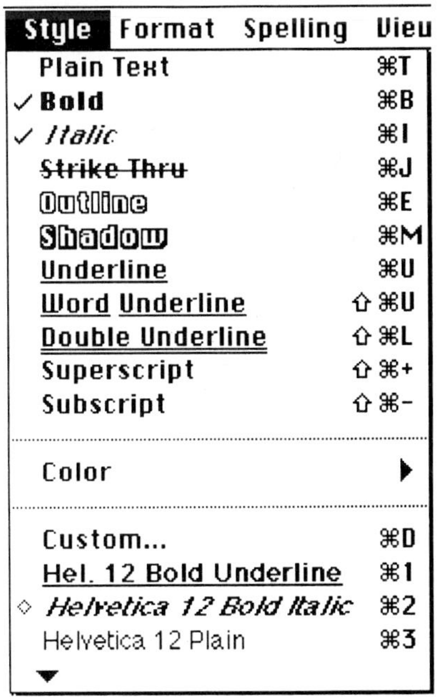

Style	Format	Spelling	View
Plain Text			⌘T
✓ **Bold**			⌘B
✓ *Italic*			⌘I
~~Strike Thru~~			⌘J
Outline			⌘E
Shadow			⌘M
Underline			⌘U
Word Underline			⇧⌘U
Double Underline			⇧⌘L
Superscript			⇧⌘+
Subscript			⇧⌘-
Color			▶
Custom...			⌘D
Hel. 12 Bold Underline			⌘1
◇ *Helvetica 12 Bold Italic*			⌘2
Helvetica 12 Plain			⌘3
▼			

Fig. 10.19. *Custom styles shown with attributes.*

The program assigns the first 10 custom styles keyboard equivalents, numbered from 1 through 9 with the tenth numbered 0. You can choose a style by pressing the Command key and the appropriate number.

When a custom style is in effect, a diamond—not a check mark—appears to the left of the custom style name in the Style menu. Check marks appear next to the styles that make up the custom style. In figure 10.19, the Bold and Italic style options are checked, and the custom style is marked with a diamond. The Font and Size menus also have the selections checked.

Searching for and Replacing Text Styles

In Chapter 5, you saw how the program permits searching for and replacing text. This powerful feature is further enhanced by the capability to search and replace text styles, with or without text. For example, you can search for each instance of a word or phrase that has been typed using the Bold and Italic style options and replace every instance with the same word or phrase, adding the Underline style option. You can search for a word or phrase of one style and replace the word or phrase with another phrase in a different style. You can search for a particular combination of styles and change to a different style or styles regardless of the text.

You can perform all these changes with the expanded Find/Change dialog box. To access the expanded Find/Change dialog box,

1. Select Find/Change from the Edit menu.

2. Click the check box to the left of the Use Attributes option.

The Find/Change dialog box expands to include all the possible text attributes that can be used in a search (see fig. 10.20).

The expanded Find/Change dialog box has five distinct sections. Each section is built from items you have seen before in previous parts of this book.

The first section—at the top of the dialog box—is the text section. Here you enter text to be found and the replacement text. Two check boxes have been added to the dialog box's text section. These boxes enable you to indicate to the program whether you want the search and replace to involve text. Both boxes initially contain an X, indicating that the program is expecting the search and replace to involve text.

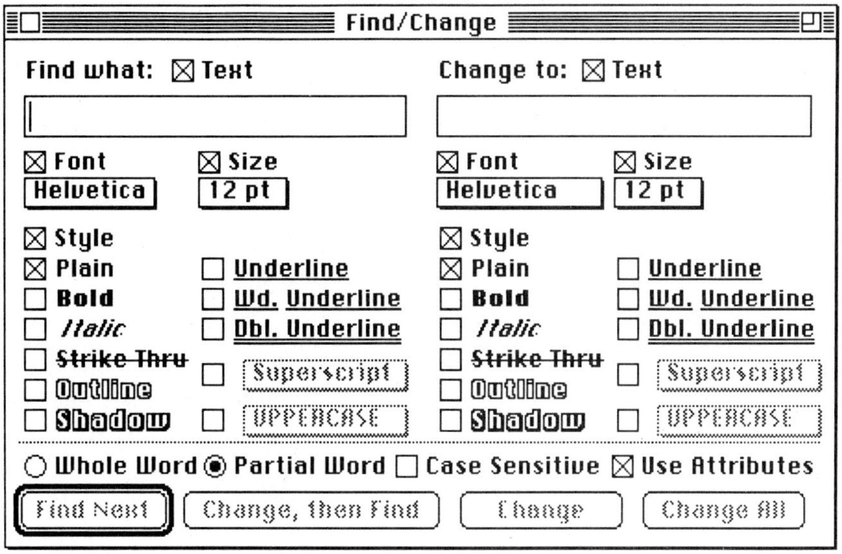

Fig. 10.20. *The expanded Find/Change dialog box.*

The next section of the dialog box involves the font and font size. This section has a total of four check boxes—two for the search item, two for the replacement item. Initially, the program expects you to specify fonts and font sizes for the search-and-replace items.

The largest section consists of the styles you can search for and use in replacements. The styles are the same as the ones in the Character dialog box, the Custom Styles dialog box, and the Style menu.

The next section contains the Whole Word, Partial Word, and Case Sensitive options. See Chapter 5 for more information about these options. The Use Attributes box is used to expand the Find/Change dialog box, as previously discussed.

Finally, the control buttons of the dialog box make up the last section. These four buttons enable you to initiate and control the search-and-replace action. To restore the Find/Change dialog box to its previous size and function, again click the box next to the Use Attributes option.

Using Attributes in General

To understand the Use Attributes option and the expanded Find/Change dialog box, try to break down your search-and-replace operation. Consider the two halves of the dialog box separately.

The Find What side determines what the program will search for. Consider these questions:

- *Are you looking for a specific word or phrase?* If you are, you must make the text section active. Type the word or phrase in the text field.

- *Are you looking for a specific font or size?* If your search is for occurrences of a particular font, such as New York, you must make the font section active. Select the font that you are searching for in the Font menu. The program displays only the fonts used in your document in the Font menu. The fonts are not displayed in their typeface (as they are in the Font menu of the menu bar). Therefore, you should know the name of the font you are searching for.

  If you are searching for the font in a particular size, make the size section active. Select the font size from the menu.

- *Are you searching for text in a particular style?* If you are looking for boldface, italic, or underlined words, make the style section active. Choose each style you are looking for. The rules for combining styles are covered in "Combining Styles," earlier in this chapter.

After you have decided the text, font, font size, and style(s) you are searching for, you should consider what—if any—change you want to make. If you do not want to make a change, leave intact the Change To section. Using this technique, you can use the Find/Change dialog box to help you locate a particular word, font use, text style, and so on.

If you want to make changes, you must ask the same questions you considered about the Find What section of the dialog box. The power of the Find/Change dialog box is tremendous. You can combine the Use Attributes options with any of the Find/Change operations discussed in Chapter 5 and perform sophisticated searches and replaces in your document.

Searching for and Replacing Fonts and Font Sizes

Using the first two sections of the expanded Find/Change dialog box, you can search for text in a particular font and size. You also can search for the font and font size, regardless of the text.

Suppose that you have used the 14-point New York font for section headings in a document, and you decide to change the headings to the 14-point London font. To accomplish this search and replace, follow these steps:

1. Select Find/Change from the Edit menu.

2. Click the Use Attributes check box to expand the Find/Change dialog box.

   You are not looking for a specific word or phrase, nor are you replacing a word or phrase. Therefore, the Find What field and the Change To field do not need the Text option.

3. Click the boxes next to Text in the Find What and Change To fields of the dialog box to remove the X's and deactivate the fields.

   The activated Font and Size defaults are fine because you are looking for a font and size. Although you are looking for New York font, you are not looking for the font in 12-point size. You must change the Size.

4. Place the mouse pointer on the Size menu.

5. Press and hold the mouse button.

6. Select the 14 pt option.

7. Place the mouse pointer on the Font menu on the Change To side of the dialog box.

8. Press and hold the mouse button. Select the London font.

9. Using the same process, select 14 pt from the Size menu on the Change To side.

   You are not concerned with the options in the style sections. In this example, you are simply searching for and replacing fonts and font sizes.

10. To deactivate the style sections, click the two boxes to the left of the two Style options.

Figure 10.21 shows the completed settings.

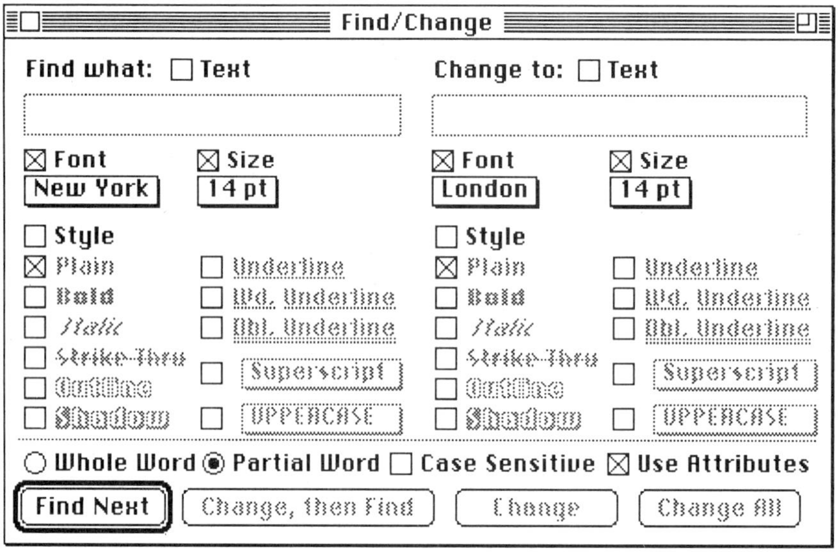

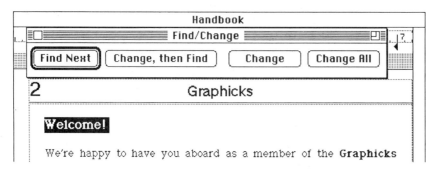

Fig. 10.21. The completed Find/Change settings.

Now you are ready to perform the search and replace:

1. Click the zoom box (the small box in the upper right corner of the dialog box). The dialog box shrinks to show only the control buttons.

2. To initiate the search, click the Find Next button.

    The first click of the Find Next button brings up a word in New York font, 14-point size (see fig. 10.22).

Fig. 10.22. The first match of the Find/Change settings.

3. To change Welcome! from New York font in 14 point to London font in 14 point, click the Change button. The font settings of Welcome! are changed (see fig. 10.23).

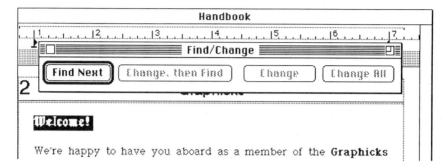

Fig. 10.23. *The font settings are changed.*

Note that the program is not looking for a word or phrase. In this example, the program is not searching for occurrences of *Welcome!* You turned off the text section of the Find What side of the dialog box, so the program is looking for styles that match the settings.

This procedure is useful when you have mixed fonts in a document and want to change a particular font in every part of your text, but you want to keep the text intact. Suppose that your document is done partly in New York font, and you have decided to change to Courier font. One method of accomplishing this change is to go through the document line by line, selecting and changing every section that is in New York font.

Using the Find/Change command, however, you can change this font quickly and easily. Follow these steps:

1. Select Find/Change from the Edit menu.

2. Click the Use Attributes check box (if an X is not already present) to expand the dialog box.

3. Deactivate all sections except the Font settings.

4. On the Find What side of the dialog box, select New York font from the Font menu.

5. On the Change To side of the dialog box, select Courier font from the Font menu.

Only the font sections of the both sides are active. The other settings are inactive, showing on-screen as grayed-out.

After the settings are made, change all text in the New York font in your document to Courier font with the following steps.

1. Click Find Next to locate the first occurrence of the font.

2. Click the Change All button.

   The program warns you that Change All operations cannot be undone by use of the Undo command. You are permitted to cancel at this point if you want. Keep in mind that you can use the Revert to Saved command to undo a Change All operation—if you save your document before attempting the operation.

3. Click OK in the warning dialog box.

The program changes every occurrence of the New York font into Courier font. This process does not affect text in any other font, nor does this process change the font size or other attributes of the text (such as boldface, underlining, and so on).

MacWrite reports the number of changes made in a dialog box. Click OK to close the dialog box. You may think that an odd number of changes is reported. Remember that the program reports the number of contiguous blocks of the same font that change, not the number of words that change.

You also can combine a font and size search with text. Suppose that you want to change each occurrence of the word *Graphicks* from New York to London font. You do not want to change the font size or the text style:

1. Select Find/Change from the Edit menu.

2. Click the Use Attributes check box (if an X is not already present) to expand the dialog box.

3. Deactivate all sections except the Font settings and the text section on the Find What side.

4. Type *Graphicks* in the text field on the Find What side.

5. Select the New York font from the Font menu on the Find What side.

6. Select the London font from the Font menu on the Change To side.

Now you can use the Find Next button to locate the next occurrence of *Graphicks* and use the Change button to change *Graphicks* from New York to London font. Note that any styling (such as boldface or underlining) remains unchanged.

Searching for and Replacing Text Styles

You can search for and replace more than fonts and font sizes—you can
locate and change text styles, such as boldface, underlining, italic, and
so on.

Suppose that your document contains the company name *Graphicks*
several times, but the name is not always in boldface. You decide that you
want to boldface every occurrence of the name. To make this change,
follow these steps:

1. Select Find/Change from the Edit menu.

2. Click the Use Attributes check box (if an X is not already present)
   to expand the dialog box.

3. Deactivate all sections except the Style settings and the text
   section on the Find What side.

4. Type *Graphicks* in the text field on the Find What side.

5. Click the Plain option in the style section on the Find What side
   of the dialog box (if an X is not already present).

6. Click the Bold option in the style section of the Change To side
   of the dialog box (see fig. 10.24).

7. Click the Find Next button.

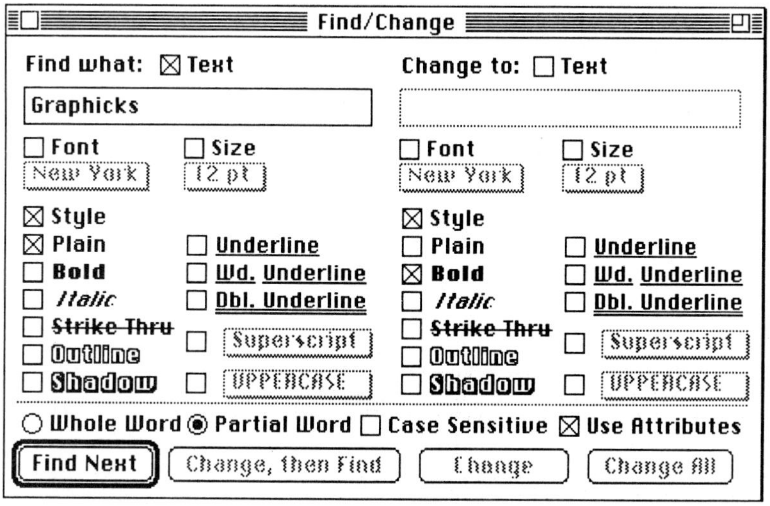

Fig. 10.24. *Changing* Graphicks *to boldface.*

The program then finds the first occurrence of *Graphicks* in plain text (not boldface, underlined, or otherwise styled).

You can use the Change, Then Find button to locate and change to boldface each occurrence of the word that is not boldfaced, viewing each before permitting the change. If you want to boldface every occurrence in one step, you can use Change All.

The Find/Change dialog box has many possible combinations. You should experiment to find out what works best for you.

Summing Up

This chapter examines the various aspects of text styles. You should now have an understanding of the functions of fonts, font sizes, and text styles.

You know how to use the Character dialog box to set the font, size, and style options. You also know how to create custom styles for your document in order to speed the process of choosing the many text options.

Finally, you have been introduced to the Find/Change dialog box's powerful Use Attributes option. This complicated option may seem intimidating at first, but you quickly appreciate its flexibility.

With fonts, font sizes, and text styles, you must do some experimenting. Many of the choices you make in these areas are subjective. The decisions often boil down to what looks good to you. Experiment with a copy of your document to find out what you can do.

Part III

Specialized Documents

Includes

Quick Start: Creating a Newsletter

Working with Columns and Graphics

Creating Tables

Quick Start: Creating a Company Mailing

Creating Form Letters

11

Quick Start:
Creating a Newsletter

You begin your exploration of the specialized documents MacWrite II can create by working with the newsletter of a fictional company. In this example, you perform the step-by-step processes of creating documents with more than one column, creating column headings, and working with graphics.

For some of these tasks, you need the Scrapbook desk accessory. If you have not installed the Scrapbook, refer to your Macintosh manuals for information on how to do so.

This chapter also shows you the MacWrite II procedure of inserting graphics files. On the MacWrite II disk, you will find a folder named Tutorial. In this folder is a file named Art. You need to copy this file to your work disk or folder that holds MacWrite II, if you have not done so already.

Choosing the Number of Columns

Before beginning any document with more than one column, decide how many columns you need. For the document in this example, you need three columns.

To define three columns in the document, follow these steps:

1. Select Page from the Format menu.

2. Press Tab four times (or double-click the Number Of field under Columns).

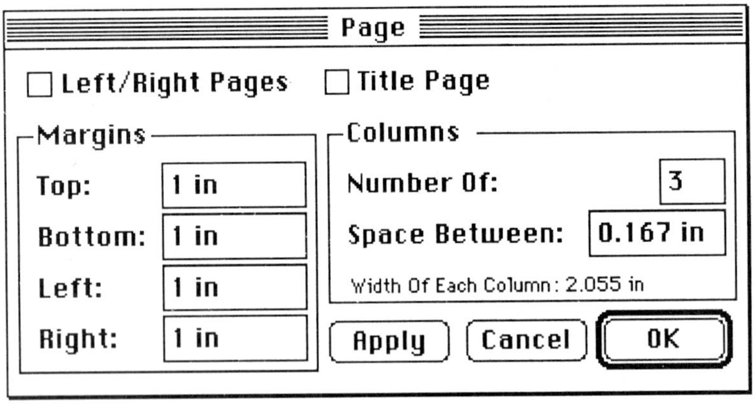

Page
Left/Right Pages
Title Page
Margins
Top: 1 in
Bottom: 1 in
Left: 1 in
Right: 1 in
Columns
Number Of: 3
Space Between: 0.167 in
Width Of Each Column: 2.055 in
Apply
Cancel
OK

Fig. 11.1. ***Defining the number of columns.***

3. Type *3* in the Number Of field (see fig. 11.1).

4. Click the OK button or press Return.

The ruler shows that the document has been divided. To see the columns, select Show Page Guides from the View menu or press Command-G (see fig. 11.2).

Document1
Page 1

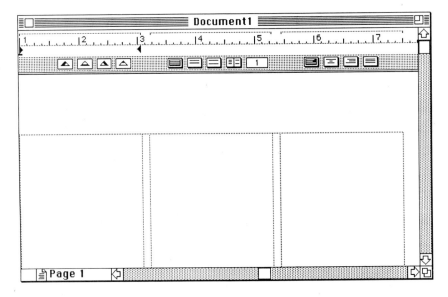

Fig. 11.2. ***When you select Show Page Guides, columns appear on-screen.***

Adding a Header

With the page properly divided, you can add text to the document. One of the first elements you add is a header. The header stretches across the columns and, in this document, contains the company name, the issue number, and the date.

Typing the Header

To create a header, follow these steps:

1. Select Insert Header from the Format menu.

2. Select centered text alignment by clicking the Center tab icon.

3. Select the New York font from the Font menu (choose another if this font is unavailable).

4. Select 24 pt from the Size menu.

5. Select Bold from the Style menu (or press Command-B).

6. Type the phrase: *The Graphicks News*.

The header automatically adjusts to accommodate the large type.

Adding the Issue Number and Date

You format the second line of the header differently from the first line. The second line contains the issue number and date. To create this part, follow these steps:

1. Press Return.

2. Select flush-left text alignment by clicking the flush-left alignment icon.

3. Select 9 pt from the Size menu (the font remains the same).

4. Select Plain Text from the Style menu (or press Command-T).

5. Type the phrase: *Volume 2; Issue 1*.

The size of the header adjusts to the smaller typeface used on this line.

6. Place a Right tab at the 7.5-inch mark on the ruler; this tab will overlap with the right indent marker (see fig. 11.3).

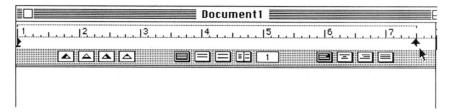

Fig. 11.3. *The rule line with a Right tab added.*

7. Press Tab.

8. Select Preferences from the Edit menu.

9. Select the date option that spells out the day and the month in full.

10. Click the OK button or press Return.

11. Select Insert Date from the Edit menu (or press Shift-Command-A).

Figure 11.4 shows the header thus far. For this figure, the page guides have been turned off. If you want to compare the appearance of your work to this figure, select Hide Page Guides from the View menu. You may want to turn the guides back on after making the comparison.

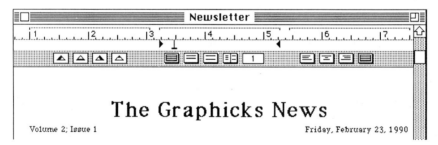

Fig. 11.4. *The newsletter header containing the title, volume and issue numbers, and date.*

Separating the Header from the Body Text

The header you created is fine. Most newsletters, however, separate the header from the text with a line. You can use two different methods to create a rule to set off the header. For the first method, you press the underscore key to draw a line across the page below the the header text. (Using the underscore is covered in the quick start in Chapter 7; you may want to refer to that chapter if you do not have a graphics package available.) The second method gives you greater flexibility. You draw a line in a graphics program and then transfer the graphic, using the Scrapbook.

As you have seen before (in Chapter 6), you can insert text by using the Scrapbook. You also can use the Scrapbook to transfer graphics into a MacWrite II document. Covering the procedures for each graphics package on the market today is not possible in this book, but the basic steps you use are outlined. Do the following:

1. Quit MacWrite II, saving the document as Newsletter.

2. Start your graphics package by double-clicking the program's icon.

   If you are using MultiFinder, which is part of the System software, you can shrink the MacWrite II window (or drag it to one side of the screen). Then start your graphics package by double-clicking the program's icon.

3. Create a new document (usually done by selecting New from the File menu).

4. Draw a 7.5-inch line from left to right.

   The thickness and other styles of the line are a matter of personal taste.

5. Select the line.

   Selection is accomplished in different ways with different graphics programs. With a program like MacDraw II, you select the line by clicking it once. Many paint programs also provide a selection tool.

6. Select Copy from the Edit menu.

7. Select Scrapbook from the Apple menu.

8. Select Paste from the Edit menu.

You now need to switch back to MacWrite II. If you are using MultiFinder, select MacWrite II from the Apple menu. If you are not using MultiFinder, follow these steps:

1. Quit the graphics package.

   The program asks whether you want to save the document containing the line. This step is unnecessary because you have stored the line in the Scrapbook.

2. Double-click the document name, Newsletter.

You now return to the point where you left off. To insert the line you saved in the Scrapbook, use the following steps:

1. Select the Scrapbook from the Apple menu.

2. Select Copy from the Edit menu.

3. Close the Scrapbook by clicking the close box, which is in the upper left corner of the screen.

4. Press Return.

   This step places the cursor on the line below the header text, the point where the graphic rule will be inserted.

5. Select Paste from the Edit menu.

The line appears below the header text (see fig. 11.5).

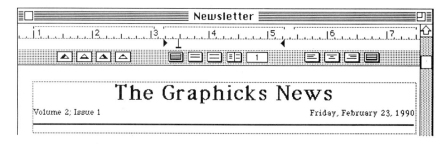

Fig. 11.5. *The rule separating the header from the body text.*

Creating a Column Heading

To begin the newsletter's first story, you want to make a heading for the column. The heading typeface is larger than the text typeface in order to draw attention to the story.

Create the column heading with the following steps:

1. Press Command-Return.

   This step moves the cursor to the start of the first column, which is the cursor's last position before the header was created.

2. Select the New York font from the Font menu.

3. Select 14 pt from the Size menu.

4. Select Bold from the Style menu (or press Command-B).

5. Type the column heading: *New Office Word Processor Chosen.*

   The heading wraps automatically to fit in the column (see fig. 11.6).

6. Press Return to move the cursor to the next line.

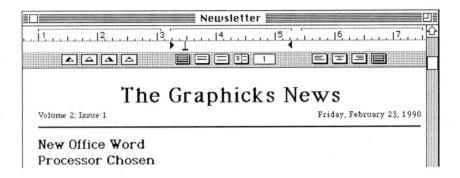

Fig. 11.6. The column heading fits in the established column width.

Adding Newsletter Text

At this point you are ready to add the text of the newsletter's first story. Before typing the text, you set the text attributes. These settings include the alignment, fonts, font sizes, and text style.

Setting the Text Formatting

Before typing the text, you need to set the text alignment, the indent marks, and the text spacing. Use the following steps:

1. Click the justified text alignment icon.

2. Drag the first-line indent mark to the 1.25-inch mark on the ruler.

As shown in figure 11.7, the text alignment is now set.

Fig. 11.7. *The ruler settings showing text alignment.*

Setting the Text Attributes

After you set the text alignment, you set the attributes that determine the appearance of the text. These settings include the font, font size, and style. Follow these steps:

1. Select New York font from the Font menu (unless a check mark is next to the font indicating that it is already selected).

2. Select 12 pt from the Size menu.

3. Select Plain Text from the Style menu (or press Command-T).

Typing the Newsletter Text

To type the text of the first newsletter story, type the following:

We have chosen MacWrite II as the word processor for office use here at Graphicks. After a long search for a program to suit our needs, we settled on MacWrite II because it has the most power and versatility and requires the least amount of time for the staff to learn.

MacWrite II has many impressive features that will delight all our word processor users.

To acquaint the office staff with the new program, we will hold a seminar Monday afternoon from 2 p.m. to 5 p.m. Topics to be covered include the program's working environment, basic document design, and document editing. We will hold a second seminar Tuesday morning from 9 a.m. to 12 noon to cover more advanced editing and page layout capabilities.

Conversion to the new program begins in two weeks. We will discuss conversion procedures at the first seminar.

Because MacWrite II is so easy to use, we don't anticipate any problems switching to it.

As you type, the program wraps the text to fit within the columns (see fig. 11.8).

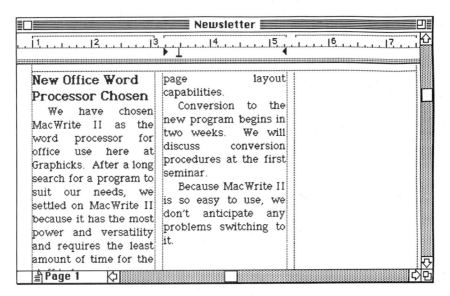

Fig. 11.8. *The newsletter text fits within the column width.*

In the middle of the last sentence in the next to the last paragraph (which begins *We will hold a second seminar Tuesday morning . . .*), the program automatically moves the cursor to the next column because the first column doesn't have enough room for the entire story.

Hyphenating Newsletter Text

Many times when you work with multiple-column documents and justified text—as in this example—you find that the program leaves extra spaces in the text. You can see an example of this spacing at the top of the second column in the sentence that ends . . . *page layout capabilities*(again see fig. 11.8).

One way you can alleviate this problem is by hyphenating the text. To hyphenate, select Auto Hyphenate from the Spelling menu. The program breaks words as needed to reduce the extra spaces (see fig. 11.9).

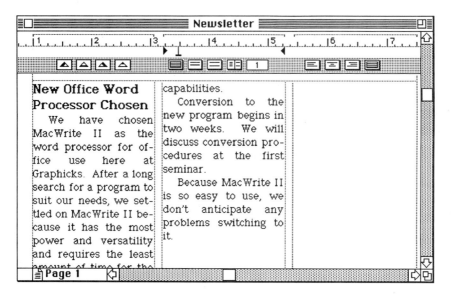

Fig. 11.9. *Auto Hyphenate reduces extra spaces caused by justification.*

Adding a Graphic

Newsletters probably use more graphics than any other kind of document. A graphic, which can be a photograph, a chart, or other illustration, adds considerably to the attractive appearance of a newsletter story.

To create a graphic for the newsletter article, do the following steps:

1. Press Return twice to add a blank line after the last paragraph of the MacWrite II story.

2. Move the first-line indent mark to the same position as the left indent mark (see fig. 11.10).

3. Select 14 pt from the Size menu.

4. Select Bold from the Style menu (or press Command-B).

5. Type the heading: *Building Complete*.

6. Press Return.

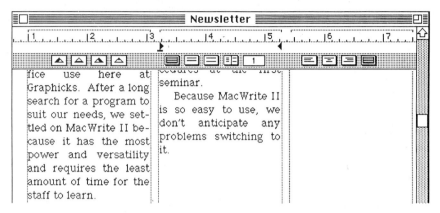

Fig. 11.10. The ruler showing the new first-line indent setting.

Inserting a Graphic

The cursor is now at the correct position for the story's graphic to be added to the document. To insert the graphic, follow these steps:

1. Select Insert File from the File menu (or press Shift-Command-I).

2. Select the file Art in the Tutorial folder by clicking the file name.

3. Click the Open button once (or press Return).

The program inserts the graphic at the cursor position (see fig. 11.11).

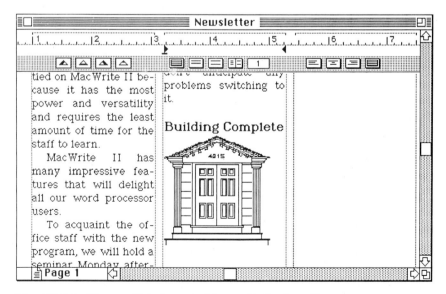

Fig. 11.11. The graphic inserted beneath the heading.

Positioning the Graphic

The graphic is not quite the same width as the column and is not centered. You correct this problem by using a Center tab. Do the following:

1. Click the graphic once.

   A box appears around the graphic indicating that it is ready for editing (see fig. 11.12).

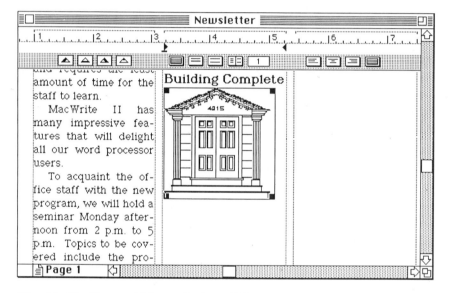

Fig. 11.12. The graphic ready for editing.

2. Click the Center tab icon.

This step moves the graphic to the center of the column. The difference is slight but helps the overall appearance of the newsletter.

Adding a Caption

Many times a caption accompanies a graphic. A caption is a short, identifying phrase that usually goes immediately below the graphic. To add a caption to the graphic, follow these steps:

1. Press Return.

   This step places the cursor below the graphic. The Center tab is still in effect.

2. Select New York font from the Font menu.

3. Select 9 pt from the Size menu.

4. Select Plain Text from the Style menu (or press Command-T).

5. Type the caption: *The New Building Entrance*.

6. Press Return.

Figure 11.13 shows the graphic with the caption added.

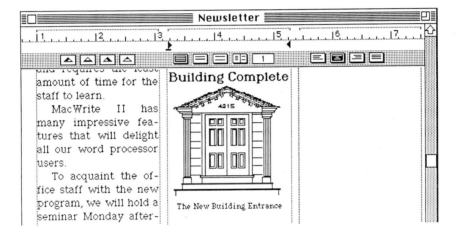

Fig. 11.13. The caption directly below the graphic.

Editing the Newsletter

Before editing the newsletter, finish writing the text. Use the following steps to format the text:

1. Click once anywhere in the first column of text except in the column heading.

2. Select Copy Ruler from the Format menu (or press Shift-Command-C).

3. Click once below the graphic's caption to return the cursor to its last position.

4. Select Apply Ruler from the Format menu (or press Shift-Command-V).

5. Select 12 pt from the Size menu.

The New York font is still selected and does not need to be selected again. Type the following text:

> The new entrance to the Graphick building is complete. This should be a relief to everyone who has dodged the construction on their way into the building.

> We think the wait has been worth it. The new entrance greatly enhances the building's appearance.

Moving the Graphic

After finishing the story about the building entrance completion, suppose that you decide that the graphic should appear in the middle of the story rather than at the beginning. You move the graphic by doing the following:

1. Click the graphic.

2. Select Cut from the Edit menu (or press Command-X).

3. Click at the end of the story's first paragraph.

4. Press Return.

5. Select Paste from the Edit menu (or press Command-V).

The graphic is inserted in the new position (see fig. 11.14). The graphic is not centered in its new location because when you pressed Return (step 4), you created a new paragraph. This paragraph took on the text formatting of the preceding paragraph, including flush-left text alignment. You also need to move the graphic's caption to the new location.

To center the graphic in its new position, use the following steps:

1. Move the first line indent mark as far left as it will move.

2. Click the center text-alignment icon.

Finally, you need to move the figure caption. Do so with the following steps:

1. Place the cursor anywhere in the caption.

2. Click the mouse button three times quickly (triple-click) to select the caption line.

3. Select Cut from the Edit menu (or press Command-X).

4. Move the mouse pointer to the immediate right of the graphic.

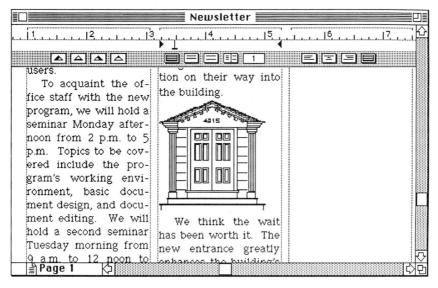

Fig. 11.14. *The graphic in its new position.*

5. Click the mouse button once, placing the cursor to the graphic's right.

6. Select Paste from the Edit menu (or press Command-V).

A blank line appears to have been added below the caption. Eliminate this line by pressing the Backspace key once.

Moving a Column

After you finish typing the stories of the newsletter, you decide that the building story should precede the word processor story. To reverse the stories' positions, do the following:

1. Place the mouse pointer to the immediate left of the first story's column heading (to the left of the words *New Office...*).

2. Drag the mouse to the right and down slightly to select the last word of the story (see fig. 11.15).

   You do not need to move through and select the entire first column before selecting the second column. When you move from the first column into the second, the program understands that you want the remainder of the first column selected.

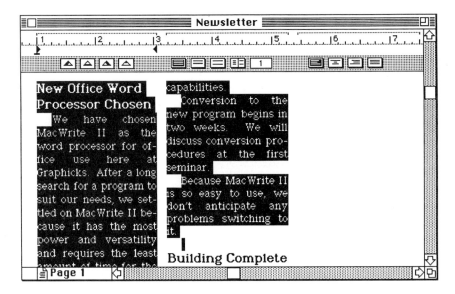

Fig. 11.15. *Selecting an entire story.*

3. Select Cut from the Edit menu (or press Command-X).

    The cut text is stored in the Clipboard, and the building story automatically moves to take the place of the word processor story.

4. Place the mouse pointer at the end of the last word of the building story.

5. Click once to place the cursor.

6. Press Return twice.

7. Select Paste from the Edit menu (or press Command-V).

When the story fills the column, the text starts at the top of the next column and fills it. The program automatically flows the text through the columns as you type or edit. Figure 11.16 shows the completed move.

Saving and Printing the Newsletter

Save the newsletter on your disk by selecting the Save command from the File menu. If you have never saved the document, the program prompts you for a name. Type *Newsletter* and press Return.

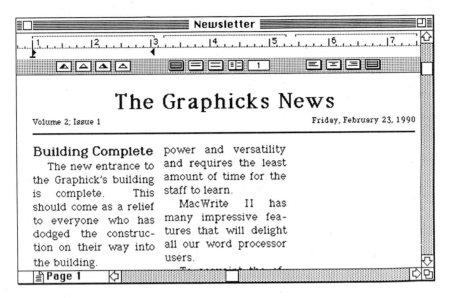

Fig. 11.16. *The newsletter after the stories have been moved.*

To print the newsletter, do the following:

1. Select Print from the File menu.

2. Click the OK button in the dialog box that appears.

When the program finishes printing, you can quit MacWrite II by selecting Quit from the File menu.

Summing Up

This chapter introduces you to documents that have more than one column and contain graphics. You have seen step-by-step how to create a newsletter, set up columns, create a heading, and enter text. You also have learned how to edit text in a multicolumn document. You have used the automatic hyphenation feature to reduce the extra space introduced by justified text.

You also have seen how to add a graphic to a document and how to move graphics within a document. Finally, you have saved and printed the sample newsletter document.

The following chapter deals with columns and graphics in greater detail.

12

Working with Columns and Graphics

Columns and graphics may seem unrelated, but they frequently are used together. Creators of documents with more than one column (often called newsletter-type documents) also tend to use graphics.

In this chapter, you learn how to divide a document into columns. Calculating column width, setting spacing between columns, and altering column settings are covered. Inserting graphics into a document also is discussed in this chapter. Other topics include inserting graphics from the Clipboard, Scrapbook, or another file, and sizing and cropping graphics.

Working with Columns

MacWrite II is capable of defining documents with up to 10 columns of equal width. The width of the columns depends on the size of the paper, the orientation of the page, and the amount of space you request between columns. The columns are *snaking*: that is, text and graphics flow from the bottom of a column to the top of the next column to the right until the page is filled.

The standard editing techniques apply to multiple-column documents. MacWrite II regards regular documents as single-column documents, so you have only a few new formatting techniques to learn.

Column Layout

Before beginning a document with multiple columns, you must decide the number of columns and the amount of space between columns. The answers to these questions depend on the kind of document you are creating and the size of the printer paper.

MacWrite columns are always of equal width—the program divides the page equally among them. You cannot have one column with a width of one inch and another with a width of six inches, for example.

Calculating Column Width

You may find that sketching your proposed page layout on a piece of paper helps. In the sketch, you can see the page as a whole and decide what settings are best.

When dividing a page into columns, you first must consider the width of the page itself. If you are working with a page that is 8.5 inches wide, dividing the page into a great many columns makes the columns too narrow. Dividing the page into 10 columns, for example, results in columns that are .7 inch wide.

You also must consider the page margins. Remember that the left and right margins reduce the space available for text and graphics (see fig. 12.1).

Fig. 12.1. *Page margins reducing available space.*

You can reduce the width of the margins and gain additional space for columns. You should keep in mind, however, that some printers cannot print close to the edges of pages. Check your printer manual to determine precisely how small the page margins can be.

You also must keep in mind the amount of space needed to separate the columns. You do not want the columns to touch. The program automatically assigns one-sixth inch between columns, but you can adjust this to as little as one-twenty-fourth inch or as much as four inches.

Because the number of columns, the space between columns, and the page margins can be adjusted at any time, you do not need to finish designing your page before creating it. You can correct mistakes. You can develop a rough design, create the document, and then alter the different factors affecting columns to achieve the appearance you want.

Setting the Number of Columns and Column Spacing

You make and change column settings in the Page dialog box. To set the number of columns in a document and the space between columns, follow these steps:

1. Select Page from the Format menu.

2. Press Tab until the cursor reaches the Number Of field in the Page dialog box.

3. Type the number of columns desired.

4. Press Tab.

5. Type the width you want between columns.

6. Click the OK button.

The program calculates and displays the width of each column as you type the values for the left and right margins, the number of columns, and the space between columns (see fig. 12.2). Using this method, you can experiment with the settings by repeating steps 2 through 5. After you have the settings you want, click the OK button to confirm the settings.

The number of columns must be a whole number from 1 to 10. If you enter an unacceptable number in the Number Of field, the program displays a dialog box notifying you of the error (see fig. 12.3). In this case, click OK in the warning dialog box and enter the correct number of columns.

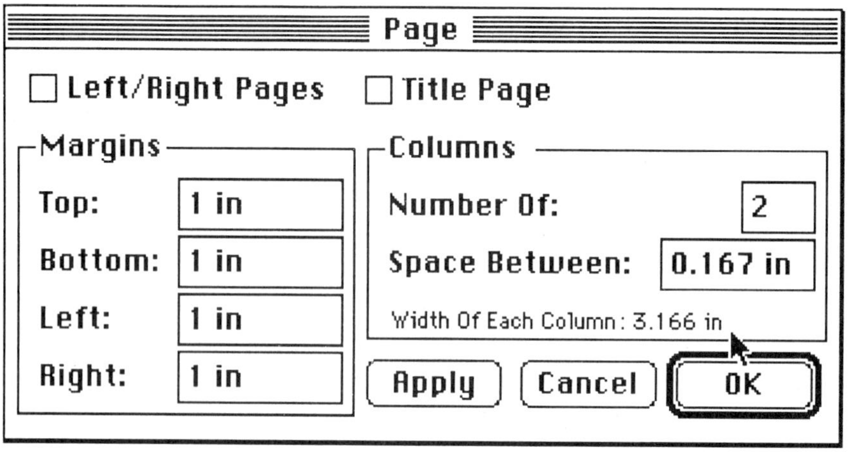

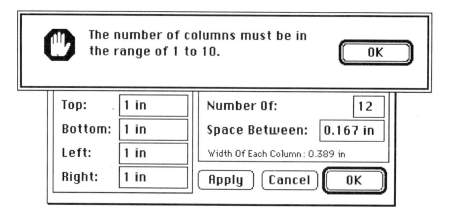

Fig. 12.2. *The Page dialog box, showing the width of each column.*

Fig. 12.3. *A warning of an invalid number of columns.*

A similar warning appears if you attempt to enter a number smaller than 0.042 (1/24th inch) or greater than 4 in the Space Between field. The upper limit of space between columns may be less than 4 inches, however, depending on the page size, page margins, and number of columns. You can tell that you have gone outside the limits when three asterisks (***) appear in the Width Of Each Column field (see fig. 12.4).

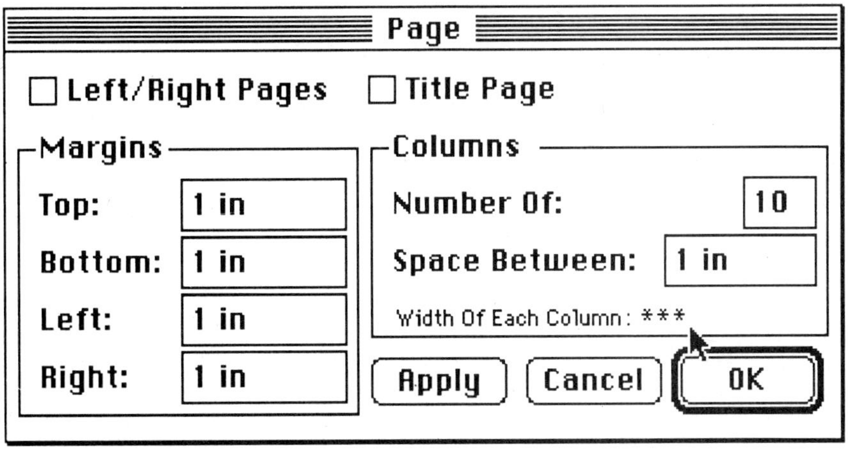

```
┌─────────────────────────────────────────────────────────┐
│ ═══════════════════════  Page  ═══════════════════════  │
│  ☐ Left/Right Pages     ☐ Title Page                    │
│  ┌Margins──────────────  ┌Columns ──────────────────    │
│   Top:      [ 1 in  ]     Number Of:          [  10 ]    │
│   Bottom:   [ 1 in  ]     Space Between:  [ 1 in  ]      │
│   Left:     [ 1 in  ]     Width Of Each Column : ***     │
│   Right:    [ 1 in  ]    ( Apply ) ( Cancel ) (( OK ))   │
└─────────────────────────────────────────────────────────┘
```

Fig. 12.4. *The warning that you have exceeded the Space Between limit.*

Another limit to consider is that the column width may not be less than one-quarter inch. If the settings in the Page dialog box result in a column width less than this amount, the program warns you with the dialog box shown in figure 12.5.

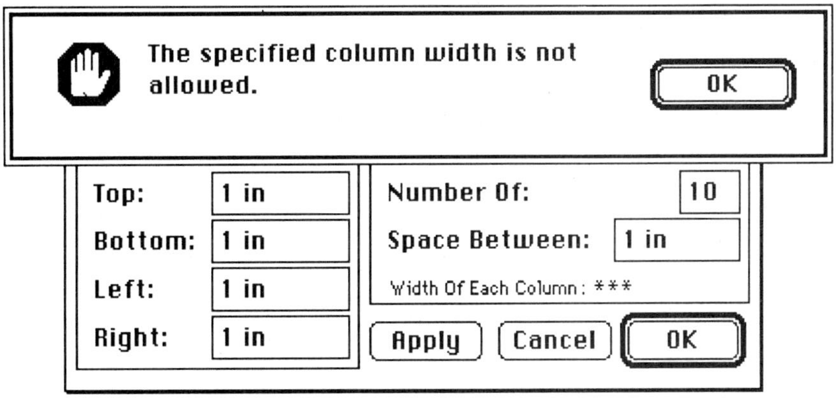

```
┌─────────────────────────────────────────────────────────┐
│  ✋     The specified column width is not                │
│         allowed.                          ( OK )         │
└─────────────────────────────────────────────────────────┘
    Top:      [ 1 in  ]     Number Of:          [  10 ]
    Bottom:   [ 1 in  ]     Space Between:  [ 1 in  ]
    Left:     [ 1 in  ]     Width Of Each Column : ***
    Right:    [ 1 in  ]    ( Apply ) ( Cancel ) (( OK ))
```

Fig. 12.5. *Warning that you have set an invalid column width.*

Changing Column Settings

Column settings are not written in stone. After creating a document, you can make changes by following the same steps you used to make the settings.

The same restrictions apply. After you click the OK button in the Page dialog box, the program reformats the document to conform to the new settings.

If you want to experiment with the number of columns or the spacing between columns, use the Apply button before you click OK. The Apply button reformats the document but leaves the Page dialog box open. Then you can return the document to its previous formatting by clicking the Cancel button, or you can make more changes and click Apply again to see their effect. If you want to confirm the new settings, click the OK button.

Column Formatting

MacWrite II "sees" little difference between a document with one column and a document with many columns. All the formatting and editing techniques discussed in this book apply equally to multiple-column documents. Besides the column settings of the Page dialog box, you need be concerned with only one command: the Insert Column Break command.

A column break is similar to a page break (discussed in Chapter 2). Page breaks separate one page from another; *column breaks* separate one column from another.

Inserting Column Breaks

When a column has been filled with text or graphics, the program normally moves to the column to the right and continues until the entire page is filled. You use the Insert Column Break command to make the program move to the next column before a column is completely filled with text or graphics.

You often use the Insert Column Break command when the normal divisions leave small amounts of text and graphics in one column and put the main body of the article in another column. Consider figure 12.6, a two-column newsletter that has the first four lines of a story in the first column and the bulk of the story in the second column.

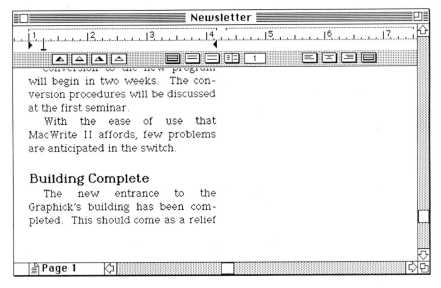

Fig. 12.6. *An unacceptable column break.*

To move the first lines of the story to the next column with the rest of the story, insert a column break before the beginning of the story. Follow these steps:

1. Place the mouse pointer immediately to the left of the first word to be moved: *Building.*

2. Press the mouse button.

3. Select Insert Column Break from the Format menu.

The program forces the text following the insertion point into the next column.

Removing Column Breaks

A column break is an invisible formatting character (discussed in Chapter 3). If you know where a column break is, removing it is simply a matter of backspacing over it.

Normally, however, a column break cannot be seen. You can use one of two methods to locate and remove a column break: show the invisible editing characters or use the Find/Change command.

To use the first method, follow these steps:

1. Select Show Invisibles from the View menu.

   The column break becomes visible. It looks like an arrow pointing down (see fig. 12.7).

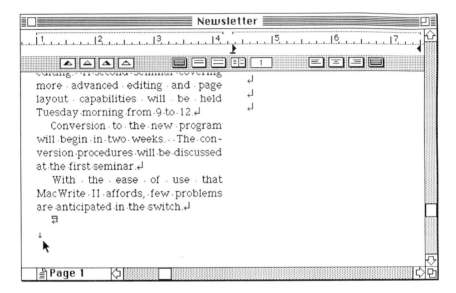

Fig. 12.7. The column break character.

2. Place the mouse pointer on the column break character.

3. Double-click the mouse button to select the character.

4. Press the Backspace key (Delete on some keyboards). The column break character is deleted.

5. Select Hide Invisibles from the View menu.

The second method involves using the Find/Change command to find invisibles. To use this method, follow these steps:

1. Select Find/Change from the Edit menu.

2. Press Command-Enter.

   The symbol \c appears in the Find What field (see fig. 12.8).

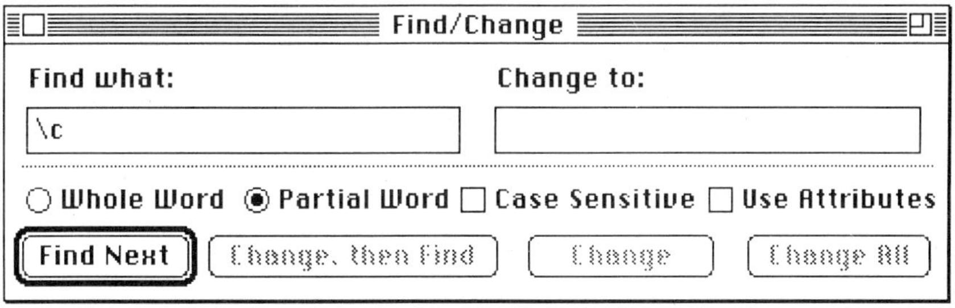

Fig. 12.8. *Searching for a column break character.*

3. Click the Find Next button.

    The program locates the first column break inserted with the Insert Column Break command. If this column break is not the break you want to delete, click Find Next to find the next column break character.

4. Click the Change button.

Because nothing has been entered in the Change To field, the program deletes the located column break character.

Adding Graphics to Your Document

Columns are one way you can dress up the appearance of your document. Graphics are another way. You can bring graphics into a MacWrite II document from a variety of sources, just as you bring in text (discussed in Chapter 6). You can bring a graphic in from the Clipboard, the Scrapbook, or another file—even if the graphic is a format other than MacWrite II.

Using the Clipboard or Scrapbook translates the graphic into a form that MacWrite II recognizes and accepts. To insert a graphic from a file of another format requires that the correct translator file be installed. (Translator files permit the program to open and read files created by other software packages. These files are discussed both in Chapter 6 and in Appendix A). For graphic files, Claris has provided translator files for MacPaint and the standard PICT format. Other translator files may be available through DataViz, as discussed in Appendix A. PICT is by far the most common graphic format on the Macintosh. Most graphics programs can work with the PICT format.

After you import the graphic, MacWrite II also offers the capability to crop and resize a graphic. Cropping enables you to cut away unneeded parts of the graphic. Resizing is simply changing the size of a graphic.

Inserting Graphics

You can insert a graphic into MacWrite II by using one of three methods.

- *The Clipboard.* Users operating under MultiFinder (part of the Macintosh System software) may find this approach most convenient.

- *The Scrapbook.* The Scrapbook provides an easy way to insert graphics, and you can store frequently used graphics in the Scrapbook, keeping them available at any time.

- *The Insert File command.* This method requires that the appropriate file translator be installed (see Appendix A).

Inserting a Graphic by Using the Clipboard

Users of MultiFinder find the Clipboard method of transferring graphics exceptionally convenient. You also can use the Clipboard method under Finder, but Finder requires a few more steps than MultiFinder. If you are uncertain about the use of MultiFinder, check the manuals provided with your computer.

After creating a graphic in your graphics program, you must select that graphic to transfer it. All graphics programs provide some sort of selection tool for this procedure. To transfer the graphic to your MacWrite document, work through the following procedures.

Beginning in the graphics package, follow these steps:

1. Select the graphic.

2. Choose Copy from the Edit menu (or press Command-C).

3. Change to the MacWrite II application.

   Note that step 3 varies according to whether you are using Finder or MultiFinder. If you are using the Finder, step 3 is done as follows:

   A. Quit the graphics package.

   B. Start MacWrite II by double-clicking the program's icon.

   C. Open the file into which the graphic is to be inserted.

   If you are using MultiFinder, the step is

   Select MacWrite II from the Apple menu.

   or

   Locate the MacWrite II icon and double-click it.

If you need further information on Finder or MultiFinder, check the manuals that accompanied your Macintosh computer.

While inside MacWrite II (and the document receiving the graphic), follow these steps:

1. Position the cursor at the location where the graphic is to be inserted.

2. Choose Paste from the Edit menu (or press Command-V).

After you choose Paste (or press Command-V), the graphic is inserted into your document. You may want to use this procedure, for example, to paste a logo created in a graphics package into the header of your document, as in figure 12.9. In this case, you must use the Insert Header command (or position the cursor in an existing header) before executing the Paste command.

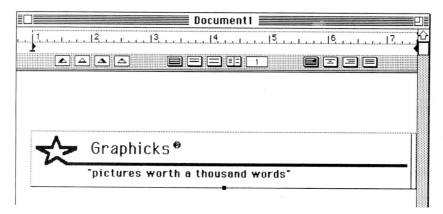

Fig. 12.9. *A sample logo brought into MacWrite from a graphics program.*

Keep in mind the size of the target area—that is, the document into which you want to place the graphic. If you create an eight-inch graphic and attempt to paste it into a three-inch column, the graphic will shrink when transferred. This shrinking sometimes occurs with undesirable results, as in figure 12.10.

Note that—as with any use of the Clipboard—the graphic is available for pasting only until the next Copy or Cut operation is performed.

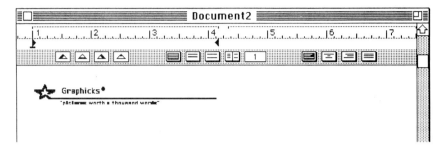

Fig. 12.10. The graphic reduced to fit a column.

Inserting a Graphic by Using the Scrapbook

Using the Scrapbook to transfer graphics is similar to using the Clipboard. You must perform a few extra steps to save the graphic to disk. The Scrapbook is a good place to store frequently used graphics because the Scrapbook contents are stored on disk and remain until you remove them.

To store a graphic in the Scrapbook, follow these steps:

1. Select the graphic.

2. Choose Copy from the Edit menu.

3. Select the Scrapbook from the Apple menu.

4. Select Paste from the Edit menu.

The graphic then appears in the Scrapbook (see fig. 12.11).

After the graphic is stored in the Scrapbook, you can recall it at any time with MacWrite II. The Scrapbook can hold more than one graphic. In figure 12.11, you see the scroll bar below the Scrapbook's window. You can scroll through the graphics stored in the Scrapbook by use of the arrows or the scroll box.

To transfer the graphic from the Scrapbook to MacWrite II, do the following:

1. Open the document into which the graphic is to be transferred.

2. Position the cursor at the point where the graphic is to be inserted.

3. Select the Scrapbook from the Apple menu.

4. Scroll until the desired graphic appears in the Scrapbook window.

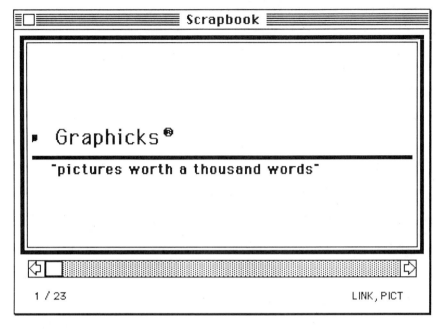

Fig. 12.11. The graphic pasted to the Scrapbook.

5. Select Copy from the Edit menu.

6. Click the close box of the Scrapbook.

7. Choose Paste from the Edit menu.

The graphic is inserted at the current cursor position.

The Scrapbook is part of the Macintosh System software. For more information, consult the manuals that came with your Macintosh.

Inserting a Graphic from a File

MacWrite II provides the capability to insert an entire file into the current document. With the Insert File command, you can insert at any location in your document a single graphic or set of graphics stored in a file.

You can insert any file format for which you have a translator file installed (see Chapter 6 and Appendix A). For example, if you have created a graphic in a program that stores data in the PICT format, you can insert the file created by this program into a MacWrite II document by using the Insert File command if you have installed the PICT translator file.

To insert a file containing a graphic, use the following steps:

1. Open the file into which the graphic is to be inserted.

2. Position the cursor at the point where the graphic is to be inserted.

3. Select Insert File from the File menu.

4. Select the file by clicking its name.

5. Click the Open button.

The graphics file is inserted at the current cursor position.

Editing Graphics

Many times you need to adjust the size or position of a graphic after inserting it into a document. Two ways exist for adjusting the size of a graphic.

Cropping is the first way of changing the size of a graphic. Cropping is similar to cutting off pieces of the graphic to save space or to emphasize part of the picture.

The other way is to resize the graphic. As you resize the graphic, you can have the program maintain the proportional size of the graphic, or MacWrite can stretch or shrink the graphic to fit the available space.

You also can cut and paste the graphic to move it to another part of the document or to another document.

Cropping a Graphic

Cropping is like taking a pair of scissors and cutting off pieces of a graphic. You may need to crop if the graphic has excess space or parts you do not need.

To crop a graphic, do the following:

1. Click the graphic. Four handles and a dotted line appear around the graphic (see fig. 12.12).

2. Place the mouse pointer on one of the four handles.

   The handle you use depends on where you want to cut the graphic. In figure 12.12, a picture of a building is shown. If you want to cut off the lower part of the building's stairs, place the mouse pointer on one of the two lower handles.

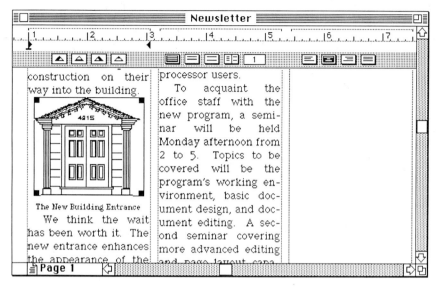

Fig. 12.12. *Displaying the graphic's editing handles.*

3. Press and hold the Option key, and press and hold the mouse button.

4. Move the pointer until the desired part of the graphic is hidden.

5. Release the Option key and the mouse button.

Figure 12.13 shows how the building graphic appears after the lower quarter inch has been cropped, hiding the stairs.

The part of the graphic that is cropped is not discarded. You can, at any time, restore the hidden part by following the same steps you used to crop the graphic. Think of the square that surrounds a graphic as a window. Cropping the graphic actually adjusts the size of the window through which the graphic is viewed. Cropping does not change the graphic itself.

Resizing a Graphic

Using the same handles that are used to crop a graphic, you can change the size of the graphic. In this case, the graphic is altered. To change the size of a graphic, do the following:

1. Click the graphic.

2. Place the mouse pointer on one of the four handles.

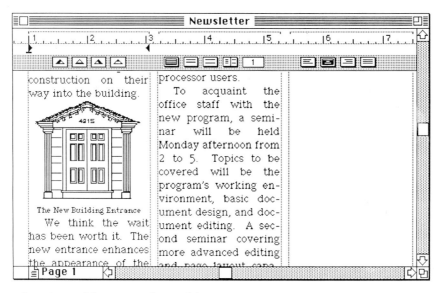

Fig. 12.13. The cropped graphic.

3. Press and hold the mouse button.

4. Move the pointer until the graphic is sized correctly.

5. Release the mouse button.

Figure 12.14 shows the graphic of a building before and after it has been resized.

Not all graphics resize well. Some graphics are distorted in an unappealing way. You should print the page on which you are working in order to determine whether the resizing produces a desirable image. Resizing should be done before performing any other operations because the Undo Picture Change command remains available until another edit operation has been performed. The Undo Picture Change in the Edit menu restores the graphic to its original size.

To increase or decrease a graphic's size while maintaining its proportion (the relative sizes of different parts of the graphic), press and hold the Shift key as you drag the mouse. Maintaining proportion enables you to increase or decrease the graphic's size without distorting the relative sizes or positions of different parts of the graphic. This feature is similar to using the enlarge or reduce controls of copy machines.

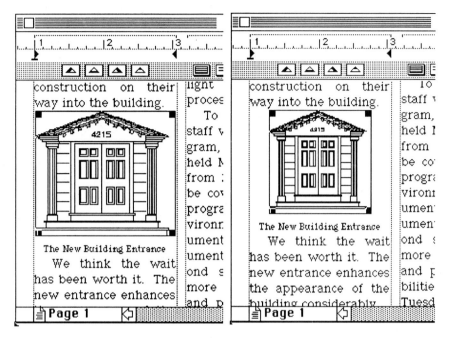

Fig. 12.14. *Resizing a graphic.*

In addition to using the mouse to resize a graphic, you can use the Scale Picture command, available in the Format menu. This command displays a dialog box that permits you to enter numerically the size to which you want the graphic to be scaled (see fig. 12.15).

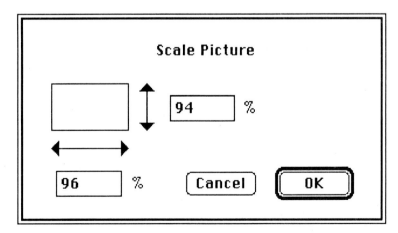

Fig. 12.15. *The Scale Picture dialog box.*

To use the dialog box, first click the graphic in order to select it. Then choose Scale Picture from the Format menu. The Scale Picture dialog box has two fields. The vertical size field has a vertical arrow next to it. Type the percentage change for the vertical height in this field. Press Tab to move the cursor to the horizontal height field, which is marked with a horizontal arrow. Then type the percentage change you want in the width of the graphic.

You can enter a number between 8 and 470 in the vertical height field and between 7 and 105 in the horizontal width field. When you click the OK button (or press Return), the graphic is resized. Click Cancel if you change your mind about resizing the graphic.

Remember that the number you are entering is a percentage. That is, if you want to double the vertical height of a graphic, enter *200* in the vertical height field.

Moving a Graphic

MacWrite II treats a graphic as if it were a single character. Therefore, you can use the Cut and Paste commands to move a graphic from one part of your document to another. To do so, use the following steps:

1. Click the graphic to select it.

2. Select Cut from the Edit menu.

3. Move the cursor to the desired location.

4. Select Paste from the Edit menu.

To duplicate a graphic, for step 2 select Copy from the Edit menu. The graphic is copied but not removed from its original position. When you then select Paste, a duplicate of the graphic is placed at the current cursor position.

Removing a Graphic

Because MacWrite II treats a graphic as if it were a single character, you can remove a graphic by backspacing. Follow these steps:

1. Place the mouse pointer at a position immediately following the graphic.

2. Press the mouse button.

3. Press the Backspace key (Delete on some keyboards).

You also can use the Clear command of the Edit menu to remove a graphic. Use the following steps:

1. Click the graphic to select it.

2. Select Clear from the Edit menu.

Immediately after a graphic has been deleted, the Undo command can restore it.

Hiding Graphics

At times, a large number of graphics may slow the scrolling of a document. When scrolling reveals pictures, the program must redraw them on the screen. If you are working solely with text and want to move quickly through a document, you can hide the graphics.

To hide graphics, choose the Hide Pictures command from the View menu. This command temporarily hides the graphics, leaving empty boxes to indicate the graphics' positions (see fig. 12.16).

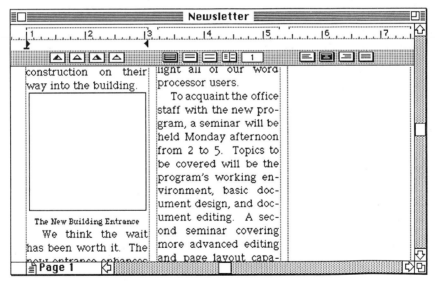

Fig. 12.16. The outline of a hidden graphic.

The graphics are not gone, merely hidden. To restore them to view, select Show Pictures from the View menu.

Summing Up

This chapter covers the column and graphics capabilities of the MacWrite II program. You have seen how you can divide a page into as many as ten columns. Calculating column width, layout, and spacing has been explored. You also have seen how to insert and remove column breaks to alter the formatting of column text and graphics.

Inserting graphics has been covered. You saw how to insert graphics from the Clipboard, how to store graphics in and insert graphics from the Scrapbook, and how to bring graphics stored in files into MacWrite II documents. You also now should understand how to resize and crop a graphic. Finally, temporarily hiding graphics in order to speed scrolling has been discussed.

13

Creating Tables

Word processor users must deal with several kinds of tables. Tables of numbers such as sales figures, tables of characters such as the ones used in this book to list MacWrite II special characters, and tables of contents are examples of the kinds of tables you may need to create.

MacWrite II does not have formal table commands, but the program allows you to create and edit tables more easily than you can with a typewriter. This chapter discusses the different features you can use to make tables.

Creating Table Headings

The table heading is the first element you create. How you create the heading depends on the type of table and the appearance you want.

Figure 13.1 shows a centered, boldfaced table heading. To create this table heading, open a new document, and work through the following steps:

1. Select the text alignment by clicking the Center tab alignment icon.

2. Select New York from the Font menu.

3. Select Bold from the Style menu.

4. Type the table heading:

    Commands for Entering Special Characters

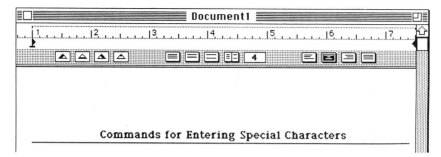

Fig. 13.1. A centered, boldfaced table heading.

If you prefer a flush-left heading, click the flush-left icon in step 1. The heading then will be against the left margin.

The type size of the table is another element you need to consider. If you prefer the table heading to be larger type than the type in the table's contents, select the font size after you select the font (see Chapter 10 for information about font sizes). Because 12-point type is the standard size used for text, you might use a 14-point type size for the heading. This slightly larger size enhances the heading's appearance without overwhelming the table's contents.

You create the line that separates the heading from the table by using the underscore key, and you move the line close to the heading with a line spacing trick. Do the following steps:

1. Press Return to start a new line.

2. Press and hold the Shift key and then press and hold the underscore key (to the right of the 0 key on every standard computer keyboard—not on the numeric keypad).

3. When the line crosses the entire page, release the Shift and underscore keys.

4. Select the heading text and the line.

5. Select Paragraph from the Format menu.

6. Use the Line Spacing pop-up menu to select the Points line spacing measure (see fig. 13.2). This option controls the space between lines.

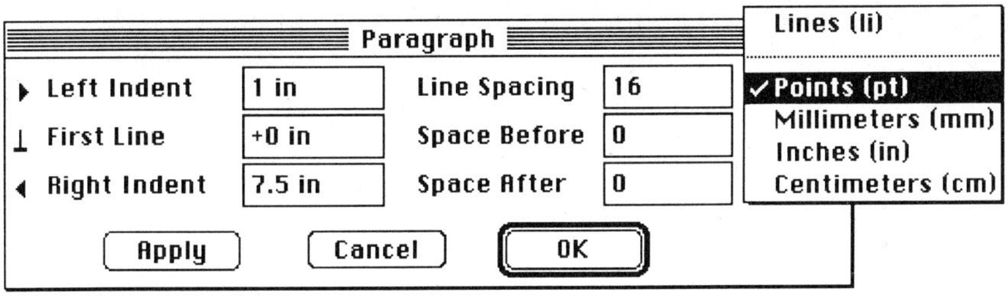

Paragraph			Lines (li)
▶ **Left Indent**	`1 in`	**Line Spacing** `16`	✓ **Points (pt)**
⊥ **First Line**	`+0 in`	**Space Before** `0`	**Millimeters (mm)** **Inches (in)**
◀ **Right Indent**	`7.5 in`	**Space After** `0`	**Centimeters (cm)**

(Apply)   (Cancel)   (OK)

Fig. 13.2. Using the Line Spacing pop-up menu to select the point size.

7. Click the OK button.

   The Line Spacing field should read 16, which corresponds to a line spacing of one.

8. Click the left side of the line spacing fine-tuning icon to reduce the space between the line of underscores and the type above it.

   Each click of the fine-tuning icon reduces the line spacing by one point. As you click the icon, you see the underscore line move closer to the heading. Continue to click the icon; the underscore line vanishes as it begins to overlap with the heading. In the example, this overlap occurs at a line spacing setting of 4 points.

9. Click the right side of the line spacing fine-tuning icon once to restore the underscore line.

The line spacing setting depends on the font you use to create the heading. There is no rule you can use to determine the correct setting. After you have determined the setting, however, you have an idea of the settings needed for different fonts. You then can enter the line spacing setting (the number of points) that suits each font.

Creating Table Columns

Tables usually consist of columns of information. To create these columns, you use tabs, not the Page command. You must decide the number of columns needed, the width of the columns, and the space between columns. You can change these items after you create the table, but the amount of editing required to make the changes can be extensive. Planning ahead saves you a considerable amount of work.

The width of your page affects the decisions you make. You must look at the amount of space available on a page in relation to the amount of space you need to create the columns. A standard 8.5-by-11-inch sheet of paper provides 6.5 inches of space. If you try to squeeze too many columns on the page, you end up with extremely small, unworkable column widths. You can recover some space by reducing page margins (which default to 1 inch on each side). However, many printers have built-in page margins and print only in a certain area of the page. Check your printer's manual to determine the print area of your printer.

You can construct larger tables by changing the page orientation (see Chapter 8). Using the landscape orientation rotates the page to a horizontal position, giving you greater page width. Rotating a standard 8.5-by-11-inch piece of paper gives you 9 inches of space with 1-inch margins. Legal-sized paper, which is 8.5-by-14 inches, allows 12 inches with 1-inch margins in landscape orientation.

To create table columns in MacWrite II, you set tabs. Setting tabs in MacWrite II is similar to setting tabs on a typewriter. MacWrite II gives you greater editing freedom than a typewriter does, however, and the program offers a variety of tab types so that you can create many different table styles. (See Chapter 2 for more information about tabs in MacWrite II.)

Figuring Tab Locations

To determine the tab locations, you must know the number of columns you want and the width of the columns. You don't have to be exact, but planning ahead means less editing later.

As an example, create a table using the heading shown in figure 13.1. The page width is 8.5 inches. The left and right margins are set at 1 inch. This leaves 6.5 inches of space for the table. The table consists of three columns. Dividing the available space among the columns yields a column width of 2.16 inches. Because the ruler is divided into eighths (unless you use another unit of measure), set the tabs for a column width of 2.25 inches. These settings are approximate, but you can adjust the tabs later if necessary.

You set the tabs by dragging the desired tab icon onto the ruler or by using the Tab dialog box. You determine the locations by adding the column width to the page margin setting and then adding this figure to each tab setting. Figure 13.3 shows the settings for the example you are creating.

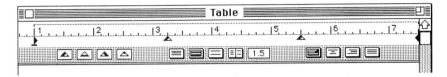

Fig. 13.3. *The tab settings for a three-column table.*

To calculate where the first tab setting goes, add the column width (2.25 inches) to the left page margin setting (1 inch). The total (3.25 inches) is your first tab setting. You figure the second tab setting by adding the column width (2.25 inches) to the first tab setting (3.25 inches), which gives you a tab setting of 5.5 inches. For the example, you use Left tabs. You can use other tab types.

Choosing Tab Types

MacWrite II provides four different tab types: Left, Center, Right, and Align On. The tab type you choose depends on the type of table you want to create.

Use the Left tab for columns of information that line up along the left side of the column. This arrangement is extremely common. Figure 13.4 shows a table that was made by using Left tabs to set the column locations.

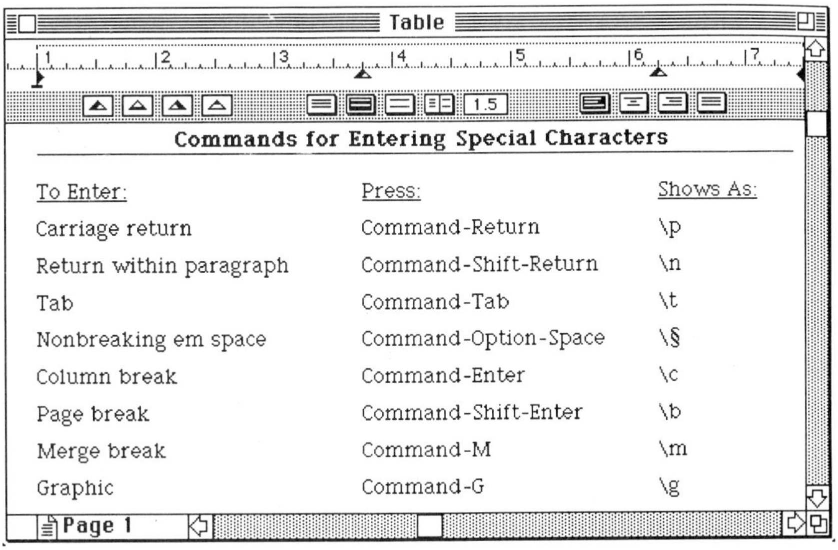

Commands for Entering Special Characters

To Enter:	Press:	Shows As:
Carriage return	Command-Return	\p
Return within paragraph	Command-Shift-Return	\n
Tab	Command-Tab	\t
Nonbreaking em space	Command-Option-Space	\§
Column break	Command-Enter	\c
Page break	Command-Shift-Enter	\b
Merge break	Command-M	\m
Graphic	Command-G	\g

Page 1

Fig. 13.4. *A table made by using Left tabs.*

Use the Right tab when you want information to line up at the right edge of a column. For example, when you create a table of contents you usually want the page numbers to line up at the right edge of the table (see fig. 13.5). You add the periods used to lead into the page numbers in the table of contents by using the tab fill character (discussed in the next section). See Chapter 2 for more information about the different types of tabs.

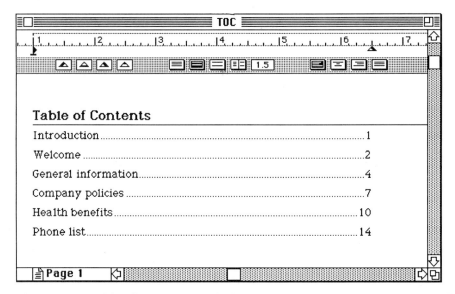

Fig. 13.5. *A table of contents created by using the Right tab for the last column.*

You can use a combination of tabs to vary the visual effect of each column. Figure 13.6 shows an invoice table that uses the Left tab to align the project codes, a Right tab for the dates, and an Align On tab for the project hours.

The Tab dialog box permits changing a tab's type, location, fill character, or align-on character (for Align On tabs). These procedures are discussed later in the chapter.

Using Tab Fill Characters

Tab fill characters are the characters that fill the blank space normally left between columns. A tab fill character can be any single character. The characters most frequently used as tab fill characters are the period and the underscore. A table's readability can be enhanced greatly by using tab fill characters.

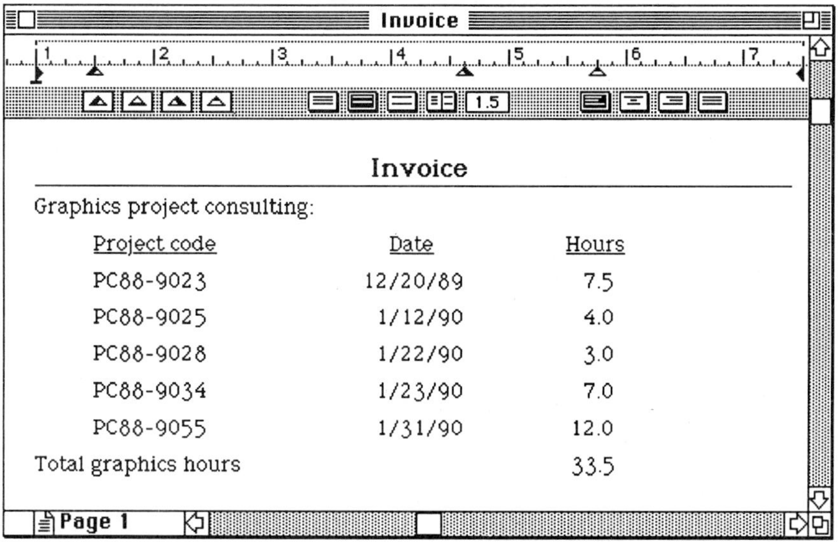

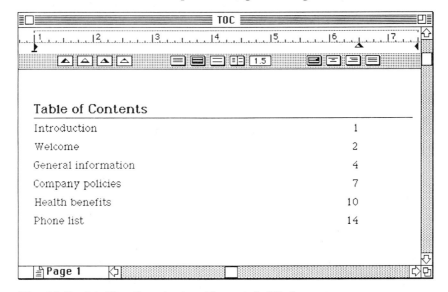

Fig. 13.6. *A table created using a Left tab, a Right tab, and an Align On tab.*

You do not need to decide the tab fill character when you set the tabs for the columns. MacWrite II allows you to add or remove a tab fill character at any time. As an example, look at the table of contents in figure 13.7. When you look at figure 13.7, your eye has difficulty traveling from the information in the first column to the page number in the second column. Tab fill characters solve this problem (again see fig. 13.5).

Fig. 13.7. *A table of contents with no tab fill characters.*

Tab fill characters can be set only in the Tab dialog box. To add tab fill characters, follow these steps:

1. Select the table text (see fig. 13.8).

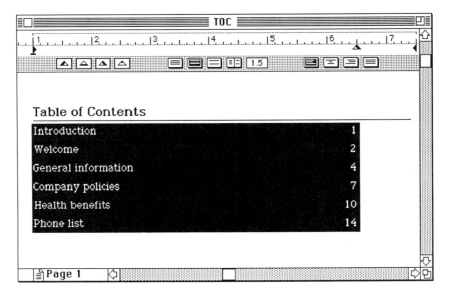

Fig. 13.8. *Select the table text in order to add tab fill characters.*

This step is important. Each paragraph (any amount of text that ends with a carriage return) may have separate formatting. If you make changes to a tab setting without selecting all the text you want the change to affect, the change is made only to the paragraph in which the cursor is located.

2. Double-click the tab to be changed.

This step brings up the Tab dialog box, which is already set to modify the tab setting (see fig. 13.9).

3. Press Tab to move the cursor to the Fill Character field.

4. Type the fill character desired. Use the underscore key for the example.

5. Click the OK button or press Return.

The tab fill characters fill the blank space between the columns, helping the reader find the page numbers that correspond to the information listed (see fig. 13.10).

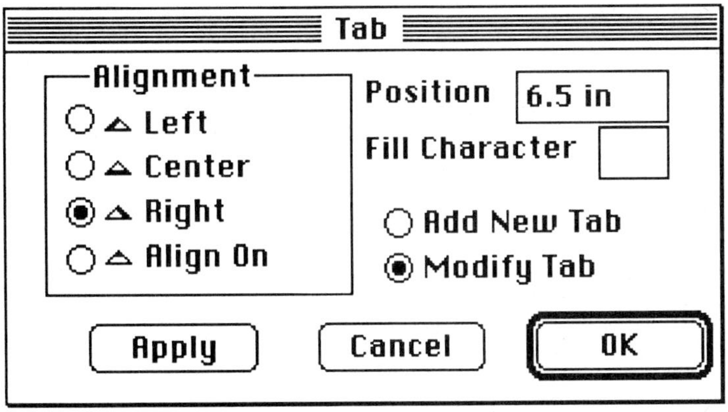

Fig. 13.9. *The Tab dialog box.*

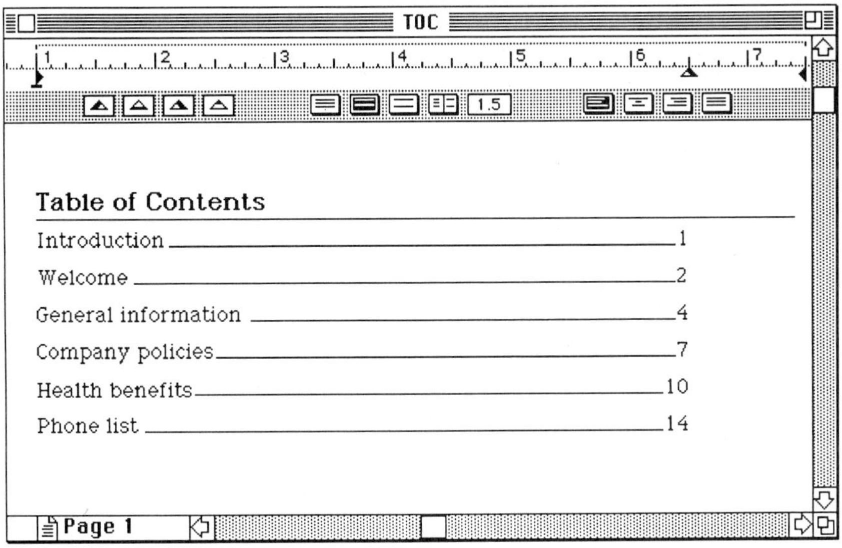

Fig. 13.10. *The underscore character used as the tab fill character.*

If you know the tab fill character you want to use, you can set the fill character when you set the tab instead of adding the fill character later. After you have placed the tab and while you are still in the Tab dialog box, perform steps 3 through 5. If you want to experiment with different characters, use the Apply button in the Tab dialog box.

Creating Column Headings

Column headings in more complicated tables, such as the invoice shown in figure 13.11, may need to be formatted differently from the column information. In figure 13.11, the column headings are done using Left tabs; the information in the columns is done with a combination of tab types.

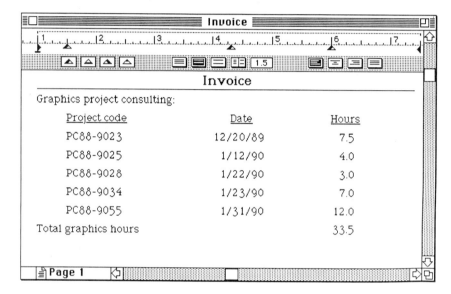

Fig. 13.11. Column headings in an invoice with formats different from the column information.

If you know before you create a table that the column headings need to be formatted differently from the column information, you can plan the different formats. Changing column headings after you create a table is easy, however.

Decide where you think that the columns should be divided and set your tabs accordingly. After adding the column headings, you can adjust them by following these steps:

1. Place the mouse pointer on the line containing the column headings.

2. Click once to place the cursor on the line (the exact location within the line is unimportant).

3. Place the mouse pointer on the tab of the column heading to be moved.

4. Press and hold the mouse button while you move the mouse; the tab follows.

5. Release the mouse button.

Repeat steps 3 through 5 until the column headings are positioned correctly.

Entering Table Information

After you set the tabs for the columns, you can enter the table's data. Entering data is simple. Suppose that you want to create the invoice shown in figure 13.11.

The tabs for the columns are in place. Because the first column was created with a tab, you begin by pressing the Tab key to reach the *Project Code* column. After typing the project code number, you press Tab to reach the *Date* column. Type the date and press Tab to move to the *Hours* column. Type the number of hours and press the Return key to begin a new line.

Keep in mind that when you use tab fill characters, a blank column will have these characters if you define a tab fill character for your preceding columns. The invoice shown in figure 13.12 has been filled out completely. The last three lines of the invoice do not need any special formatting. To add these lines, you type each line without pressing Tab first. This action places the lines against the left margin. When you press Tab after typing the line *Total graphics hours,* the blank space fills with the tab fill character. Press Tab a second time without typing any information in the *Date* column, and the tab fill characters stretch across to the *Hours* column.

This unbroken line of leaders occurs only if you select a tab fill character for all the tabs leading to the last column. Otherwise, blank spaces appear in the line. Because the last two tabs in the invoice document use the period as a fill character, the period character stretches across the blank *Date* column on the last three lines of the invoice table.

Editing Tables

Planning ahead reduces the amount of editing a table needs, but some editing usually is required. Editing tables can be tedious, but you will find that the task is much easier in MacWrite II than on a typewriter.

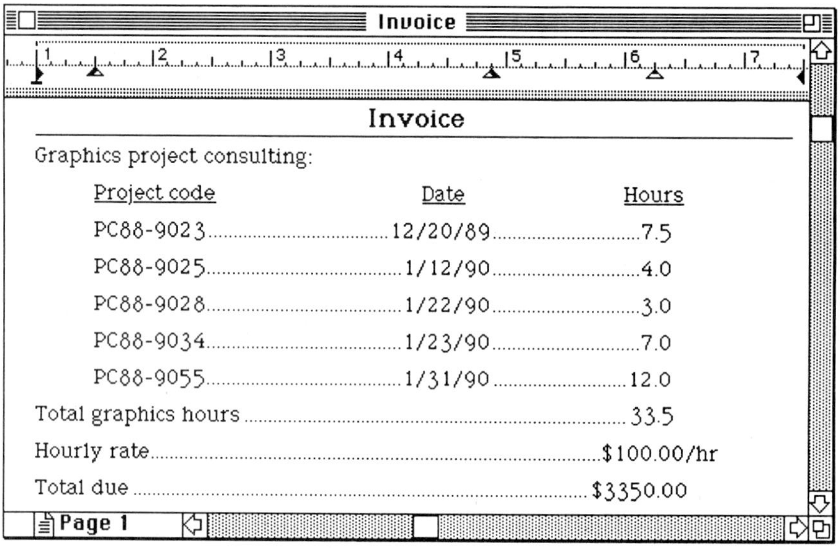

Fig. 13.12. The completed invoice.

Necessary changes you may want to make include adding, removing, and moving columns or rows, and changing the tab attributes (type of tab and fill character).

Editing Columns

Making changes to columns is the most difficult part of working with tables in MacWrite II. You must deal separately with each row of each column because MacWrite II has no column-oriented commands. After you are familiar with the procedures for changing columns, however, you can make changes quickly.

Adjusting Column Widths

Adjusting a column's width or position is easy. In figure 13.13, the columns are spaced unevenly. To space the columns evenly, you adjust the column locations.

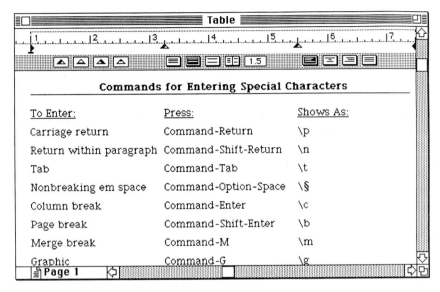

Fig. 13.13. *The column widths in this table need to be adjusted.*

Suppose that you decide to move the last column (*Shows As:*) farther to the right. To adjust the column, follow these steps:

1. Select the entire table text.

   This step is important because changes made to formatting apply only to the paragraph where the cursor is located unless you select more than one paragraph.

2. Place the mouse pointer on the tab at the 5.5-inch mark.

3. Press and hold the mouse button.

4. Move the tab to the 6.25-inch mark; the tab icon follows.

5. Release the mouse button.

The column moves to the new position (see fig. 13.14).

As long as the text is highlighted, you can repeat steps 2 through 5 for the same column or any other column until you achieve the spacing you want. Similar steps were followed to move the second column in the figure from the 3.25-inch position to the 3.75-inch mark.

Moving a column from one location to another is more complicated. You must first remove the column then add it again in the new location. Removing and adding columns is covered in the following sections.

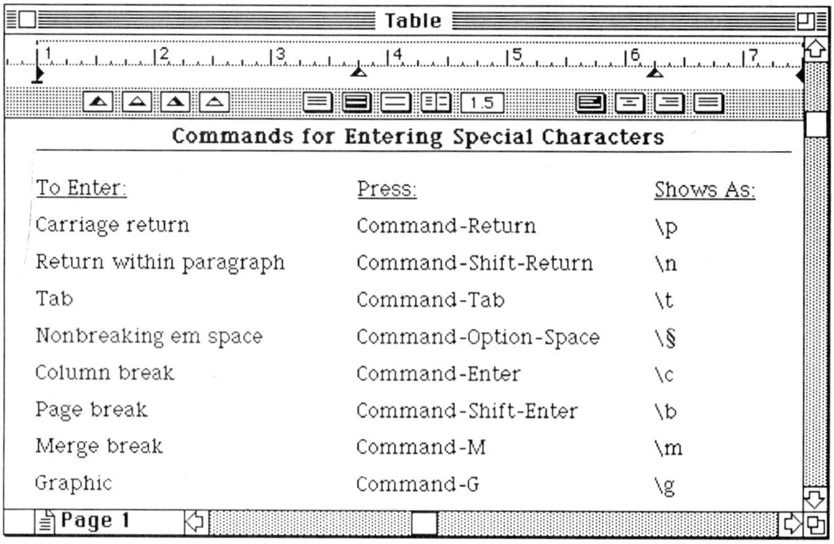

Commands for Entering Special Characters

To Enter:	Press:	Shows As:
Carriage return	Command-Return	\p
Return within paragraph	Command-Shift-Return	\n
Tab	Command-Tab	\t
Nonbreaking em space	Command-Option-Space	\§
Column break	Command-Enter	\c
Page break	Command-Shift-Enter	\b
Merge break	Command-M	\m
Graphic	Command-G	\g

Fig. 13.14. *The column has been moved.*

Adding a Column

To add a column, you first make room for the column by adjusting column widths (as discussed in the preceding section). You then add a new tab for the column. The entire table body should remain selected when you add the tab. Look at the invoice in figure 13.15 for an example.

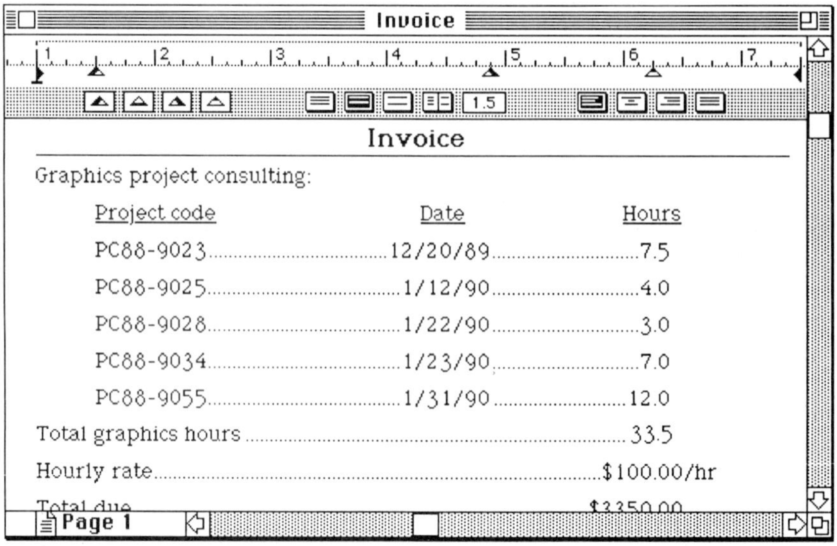

Invoice

Graphics project consulting:

Project code	Date	Hours
PC88-9023	12/20/89	7.5
PC88-9025	1/12/90	4.0
PC88-9028	1/22/90	3.0
PC88-9034	1/23/90	7.0
PC88-9055	1/31/90	12.0
Total graphics hours		33.5
Hourly rate		$100.00/hr
Total due		$3350.00

Fig. 13.15. *This invoice needs a fourth column.*

You decide to add a column that lists the person who worked on the project. This column will be only a few characters wide because you plan to use the initials of the person assigned to the project. This new column will follow the *Project Code* column. Use the following procedure:

1. Select the column heading line.

   In the example in figure 13.15, you want to select and change the information columns and the headings separately because they each have different formatting.

2. Move the *Date* column to the right to make room for the new column.

   The amount of space needed depends on the width of the new column. For the example, .5 inch is sufficient.

3. Place a tab for the new column header.

   Initially, this tab causes the formatting of the other columns to change. This change is not a problem.

4. Place the mouse pointer at the end of the *Project Code* column.

5. Click once.

6. Press Tab and type the new column heading.

The last step moves the other column headings back to their correct locations (see fig. 13.16).

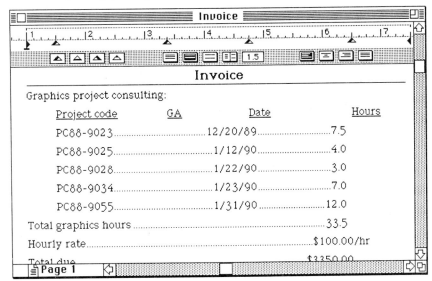

Fig. 13.16. *The invoice now has four columns instead of three.*

You use the same procedure to add data to the new column. When adding the new data column, select the column information text. Then proceed with steps 2 and 3. Repeat steps 4 through 6 for each line of column data.

Removing a Column

The procedure for removing a column is similar to the procedure for adding a column. You deal with each row separately, but you can remove the tab for the column from all lines at one time.

Follow these steps:

1. Select the table text.

   As discussed in the preceding section, the data text and heading text must be selected and worked on separately if they have different formatting.

2. Remove the column's tab.

3. Place the mouse pointer on the data item to be removed.

4. Double-click to select the data.

5. Press Backspace twice.

Repeat steps 3 through 5 for each row of the table. You must press Backspace twice, first to remove the data and then to remove the extra tab character. You may have to adjust the remaining column positions to space them evenly across the page.

Editing Rows

Making changes to rows is much easier than making changes to columns. MacWrite II considers each row of the table a paragraph because each row contains a carriage return. Therefore, you edit rows the same way you edit paragraphs.

Adding a Row

To add a row, follow these steps:

1. Place the mouse pointer at the end of the row that precedes the location where you want to place a new row.

2. Press Return to begin a new line.

3. Enter the information for the new row.

Removing a Row

To remove a row, you use the same steps that you use to remove any line created in MacWrite II. Follow these steps:

1. Place the mouse pointer on the row to be removed (the exact location is unimportant).

2. Triple-click to select the row.

3. Press Backspace.

You can remove several rows at a time by using the standard selection techniques discussed in Chapter 3.

Changing Tabs

You can change a tab's type or fill character at any time. If you find that you want to use a Center tab instead of a Left tab for a column, you can do so quickly and easily. Use the following steps to change a tab:

1. Select the table text.

   Select all the text that contains the column you want to change.

2. Double-click the tab you want to change.

   The Tab dialog box appears.

3. Click the tab type you want.

   Or

   Press Tab to move the highlighting to the Fill Character field and type the desired fill character.

4. Click the OK button or press Return.

Summing Up

This chapter discusses ways to create and edit tables in MacWrite II. Although MacWrite II does not have specific table-oriented commands, many of the program's features can be used to create and edit tables.

You have seen ways to set up and edit tables, column headings, columns, and rows. The chapter explains how to determine tab positions and types for columns and how to enter table data.

Three tables have been used as examples. From these examples and the procedures discussed, you should be ready to create a variety of tables.

14

Quick Start: Creating a Company Mailing

One of the most powerful features in MacWrite II is the capability to create form letters. A *form letter* is a letter in which information, such as names and addresses, is replaced by fields. The program draws information from a data file and inserts the information into the field.

You have seen form letters. As direct-mail marketing has become more sophisticated, the number of "personalized" computer letters has increased. Because of the form-letter capabilities of word processors, companies routinely send letters with the names and addresses of the recipients drawn from a mailing list.

MacWrite II can create personalized mailings by creating a form letter and using a list of names and addresses to create a personalized letter for each individual on the list. For more information on form letters, see Chapter 15.

In this quick start, you are creating a form letter for a company mailing. The letter is sent to the company employees.

Creating the Data File

In order to use a form letter, you must create a list of names and addresses from which the program draws information. Creating the data file is the easiest part of form letters. You create a file with columns of names, street addresses, cities, and the like, for the company employees.

To create the data file, follow these steps:

1. Place Left tabs at the following inch marks: 2, 3, 5, 6.5, and 7.

2. Type *First Name* and press Tab.

3. Type *Last Name* and press Tab.

4. Type *Street Address* and press Tab.

5. Type *City* and press Tab.

6. Type *State* and press Tab.

7. Type *ZIP* and press Return.

You have entered the headings for the data file. The tabs are set to create columns for each item in a record. The first line contains the headings that identify the type of information entered in each column. Figure 14.1 shows the data file at this stage.

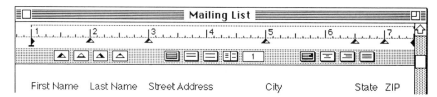

Fig. 14.1. The data file headings.

You now enter the data itself. Enter the names and addresses as listed in figure 14.2. Type each item and then press Tab. At the end of each line, press Return. Each line is called a *record*.

After you have typed all the names and addresses, save the mailing list data file with the following steps:

1. Click the close box of the document.

2. Click the Yes button in the dialog box that appears (or press Return).

3. Type the name *Mailing List* for the file, and press Return.

The document is saved and closed. You are now ready to create the form letter itself.

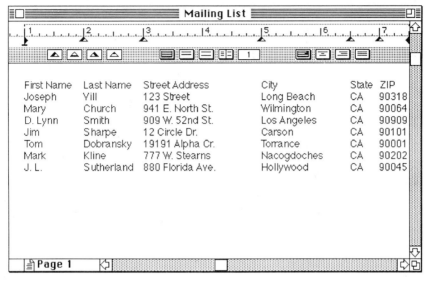

Fig. 14.2. *The completed data file.*

Creating the Form Letter

The information from the mailing list file is inserted into the form letter. Fields in the letter specify where the information is placed.

Use the following steps to open a file and begin the letter:

1. Select New from the File menu.

2. Place a Left tab at the 4.5-inch position.

3. Press Tab.

4. Type the date.

5. Press Return twice.

The letter is ready to be addressed. The program will insert the information from the mailing list file here when you perform the merge operation. The first line of the address consists of the name of the addressee. Instead of typing the name, follow these steps:

1. Select Open Merge Data File from the File menu.

   After you choose the Open Merge Data File command, you do not have to do so again. The data file remains open.

2. Click the filename Mailing List (see fig. 14.3).

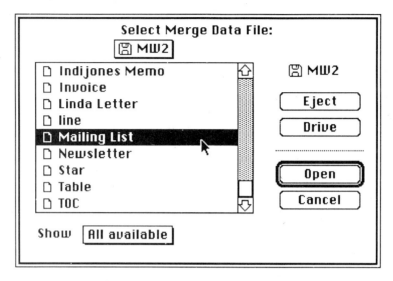

***Fig. 14.3.** Selecting the merge data file.*

3. Click the Open button.

The Insert Merge Field dialog box appears (see fig. 14.4). Under Field Name, you see the names of the columns you created in the Mailing List data file. Note that the field First Name is already highlighted by the program.

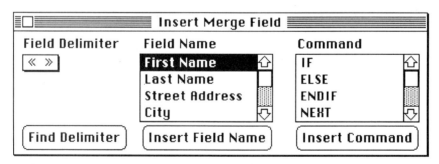

***Fig. 14.4.** The Insert Merge Field dialog box.*

4. Click the Insert Field Name button to insert the First Name field.

The program inserts the First Name field into the document (see fig. 14.5). During the merge operation, the program will read the data file, find the data in the First Name field, and replace the field with the data.

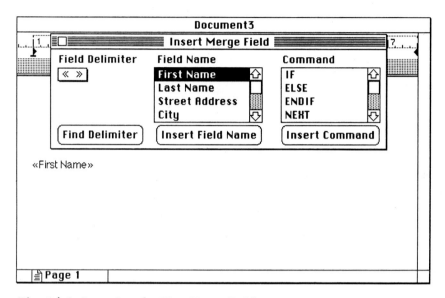

Fig. 14.5. *Inserting the First Name field.*

You also need the person's last name. Continue with the following:

1. Click the close box of the Insert Merge Field dialog box.

2. Select Insert Merge Field from the File menu (or press Shift-Command-M).

   The Insert Merge Field dialog box reappears.

3. Double-click the Last Name field in the Field Name list.

   Double-clicking has the same effect as clicking the field name and then clicking the Insert Field Name button.

4. Close the Insert Merge Field dialog box by clicking the close box.

You are returned to your document. Finish the name part of the address by pressing Return. Figure 14.6 shows the form letter so far.

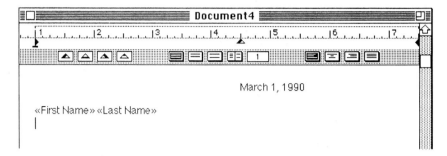

Fig. 14.6. The beginning of the form letter.

You are now ready to insert the street address. This line consists of one item of information. Use the following steps:

1. Select Insert Merge Field from the File menu (or press Shift-Command-M).

2. Double-click the field Street Address.

   The last line of the address contains the city, state, and ZIP code. Note that the State and ZIP fields do not show in the Field Name list at first. You must scroll the list to select them.

3. Double-click the City field name.

4. Scroll the Field Name list by clicking a few times on the down scroll arrow.

5. Double-click the State field name.

6. Double-click the ZIP field name.

7. Click the close box of the dialog box.

Figure 14.7 shows the partially completed form letter.

Note that in figure 14.7, the fields have been entered on a single line without punctuation. Adding the punctuation now— instead of while entering the fields—saves a few steps. You now enter the punctuation with the following steps:

1. Click once between the First Name and Last Name fields.

2. Press the space bar once.

3. Click once between the Last Name and Street Address fields, and press Return.

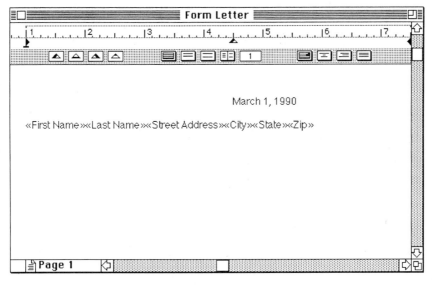

Fig. 14.7. The partially entered address lines.

4. Click once between the Street Address and City fields, and press Return.

5. Click once between the City and State fields.

6. Press the comma and then the space bar.

7. Click once between the State and ZIP fields, and press the space bar once.

The inside address part of the letter is now completed (see fig. 14.8). The field names are enclosed by angle brackets. These brackets tell the program to substitute information from the data file for these fields.

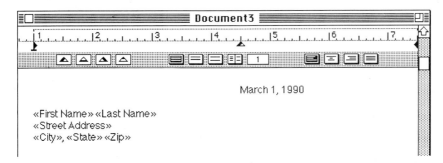

Fig. 14.8. The completed form letter inside address.

You are now ready to add the greeting to the form letter. You want the letters to have a personal, informal touch, so the first name of the addressee is necessary. Use the following steps:

1. Type *Dear* followed by a space.

2. Select Insert Merge Field from the File menu.

   You may not see the First Name field in the Field Name list. Click the up arrow until the field name moves into view.

3. Double-click the First Name field.

4. Click the close box, type a comma, and press Return twice.

You are now ready to add the body of the letter. Follow these steps:

1. Place a left Tab at the 1.5-inch position.

2. Press Tab.

3. Type the following paragraph:

   You are invited to join us in a farewell party for Linda South. After three years with us, Linda has accepted a position with Imajiz Inc. We'll all be sorry to see her go but wish her luck in her future endeavors.

4. Press Return, press Tab, and type the second paragraph:

   The party will take place next Friday (March 9th) after work at the Chicago Pizza Factory. The company is picking up the tab for dinner. So come join us in wishing Linda our best for the future.

5. Press Return twice.

6. Press Tab twice.

7. Type *February Deb, Personnel*.

The completed letter is shown in figure 14.9.

You should now save the letter. You do not want to close the form letter document. Follow these steps:

1. Select Save from the File menu (or press Command-S).

2. Type the name *Form Letter*.

3. Click the Save button.

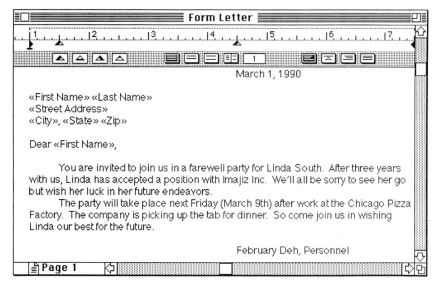

Fig. 14.9. *The completed form letter.*

Printing the Mailing

After the file has been saved, you can use it to generate form letters. By merging the form letter with the mailing list file, you create one letter for each record in the mailing list file.

The program knows which files to use because the form letter file is still open, and you have chosen the data file by using the Open Merge File command. If you had just started the program, you would need to perform these two Open commands to indicate to MacWrite II which files to use.

Use the following steps to print the letters:

1. Select Merge from the File menu.

    The Merge dialog box appears (see fig. 14.10).

2. Click the Merge button (or press Return).

3. Click the OK button in the Print dialog box.

The program proceeds to print the form letters (see fig. 14.11). In each letter, the program replaces the field names with the data that corresponds to that field.

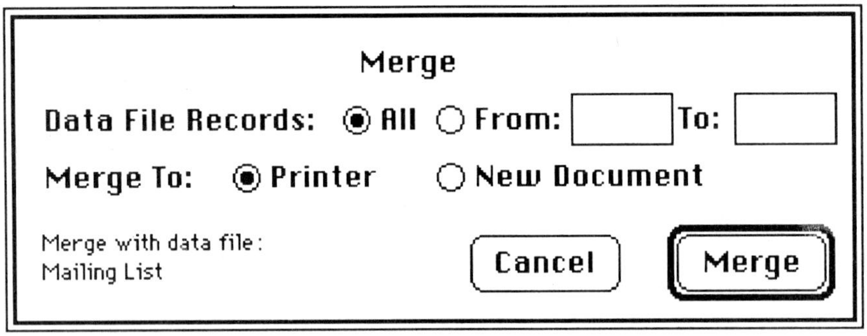

Fig. 14.10. The Merge dialog box.

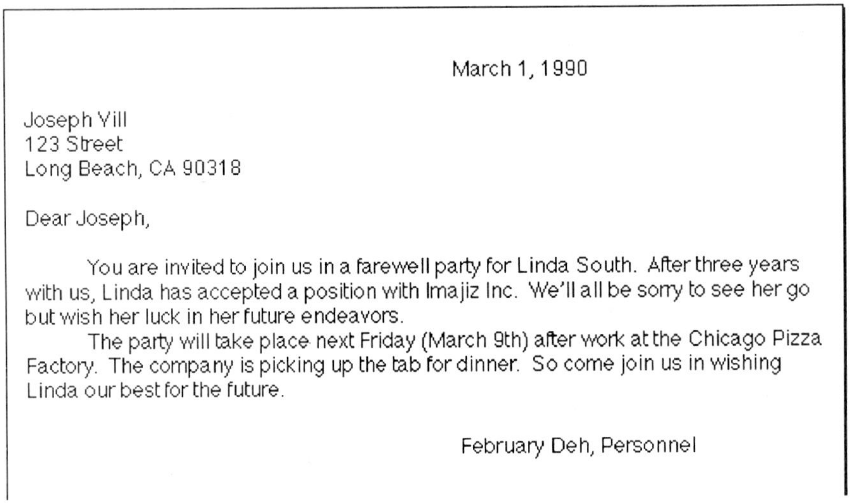

March 1, 1990

Joseph Vill
123 Street
Long Beach, CA 90318

Dear Joseph,

You are invited to join us in a farewell party for Linda South. After three years with us, Linda has accepted a position with Imajiz Inc. We'll all be sorry to see her go but wish her luck in her future endeavors.

The party will take place next Friday (March 9th) after work at the Chicago Pizza Factory. The company is picking up the tab for dinner. So come join us in wishing Linda our best for the future.

February Deh, Personnel

Fig. 14.11. The first printed form letter.

After the printing ends, you leave MacWrite II by selecting Quit from the File menu.

In this chapter, you have seen the basic steps for creating a data file and a form letter file. You also have seen how the Merge command brings the two files together to create printed form letters. Many other options are available to you in creating form letters. These options are explored in the next chapter.

15

Creating Form Letters

Chapter 14 gives an example of a simple, straightforward use of form letters. The chapter—although illustrating a common use of form letters—barely does justice to the power and flexibility of this part of MacWrite II. This chapter covers the form letter capabilities of the program in greater depth.

In addition to the capability to draw information from a merge data file and place that information into a form letter, MacWrite II is capable of responding to commands to alter the information and form of a letter according to the data in the merge data file. MacWrite II also can bring in a mailing list or other data created by other programs. You can use data created using another word processor, the MS Works database, or other database programs.

This chapter also presents three methods available for creating form letters and covers the different field delimiters (characters used to set off form letter fields). Finally, the text discusses the program's range feature, which enables you to choose a range of data to be used.

Creating Data Files

To use the form letter feature of MacWrite II, you must have a data file. This file is basically an organized list of facts from which the program draws when printing (also called merging) your form letter document. In Chapter 14, the example uses a list of names and addresses as the data file. This example is a common use but not the only one by far.

A data file consists of a series of records, which are lines of information. Each *record* ends with a carriage return character. A record contains several items of information separated by tabs. Each item is called a *field*.

The first line of a data file must contain the names of each data item (field). This first line of column headings (field names) is the bridge used by the program to identify the data items. The records below contain the needed data. The data items (fields) in the records must be entered in the same order as the items (field names) in the headings line.

Specifying Data Categories

As stated, the first line of a data file must identify the items on the subsequent lines (records). This requirement means that you must determine the data items before you create the data file.

In the example in Chapter 14, the data items are

First Name
Last Name
Street Address
City
State
ZIP

These items were chosen because the form letter created in that chapter is a company mailing. The names and addresses changed from letter to letter. The categories chosen correspond to the separate items of an address. The first and last names of the addressee are separated so that the first name can be used in the letter's greeting. The data file's first line then identifies each item, as seen in figure 15.1. The names of the items are called the field names.

Now suppose that you want to create a more formal mailing. A cover letter to accompany promotional material is a good example. Consider the different data items you will need.

First, like the example in Chapter 14, the letter is a mailing, and each letter will be addressed differently. This factor requires that some of the data items be the same for both examples. You again need the street address, city, state, and ZIP code for each individual to whom you want the mailing to go.

Because this mailing is a more formal mailing and is directed to people in a company, you will need a more formal greeting. A business letter does not start out *Dear Joe* but uses the more formal *Dear Mr. Vill*. The first and last name will be used separately. This requirement tells you that you will need a First Name field and a Last Name field. In addition to the separate First and Last Name fields, you will need a field for the title. This field will contain the person's title: *Mr.*, *Ms.*, *Dr.*, and the like. You label this field Title.

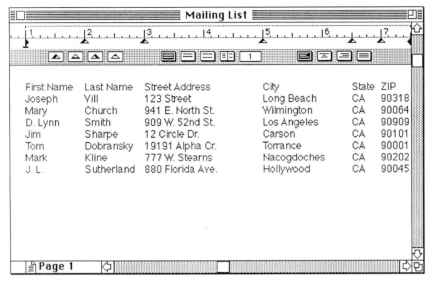

Fig. 15.1. *A sample data file.*

At the same time, you realize that you need the position the person holds in the company. In addition to placing this information in the address, you want the form letter to include a first line that says, "In your position as [position] with [company], you know...." Obviously, the data file must contain the position of the addressee. This field can be called Position. You could use Company Title or something along those lines, but the best practice is to keep field names short.

Finally, you realize that you must include the name of the company. This inclusion will be held in a field called Company.

You have decided on the following data items:

Title
Position
First Name
Last Name
Company
Street Address
City
State
ZIP

The order and number of the categories is not important. What is important is to consider your planned form letter and determine the data items you will need. One helpful technique is to create a rough draft of the form letter. Then you can examine the letter and determine the data items you need and the order in which you want to enter the items.

The names of the data items (field names) are important. When you are creating the form letter document, you must choose the field names from the scrolling list of the Insert Merge Field dialog box. The names you give the data items will appear in this list in the order in which you enter them in the first line of the data file. Use field names that you can recognize immediately.

Separating Data Fields

When you enter data into a file to be used with a form letter, you must separate the data fields from each other. In MacWrite II, you have two ways to separate data fields. In Chapter 14, the separator—also called data delimiter—was a tab. You separated each data field from the next by pressing the Tab key.

The program also allows the use of a comma to separate data fields. This usage is included mostly to provide compatibility between MacWrite II and other programs. If you create and maintain your data file with MacWrite II, you most likely will want to use the tab as your data delimiter. The reason for this preference becomes plain in the data file shown in figure 15.2.

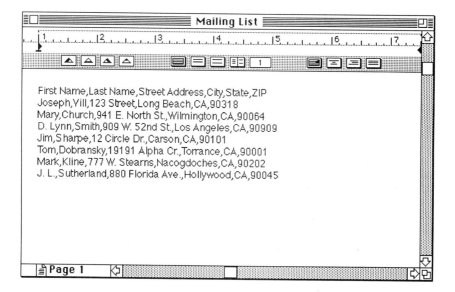

Fig. 15.2. A data file using the comma as a data delimiter.

Although the data file shown in the figure is completely valid in MacWrite II, reading the file can be difficult. Editing and maintaining such a file is tedious. Referring to figure 15.1, you see the same file using the tab as a data delimiter. Obviously, you can read and edit this file much more easily.

Many programs, however, use the comma to separate data. This fact is why the comma is included as a data delimiter.

Creating the Data File

After you have determined the data fields you want to use in your form letter, you are ready to create the data file itself. The general steps are as follows:

1. Select New from the File menu.

2. Place Left tabs on the ruler to position the data fields in columns. (This step enhances the readability of the file.)

3. Type the first line—the headings identifying the data fields. Use any order that is logical and useful for you.

4. Type the data records. Remember that the data fields must be entered below the corresponding column headings.

5. Save the data file.

When a data file is being created or edited, it is simply another file so far as MacWrite II is concerned. The purpose of using tabs is for your convenience—to align the data fields into columns. The process is similar to creating tables. (You may want to review Chapter 13, which covers tables.) Of course, a data file has no header as a table does; however, the data fields of the file are created in a similar way.

You do not have to limit yourself to a single line for a data record, but you must end each record with a carriage return (that is, press the Return key). The data crossing onto a second line causes no problem (see fig. 15.3).

The file in figure 15.3 is shown with the Show Invisibles command on. Showing the invisibles helps you see the tabs that separate data fields and the carriage return that ends each record. The records of the file shown in the figure are so long that they have wrapped to the next line. No carriage return follows the company name. Instead, a tab separates the Company field and the Street Address field. The carriage return is after the ZIP field of each record.

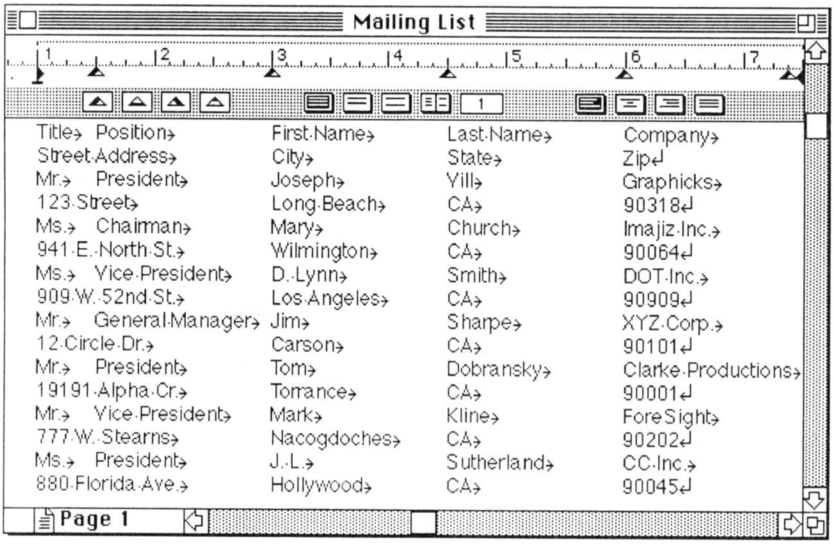

Fig. 15.3. Records of data may wrap to following lines.

Always remember that the first line of the data file *must* contain the names of the fields. This line is the line MacWrite II reads to obtain the field names when you select the Open Merge Data File command in the File menu. If you open a merge data file and find that the field names are something unexpected, you probably omitted the first line.

Importing Other Data Files

If you maintain a database in some other program, you may be able to use this database as the merge data file. You can use as merge data files the files from two types of programs:

- *Other word processors.* Recall that the MacWrite II program is capable of working with any file for which the program has a translator.

- *Database programs.* The easiest to use of these files are the files created by the Microsoft Works database program. MacWrite II is capable of working with these files directly. To use other database programs, you must export the information to an intermediate file.

Importing from Word Processors

The rules for using files from other word processors as merge data files are the same as the rules for using the files as regular documents (see Chapter 6). You must install the translator for that word processor. After the translator is installed, you can open the merge data file created by the other word processor.

When you select the Open Merge Data File command, you see the Select Merge Data File dialog box (see fig. 15.4). This dialog box enables you to choose the data file to be used with your form letter.

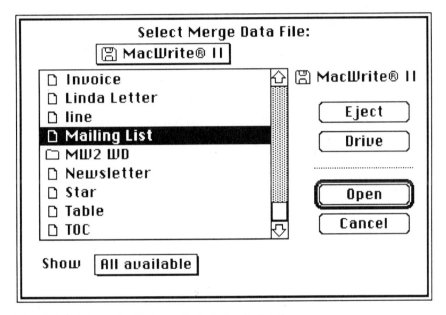

Fig. 15.4. *The Select Merge Data File dialog box.*

Like the standard Open Document dialog box, this dialog box has a pop-up Show menu at the bottom. Through this menu, you choose the format of files you want to view (see Chapter 6 for more details about using other formats). By default, this menu lets you view all files the program is capable of opening. You simply select the file you want to use as your merge data file and click the OK button.

If you want to view only the files of a particular format, follow these steps:

1. Place the mouse pointer on the Show menu (the shadowed box, not the word Show).

2. Press and hold the mouse button.

3. Move the mouse up or down until the format you want is highlighted.

4. Release the mouse button.

The program displays only the files in the format you choose. This feature helps you locate a file if you have a large number of files available.

To create data files in other word processors, you use the same procedures you use to create files in MacWrite II. The first line must contain the field names. The data fields are separated by tabs (or commas). Each data record ends with a carriage return.

If you do not have the translator for a particular word processor, you can do one of two things. You can purchase the translator from a company such as DataViz, or you can save the data file in text format. Consult the manual of the word processor to learn this procedure. (Some manuals call a text file an ASCII file.) MacWrite II recognizes all text files regardless of the program that created them. (Not all word processors create text files the same way. Some programs remove the tab character and replace it with spaces; these word processing files do not work with MacWrite II merge files.)

From a Microsoft Works Database

If you use the Microsoft Works database, you can use these files directly. No special procedures are necessary other than to make sure that the Works translator is installed. To use a Works file as your merge data file, simply do the following:

1. Choose Open Merge Data File from the File menu.

2. Click once on the Works database file name to highlight it.

3. Click the Open button.

The field names you have defined in your database appear in the Insert Merge Field list. You then insert them into your form letter.

Importing from Other Programs

To use information from any database other than Works or from a program that is not a word processor, you must store the data in a file MacWrite II can read.

You are not necessarily limited to database programs as such. Many programs are capable of storing information in a format MacWrite II can read. One example of a program that can store information for MacWrite II is the popular Dollars and Sense personal finance management program of Monogram Software.

To determine whether your database or other program can store data in a format MacWrite II can use, look in the software manual for an export feature. This feature stores the program's data in a text file that can be read by many other programs.

Make sure that the program exports text in a tab-delimited or comma-delimited format. Tab-delimited indicates a data file that separates data fields with tab characters and ends the data record with a carriage return. Comma-delimited also ends the data record with a return but separates data fields with commas.

The tab-delimited format is preferable because you may need to edit the file format before attempting to use the file as a merge data file. Attempting to use a file from another program may result in an error message like the message in figure 15.5.

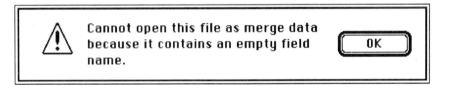

Fig. 15.5. MacWrite II notifies of an error.

The error message in the figure indicates that a record in the data file has two consecutive tabs (or commas). Recall that tabs (or commas) separate data fields. The first line must contain the data field names. A blank field name is not permitted.

In a case like this example, you need to open the data file as a regular document (using the Open command in the File menu) and edit the file. Use the Show Invisibles command in the View menu to see the tab and return characters when editing (see Chapter 3 for more on invisible characters).

Creating Form Letters

Form letters are the documents into which the data from the merge data file is inserted. You indicate the locations where the data is to be inserted by placing merge fields in the document. Merge fields act as place holders, showing the item of data that is to be entered at this point when the two files are merged.

Keep in mind that when you merge the form letter with the data file, one copy of the form letter is generated for each data record (except for the first line, which serves solely to name the data fields).

You can use one of three methods in creating a form letter. You will need to experiment to determine the best method for your needs. Each technique is described in this chapter.

With the first method, you type the field names directly into the form letter without using the Insert Merge Field command. This method is quicker than the other two but carries with it greater possibility of error. You may accidentally type an incorrect field name.

The second method is the slowest but easiest and most error free. You saw this method in the example of Chapter 14. This method requires the use of the Insert Merge Field command to place each merge field in the form letter document.

The third method is a compromise between these two methods. You insert the field delimiters to indicate the location of each merge field as you type the form letter but do not insert the field names until you have finished creating the form letter.

Using Different Merge Field Delimiters

Some fonts do not have the double less-than and greater-than symbols used by MacWrite II as the default merge field delimiters. Although you can use the symbols even if the font does not contain them, switching to another field delimiter is the best technique. If you use the double less-than or greater-than symbol in your text, you also need to use a different symbol for the merge fields.

The Field Delimiter pop-up menu provides a choice of two field delimiters (brackets and braces) besides the standard double greater-than and less-than symbols.

To change to another merge field delimiter, use the following steps:

1. Select Insert Merge Field from the File menu (or use Shift-Command-M).

2. Place the mouse on the Field Delimiter menu.

3. Press and hold the mouse button.

4. Move the mouse up or down to select the desired field delimiter (see fig. 15.6).

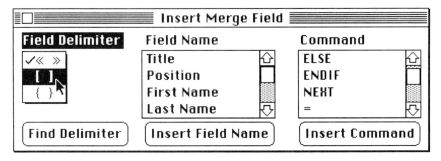

Fig. 15.6. *Choosing a merge field delimiter.*

5. Release the mouse button.

You must choose the field delimiter before you insert any merge fields. Changing the field delimiter by use of the Insert Merge Field command does not change any fields that have already been inserted.

If you need to change fields that have already been inserted, use the Find/Change command in the Edit menu (see Chapter 5).

Typing the Field Names

Typing the field names is the quickest method for touch-typists. With this method, you use the keyboard to enter the data field names as you type the form letter. You must be careful about the spelling of the data field names. They must be spelled *exactly* as they appear in the merge data file.

If you spell a data field name incorrectly, the program does not notify you of an error. Instead, the program skips the field. Note figure 15.7, where a merged file is shown.

The first line of the address shows as Mr. ‹‹Frist Name›› Vill. In the form letter, the data field name First Name has been misspelled. The program assumes that the field name is simply part of the form letter text because the program finds no data field with the same name. The program therefore prints the text as it is.

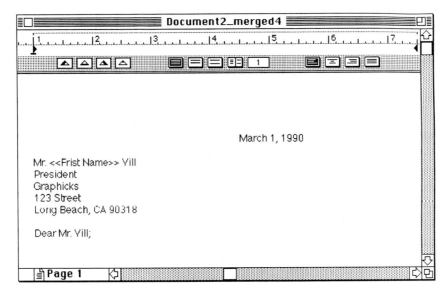

Fig. 15.7. *An incorrect field name causes errors.*

A merge printing of a form letter can be difficult to halt—especially if your merge data file is large. The best policy, therefore, is to make certain of the field name spellings before beginning a merge printing (see "Producing the Form Letter," later in this chapter).

With that warning in mind, work through the following steps to create a form letter by this method:

1. Select New from the File menu.

2. Format the document.

3. Type the document text, inserting merge field names where needed.

4. Save the file.

These steps are the same as for creating any other document except when you need to insert a merge field. The only variation comes in step 3. When you reach a point where you need to insert a merge field name, use the following steps:

1. Type two less-than symbols (<<).

2. Type the field name as entered in the first line of the merge data file.

Whether the merge field name is in upper- or lowercase letters is not important. What is important is that the spelling is correct.

3. Type two greater-than symbols (>>).

As an alternative, you can use the following steps to insert the merge field names:

1. Press Option-\ (backslash key) to enter two less-than symbols (<<).

2. Type the field name.

3. Press Shift-Option-\ (backslash) to enter two greater-than symbols (>>).

This technique speeds data entry by reducing the number of keystrokes you use to enter a field name. Note, however, that if you use different field delimiters, these steps will not work. You need actually to type the field delimiter instead of using the Option-\ and Shift-Option-\ key combinations.

Some fonts do not contain the symbols generated by these two key combinations. This lack does not stop MacWrite II from recognizing them as field delimiters. However, the field delimiters will appear as boxes in the text (see fig. 15.8).

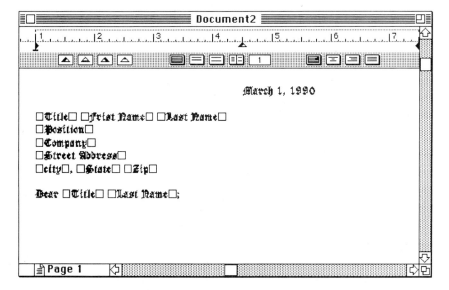

Fig. 15.8. The field delimiters appear as boxes.

Although the program still recognizes the field delimiters, the best policy in a case like this to choose one of the other field delimiters for your form letter (see "Using Different Merge Field Delimiters," in this chapter).

Using the Insert Merge Field Command

Using the Insert Merge Field command is the best technique if you are uncertain of the merge field names. You must use the Insert Merge Field command each time you need to place a merge field name in your form letter. You will be ensured that the merge field names are correctly spelled, but the process can be time-consuming. Before the Insert Merge Field becomes available, you must open the merge data file.

Format the form letter document and type the text as you type any other document. When you are ready to insert a field name, make sure that the merge data file is open and follow these steps:

1. Select Insert Merge Field from the File menu (or press Shift-Command-M).

2. Highlight the merge field name you want to insert (see fig. 15.9).

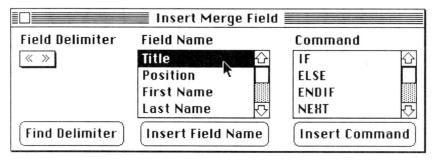

Fig. 15.9. *Selecting a merge field name.*

3. Click the Insert Field Name button.

You can combine steps 2 and 3 into a single step: Double-click the merge field name. Either version of this procedure inserts the field name with field delimiters at the current cursor position.

4. Click the close box of the Insert Merge Field dialog box.

To save some time with this method, use the following step instead of step 4: Click in the form letter document. This step hides the Insert Merge Field dialog box but does not close it. This technique can save floppy disk users the moment or two required to open the dialog box.

Using a Combination Method

The third method of creating form letters combines the other two. This technique gives the speed of the first method while preserving the accuracy of the second.

Format and type the form letter as any other document. When you need to insert a merge field name, follow these steps:

1. Type the left field delimiter.

   You can type two less-than symbols or press Option-\, as described in the first method.

2. Type the right field delimiter.

   You can type two greater-than symbols or press Shift-Option-\, as discussed for the first method.

These steps insert the field delimiters where a merge field is located but do not provide the field name. You add the field names after the document is completed.

Figure 15.10 shows the inside address of a form letter entered using this approach. The address is ready for the field names to be inserted.

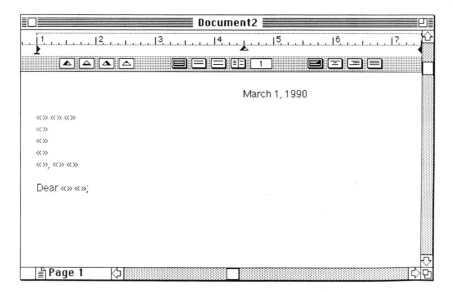

Fig. 15.10. *The beginning of a form letter before field names are inserted.*

After you have completed the form letter, you use the Insert Merge Field command to insert the field names. Follow these steps:

1. Select Insert Merge Field from the File menu (or use Shift-Command-M).

2. Click the Find Delimiter button.

   The program locates and highlights the first occurrence of the field delimiters and highlights the pair (see fig. 15.11).

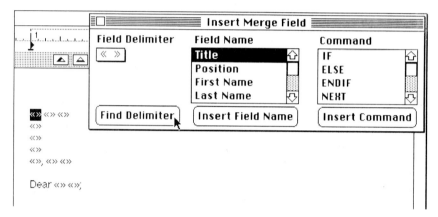

Fig. 15.11. *The first pair of field delimiters found.*

3. Select the field name to be inserted.

4. Click the Insert Field Name button.

The program inserts the field name between the two field delimiters. Repeat steps 2 through 4 until all field names have been placed in the document.

Locating Field Delimiters

If your form letter is long, you may find locating merge fields a tedious process. To find the fields quickly, you can use the Find Delimiter button in the Insert Merge Field dialog box.

Use the following steps:

1. Select Insert Merge Field from the File menu (or use Shift-Command-M).

2. Click the Find Delimiter button.

The program locates and highlights the first merge field after the current cursor position. While a merge field is selected, you can change the field name by selecting the desired field name in the list in the dialog box and clicking the Insert Field Name button (or you can double-click on the field name). After making the change, you click Find Delimiter to find the next field. When the program reaches the end of the document, the program beeps and returns to the first merge field in the document.

Using the Merge Field Commands

MacWrite II provides a powerful set of commands that can be used to alter a form letter according to the data in the merge data file. The program enables you to compare the value of a merge field with a value you enter and to print text according to the results of the test.

Although you do not have to use commands to create and use form letters, commands can be useful. You may need to experiment to understand fully how to use the commands.

The IF Statement

Everyone is familiar with IF statements. They are used commonly in everyday speech. You hear them in phrases such as "If you run that red light, you'll get a ticket." Although the structure of an IF statement in MacWrite II is slightly different from the structure of common speech, the concept is the same.

An IF statement in MacWrite II enables you to include text in a form letter based on whether a condition is true or false. When the condition is met, the statement is true, and the text is printed. When the statement is false, the text is not printed. Every IF statement must be followed by an ENDIF statement.

The basic structure of an IF statement is as follows:

<<IF condition>> text to print <<ENDIF>>

A condition is made up of a merge data field name, an operator (also called a command because it is listed in the Command list of the Insert Merge Field dialog box), and a value with which the merge data is to be compared.

Using Operators

MacWrite II provides eight operators (called commands in the dialog box), which can be used in the condition part of an IF statement:

Operator	Meaning
=	Equal to
<>	Not equal to
<	Less than
<=	Less than or equal to
>	Greater than
>=	Greater than or equal to
CONTAINS	Contains the following text
NOT	Opposite of the following

The first six can be used to compare the value of a merge data field to a particular value. For example, suppose that you are sending a mailing that includes a toll-free number valid only for California customers. In the text of the form letter, you include a line similar to the following:

<<IF State = "CA">> Use our toll-free number for fast, friendly service. Call 1-800-555-9090. <<ENDIF>>

As the program reads each line of the merge data file, the program checks the data in the State field to determine whether the State data is equal to CA. If the State data is equal to CA, the program prints the text contained between the IF statement and the ENDIF statement. If the State data is anything else, the program does not print the text.

Many businesses have different sales people for different areas of the country. To customize the form letter according to a region, you can use several IF statements:

Call <<IF State = "CA">> Jim Kearns <<ENDIF>> <<IF State = "OR">> Jim Kearns <<ENDIF>> <<IF State = "TX">> Tom Jones <<ENDIF>> at 1-800-555-9090 to open an account.

Admittedly, this statement can get complex if you have to accommodate 50 states. At the same time, this example shows just how detailed your customization of a form letter can become. The preceding example prints the name *Jim Kearns* if the customer resides in California or Oregon and the name *Tom Jones* if the customer is located in Texas.

The not-equal-to operator can be used when you have a situation where you want to print text only if something is not true. An example of this situation is the toll-free number example. If your business has a toll-free number only for customers outside the state of California, you can use the following:

<<IF State <> "CA">> Call us at 1-800-555-9090 for fast, friendly service. <<ENDIF>>

Now the program prints the toll-free number only if the State data is not equal to CA.

Note that the value to which you are comparing the data is enclosed in quotation marks. The quotation marks act as separators for the data, indicating to MacWrite II the beginning and end of the data. You do not have to enclose numbers in quotation marks, but you *must* enclose letters in quotation marks. If you do not, you receive the error message shown in figure 15.12.

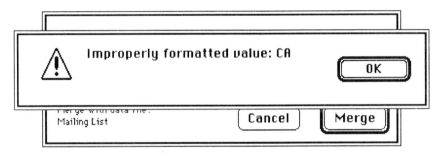

Fig. 15.12. *An incorrect value is detected.*

The program is indicating that the value *CA* is improperly formatted. That is, the value is not enclosed in quotation marks. Numbers may be entered either way. The following statements are equally valid:

<<IF Area Code = 213>> Drop by our open house this Saturday! <<ENDIF>>

<<IF Area Code = "213">> Drop by our open house this Saturday! <<ENDIF>>

The rest of the first six operators operate as you might expect. The greater-than operator (>) checks to see whether the merge data is larger than the value to which the merge data is compared. An example is

<<IF ZIP > 90000>> Visit one of our show rooms. More than 100 locations throughout the West. <<ENDIF>>

The program prints the text only if the ZIP value is higher than 90000.

The less-than operator (<) causes the text to print only if the merge data is lower than the value to which the merge data is compared. The greater-than-or-equal-to operator (>=) prints text if the value is bigger *or* the same. The less-than-or-equal-to operator (<=) performs a similar function. The text is printed if the merge data is lower or the same.

The CONTAINS operator is unusual. It permits you to print text if a data field contains a specified piece of text. Suppose that the data file contains a Phone Number field. This field is the entire number including the area code in parentheses. You can use a statement such as this:

<<IF Phone Number CONTAINS "(213)">> Come to our open house this Saturday from 10 to 2! <<ENDIF>>

MacWrite II prints the text only if the phone number has a 213 area code enclosed in parentheses. The program searches each value of the Phone Number field to determine whether the string *(213)* occurs anywhere in the merge data. If the program finds the string, the condition is considered true, and the text prints.

The NOT operator allows you to specify the opposite of a condition. You may use NOT as in the following statement:

<<IF NOT State = "CA">> Call us toll free at 1-800-555-9090 <<ENDIF>>

This statement tells the program to print the text if the State is not equal to CA.

Using the NEXT Command

Normally, MacWrite II creates a new form letter for each data record in your merge data file. At times, however, you may want to use the data from more than one record in a single form letter.

The NEXT command causes the program to proceed immediately to the next record in the merge data file. When MacWrite II encounters this command in a form letter, the program moves to the next data record but remains in the same form letter.

An example of using the NEXT command is to use the data file shown in figure 15.3 to create a printed mailing list. Consider figure 15.13, which shows the merge fields for the list.

When you place the NEXT command at the end of each address in the form letter, the program selects the next data record before filling in the information of the merge fields following the NEXT command. Figure 15.14 shows the resulting list.

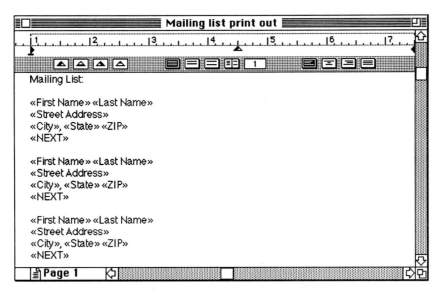

Fig. 15.13. *A "form letter" for a printed mailing list.*

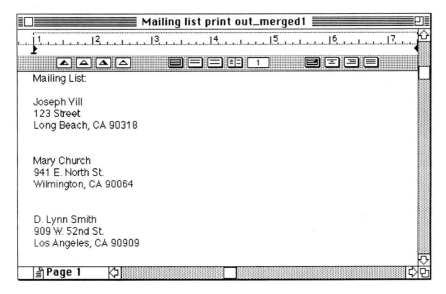

Fig. 15.14. *The mailing list.*

Inserting the IF Statement

You can use one of several ways to enter IF statements in your form letter. These methods correspond closely to the methods outlined for creating form letters.

The first method is to type the IF statement. Follow these steps:

1. Type the left field delimiter.

   You can type the double less-than symbol (or press Option-\) or type another left field delimiter (either [or {).

2. Type IF (upper- or lowercase) followed by a space.

3. Type the name of the merge data field followed by a space.

4. Type the operator.

   If you use the NOT operator, you must type it immediately after IF.

5. Type the value to which you want to compare the merge data.

6. Type the right field delimiter followed by a space.

7. Type the text you want to be printed if the condition is true; type a space.

8. Type the left field delimiter, type *ENDIF*, and type the right field delimiter.

This procedure is the quickest (especially for touch-typists), but if you mistype anything, the program may print strangely or give you an error message when you attempt to merge the data file with the form letter.

As an alternative, you can use the Insert Merge Field dialog box to enter commands. Perform the following steps:

1. Select Insert Merge Field from the File menu.

2. Select the IF command.

3. Click the Insert Command button.

4. Select the field name.

5. Click the Insert Field Name button.

6. Select the operator (from the Command list).

7. Click the Insert Command button.

   The Insert Merge Field dialog box closes automatically. Type the value to which you want to compare the merge data.

8. Place the mouse pointer to the right of the right field delimiter.

9. Click the mouse button once.

   This step places the cursor outside the field delimiters.

10. Type the text to be printed if the condition is true.

11. Select Insert Merge Field.

12. Select the ENDIF command.

13. Click the Insert Command button.

The Insert Merge Field dialog box closes.

Steps like 2 and 3 can be combined into one step. In any of the preceding steps, you can double-click on the command or field name to insert it into your form letter, skipping the use of the Insert Command button.

Compound IF Statements

At times, you may want to have two different texts to print depending on whether a condition is true or false. At other times, you may want to combine conditions. These situations require compound IF statements.

Using the ELSE Statement

In the case of a toll-free number, you may have one number for use within the state and another number for the rest of the country. You can use the ELSE statement to print the number depending on the state of the addressee. Consider the following:

> <<IF State = "CA">> Call us toll free at 1-800-555-9090.
> <<ELSE>> Call us toll free at 1-800-555-8888 <<ENDIF>>

This statement tells the program to do the following:

> If the State data is equal to CA, print the phrase "Call us toll free at 1-800-555-9090."

> Otherwise, print the phrase "Call us toll free at 1-800-555-8888."

The text that follows an ELSE statement is printed if the condition of the IF statement is false.

Using Conjunctions

MacWrite II offers two conjunctions: OR and AND. These conjunctions enable you to combine conditions to create a new condition. For example, your business may be required to collect sales tax for goods sold to customers living in California and Texas but in no other state. You use the following statement:

<<IF State = "CA" OR State = "TX">> Please include sales tax. <<ENDIF>>

This statement tells the program to print the phrase if the State data equals either CA or TX. If the State is any other value, the program does not print the text.

As an example of the use of the AND conjunction, suppose that you want to direct local callers to your local number instead of the toll-free number. You can use the following:

<<IF State = "CA" AND Area Code = 213>> Call us at 555-9000. <<ENDIF>>

Callers outside your local area code but in California can be directed to the state toll-free number with the following statement:

<<IF State = "CA" AND Area Code <> 213>> Call us toll free at 1-800-555-9090 <<ENDIF>>

This statement prints the text if the State data is equal to CA and the Area Code data is *not* equal to 213.

The ELSE statement can be added to a compound IF statement to print text if the condition is found to be false.

Using Parentheses

Parentheses help you control the order in which the program evaluates conditions in a compound IF statement. Conditions you want evaluated first are enclosed in parentheses.

As an example consider the following:

<<IF County = "Los Angeles" AND (Area Code = 213 OR Area Code = 818>> Watch for special offer in the Sunday paper. <<ENDIF>>

MacWrite II first considers the Area Code data. If the Area Code is equal to 213 or 818, the statement in the parentheses is considered true. Then if the County data is equal to Los Angeles, the entire statement is considered true and the text is printed. If the area code is neither 213 nor 818 or if the county is not Los Angeles, the statement is false.

A statement of this kind prints the text only for the addresses in the 213 or 818 area codes in the county of Los Angeles. Compare the preceding statement with the following:

<<IF County = "Los Angeles" AND Area Code = 213 OR Area Code = 818>> Watch for special offer in the Sunday paper. <<ENDIF>>

This statement prints the text for addressees who are in Los Angeles County and have a 213 area code *or* the addressees who have an 818 area code regardless of the county in which they reside.

Producing the Form Letter

After you have created the merge data file and the form letter, you are ready to put the form letter to work. MacWrite II provides a few options for using form letters. These options allow you to print all the form letters, print only some form letters using a range of the data of the merge data file, or send the form letters to another file instead of the printer.

Printing Form Letters

The most straightforward use of a form letter is to merge it with the data file and print one form letter for each record in the data file. To print form letters, open both the form letter document and the merge data file. Then follow these steps:

1. Select Merge from the File menu.

   The Merge dialog box appears (see fig. 15.15).

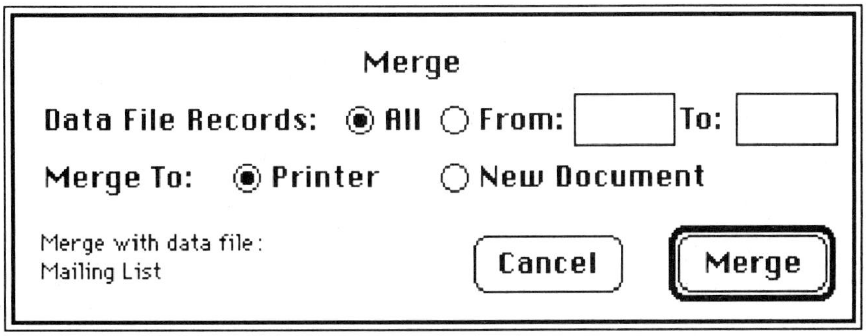

```
┌─────────────────────────────────────────────────────────┐
│                          Merge                           │
│                                                          │
│  Data File Records:  ◉ All  ○ From: [      ]  To: [      ]│
│                                                          │
│  Merge To:   ◉ Printer      ○ New Document               │
│                                                          │
│  Merge with data file:          ┌──────────┐ ┌──────────┐│
│  Mailing List                   │  Cancel  │ │  Merge   ││
│                                 └──────────┘ └──────────┘│
└─────────────────────────────────────────────────────────┘
```

Fig. 15.15. The Merge dialog box.

2. Click the Merge button (or press Return).

   The Print dialog box for your printer appears.

3. Click the OK button (or press Return).

The program begins to print the form letters. You can cancel printing after it has begun by pressing Command-. (period). You may have to hold the keys down for a short while to cause the program to stop printing the form letters. Although Command-. is the standard Macintosh way to cancel printing, this key combination does not always work efficiently in MacWrite II.

Printing a Range of Form Letters

Instead of printing a form letter for every record in your merge data file, you may want to print letters for a particular group of records in the file. In the Merge dialog box, you can specify a range of data records to be printed. You can set a range only of contiguous records (that is, records that follow one after another).

Use the following steps:

1. Select Merge from the File menu.

2. In the From box, type the number of the first merge data file record to be used.

   For example, to begin printing form letters with the tenth record, type *10*.

3. Press Tab.

4. In the To box, type the number of the last merge data file record to be used.

   As an example, type *30* to end the printing with the thirtieth record of the data file.

5. Click the Merge button (or press Return).

   The Print dialog box for your printer appears.

6. Click the OK button (or press Return).

You can cancel printing by pressing Command-. (period). You may need to hold down the keys for a while before the program stops printing.

Sending Form Letters to a Document File

Because canceling the printing of form letters is difficult, you may want to send the form letters to a document file first to determine whether your form letter works as you intended. This test can save a great deal of time and frustration. To send form letters to a document file instead of the printer, do the following:

1. Select Merge from the File menu.

2. Click the New Document option.

3. Click the Merge button once (or press Return).

A new document containing the form letters appears in a new document window. The merged form letters can be reviewed, edited, or printed just like any other MacWrite II document. You also can use the Range option for sending letters to a document.

Summing Up

This chapter is concerned with the form letter capability of MacWrite II. You have seen how to create a merge data file or import data from another program. The chapter discusses three methods of creating form letter documents and explores the Insert Merge Field dialog box options.

The form letter commands have been covered. You now know how to customize your form letters according to the data in your data file. You have seen how to use the IF statement, operators, and the ELSE statement.

Finally, the text has covered the merge options for printing form letters. You have learned how to print form letters for the entire data file or for a range of data file records, and how to print form letters to either the printer or a new document.

Installing MacWrite II

Before using MacWrite II, you must install the program on your system. For hard disk users, installation is an easy process of copying files to the appropriate folders. Floppy disk users face some choices. Because the program comes on three disks (as of the release of Version 1.1), you must choose which parts of the program you need.

Reviewing the Minimum System Requirements

At the very least, you need a Macintosh Plus computer with two 800K drives. Any of the newer Macintosh systems, such as the SE and beyond, satisfy the system requirements of the program.

Although you can use the program without a printer, word processing is of little use if you do not have a way to print the documents you create. A wide variety of printers are on the market today, and all but the most specialized types (such as plotters) work well with MacWrite II. If you need high-resolution printing for your text and graphics, you should consider one of the many laser printers available. Color is available only on printers with color capability.

A hard disk drive is helpful but not required unless you want to use the Word Finder thesaurus program (see Chapter 5). A hard disk increases the program's operating speed and enables you to store more documents.

A large-screen monitor can be beneficial, but it is not required for running the program. Many larger monitors provide the capability of viewing an entire page (or even two) at one time—a capability that can be a great help when you are working with documents.

The most recent System software (as of the writing of this book, System 6) is recommended. Because of the special requirements of the upcoming System 7, many users will be unable to upgrade to this new system. These users can remain with System 6, however, because the program operates well under this release.

Installing the MacWrite II Package

The MacWrite II program comes on three 800K floppy disks (as of release 1.1). These disks contain the following program files:

- MacWrite II disk
  MacWrite II
  Main Dictionary
  User Dictionary
  MacWrite II Hyphenation
  Stationery Templates (within a folder)
  Tutorial (contains a few MacWrite II documents)

- MacWrite II Reference disk
  Claris Translators (a folder of translator files)
  Thesaurus (a folder of Word Finder thesaurus files)

- MacWrite II Help disk
  MacWrite II Help
  MacWrite II Help System
  MacLink Plus/Bridge (a folder of MacLink Plus files)

Installing MacWrite II on a Floppy Disk System

Floppy disk users need to determine the features they need most in order to decide how to install the program. Unfortunately, not all the files fit on one disk. (You may want to create more than one MacWrite II disk with different features on each.) Because you need to understand the program to choose the features you need, the basic installation is discussed first to enable you to begin working with the program.

This procedure is based on the assumption that you have some familiarity with the Macintosh operating system. If you are new to the Macintosh, read the manuals that come with the computer and work through the tutorial provided by Apple.

Basic Installation

To create a MacWrite II working disk, follow these steps:

1. Insert a blank disk into one of the disk drives.

    The Macintosh informs you that it is unable to read the disk. You are offered the choice of initializing the disk as a one-sided or two-sided disk.

2. Click the Two-sided button.

    You are informed that the disk will be erased. Because the disk is blank, erasure is not a problem.

3. Click Erase. You are now asked to name the disk.

4. Type *MacWrite II Work Disk* and press Return; the system then formats the disk.

5. Click the System disk icon.

6. Select Eject from the File menu (or press Command-E).

7. Insert the MacWrite II disk into the drive from which the System disk was ejected.

    The MacWrite II program files appear (see fig. A.1).

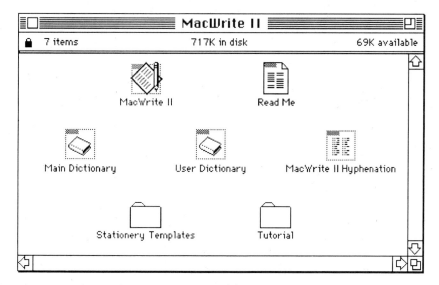

Fig. A.1.** **The MacWrite II program files.

8. Press and hold the Shift key.

9. Place the mouse pointer on the MacWrite II icon and click once.

   The MacWrite II program darkens (see fig. A.2). Continue to hold down the Shift key.

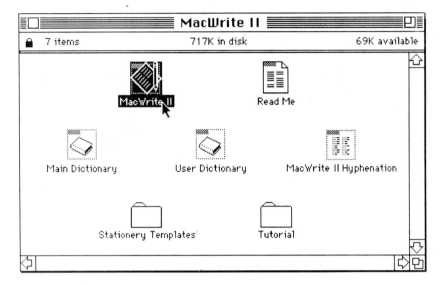

Fig. A.2. Selecting the MacWrite II program.

10. Place the mouse pointer on the Main Dictionary icon and click once. This file also darkens.

11. Place the mouse pointer on the User Dictionary icon and click once.

12. Release the Shift key.

13. Place the mouse pointer on the MacWrite II program.

14. Press and hold the mouse button.

15. Move the mouse until the mouse pointer is over the MacWrite II Work Disk.

    Outlines of the selected files move with the mouse pointer. When the mouse pointer is over the MacWrite II Work Disk, the disk picture (icon) darkens.

16. Release the mouse button.

    The computer informs you that it is copying the files to the new disk.

17. Place the mouse button on the MacWrite II disk icon (not the Work Disk) and click once.

18. Select Eject from the File menu.

19. Insert the System disk into the disk drive.

The MacWrite II Work Disk is ready to use. This disk enables you to work with the features discussed in this book, except for the Word Finder thesaurus (covered in Chapter 5) and the use of other program formats (parts of Chapters 6 and 12).

Translators (discussed in Chapters 6 and 12) can be installed if your System disk has sufficient space. You cannot use the Word Finder thesaurus on a two-drive system (unless you have more than one megabyte of memory and use a RAM disk).

Translators

Chapters 6, 12, and 15 of this book discuss, in the context of the features covered, using files created by other programs. If you are going to be sharing files between MacWrite II and other programs, you need to install the translators for those programs. To do so, follow these steps:

1. Place the mouse pointer on your System disk icon.

2. Double-click to open the disk.

3. Select New Folder from the File menu. A new folder named Empty Folder appears.

4. Type *Claris Translators*.

5. Insert the MacWrite II Reference disk.

6. Place the mouse pointer on the Claris Translators folder icon of the MacWrite II Reference disk.

7. Double-click to open the folder.

    The translator file icons appear (see fig. A.3).

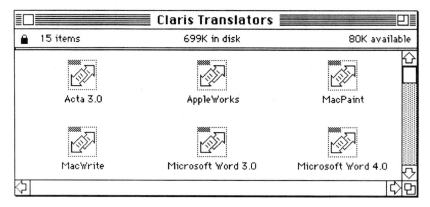

Fig. A.3. *The translator file icons.*

8. Press and hold the Shift key.

9. Place the mouse pointer on the icon of the first translator file to be copied and click once.

   For this book, you should copy at least the PICT translator. Repeat step 9 for each translator file you need.

10. Release the Shift key.

11. Place the mouse pointer on any of the darkened files.

12. Press and hold the mouse button.

13. Move the mouse pointer to the Claris Folder on your System disk (the Claris Folder darkens).

14. Release the mouse button. The files are then copied.

15. Place the mouse pointer on the MacWrite II Reference disk icon and click once.

16. Select Eject from the File menu.

If you plan to use translator files from DataViz (the MacLink Plus program), use the same procedure to copy the MacLink Plus/Bridge file (in the MacLink Plus/Bridge folder on the MacWrite II Help disk) into the Claris Folder on your System disk.

General Tips for Floppy Disk Users

If you are using floppy disks, you should copy only the files you need. Obviously, you need the MacWrite II program itself. If you want to use the spelling-checking capability of the program (Chapter 4), you also need to have the Main Dictionary and User Dictionary files on your MacWrite II Work Disk.

You do not need to copy the MacWrite II Hyphenation file to your working disk unless you want to use the hyphenation feature (Chapter 5). If you do not need to share files between MacWrite II and other programs, you do not need to copy any of the translator files.

Floppy disk users who have a RAM disk may use the Word Finder thesaurus by creating a Thesaurus disk. Copy the WF Large Thesaurus file from the Thesaurus folder on the MacWrite II Reference disk to a disk of its own. Insert this disk when you want to use the Word Finder thesaurus desk accessory. For installation instructions for the desk accessory, see the section on hard disk installation of the program.

The help system is unavailable unless you have a hard drive or RAM disk. If you do have a RAM disk, copy the Claris Help System file into your System Folder and then copy the file MacWrite II Help from the MacWrite II Help disk to a separate disk. Insert this disk before choosing Help from the Apple menu in the program.

Installing MacWrite on a Hard Disk

Installing the program on a hard disk drive is easy. The procedure consists mostly of copying files from the MacWrite II disks to the hard disk. Use the following steps to ready the MacWrite II program for use on your hard drive:

1. Double-click the hard drive icon to open it.

2. Select New Folder from the File menu.

3. Type *MacWrite II Folder.*

4. Double-click the MacWrite II folder icon to open the folder (see fig. A.4).

5. Insert the MacWrite II disk into the drive.

6. Double-click the MacWrite II disk icon to open the disk.

7. Choose Select All from the Edit menu.

8. Place the mouse pointer on the MacWrite II file.

9. Press and hold the mouse button, and move the mouse pointer, dragging the file outlines, onto the MacWrite II Folder.

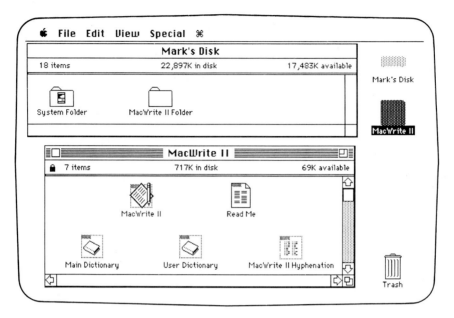

Fig. A.4. The MacWrite II folder.

10. When the folder darkens, release the mouse button.

    The files are copied into the folder.

11. Click the MacWrite II disk icon once.

12. Select Eject from the File menu.

13. Insert the MacWrite II Help disk in the drive.

14. Click the MacWrite II Help file icon once.

15. Press and hold the Shift key, and click the Claris Help System file icon once (see fig. A.5).

16. Release the Shift key.

17. Place the mouse pointer on the MacWrite II Help file.

18. Press and hold the mouse button, and move the mouse pointer, dragging the file outlines, onto the MacWrite II folder.

19. When the folder darkens, release the mouse button.

    The files are copied into the folder. If you are going to use the translator files, skip the following steps and proceed to the next section.

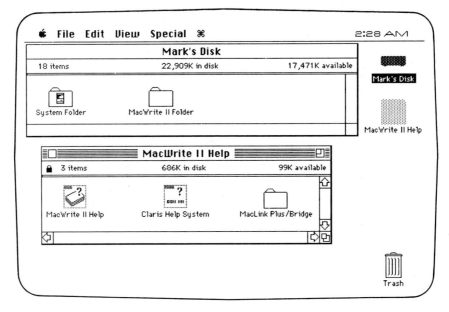

Fig. A.5. *Selecting the help files.*

20. Click the MacWrite II Help disk icon once.

21. Select Eject from the File menu.

Installing Translator Files

Use the following steps if you plan to share files between MacWrite II and other programs:

1. Double-click the System Folder icon on your hard drive to open it.

2. Select New Folder from the File menu.

3. Type *Claris Translators*.

4. Insert the MacWrite II Help disk, and double-click the disk icon to open it.

5. Double-click the MacLink Plus/Bridge folder to open it.

6. Place the mouse pointer on the MacLink Plus/Bridge file.

7. Press and hold the mouse button, and move the mouse pointer onto the Claris Translators folder on your hard drive.

8. When the folder darkens, release the mouse button.

   The file is copied.

9. Click the MacWrite II Help disk icon once.

10. Select Eject from the File menu.

11. Insert the MacWrite II Reference disk into the drive.

12. Double-click the Claris Translators folder on the MacWrite II Reference disk to open it (see fig. A.6).

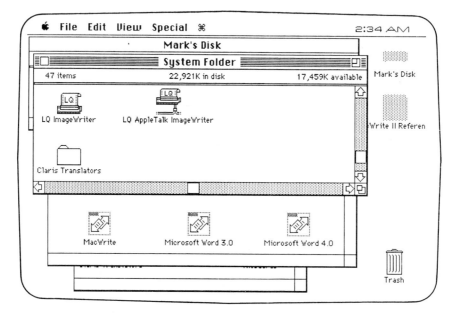

Fig. A.6. *Adding the Claris Translators folder.*

13. Choose Select All from the Edit menu; all the icons darken (see fig. A.7).

14. Place the mouse pointer on any of the darkened icons.

15. Move the mouse pointer to the Claris Translators folder on your hard drive.

16. When the folder darkens, release the mouse button.

    The files are copied. If you want to use the Word Finder thesaurus, skip the following steps and proceed to the next section.

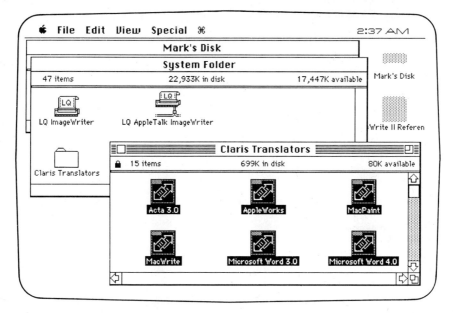

Fig. A.7. *Selecting the translator files.*

17. Click the MacWrite II Reference disk icon once.

18. Select Eject from the File menu.

Installing the Word Finder Thesaurus

Installing the thesaurus system requires the use of the Font/DA Mover program. This program has been provided by Claris on the MacWrite II Reference disk, although the program is part of the Apple System software.

Follow these steps to install the thesaurus:

1. Insert the MacWrite II Reference disk.

2. Double-click the Thesaurus folder to open it (see fig. A.8).

3. Place the mouse pointer on the WF Large Thesaurus file icon.

4. Press and hold the mouse button, and move the mouse pointer to the System Folder on your hard drive.

5. When the folder darkens, release the mouse button.

   The file is copied.

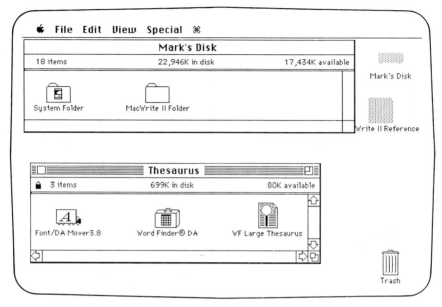

Fig. A.8. *Preparing to copy the thesaurus.*

6. Place the mouse pointer on the Word Finder DA icon, and double-click.

   The Font/DA Mover program starts (see fig. A.9).

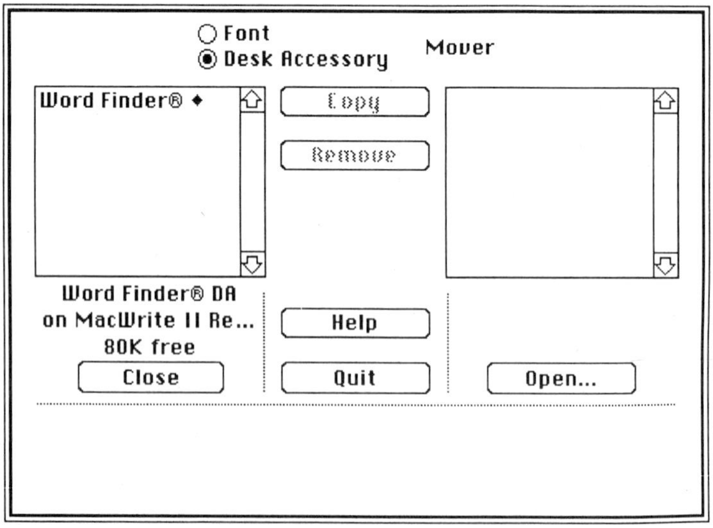

Fig. A.9. *The Font/DA Mover screen.*

7. Click the Open button.

8. Click the Drive button until your hard drive appears.

9. Double-click the System Folder.

   You see the System file in the list box of the dialog box.

10. Double-click the System file icon.

11. Click the Word Finder desk accessory listed in the left-hand list box (see fig. A.10).

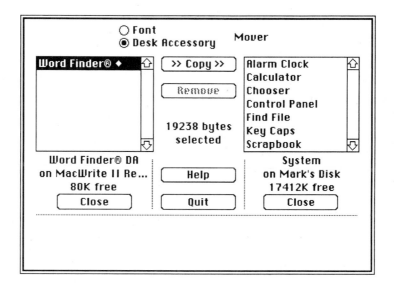

Fig. A.10. *Copying the Word Finder disk accessory.*

12. Click Copy.

    The desk accessory is copied into your System file.

13. Click Quit.

14. Click the MacWrite II Reference disk once.

15. Select Eject from the File menu.

You have now completed the installation of the MacWrite II program. You are ready to begin your exploration of the program.

Quick Reference: Procedures

This section contains quick, step-by-step instructions for the major procedures for using MacWrite II. Keyboard equivalents for an operation are shown in parentheses. Alternative steps for many procedures are given.

Working with Documents

Opening a Document

1. Select New from the File menu (Command-N) to create a new document.

Or

1. Select Open from the File menu (Command-O) to open an existing document.

2. Double-click the document name.

Closing a Document

1. Select Close from the File menu (Command-W).

Or

1. Click the close box in the upper left corner of the document window.

Saving a Document

1. Select Save (Command-S) from the File menu. If the document has not been saved previously, type a name for the document, and press Return.

Or

1. To save a copy of the document under a different name, select Save As from the File menu, type a name for the document, and press Return.

Reverting to the Last Saved Version

1. Select Revert to Saved from the File menu.

2. Click OK (press Return).

Inserting a File into a Document

1. Select Insert File from the File menu (Shift-Command-I).

2. Double-click the file name.

Opening a Merge Data File

1. Select Open Merge Data File from the File menu.

2. Double-click the file name.

Switching to Another Open Document

1. Select document name from the View menu.

Viewing Invisible Formatting Characters

1. Select Show Invisibles from the View menu (Command- semicolon).

Hiding Invisible Formatting Characters

1. Select Hide Invisibles from the View menu (Command-semicolon).

Viewing Reduced Size

1. Select Reduced Size from the View menu (Command-R).

Viewing Normal Size

1. Select Actual Size from the View menu (Command-R).

Printing Documents

Printing a Document

1. Select Print from the File menu (Command-P).

2. Click OK (press Return).

Printing a Form Letter

1. Select Merge from the File menu.

2. Click Merge (press Return).

3. Click OK (press Return).

Working with Text

Selecting Text

1. Place the mouse pointer at the beginning of the text.

2. Press and hold the mouse button.

3. Move the pointer to the end of the text.

4. Release the mouse button.

Selecting the Entire Document

1. Choose Select All from the Edit menu (Command-A).

Deleting Text

1. Select the text.

2. Select Clear from the Edit menu (press Backspace).

Copying Text

1. Select the text.

2. Select Copy from the Edit menu (Command-C).

3. Click where the text is to be copied.

4. Select Paste from the Edit menu (Command-V).

Moving Text

1. Select the text.

2. Select Cut from the Edit menu (Command-X).

3. Click where the text is to be moved.

4. Select Paste from the Edit menu (Command-V).

Searching for Text

1. Select Find/Change from the Edit menu (Command-F).

2. Type the text to be searched for.

3. Click Whole Word to search for whole words, Partial Word to find a part of a word, Case Sensitive to match upper- and lowercase letters.

4. Click Find Next (press Return).

Searching and Replacing Text

1. Select Find/Change from the Edit menu (Command-F).

2. Type the text to be searched for.

3. Press Tab and type the text to replace the located text.

4. Click Whole Word to search for whole words, Partial Word to find a part of a word, Case Sensitive to match upper- and lowercase letters.

5. Click Find Next (press Return).

6. Click Change to change only this occurrence; Change, Then Find to change this occurrence and locate the next; Change All and then OK to change every occurrence.

Inserting the Date

1. Select Insert Date from the Edit menu (Shift-Command-A).

Setting the Date Format

1. Select Preferences from the Edit menu.

2. Click the desired format.

3. Click Always Update to have the date updated, Never Update to have it left as inserted.

4. Click OK (press Return).

Inserting the Time

1. Select Insert Time from the Edit menu (Shift-Command-T).

Inserting the Page Number

1. Select Insert Page # from the Edit menu (Shift-Command-P).

Setting the Starting Page Number

1. Select Preferences from the Edit menu.

2. Type the starting page number.

3. Click OK (press Return).

Setting the Page Number Format

1. Select Preferences from the Edit menu.

2. Click Current Page # to have just the page number, Current of Total to have a page number and the total number of pages.

3. Click OK (press Return).

Selecting Fonts and Styles

Selecting a Font

1. Choose the font from the Font menu.

Selecting a Font Size

1. Choose the size from the Size menu.

Or

1. Choose Other from the Size menu (Shift-Command-O).

2. Type the font size.

3. Click OK (press Return).

Boldfacing Text

1. Select Bold from the Style menu (Command-B).

2. Type the text.

Or

1. Select the text.

2. Select Bold from the Style menu (Command-B).

Italicizing Text

1. Select Italic from the Style menu (Command-I).

2. Type the text.

Or

1. Select the text.

2. Select Italic from the Style menu (Command-I).

Underlining Text

1. Select Underline (Command-U), Word Underline (Shift-Command-U), or Double Underline (Shift-Command-L) from the Style menu.

2. Type the text.

Or

1. Select the text.

2. Select Underline (Command-U), Word Underline (Shift-Command-U), or Double Underline (Shift-Command-L) from the Style menu.

Superscripting or Subscripting Text

1. Select Superscript (Shift-Command-plus) or Subscript (Shift-Command-minus) from the Style menu.

2. Type the text.

Or

1. Select the text.

2. Select Superscript (Shift-Command-plus) or Subscript (Shift-Command-minus) from the Style menu.

Choosing Color

1. Select Color from the Style menu; continue to hold down the mouse button.

2. Move into the Color menu and select the desired color.

3. Type the text.

Or

1. Select the text.

2. Select Color from the Style menu; continue to hold down the mouse button.

3. Move into the Color menu and select the desired color.

Setting All Text Attributes at Once

1. Select Character from the Format menu (Shift-Command-D).

2. Choose font, font size, and font color.

3. Click the desired text attributes.

4. Click OK (press Return).

Creating a Custom Text Style

1. Select Custom from the Style menu (Command-D).

2. Select the font, font size, and font color.

3. Click each desired font style attribute.

4. Type the custom style name.

5. Click Add (press Return).

6. Click OK.

Changing a Custom Text Style

1. Select Custom from the Style menu (Command-D).

2. Click the style name.

3. Select the font, font size, and font color.

4. Click the desired font style attributes.

5. Click Modify.

6. Click OK.

Removing a Custom Text Style

1. Select Custom from the Style menu (Command-D).

2. Click the style name.

3. Click Remove.

4. Click OK.

Searching for Text Attributes

1. Select Find/Change from Edit menu (Command-F).

2. Click Use Attributes.

3. Click to place or remove the X in attributes needed or not needed, respectively.

4. Click Find Next.

Searching and Replacing Text Attributes

1. Select Find/Change from Edit menu (Command-F).

2. Click Use Attributes.

3. Click to place or remove the X in attributes needed or not needed for search, respectively.

4. Click to place or remove the X in attributes needed or not needed for replacement, respectively.

5. Click Find Next.

6. Click Change to change one occurrence; Change, Then Find to change and then locate next occurrence; Change All and then OK to change every occurrence.

Formatting Pages

Creating Left/Right Pages

1. Select Page from the Format menu.

2. Click the Left/Right Pages option.

3. Click OK (press Return).

Viewing Left/Right Pages

1. Select Side By Side from the View menu.

2. Select again to return to normal view.

Setting Page Margins

1. Select Page from the Format menu.

2. Type the top margin setting, press Tab, type the bottom margin setting, press Tab, type the left (or inside) margin setting, press Tab, and type the right (or outside) margin setting.

3. Click OK (press Return).

Viewing Page Margins

1. Select Show Page Guides from View menu (Command-G).

2. Select again to return to normal view.

Adding a Title Page

1. Select Page from the Format menu.

2. Click the Title Page option.

3. Click OK (press Return).

Setting the Number of Columns

1. Select Page from the Format menu.

2. Press Tab four times, type the number of columns, press Tab, and type the amount of space between columns.

3. Click OK (press Return).

Inserting a Page Break

1. Click where the page is to end.

2. Select Insert Page Break.

Removing a Page Break

1. Click at the beginning of the page after the page break.

2. Press Backspace.

Or

1. Select Show Invisibles from the View Menu (Command-semicolon).

2. Double-click the page break character.

3. Press Backspace.

Inserting a Column Break

1. Click where the column is to end.

2. Select Insert Column Break from the Format menu.

Removing a Column Break

1. Click at beginning of column after column break.

2. Press Backspace.

Or

1. Select Show Invisibles from the View Menu (Command-semicolon).

2. Double-click column break character.

3. Press Backspace.

Inserting a Header

1. Select Insert Header from Format menu.

2. Type the header text.

Removing a Header

1. Select Remove Header from the Format menu.

2. Click OK.

Resizing a Header

1. Click once in the header.

2. Place the mouse pointer on the small black square in the center of the header boundary.

3. Press and hold the mouse button, drag the header to the new size, and release the button.

Inserting a Footer

1. Select Insert Footer from the Format menu.

2. Type the footer text.

Removing a Footer

1. Select Remove Footer from the Format menu.

2. Click OK.

Resizing a Footer

1. Click once in the footer.

2. Place the mouse pointer on the small black square in the center of the footer boundary.

3. Press and hold the mouse button, drag the footer to the new size, and release the button.

Inserting a Footnote

1. Select Insert Footnote from the Format menu.

2. Type the footnote.

3. Press Command-Return to return to last cursor position.

Using Special Footnote Characters

    1. Turn off the Auto Number Footnotes option.

For each footnote,

    2. Select Insert Footnote from the Format menu.

    3. Type the footnote reference character.

    4. Click OK.

    5. Type the footnote.

    6. Press Command-Return to return to last cursor position.

Turning Auto Numbering of Footnotes On or Off

    1. Select Preferences from Edit menu.

    2. Click the Auto Number Footnotes option.

    3. Click OK.

Positioning the Footnote Print Position

    1. Select Preferences from the Edit menu.

    2. Click the End of Page or End of Document option.

    3. Click OK.

Formatting Paragraphs

Setting Paragraph Indents

    1. Select Paragraph from the Format menu.

    2. Type the left indent setting, press Tab, type the first-line indent setting, press Tab, and type the right indent setting.

    3. Click OK (press Return).

Or

    1. Drag the indent marker in the ruler to the new location.

Creating a Hanging First-Line Indent

    1. Select Paragraph from the Format menu.

    2. Press Tab and then type a negative setting in the First Line indent box.

Or

1. Drag the left indent marker to a new location.

2. Drag the first-line indent marker to the left.

Setting Line Spacing

1. Select Paragraph from the Format menu.

2. Press Tab three times, and then type the line spacing setting.

3. Click OK (press Return).

Or

1. Click the single-space, double-space, or triple-space icon.

Or

1. Click the left half of the line spacing fine-tuning icon to decrease the line spacing, or click the right half to increase the line spacing.

Changing the Line Spacing Unit of Measure

1. Select Paragraph from the Format menu.

2. Place the mouse pointer on the line spacing unit of measure pop-up menu.

3. Press and hold the mouse button, and then select the unit of measure.

4. Click OK (press Return).

Setting Space Before or After a Paragraph

1. Select Paragraph from the Format menu.

2. Press Tab four times, and then type the amount of space before the paragraph.

3. Press Tab once and type the amount of space after the paragraph.

4. Click OK (press Return).

Setting Tabs

1. Select Tab from the Format menu.

2. Click Left, Center, Right, or Align On.

3. Type the position of the tab.

4. Click Apply and repeat steps 2 and 3 for more tabs.

5. Click OK (press Return).

Or

1. Place the mouse pointer on the tab icon.

2. Press and hold the mouse button.

3. Drag the tab icon onto the ruler.

4. Release the mouse button.

Modifying Tabs

1. Select Tab from the Format menu.

2. Click the tab to be modified.

3. Click Tab Type and type new position, or press Tab and type the new fill character.

4. Click OK (press Return).

Or

1. Double-click the tab to be modified.

2. Click Tab Type and type new position, or press Tab and type the new fill character.

3. Click OK (press Return).

To move to a tab stop only,

1. Place the mouse pointer on the tab icon in the ruler.

2. Press and hold the mouse button.

3. Drag to the new location.

4. Release the mouse button.

Copying a Ruler

1. Click the paragraph with the ruler settings to be copied.

2. Select Copy Ruler from the Format menu (Shift-Command-C).

3. Click the paragraph where the ruler settings are to be applied.

4. Select Apply Ruler from the Format menu (Shift-Command-V).

Checking Spelling

Installing the Main Dictionary

1. Select Install Dictionaries from the Spelling menu.

2. Click the Main option.

3. Double-click the main dictionary name.

Installing the User Dictionary

1. Select Install Dictionaries from the Spelling menu.

2. Click the User option.

3. Double-click the user dictionary name.

Removing the User Dictionary

1. Select Install Dictionaries from the Spelling menu.

2. Click the User option.

3. Click None.

Creating a New User Dictionary

1. Select Install Dictionaries from the Spelling menu.

2. Click the User option.

3. Click New.

4. Type the user dictionary name.

5. Click Save (press Return).

Checking the Spelling in a Document

1. Select Check All from the Spelling menu (Command-equal sign).

2. Double-click a listed spelling correction (or press Command and the number next to the correction you want).

   Or

   Type the new spelling and click Replace (press Return).

3. Repeat until done, and then click Done (press Return).

Adding Words to the User Dictionary

1. Click Learn in the Spelling dialog box.

Or

1. Select User Dictionary from the Spelling menu.

2. Type the word to be added.

3. Click Add (press Return).

4. Click OK.

Removing Words from the User Dictionary

1. Select User Dictionary from the Spelling menu.

2. Click the word to be removed.

3. Click Remove.

4. Click OK.

Checking the Spelling of a Page Element

1. Click in page element.

2. Select Check Header, Check Footer, Check Footnotes, Check Main Body (depending on the element you want to check).

Checking the Spelling of a Text Selection

1. Select text.

2. Select Check Selection from the Spelling menu (Command-K).

Checking Spelling as You Type

1. Select Spelling Options from the Spelling menu.

2. Click Beep On Questionable Settings.

   Or

   Click Flash Menu Bar on Questionable Settings.

3. Click OK (press Return).

Looking up the Questioned Word

When using the Spell As You Type option:

1. Select Spell Word from the Spelling menu (Command-Y).

2. Double-click the correct spelling.

   Or

   Type the new spelling and click Replace (press Return).

Hyphenating Your Document

Hyphenating a Document

    1. Select Auto Hyphenate from the Spelling menu.

Turning Off Hyphenation

    1. Select Auto Hyphenate from the Spelling menu.

Entering a Hyphenation Exception

    1. Select Hyph. Exceptions from the Spelling menu.

    2. Type the word with hyphens.

    3. Click Add (press Return).

    4. Click OK.

Removing a Hyphenation Exception

    1. Select Hyph. Exceptions from the Spelling menu.

    2. Click the exception to be removed.

    3. Click Remove.

    4. Click OK.

Inserting a Discretionary Hyphen

    1. Press Command-hyphen.

Working with Graphics

Inserting a Graphic

    1. Click where the graphic is to be inserted.

    2. Select Insert File from the File menu (Shift-Command-I).

    3. Double-click the name of the graphic file.

Or

    1. Click where the graphic is to be inserted.

    2. Select Scrapbook from the Apple menu.

    3. Select Copy from the Edit menu (Command-C).

    4. Click the close box of the Scrapbook.

    5. Select Paste from the Edit menu (Command-V).

Scaling a Graphic

1. Click the graphic.

2. Place the mouse pointer on one of the four black, square handles in the corner of the graphic.

3. Press and hold the Shift key to maintain the graphic's proportions.

4. Press and hold the mouse button; then move the mouse to change the graphic's size.

5. Release the mouse button.

Or

1. Click the graphic.

2. Select Scale Picture from the Format menu.

3. Type the vertical percentage to scale, press Tab, and then type the horizontal percentage to scale.

4. Click OK (press Return).

Cropping a Graphic

1. Click the graphic.

2. Place the mouse pointer on one of the four black, square handles in the corner of the graphic.

3. Press and hold the Option key.

4. Press and hold the mouse button; then move the mouse to crop the graphic.

5. Release the mouse button.

Creating Form Letters

Opening a Merge Data File

1. Select Open Merge Data file from the File menu.

2. Double-click the file name.

Inserting a Merge Field

1. Select Insert Merge Field from the File menu (Shift-Command-M).

2. Click the field name.

3. Click Insert Field Name.

Inserting a Merge Command

1. Select Insert Merge Field from the File menu (Shift-Command-M).

2. Click the command.

3. Click the Insert Command button.

Changing the Merge Field Delimiter

1. Select Insert Merge Field from the File menu (Shift-Command-M).

2. Place the mouse pointer on the Field Delimiter menu.

3. Press and hold the mouse button.

4. Highlight the delimiter; then release the mouse button.

Finding a Merge Field

1. Select Insert Merge Field from the File menu (Shift-Command-M).

2. Select delimiters from the Field Delimiter menu (if not already displayed).

3. Click Find Delimiter.

Printing Form Letters

1. Select Merge from the File menu.

2. Click Merge (press Return).

3. Click OK (press Return).

Printing a Range of Form Letters

1. Select Merge from the File menu.

2. Type the number of the first data record, press Tab, and then type the number of the last data record.

3. Click Merge (press Return).

4. Click OK (press Return).

Printing Form Letters to a Document File

1. Select Merge from the File menu.

2. Click the New Document option.

3. Click Merge (press Return).

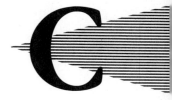

Menu-by-Menu Reference Guide

This guide displays each menu in MacWrite II with a short explanation of the functions of the available commands. References to the chapters in which these commands are discussed are given in parentheses.

The Apple Menu

The Apple menu varies according to the desk accessories you have installed in your Apple System file. The options also are affected by whether you use MultiFinder (see your Macintosh manual for more information). Your menu may not appear exactly as shown in figure C.1, therefore, but two items—About MacWrite II and Help—are constant.

```
 ╔══╗
 ║ ⬤ ║
 ╠══╩═══════════════════╗
 ║ About MacWrite II...  ║
 ║ Help...          ⌘?  ║
 ╟┄┄┄┄┄┄┄┄┄┄┄┄┄┄┄┄┄┄┄┄┄┄╢
 ║ Chooser              ║
 ║ Control Panel        ║
 ║ Find File            ║
 ║ Key Caps             ║
 ║ Scrapbook            ║
 ║ Word Finder® ◆       ║
 ╚══════════════════════╝
```

Fig. C.1. *The Apple menu.*

The commands available from the Apple Menu and their functions are

- *About MacWrite II.* Brings up a window with general information about the program, including the version number

- *Help.* Starts the Claris Help system (Appendix A discusses installation of this system.)

- *Word Finder* (a desk accessory provided with MacWrite II). Brings up the Word Finder thesaurus (Chapter 5 and Appendix A). Word Finder must be installed before it can appear (see Appendix A)

The File Menu

The File menu contains the commands for opening, closing, saving, and printing document files (see fig. C.2).

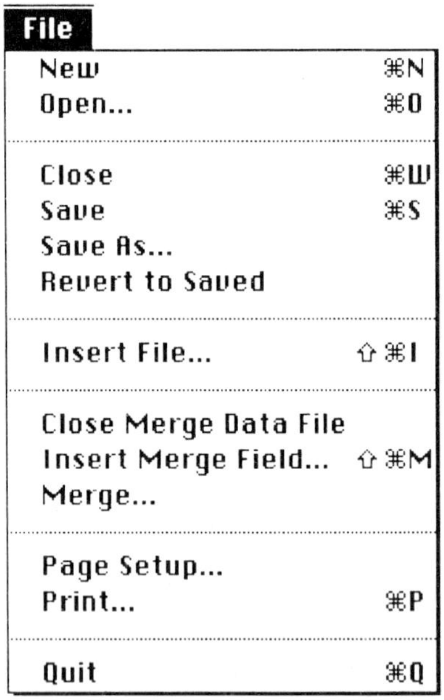

```
File
  New                     ⌘N
  Open...                 ⌘O

  Close                   ⌘W
  Save                    ⌘S
  Save As...
  Revert to Saved

  Insert File...        ⇧⌘I

  Close Merge Data File
  Insert Merge Field... ⇧⌘M
  Merge...

  Page Setup...
  Print...                ⌘P

  Quit                    ⌘Q
```

Fig. C.2. The File menu.

The commands available from the File menu are

- *New.* Creates a new, blank document (Chapter 2)

- *Open.* Opens an existing MacWrite II or other document (Chapter 6)

- *Close*. Closes the current document (Chapter 2)

- *Save*. Saves the current document to disk (Chapters 2 and 6)

- *Save As*. Saves a copy of the current document to disk (Chapters 2 and 6)

- *Revert to Saved*. Returns the current document to the version last saved to disk (Chapter 2)

- *Insert File*. Inserts another file into the current document (Chapters 6 and 12)

- *Open/Close Merge Data File*. Opens or closes the merge data file for use in a form letter (Chapter 15)

- *Insert Merge Field*. Inserts a merge data field into the document (Chapter 15)

- *Merge*. Prints form letters, combining the merge data file and the form letter (Chapter 15)

- *Page Setup*. Brings up a dialog box that enables you to set printer options (Chapter 2)

- *Print*. Prints the current document (Chapter 2)

- *Quit*. Quits MacWrite II

The Edit Menu

Figure C.3 shows the Edit menu.

The commands available from the Edit menu include

- *Undo*. Changes according to the last operation performed. Selecting it causes the program to reverse the last operation (Chapter 3).

- *Cut*. Cuts selected text or graphic from the document and stores in the Clipboard (Chapters 3, 6, and 12)

- *Copy*. Copies selected text or graphic to the Clipboard (Chapters 3, 6, and 12)

- *Paste*. Places the text or graphic in the Clipboard into the document at the current cursor position (Chapters 3, 6, and 12)

- *Clear*. Deletes the selected text (Chapter 3)

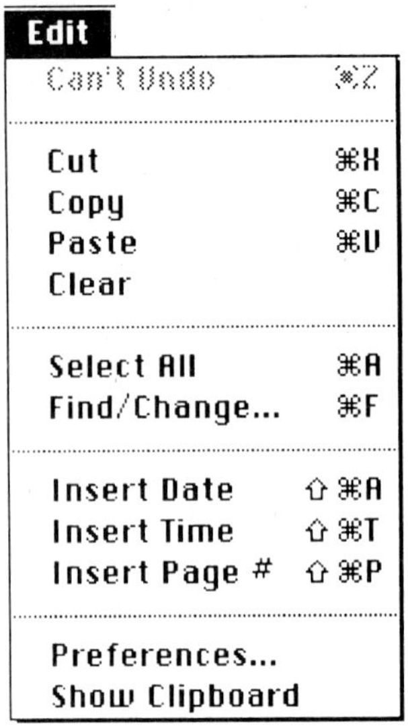

```
╔═══════════════════════════════╗
║ Edit                          ║
╟───────────────────────────────╢
║ Can't Undo           ⌘Z       ║
║ ·····························  ║
║ Cut                  ⌘H       ║
║ Copy                 ⌘C       ║
║ Paste                ⌘U       ║
║ Clear                         ║
║ ·····························  ║
║ Select All           ⌘A       ║
║ Find/Change...       ⌘F       ║
║ ·····························  ║
║ Insert Date        ⇧⌘A        ║
║ Insert Time        ⇧⌘T        ║
║ Insert Page #      ⇧⌘P        ║
║ ·····························  ║
║ Preferences...                ║
║ Show Clipboard                ║
╚═══════════════════════════════╝
```

Fig. C.3. The Edit menu.

- *Select All.* Selects all text and graphics in the document (Chapter 3)

- *Find/Change.* Brings up a window that enables you to search for and optionally replace text and text attributes (Chapters 5 and 10)

- *Insert Date.* Inserts the current date into the document (Chapter 9)

- *Insert Time.* Inserts the current time into the document (Chapter 9)

- *Insert Page #.* Inserts the page number into the document (Chapter 9)

- *Preferences.* Enables you to make preferred settings, including the unit of measure (Chapter 2), date, time, page number, and footnote numbering settings (Chapter 9)

- *Show Clipboard.* Displays the contents of the Clipboard (Chapters 3, 6, and 12)

The Font Menu

The Font menu varies according to the fonts you have installed in your System file (see fig. C.4). The fonts are displayed in their actual typeface and appear in your document as shown in the menu. The selected font has a check mark to the left of it. MacWrite II automatically selects Helvetica for new documents, but this default selection may be changed at any time. Chapter 10 discusses fonts.

Fig. C.4. *The Font menu.*

The Size Menu

The Size menu enables you to select the size of the font you have chosen in the Font menu (see fig. C.5). The font sizes that have been installed in your System file are displayed in outlined type in the menu; these sizes produce the best results. See Chapter 10 for information on this menu.

Besides the different size options, the Size menu contains only one command:

  • *Other*. Enables you to enter any font size from 2 to 500 points

The Style Menu

The Style menu enables you to choose the text styling for the current font (see fig. C.6). Chapter 10 provides a discussion of this menu.

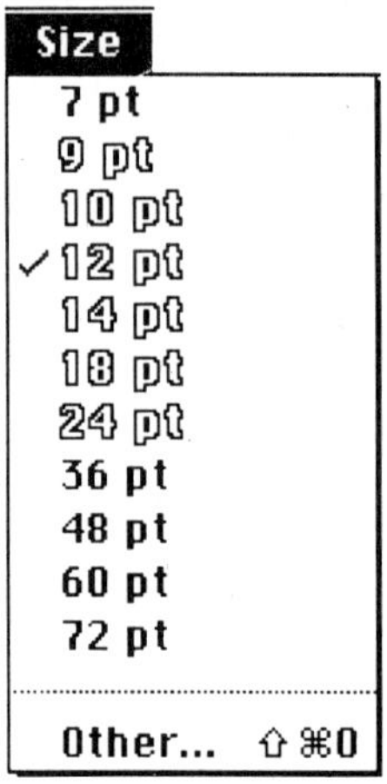

***Fig. C.5.** The Size menu.*

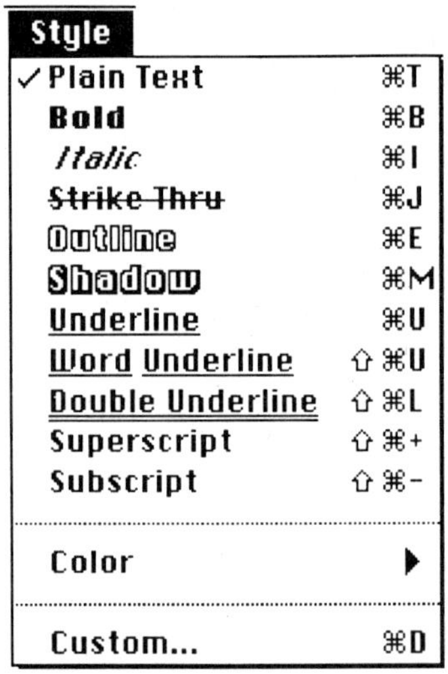

***Fig. C.6.** The Style menu.*

The commands available from the Style menu are

- *Plain Text.* Uses the base font without attributes

- *Bold.* Boldfaces the current font

- *Italic.* Italicizes the current font

- *Strike Thru.* Draws a line through the selected text

- *Outline*. Changes the current font to an outline font

- *Shadow*. Places a shadow on the current font

- *Underline*. Underlines the text

- *Word Underline*. Underlines individual words in the text, does not underline spaces

- *Double Underline*. Places two lines under the text

- *Superscript*. Raises the text to superscript position

- *Subscript*. Lowers the text to subscript position

- *Color*. Enables you to choose the color of text

- *Custom*. Enables you to create a custom text style

The Format Menu

The Format menu consists of various formatting commands (see fig. C.7).

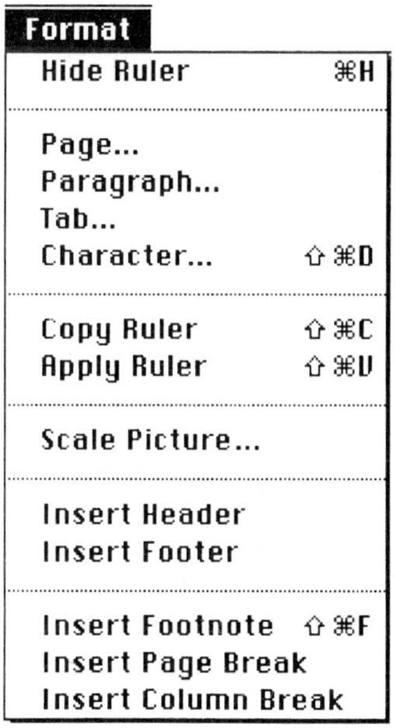

Format	
Hide Ruler	⌘H
Page...	
Paragraph...	
Tab...	
Character...	⇧⌘D
Copy Ruler	⇧⌘C
Apply Ruler	⇧⌘U
Scale Picture...	
Insert Header	
Insert Footer	
Insert Footnote	⇧⌘F
Insert Page Break	
Insert Column Break	

***Fig. C.7.** The Format Menu.*

The commands available from the Format menu are

- *Hide/Show Ruler.* Hides or shows the ruler at the top of the document window

- *Page.* Opens the Page dialog box, enabling you to set the page margins (Chapter 2), number of columns (Chapter 12), and left/right pages (Chapter 8) and to create a title page (Chapter 9)

- *Paragraph.* Opens the Paragraph dialog box, enabling you to set the paragraph indents, line spacing, and space before and after paragraphs (Chapter 2)

- *Tab.* Opens the Tab dialog box, enabling you to set and modify tabs (Chapter 3)

- *Character.* Opens the Character dialog box, enabling you to define text attributes (Chapter 10)

- *Copy Ruler.* Copies the current ruler settings, used with Apply Ruler (Chapter 3)

- *Apply Ruler.* Applies the last copied ruler settings to the current paragraph (Chapter 3)

- *Scale Picture.* Enables you to change the size of the selected graphic by entering scaling numbers (Chapter 12)

- *Insert Header.* Inserts a header into the document (Chapter 9)

- *Insert Footer.* Inserts a footer into the document (Chapter 9)

- *Insert Footnote.* Inserts a footnote at the current cursor position (Chapter 9)

- *Insert Page Break.* Ends the current page and places the cursor on a new page (Chapter 2)

- *Insert Column Break.* Ends the current column and places the cursor in a new column (Chapter 12)

The Spelling Menu

The Spelling menu, shown in figure C.8, contains the commands used for checking spelling (Chapter 4) and hyphenation (Chapter 5).

```
┌─────────────────────────────────────┐
│ Spelling                            │
├─────────────────────────────────────┤
│ Check All...              ⌘=        │
│ Check Main Body...                  │
│ Check Selection...        ⌘K        │
│ ..................................  │
│ Spell Word...             ⌘Y        │
│ Spelling Options...                 │
│ ..................................  │
│ Install Dictionaries...             │
│ User Dictionary...                  │
│ ..................................  │
│ Auto Hyphenate                      │
│ Hyph. Exceptions...                 │
└─────────────────────────────────────┘
```

Fig. C.8. The Spelling menu.

The commands available from the Spelling menu are

- *Check All.* Checks the spelling of the entire document

- *Check Main Body.* Changes according to the document element in which the cursor currently resides (header, footer, footnote) and checks that element only

- *Check Selection.* Checks the spelling of selected text

- *Spell Word.* Produces alternative spellings for a word questioned by the on-line spelling check

- *Spelling Options.* Brings up a dialog box that enables you to set various spelling options, including turning on or off the on-line spelling check

- *Install Dictionaries.* Enables you to install the Main and User Dictionaries for checking spelling

- *User Dictionary.* Enables you to edit the currently installed User Dictionary

- *Auto Hyphenate.* Hyphenates the current document

- *Hyph. Exceptions.* Enables you to enter the hyphenation of certain words to override the program's hyphenation rules

The View Menu

The View menu contains various commands that determine the way the current document is displayed (see fig. C.9).

```
┌─────────────────────────┐
│ ▐ View ▌                 │
├─────────────────────────┤
│ Show Invisibles      ⌘;  │
│ Show Page Guides     ⌘G  │
│ Hide Pictures            │
├─────────────────────────┤
│ Reduced Size         ⌘R  │
│ Side By Side             │
├─────────────────────────┤
│ Document1                │
└─────────────────────────┘
```

Fig. C.9. The View menu.

The commands available from the View menu are

- *Show/Hide Invisibles.* Displays or hides the invisible formatting characters (Chapters 3 and 6)

- *Show/Hide Page Guides.* Displays or hides the page guides that show the page margins (Chapter 6)

- *Show/Hide Pictures.* Displays or hides the graphics in the current document (Chapters 6 and 12)

- *Reduced Size/Actual Size.* Shrinks or expands the current document to enable you to view it in its entirety or at normal size (Chapter 6)

- *Side By Side.* Enables you to work with left and right pages side by side (Chapter 6)

At the bottom of the menu, each open document is listed by name. You can bring a document forward, making it the current document by selecting the document name.

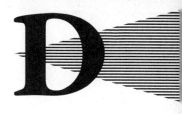

Window-by-Window Reference Guide

This appendix summarizes the MacWrite II windows. The operation of each window is explained briefly, and the chapter that covers the window is given in parentheses.

Document Window

The document window is where the text and graphics of your document are displayed and manipulated (see fig. D.1). The document window is discussed in Chapters 2 and 6.

The main parts of the document window are as follows:

- *Title bar.* Contains the document name, the close box (to the left), and the zoom box (to the right)

- *Close box.* Closes the window

- *Zoom box.* Resizes the window quickly

- *Ruler.* Sets the page margins, paragraph indent settings, and tabs

- *Icon bar.* Contains the tab, line spacing, and text alignment icons

- *Text area.* Contains the text and graphics of the document

- *Scroll bars.* Move the document in the window

- *Page number indicator.* Shows the current page number and indicates whether the page is a left or right page

- *Size box.* Adjusts the size of the window

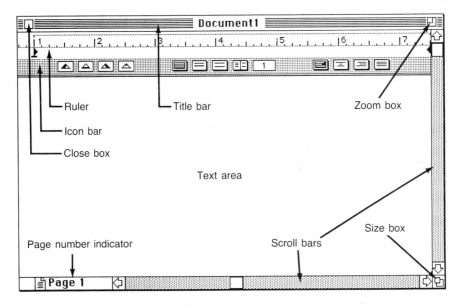

Fig. D.1 *The document window.*

Open Document Dialog Box

The Open Document dialog box enables you to open a document file (see fig. D.2). You see this dialog box (with slightly different names) after you select the Open command (Chapter 6), the Insert File command (Chapters 6 and 12), or the Open Merge Data File command (Chapter 15), but the function is always the same. Your Macintosh manual also discusses this dialog box.

The main parts of the Open Document dialog box are as follows:

- *Disk/Folder name.* Displays the current disk or folder name; enables you to change folders (Macintosh manual)

- *List box.* Lists the files in the current folder or on the current disk (Macintosh manual)

- *Show menu.* Enables you to display only certain types of files, as you designate (Chapter 6)

- *Current disk.* Displays the name of the current disk drive (Macintosh manual)

- *Eject.* Ejects the current floppy disk (Macintosh manual)

- *Drive.* Changes to another disk drive (you also can press the Tab key, Macintosh manual)

- *Open.* Opens the selected file in the list box (you also can press Return, Macintosh manual)

- *Cancel.* Closes the dialog box, performs no operations (Macintosh manual)

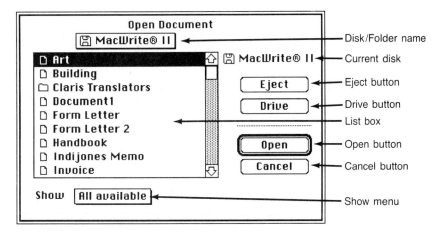

Fig. D.2. *The Open Document dialog box.*

Save Dialog Box

The Save dialog box appears after you select the Save command after creating a new document or converting a document to MacWrite II from another format, or after you select the Save As command (Chapters 2 and 6). This dialog box enables you to save the file to disk, name the file, save a copy of the file, save only a selection of the file, or save the file in a different format (see fig. D.3). Parts of the dialog box that appear only after choosing the Save As command are indicated by the notation *(Save As)*.

The Save dialog box contains the following parts:

- *Disk/Folder name.* Displays current disk or folder name, enables you to change the current folder (Macintosh manual)

- *List box.* Lists files in the current folder or on current disk (Macintosh manual)

- *Save As menu.* Selects the format in which the document or selection is saved (Save As, see Chapter 6).

- *Document name.* Names the document or selection (Chapter 2)

- *Entire Document/Selection Only.* Saves the entire document or only a selection (Save As, see Chapters 3 and 6)

- *Current disk.* Displays the name of the current disk drive (Macintosh manual)

- *Eject.* Ejects the current floppy disk (Macintosh manual)

- *Save.* Saves the document or selection (you also can press Return, see Macintosh manual and Chapter 2)

- *Cancel.* Cancels the Save or Save As operation, closing the dialog box

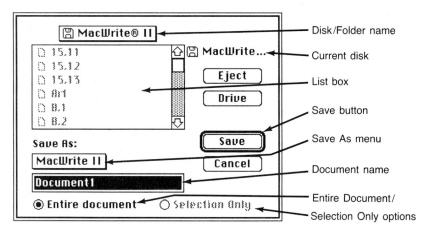

Fig. D.3. *The Save dialog box.*

Insert Merge Field Dialog Box

Discussed fully in Chapter 15, the Insert Merge Field dialog box enables you to insert a merge field into a form letter (see fig. D.4).

The main parts of the Insert Merge Field dialog box are the following:

- *Field Delimiter menu.* Specifies one of three delimiters used to separate merge fields

- *Field Name list box.* Lists the names of the fields as defined in your merge data file

- *Command list box.* Lists the MacWrite II form letter commands

- *Find Delimiter.* Finds the next delimiter in your document
- *Insert Field Name.* Inserts the field name selected in the Field Name list box into your document
- *Insert Command.* Inserts the command selected in the Command list box into your document

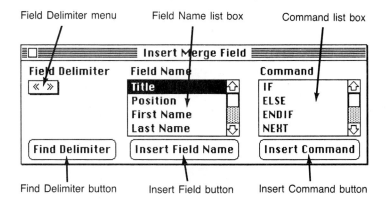

Fig. D.4. The Insert Merge Field dialog box.

Merge Dialog Box

The Merge dialog box is discussed in Chapter 15. From this dialog box, you set the range of records you want to use from your merge data file, direct the form letters to a file or the printer, and begin merging the form letter and the data file (see fig. D.5).

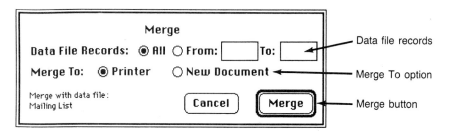

Fig. D.5. The Merge dialog box.

The options available from the Merge dialog box are as follows:

- *Data File Records.* Specifies a range of data records to be used in the form letter merge or specifies that all records are to be used

- *Merge To.* Sends the form letters to the printer or a new document file

- *Merge.* Begins the merge operation (you also can press Return)

- *Cancel.* Closes the dialog box, performs no operation

Find/Change Dialog Box

The Find/Change dialog box enables you to search for and replace text and text attributes. Figure D.6 shows the dialog box in its expanded form; it is discussed in Chapters 5 and 10.

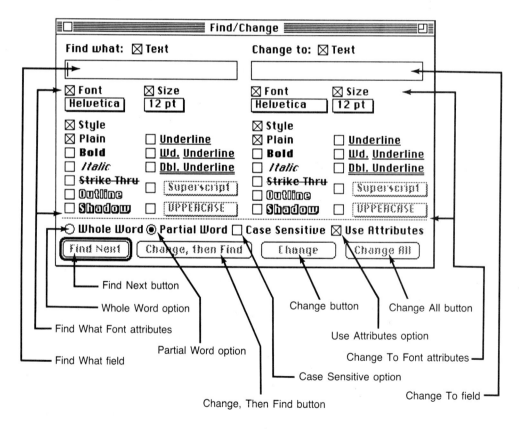

Fig. D.6. *The expanded Find/Change dialog box.*

The Find/Change dialog box contains the following parts:

- *Find What field.* Contains text to be searched for
- *Find What Font attributes.* Selects the font, font size, and font style(s) to be searched for
- *Change To field.* Contains text to replace located text
- *Change To Font attributes.* Selects the font, font size, and font style(s) to be applied to located text or the text in the Change To field
- *Whole Word.* Searches only for whole words
- *Partial Word.* Searches for partial and whole words
- *Case Sensitive.* Searches only for text that matches the case of the Find What text
- *Use Attributes.* Expands or contracts the dialog box to include or exclude the Find What and Change To font attribute settings
- *Find Next button.* Locates the next occurrence of text that matches the Find What settings
- *Change, Then Find.* Changes the currently selected text according to the Change To settings and then locates the next occurrence of text matching the Find What settings
- *Change.* Changes the current located text only
- *Change All.* Changes every occurrence of text that matches the Find What settings according to the Change To settings

Preferences Dialog Box

The Preferences dialog box enables you to specify preferred settings (see fig. D.7).

The major parts of the Preferences dialog box are the following:

- *Measure menu.* Sets the unit of measure (Chapter 2)
- *Date Format.* Sets the date format (Chapter 9)
- *Date & Time.* Sets the date and time to update continuously or remain as inserted (Chapter 9)
- *Smart Quotes.* Turns on or off the Smart Quotes option (Chapter 5)

- *Fractional Character Widths.* Sets the program to adjust character widths for laser printers

- *Page Number.* Sets the page number format and starting page number (Chapter 9)

- *Footnotes.* Sets the footnote position and numbering (Chapter 9)

- *Cancel.* Closes the dialog box, performs no operation

- *OK.* Saves changes and closes the dialog box

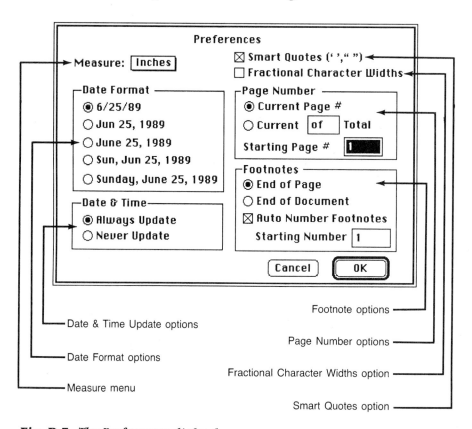

Fig. D.7. *The Preferences dialog box.*

Custom Style Dialog Box

The Custom Style dialog box enables you to create a custom style (see fig. D.8). Chapter 10 discusses this dialog box.

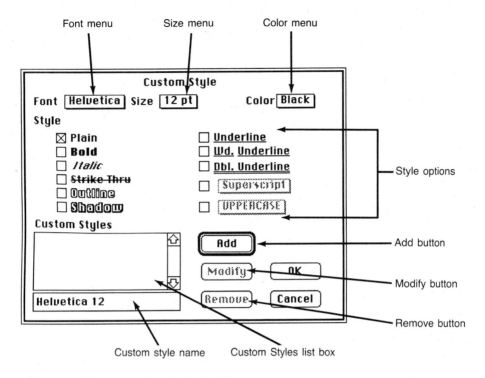

Fig. D.8. *The Custom Style dialog box.*

The major parts of the Custom Style dialog box are as follows:

- *Font pop-up menu.* Selects the font
- *Size pop-up menu.* Selects the font size
- *Color pop-up menu.* Selects the font color
- *Style.* Sets desired style options
- *Custom Styles.* Lists the current custom styles
- *Custom style name.* Contains a name for a new custom style
- *Add.* Adds the new style to the Custom Styles list
- *Modify.* Change the custom style selected in the Custom Styles list
- *Remove.* Removes the custom style selected in the Custom Styles list
- *OK.* Accepts changes and closes the dialog box
- *Cancel.* Discards changes and closes the dialog box

Page Dialog Box

The Page dialog box contains page settings you can make (see fig. D.9).

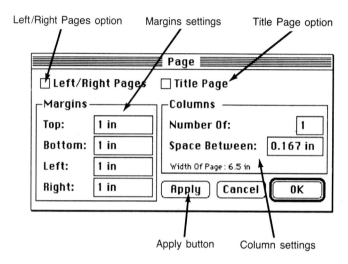

Fig. D.9. The Page dialog box.

The major parts of the Page dialog box are the following:

- *Left/Right Pages.* Sets the document to contain left and right pages (Chapter 8)

- *Margins.* Sets the page margins (Chapter 2)

- *Title Page.* Adds a title page to the document (Chapter 9)

- *Columns.* Sets the number of columns and space between columns (Chapter 12)

- *Apply.* Applies the current settings to the document but does not close the dialog box

- *Cancel.* Discards any changes and closes the dialog box

- *OK.* Applies the current settings to the document and closes the dialog box

Paragraph Dialog Box

The Paragraph dialog box controls paragraph settings (see fig. D.10). It is discussed in Chapter 2.

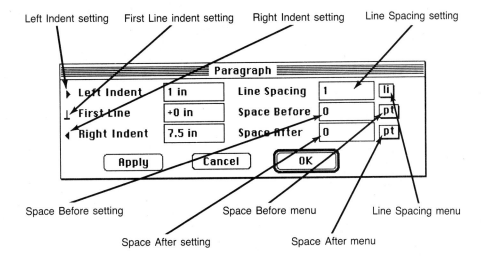

Fig. D.10. *The Paragraph dialog box.*

The major parts of the paragraph dialog box are as follows:

- *Left Indent.* Sets the left edge of the paragraph

- *First Line.* Sets the indention of the first line of the paragraph

- *Right Indent.* Sets the right edge of the paragraph

- *Line Spacing.* Sets the line spacing of the paragraph

- *Line Spacing pop-up menu.* Changes the unit of measure for paragraph line spacing

- *Space Before.* Sets the amount of space to precede the paragraph

- *Space Before pop-up menu.* Changes the unit of measure for spacing before the paragraph

- *Space After.* Sets the amount of space to follow the paragraph

- *Space After pop-up menu.* Changes the unit of measure for spacing after the paragraph

- *Apply.* Applies the settings to the selected paragraph(s) but does not close the dialog box

- *Cancel.* Discards any changes made and closes the dialog box

- *OK.* Applies the settings to the selected paragraph(s) and closes the dialog box

Tab Dialog Box

The Tab dialog box enables you to enter the type, position, and fill character for a tab (see fig. D.11). You also can modify existing tabs. It is discussed in Chapter 8.

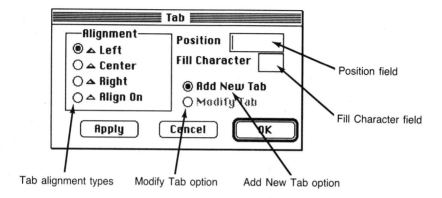

Fig. D.11. *The Tab dialog box.*

The Tab dialog box includes the following parts:

- *Alignment.* Sets the tab type you want to use or change to

- *Position.* Specifies the position for the tab

- *Fill Character.* Specifies a single character to fill the empty space preceding the tab

- *Add New Tab.* Adds new tabs

- *Modify Tab.* Modifies existing tabs, active when a tab icon on the ruler is clicked

- *Apply.* Places the tab on the ruler but does not close the dialog box

- *Cancel.* Discards any changes made and closes the dialog box

- *OK.* Accepts changes made and closes the dialog box

Character Dialog Box

The Character dialog box enables you to set all the font attributes at one time instead of choosing them individually from the Font, Size, and Style menus (see fig. D.12). This box is discussed in Chapter 10.

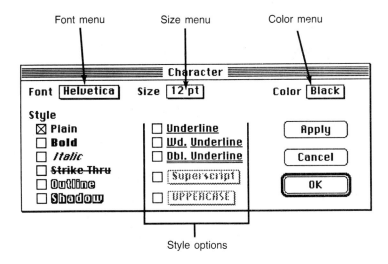

Fig. D.12. *The Character dialog box.*

The Character dialog box includes the following parts:

- *Font pop-up menu.* Sets the font

- *Size pop-up menu.* Sets the font size

- *Color pop-up menu.* Sets the font color

- *Style.* Specifies all the style attributes you want to use

- *Apply.* Applies the settings to selected text but does not close the dialog box

- *Cancel.* Discards any changes made and closes the dialog box

- *OK.* Applies the settings to the selected text (or future text typed) and closes the dialog box

Spelling Dialog Box

The Spelling dialog box appears when the spelling-checking feature of the program is active (see fig. D.13). The questioned word appears with suggested spellings. This dialog box is discussed in Chapter 4.

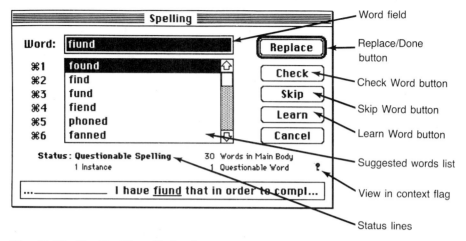

Fig. D.13. *The Spelling dialog box.*

The major parts of the Spelling dialog box are as follows:

- *Word field.* Displays the word MacWrite II does not recognize

- *Suggested words list.* Displays suggested spellings of the questioned word; select one by double-clicking or holding down the Command key and pressing the number indicated

- *Replace/Done.* Replaces the questioned word with the highlighted suggested spelling or what you type in the Word field. Changes to Done when spelling checking is finished; you click it to close the dialog box.

- *Check.* Checks the word typed in the Word field

- *Skip.* Ignores the questioned word and proceeds to the next

- *Learn.* Adds the questioned word to the user dictionary

- *Cancel.* Ends the spelling checking, does not cancel previous changes

- *Status lines.* Indicate the current status of the spelling checking

- *View in context flag.* Shows the word in context

Spelling Options Dialog Box

The Spelling Options dialog box enables you to set the various spelling options (see fig. D.14). It is discussed in Chapter 4.

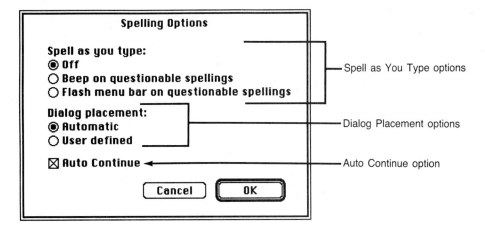

Fig. D.14. *The Spelling Options dialog box.*

The Spelling Options dialog box includes the following parts:

- *Spell as You Type.* Turns on or off the on-line spelling checker controlling how the program notifies you of a possible misspelled word

- *Dialog Placement.* Selects where the spelling dialog box appears

- *Auto Continue.* Determines whether the program automatically proceeds to the next document element or pauses to ask whether you want to continue

- *Cancel.* Discards changes and closes the dialog box

- *OK.* Accepts changes and closes the dialog box

Select Dictionary Dialog Box

The Select Dictionary dialog box enables you to install a main or user dictionary or create a new user dictionary (see fig. D.15). It is discussed in Chapter 4.

The Select Dictionary dialog box includes the following parts:

- *Select Dictionary.* Specifies Main or User to indicate whether you are installing a main or user dictionary

- *Dictionary list box.* Lists the names of the dictionaries on the current disk

- *Eject.* Ejects the current floppy disk

- *Drive.* Switches to another disk drive

- *OK.* Installs the dictionary selected in the Dictionary list box and closes the dialog box

- *Cancel.* Closes the dialog box without performing any operation

- *None.* Shows only if the User option is clicked, removes any installed User Dictionary

- *New.* Shows only if the User option is clicked, creates a new User Dictionary

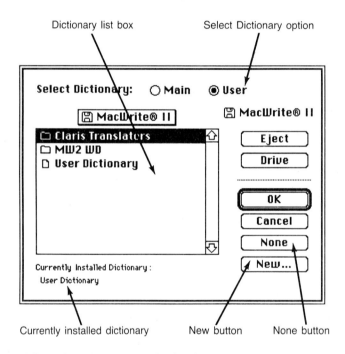

Fig. D.15. *The Select Dictionary dialog box.*

User Dictionary Dialog Box

The User Dictionary dialog box enables you to edit the currently installed user dictionary (see fig. D.16). It is discussed in Chapter 4.

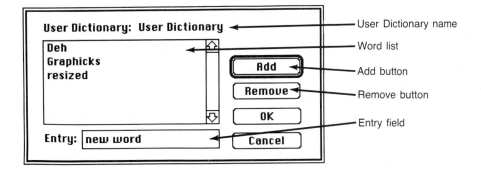

Fig. D.16. *The User Dictionary dialog box.*

The major parts of the User Dictionary dialog box are

- *User Dictionary.* Displays the name of the current user dictionary
- *Word list.* Lists the words in the user dictionary
- *Entry.* Contains a word to be added or removed from the User Dictionary
- *Add.* Adds the word in the Entry field to the dictionary
- *Remove.* Removes the word selected in the Word list or typed in the Entry field
- *OK.* Accepts changes made to the dictionary and closes the dialog box
- *Cancel.* Discards the changes made and closes the dialog box

Hyphenation Exceptions Dialog Box

The Hyphenation Exceptions dialog box enables you to enter hyphenated words to show the program where to divide them (see fig. D.17). It is discussed in Chapter 5.

The major parts of the Hyphenation Exceptions dialog box are as follows:

- *Word list.* Lists the hyphenated words you have entered
- *Entry.* Contains the word to be added or removed (with hyphens placed as you want them)
- *Add.* Adds the word in the Entry field to the word list
- *Remove.* Removes the highlighted word from the word list

- *OK.* Accepts changes made to the word list
- *Cancel.* Discards changes made to the word list and closes the dialog box

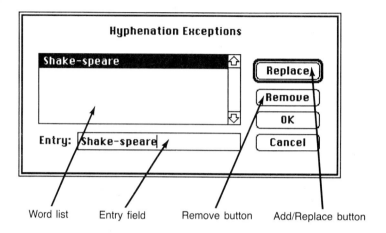

Word list   Entry field   Remove button   Add/Replace button

Fig. D.17. *The Hyphenation Exceptions dialog box.*

Glossary of Terms

Align On tab. A tab stop that aligns text on a particular character, such as a decimal point.

Alignment. The horizontal positioning of text. See also *Center, Flush left, Flush right, Justified*.

AND. A conjunction that joins two conditions in a compound IF statement. Both conditions must be true for the statement to be true.

Application. A program, such as MacWrite II, that performs a specific function on a computer.

ASCII. American Standard Code for Information Interchange. A standard way of representing text used by computers to share information.

ASCII file. A file formatted according to the ASCII standards, that contains only letters, numbers, and other characters but no formatting except tabs and carriage returns. See also *ASCII*.

Attribute. A certain feature of text such as boldface, italic, and so on. Attributes are set in the Style menu.

Automatic stationery. A MacWrite II file in the System Folder, that has settings to be applied to all new documents created by the program. You can override these settings by holding down the Option key while you select New from the File menu.

Back up. To create a copy of a file in case the original is damaged.

Boldface. A text attribute in which letters are thickened to darken them.

Button. In a dialog box, an oval containing words. A button is clicked to perform the named function.

Center. To place text midway between the left and right margins of a page.

Center tab. A tab stop that causes text to center around the location of the tab.

Centimeter (cm, c). A metric measure approximately 0.39 inch and about 28.35 points. See also *Point.*

Check box. In a dialog box, a small box that acts as a switch (or toggle) for an option. The option is on when an X is in the box. Clicking the check box adds or removes the X.

Click. To place the mouse pointer on an item on-screen and quickly press and release the mouse button once.

Clipboard. A temporary storage area that holds text cut or copied from a document by use of the Edit menu commands Cut or Copy; part of the Macintosh System software. Data in Clipboard is lost when the computer is turned off.

Close box. The small box in the upper left corner of a window, that when clicked, closes the window.

Column. The vertical arrangement of text on a page. A document can contain from one to ten columns of equal width.

Column break character. A formatting character that forces a column to end before MacWrite II normally would end it; subsequent text moves to the next column.

Command key. The key used by the Macintosh to perform a command from the keyboard; has a four-leaf clover symbol on the key.

Crop. To hide part of a graphic by dragging the handle of the graphic's frame.

Cursor. The blinking vertical bar that indicates where text will be placed when typed.

Custom style. A combination of text styles named by the user.

Database. An organized collection of information stored in a file that can be accessed in various ways. Also a program that stores and retrieves information in this format.

Default. Automatic choices made by a program concerning certain options. For example, Helvetica is the default font for new documents.

Delimiter. A character that indicates the beginning and end of a command, command statement, or merge data field.

Desk accessory. A small program that can be accessed through the Apple menu. Some desk accessories are the Alarm Clock, Scrapbook, and the Control Panel.

Dialog box. A window that contains commands and options. Usually displayed by selecting a command and usually requires some response.

Dictionary. A set of words used to check the spelling of a document. MacWrite II can use two at a time—Main (provided by Claris) and User (created by the user).

Discretionary hyphen (Command-hyphen). An invisible hyphen that the program uses to divide a word at the end of a line, if needed.

Disk. The magnetic media used to store information. Macintosh uses the hard-shell 3.5-inch removable disks and the nonremovable hard drive.

Document. A collection of text, graphics, and formatting stored in a file on disk.

Document element. An individual part of a document, such as page, paragraph, header, footer, footnote, and so on.

Dot-matrix printer. A printer that creates an image on paper by striking a ribbon with small needlelike rods or by spraying ink through small holes.

Double-click. To place the mouse pointer on an item on-screen and quickly press and release the mouse button twice.

Drag. To place the mouse pointer on an item on-screen, press and hold the mouse button, and move the mouse pointer, usually moving across the screen the item on which the pointer was placed, or moving the pointer through a menu to choose a command.

ELSE statement. A line of text printed when the IF condition is false; also the word ELSE itself, which indicates the beginning of text to be printed.

Em space. A space that is the same width as the capital letter M in a font.

En space. A space that is one-half the width of the capital letter M in a font.

Export. To save a document (or other information) to a file that can be used by another program.

Field. An area in which text may be typed or an area in a form letter into which data is brought from a data file. See *Merge field*.

File. A collection of information stored on a disk and indicated by an icon on the screen.

Fill character. A character that fills the empty space preceding a tab; used frequently in tables of contents.

Finder. Part of the Macintosh System software that manages files and icons.

First-line indent. A specified amount of space that the first line of a paragraph is shifted relative to the other lines of the paragraph.

Floppy disk. A removable magnetic media that holds information; the Macintosh uses 3.5-inch hard-shell floppy disks.

Flush left. A text alignment that produces a straight left edge but a ragged right edge in a paragraph.

Flush right. A text alignment that produces a straight right edge but a ragged left edge in a paragraph.

Folder. An icon on a disk that holds files for the purposes of organizing files.

Font. A particular style of letters grouped under a single name.

Footer. Text and graphics printed at the bottom of every page (or every left page or every right page) of a document but not printed on the title page of a document.

Footnote. A note printed at the bottom of a page or the end of a document, referred to by a number or other symbol in the main document text.

Footnote reference. A small number or symbol in the main text of a document, referring the reader to a footnote.

Form letter. A letter with fields that are filled in by information contained in a merge data file, used to create mailings and similar items.

Formatting characters. See *Invisibles*.

Graphic. A picture included in a document.

Hanging indent. A paragraph format in which the first line of a paragraph extends to the left of the other lines of that paragraph.

Hard disk. A magnetic storage medium that is contained in a computer or a separate box that stores large amounts of information. Hard disks usually are not removable. See *Floppy disk*.

Header. Text and graphics printed at the top of every page (or every left page or every right page) of a document, but not printed on title pages.

Highlight. To surround text or graphics with a dark band, also called selecting. See *Select*.

Hyphen (-). A punctuation mark used to indicate where a word may be divided. See also *Discretionary hyphen, Nonbreaking hyphen*.

Hyphenate. To divide a word into syllables, usually to split a word between lines of text. MacWrite II provides automatic and manual hyphenation.

Hyphenation exception. A word entered by the user indicating the way a word is to be divided. A hyphenation exception overrides the built-in hyphenation rules of MacWrite II.

I-beam pointer. The vertical bar the mouse arrow becomes when in a text area; used to make selections. See also *Insertion point, Mouse pointer*.

Icon. An on-screen picture used to indicate a file on a disk or an item that performs a specific function.

IF statement. A conditional statement. MacWrite II uses IF statements to print text when a condition is found to be true.

ImageWriter. The brand name for dot-matrix printers made by Apple Computer, Inc.

Import. To use a file created by another program.

Inch (in, i, ″). A measurement approximately equal to 2.54 centimeters.

Inch decimal (in, i, ″). A measurement using inches but dividing each inch into tenths instead of the usual eighths.

Insertion point. The place at which text or graphics will be placed, indicated by a blinking vertical bar. See also *Cursor, I-beam pointer*.

Invisibles. Characters that control formatting, such as tabs, carriage returns, page breaks, and the like; not seen unless the Show Invisibles command is invoked.

Italic. A type style in which the letters are slanted.

Justified. An alignment where the left and right edges of a paragraph are straight.

Landscape. A paper orientation where a document is printed with the long edges of the paper at the top and bottom.

Laser printer. A high-resolution printer that uses a laser to create an image on paper.

LaserWriter. The brand name for laser printers made by Apple Computer, Inc.

Left indent. The position of the left edge of text.

Left tab. A tab stop that causes the left edge of text to align to its position.

Left/right pages. Pages meant to be bound together in book style. These pages have large inside margins to allow for binding.

Line (li). A unit of measure that corresponds to the normal height of letters in a font.

Line spacing. The amount of room allocated to a line of text.

Maclink Plus. A program by DataViz that permits exchanging files among different computer and program formats.

Main body. The bulk of text and graphics in a document.

Margin. A specified edge on a page beyond which text and graphics cannot go.

Menu. A collection of commands grouped under a name at the top of the screen. Menu commands can be accessed by use of the mouse or the keyboard. See also *Pop-up menu.*

Menu bar. The top part of the Macintosh window, that contains the main menus of a program.

Merge. To cause information from a data file to be inserted into a form letter.

Merge data file. A collection of information that is to be inserted into a form letter.

Merge field. A space in a form letter that receives specific information from a data file.

Millimeter (mm, m). A metric unit of measure equal to approximately 0.039 inch.

Mouse. A pointing device that rolls or slides, moving a pointer on the computer screen; may contain one or more buttons.

Mouse button. The button on a mouse, pressed to initiate a command or action.

Mouse pointer. The arrow or I-beam that moves on the screen as the mouse is moved. See *I-beam pointer.*

Nonbreaking hyphen (Command-Option-hyphen). A hyphen placed between two words (or other amounts of text) that is not to be divided by the program.

Nonbreaking space (Command-space). A space placed between two words that are not to be separated by the program.

On-line spelling check. The MacWrite II option that checks the spelling of each word as it is typed.

Operator. A character or characters that indicate a comparison between two values, such as $=$, $>$, $<$, and so on. Listed in the Command list box of the Insert Merge Field dialog box. Used in IF statements. See *IF statement*.

Option key. The key labeled "Option" or "Opt" and in MacWrite II used to modify the meaning of certain mouse operations.

Option-click. To place the mouse pointer on something, hold down the Option key, and press the mouse button.

OR. A conjunction that joins two conditions in an IF statement. The statement is true if either condition is true.

Orientation. The direction a document is printed on a page. See also *Landscape*, *Portrait*.

Outline. A text attribute that uses lines around the normal shape of a letter.

Page. A collection of text, graphics, and formatting that corresponds to a sheet of paper.

Page break. An invisible formatting character that forces a page to end and following text to move to the next page.

Page guide. Lines on a page that indicate the location of the margins.

Paragraph. Any amount of text or graphics that ends with a return character.

Pica (p). A unit of measure that corresponds to 1/6th inch, or 12 points.

PICT. A format used by Macintosh programs to store graphics.

Plain text. A text style that is the font itself only.

Point (pt). A unit of measure that corresponds to 1/72nd inch; 12 points make a pica.

Pop-up menu. A shadowed box in a dialog box or window; permits choices through the menu that appears when the user places the mouse pointer on the box and presses the mouse button.

Portrait. A paper orientation where the document is printed with the short edges of the paper at the top and bottom.

Printer. A device that transfers documents to paper.

Quadruple-click. To place the mouse pointer on an item on-screen and quickly press and release the mouse button four times.

Resize. To change the size of a window or graphic.

Right indent. The position of the right edge of text.

Right tab. A tab stop that causes the right edge of text to align on the tab position.

Ruler. The top part of the MacWrite II document window that contains the measurements, indent markers, and tab stops.

Scale. To adjust the size of a graphic by dragging a handle on the frame surrounding the graphic. To maintain proportion, hold down the Command key while dragging.

Scrapbook. A desk accessory that permits you to store text and graphics on disk for later use.

Scroll. To move a document or list up, down, left, or right within a window, by clicking a scroll arrow or scroll bar or by dragging a scroll box. See *Scroll arrow, Scroll bar, Scroll box.*

Scroll arrow. A small arrow in the scroll bar, that moves a document or list within a window when clicked. See *Scroll, Scroll bar, Scroll box.*

Scroll bar. The up and down (or left and right) arrows, the gray bar, and the scroll box that permit movement of a document or list. Located along the bottom or the right side of a window or list.

Scroll box. The small box in a scroll bar that may be dragged to move a document or list quickly. See *Scroll, Scroll arrow, Scroll bar.*

Select. To indicate a portion of text or a graphic on which an operation is to be performed. See *Highlight.*

Selection. A block of text or graphics on which an operation is to be performed.

Shadow. A text style where letters have a dark edge giving the appearance of a shadow behind them.

Shift-click. To place the mouse pointer on something on-screen, hold down the Shift key, and press and release the mouse button.

Size box. The box in the lower right corner of a window, that permits a window's size to be adjusted.

Small caps. A text style where the usually lowercase letters are the same size as lowercase letters but are capitalized and the normally capital letters are the usual size.

Smart Quotes. A MacWrite II option that encloses text in "curly" opening and closing quotation marks instead of the usual straight quotation marks.

Spelling check. To verify the correctness of word spelling in a document. MacWrite II performs a spelling check by comparing the words in a document with words in a dictionary.

Stationery. A MacWrite II document file that contains formatting. When a stationery document is opened, MacWrite creates a copy to permit a document to be created using the formatting of the stationery file.

Strike thru. A text style where a horizontal line is drawn through the letters.

Style. The appearance, or way text looks. Style includes such elements as boldface, italic, and underlining.

Subscript. A text style where letters or numbers are positioned below the normal text line.

Superior. A text style where letters or numbers are raised above the normal text line but do not extend above text.

Superscript. A text style where letters or numbers are raised above the normal text line.

Synonym. A word that means the same as another word.

System software. Software that tells a computer how to perform basic operations.

System file. The Macintosh file that contains the basic operating instructions, fonts, and desk accessories.

Tab. A position on a ruler to which the cursor moves when the Tab key is pressed.

Text. Letters, spaces, carriage returns, and other nongraphic items in a document.

Text alignment. The positioning of a paragraph's text. See also *Flush left, Flush right, Center, Justified*.

Text attributes. Various settings that affect the way text appears. Attributes include boldface, italic, and underlining. See also *Style*.

Text file. A file that contains only letters, numbers, spaces, punctuation marks, and basic formatting, such as tabs and carriage returns, and does not contain special formatting, such as fonts, styles, page breaks, and the like. See also *ASCII file*.

Thesaurus. A collection of related words (synonyms).

Title page. The first page in a document; does not have a header, footer, footnotes, or more than one column.

Translator. A file that tells a program how to read another program's files.

Triple-click. To place the mouse pointer on an item on-screen and quickly press and release the mouse button three times.

Typeface. The unique appearance of a font (set of letters).

Underline. A line drawn under text and spaces.

Unit of measure. A system of measurement, for example, inch, millimeter, point, and so on.

Window. A frame in which a document is displayed.

Word processor. A computer program that permits the manipulation of text and graphics for the purpose of creating a document.

Word underline. Lines drawn below words but not the spaces between the words.

Word Finder. The thesaurus provided with MacWrite II. See also *Synonym*, *Thesaurus*.

Zoom box. The box in the upper right corner of a window that changes the size quickly.

Index

< (less than) operator, 396-398
<= (less than or equal to) operator, 396-398
<> (not equal to) operator, 396-398
= (equal to) operator, 396-398
> (greater than) operator, 396-398
>= (greater than or equal to) operator, 396-398

A

A4 Letter size paper, 232
adjusting table column width, 362-363
align on tabs, 100-101, 355-357, 467
aligning text, 59-60, 216-218
alignment, 467
AND Merge Field conjunction, 402, 467
Apple menu, 439-440
  Control Panel, 273-274
  Key Caps option, 265-267
  Word Finder option, 151-152, 159
application, 467
Apply Ruler (Format menu) option, 106-107
applying styles, 297
ASCII, 467
ASCII file, 467
attribute, 467
Auto Hyphenate (Spelling menu) option, 162-163, 321-322
automatic features
  footnote numbering, 262-264
  hyphenation, 162-165, 321-322
  stationery, 197-198, 467

B

B5 Letter size paper, 233
backup files, 467
Bold (Style menu) option, 208-209, 224, 290
boldface, 208-209, 224, 425, 467
button, 467

C

calculating
  column width, 332-335
  tab locations in tables, 354-355
canceling printing, 72
captions, 324-325
case sensitivity
  searching and replacing text, 141-142
center tabs, 355-357, 468
centered text, 59-60, 468
centering headers, 315-316
Character (Format menu) option, 293
Character dialog box, 292-296, 460-461
Check All (Spelling menu) option, 24-26, 117
check box, 468
Check Selection (Spelling menu) option, 123
checking spelling, 24-26, 115-132, 434
  adding words to dictionary, 435
  Auto Continue option, 131-133
  checking parts of documents, 122-123
  checking single words, 124-125
  completing, 121-122

G

H

Q

R

U

V